PURGATORY:
Doctrinal, Historical and Poetical

BY
MRS. J. SADLIER

INTRODUCTION

I have written many books and translated many more on a great variety of subjects, nearly all of which, I thank God now with all my heart, were more or less religious, at least in their tendency; but the circle of these my life-long labors seems to me incomplete. One link is wanting to the chain, and that is a work specially devoted to the souls in Purgatory. This omission I am anxious to supply while the working days of my life are still with me, for, a few more years, at most, and for me "the night cometh when no man can work."

As we advance into the vale of years and journey on the downward slope, we are happily drawn more and more towards the eternal truths of the great untried world beyond the grave. Foremost amongst these stands out more and still more clearly, in all its awful reality, the dread but consoling doctrine of Purgatory. When we have seen many of our best beloved relatives, many of our dearest and most devoted friends—those who started with us in "the freshness of morning" on the road of life, which then lay so deceitfully fair and bright before them and us—they who shared our early hopes and aspirations, and whose words and smiles were the best encouragement of our feeble efforts—when we have seen them sink, one by one, into the darkness of the grave, leaving the earth more bleak and dreary year by year for those who remain—then do we naturally follow them in spirit to those gloomy regions where one or all may be undergoing that blessed purification which prepares them for the eternal repose of Heaven.

Of all the divine truths which the Catholic Church proposes to her children, assuredly none is more acceptable to the pilgrim race of Adam than that of Purgatory. It is, beyond conception, dear and precious as one of the links that connect the living with the vanished dead, and which keeps them fresh in the memory of those who loved them on earth, and whose dearest joy it is to be able to help them in that shadowy border-land through which, in pain and sorrow, they must journey before entering the Land of Promise, which is the City of God, seated on the everlasting hills.

When I decided on adding yet another to the many books on Purgatory already existing even in our own language, I, at the same time, resolved to make it as different as possible from all the others, and thus fill up a void of which I have long been sensible in our English Purgatorial literature. Doctrinal works, books of devotion, e have in abundance, but it is, unhappily, only the pious, the religiously-inclined who will read them. Knowing this, and still desirous to promote devotion to the Holy Souls by making Purgatory more real, more familiar to the general reader, I thought the very best means I could take for that end would be to make a book chiefly of legends and of poetry, with enough of doctrinal and devotional matter to give a substantial character to the work by placing it on the solid foundations of Catholic dogma, patristic authority, and that, at the same time, of the latest divines and theologians of the Church, by selections from their published writings.

I have divided the work into five parts, viz.: Doctrinal and Devotional, comprising extracts from Suarez, St. Catherine of Genoa,

St. Augustine, St. Gertrude, St. Francis de Sales, of the earlier and middle ages; and from Archbishop Gibbons, Very Rev. Faá di Bruno, Father Faber, Father Muller, C.S.S.R., Father Binet, S.J., Rev. J. J. Moriarty, and others.

The Second Part consists of Anecdotes and Incidents relating to Purgatory, and more or less authentic. The Third Part contains historical matter bearing on the same subject, including Father Lambing's valuable article on "The Belief in a Middle State of Souls after Death amongst Pagan Nations." The Fourth Part is made up of "Thoughts on Purgatory, from Various Authors, Catholic and non-Catholic," including Cardinals Newman, Wiseman, and Manning; the Anglican Bishops Jeremy Taylor and Reginald Heber, Dr. Samuel Johnson, William Hurrell Mallock, Count de Maistre, Chateaubriand.

The Fifth and last part consists of a numerous collection of legends and poems connected with Purgatory. Many of these are translated from the French, especially the *Légendes de l'Autre Monde,* by the well-known legendist, J. Colin de Plancy. In selecting the legends and anecdotes, I have endeavored to give only those that were new to most English readers, thus leaving out many legends that would well bear reproducing, but were already too well known to excite any fresh interest.

In the poetical section I have represented as many as possible of the best-known poets, from Dante down, and some poems of rare beauty and merit were translated from French and Canadian poets by my daughter, who has also contributed some interesting articles for the historical portion of the work. As may be supposed, this book is the fruit of much research. The collection of the material has necessarily been a work of time, the field from which the gleanings were made being so vast, and the selections requiring so much care.

As regards the legendary portion of the work, whether prose or poetry, the reader will, of course, understand that I give the legends precisely for what they are worth; by no means as representing the doctrinal belief of Purgatory, but merely as some of the wild flowers of poetry and romance that have grown, in the long lapse of time, from the rich soil of faith and piety, amongst the Catholic peoples of every land—intensified, in this instance, by the natural affection of the living for their dear departed ones, and the solemn and shadowy mystery in which the dead are shrouded when once they have passed the portals of eternity and are lost to mortal sight. Some of these legends, though exceedingly beautiful, will hardly bear close examination in the light of Catholic dogma. Of this class is "The Faithful Soul," of Adelaide Procter, which is merely given here as an old French legend, nearly connected with Purgatory, and having really nothing in it contrary to faith, though in a high degree improbable, but yet from its intrinsic beauty and dramatic character, no less than the subtle charm of Miss Procter's verse, eminently worthy of a place in this collection. The same remark applies more or less to some of Colin de Plancy's legends, notably that of "Robert the Devil's Penance," and others of a similar kind, as also T. D. McGee's "Penance of

Don Diego Rias" and Calderon's "St. Patrick's Purgatory"—the two last named bearing on the same subject. Nevertheless, they all come within the scope of my present work and are, therefore, presented to the reader as weird fragments of the legendary lore of Purgatory.

Taken altogether, I think this work will help to increase devotion to the Suffering Souls, and excite a more tender and more sensible feeling of sympathy for them, at least amongst Catholics, showing, as it does, the awful reality of those purgative pains awaiting all, with few or no exceptions, in the after life; the help they may and do receive from the good offices of the living, and the sacred and solemn' duty it is for Christians in the present life to remember them and endeavor to relieve their sufferings by every means in their power. To answer this purpose I have made the dead ages unite their solemn and authoritative voice with that of the living, actual present in testimony of the truth of this great Catholic dogma. The Saints, the Fathers, the Doctors of the Church in the ages of antiquity, and the prelates and priests of our own day all speak the same language of undoubting faith, of solemn conviction regarding Purgatory,—make the same earnest and eloquent appeal to the faithful on behalf of the dear suffering souls. Even the heathen nations and tribes of both hemispheres are brought forward as witnesses to the existence of a middle state in the after life. Nor is Protestantism itself wanting in this great and overwhelming mass of evidence, as the reader will perceive that some of its most eminent divines and secular writers have joined, with no hesitating or faltering voice, in the grand *Credo* of the nations and the ages in regard to Purgatory.

What remains for me to add except the earnest hope that this book may have the effect it is intended to produce by bringing the faithful children of the Church to think more and oftener of their departed brethren who, having passed from the Militant to the Suffering Church, are forever crying out to the living from their darksome prison—"Have pity on us, have pity on us, at least you who were our friends, have pity on us, for the hand of the Lord is heavy upon us!"

PART I.
DOCTRINAL AND DEVOTIONAL.

"But now, brethren, if I come to you, speaking with tongues: what shall I profit you, unless I speak to you either in revelation, or in knowledge, or in prophecy, or in doctrine?"

—ST. PAUL, I. COR. PURGATORY:
DOCTRINAL AND DEVOTIONAL.
DOCTRINE OF SUAREZ ON PURGATORY.
THE PLACE.

It is a certain truth of faith that after this life there is a place of Purgatory.

Though the name of Purgatory may not be found in Holy Scripture, that does not matter, if we can show that the thing meant by the name can be found there; for often the Church, either because of new heresies, or that the doctrine of the faith may be set forth more clearly and shortly, gives new and simple names, in which the mysteries of the faith are summed up. This is evident in the cases of the Holy Trinity, the Incarnation, and the Holy Eucharist.

The doctrine of Purgatory is proved by:—the Old Testament, the New Testament, the Councils of the Church, especially those of Florence and of Trent, the Fathers and Tradition, and by theological reasons.

WHERE PURGATORY IS.

Nothing is said in Holy Scripture about this place, nor is there any definition of the Church concerning it. The subject, therefore, comes within the range of theological discussion. Theologians, however, suppose Purgatory to be a certain corporeal place, in which souls are kept till they pay fully the debt which they owe. It is true that they do not in themselves need a corporeal place, since they are spirits; but yet, as they are in this world, they must, of necessity, be in some corporeal place—at any rate, with regard to substantial presence. Thus we see that God, in His providence, has made definite places for the Angels, according to the difference of their states. Gehenna is prepared for the devil and his angels, whereas the empyreal Heaven is made for the good angels. In this way, it is certain that the souls, paying their debt, are kept in a corporeal place. This place is not heaven, for nothing that is defiled enters there; nor is it hell, for in hell there is no redemption, and from that place no souls can be saved.

PAIN OF LOSS AND SENSE.

The pain of loss is the want of the vision of God and of the whole of our everlasting beatitude. The pain of sense is the suffering of punishment specially inflicted over and above the loss of the beatitude of Heaven.

We must assert that the souls in Purgatory suffer the pain of loss, tempered by hope, and not like the souls in hell, which have no hope.

In the pain of sense we can distinguish two things. There is the sorrow which follows closely the want or delay of the vision of God, and has that for its object. There is also another pain, as it were outward, and this is proportioned to the sensible pain which is caused in us by fire, or any like action, contrary to nature and hurtful to it. That in Purgatory this sorrow does follow the loss of God is most certain; for that loss, or delay, is truly a great evil, and is most keenly felt to be such by those souls that with all their strength love God and long to see Him. Therefore, it is impossible for them not to feel the greatest sorrow about that delay.

* * * * *

We must assert that, besides the pain of loss and the sorrow annexed to it, there is in Purgatory a proper and peculiar pain of sense. This is the more common judgment of the scholastics; and seems to be received by the common judgment and approbation of the Church. Indeed, the equity of the avenging justice of God requires this. The sinner, through inordinate delight in creatures and affection for them, deserves a punishment contrary to that delight; and if in this life he has not made full satisfaction, he must be punished and freed by some such pain as this, which we call the pain of sense. Theologians in common teach this, and distinguish a proper pain of sense from the sorrow caused by the want of the vision of God. Thus they distinguish spiritual pains, such as sorrow for the delay of the vision, and remorse of conscience, from corporeal pains, which come from the fire, or any other instrument of God. These corporeal pains we comprehend under the pain of sense.

* * * * *

Whether, besides the fire, other corporeal things, such as water and snow, are used as instruments for punishing the souls is uncertain. Bede says that souls in Purgatory were seen to pass from very great heat to very great cold, and then from cold to heat. St. Anselm mentions these punishments disjunctively. He says, "or any other kind of punishments." We cannot, therefore, speak of this with certainty.

THE PAIN OF LOSS.

In this matter we may look at the pain of loss as well as the pain of sense. It is certain that the pain of loss is very sharp, because of the greatness of the good for which they wait. True, it is only for a time; yet it is rightly reckoned, as St. Thomas taught, a greater evil than any loss in this life. He and other theologians with him mean that the sorrow also which springs from the apprehension of this evil is greater than any pain or sorrow here. Hence, they conclude that the pain of loss in every way exceeds all pains of this life; for they think, as I have already noted, that this sorrow pertains to the pain of loss, and therefore they join this pain with privation, that the punishment may be greater in every way.... The vision of God and the beatitude of heaven are such that the possession of them, even for a day, could exceed all goods of this life taken together and possessed for a long time.... Therefore, even a short delay of such a good is a very heavy sorrow, far exceeding all the pains of this life. The Holy Souls well understand and weigh the greatness of this evil; and very piercing is the pain they feel, because they know that they are suffering through their own negligence and by their own fault.... There are, however, certain things which would seem to have power to lessen their pain:

1. They are certain of future glory. This hope must bring them much joy; as St. Paul says, "rejoicing in hope." (Roms. xii. 12.)

2. There is the rightness of their will, by which they are conformed to the justice of God. Hence, it follows that, in a certain sense, their pain is voluntary, and thus not so severe.

3. By the love of God they not only bear their punishment, but rejoice in it, because they see that it is the means of satisfying God and being brought to Heaven.

4. If they choose, they can turn their thoughts from the pain of delay, and give them very attentively to the good of hope. This would bring them consolation.

7

THE PAIN OF SENSE.

It is the common judgment of theologians, with St. Augustine, St. Thomas, and St. Bonaventure, that this pain is bitterer than all pain of this life…. Theologians, in common with St. Thomas and St. Bonaventure, teach that the pain of Purgatory is not in any way inflicted by devils. These souls are just and holy. They cannot sin any more; and, to the last, they have overcome the assaults of the devils. It would not, therefore, be fitting that such souls should be given into their power to be tormented by them. Again, when the devils tempt wayfarers, they do it because they hope to lead them into sin, however perfect they may be; but they could have no such hope about the souls in Purgatory, and so would not be likely to tempt them. Besides, they know that their temptations or harassings would have an effect not intended by them, and would bring the souls from Purgatory to Heaven more quickly.

* * * * *

It is the common law that souls in Purgatory, during the whole time that they are there, cannot come out from the prison, even if they wish; The constant closing of the prison-doors is a part of the severity of their punishment. So teach St. John Chrysostom, St. Athanasius, and St. Augustine…. The reason for this is the law of the justice of God. The souls of the lost are kept in prison by force and against their will. The souls in Purgatory stay there willingly, for they understand the just will of God and submit to it. This law, however, can be sometimes dispensed with; and so St. Augustine holds it to be probable that there are often true apparitions of the Holy Souls by the permission of God…. It is true that, as a rule, these are apparitions of souls, who, by a special decree of God, are suffering their Purgatory somewhere in this world…. One thing, however, we must note in these cases. When such a permission is given, the pain of the soul is not interrupted. This is not only seen from the visions themselves, but is what reason requires.

* * * * *

Here occurs the question whether the Holy Souls pray for us and can gain anything for us by merit of congruity, or, at least, impetrate it for us, as others prefer to say. Some have said that they do not thus pray for us, because it is not fitting to their state, in that they are debtors and, as it were, kept in prison for their debts; and also because they do not see God, and so do not know what is done here. They might know such things by special revelations, but revelations of this kind are not due to their state. But surely their penal state does not necessarily hinder the Holy Souls from praying for, and impetrating for us. They are holy and dear to God; and they love us with charity, remembering us, and knowing, at least in a general way, the dangers in which we live; they understand also how greatly we need the help of God: why, then, should they not be able to pray for us, even though in another way they are paying to God their debt of punishment? For we also in this life are debtors to God, and yet we pray for others…. Besides, we may well believe that the Holy Angels make revelations to the souls in Purgatory about their relatives or friends still living on this earth. They will do this for the consolation of the Holy Souls, or that they may know what to ask for us in particular cases, or that they may know of our prayers for them.

ST. CATHARINE OF GENOA ON PURGATORY.

This Holy Soul, while still in the flesh, was placed in the purgatory of the burning love of God, in whose flames she was purified from every stain, so that when she passed from this life she might be ready to enter the presence of God, her most sweet love. By means of that flame of love she comprehended in her own soul the condition of the souls of the faithful in Purgatory, where they are purified from the rust and stain of sins, from which they have not been cleansed in this world. And as in the purgatory of that divine flame she was united with the divine love and satisfied with all that was accomplished in her, she was enabled to comprehend the state of the souls in Purgatory, and thus discoursed concerning it:

"As far as I can see, the souls in Purgatory can have no choice but be there; this God has most justly ordained by His divine decree. They cannot turn towards themselves and say, 'I have committed such and such sins for which I deserve to remain here;' nor can they say, 'Would that I had refrained from them, for then I should at this moment be in Paradise;' nor again, 'This soul will be released before me;' or, 'I shall be released before her.' They retain no memory of either good or evil respecting themselves or others which would increase their pain. They are so contented with the divine inspirations in their regard, and with doing all that is pleasing to God in that way which he chooses, that they cannot think of themselves, though they may strive to do so. They see nothing but the operation of the divine goodness which is so manifestly bringing them to God that they can reflect neither on their own profit nor on their hurt. Could they do so, they would not be in pure charity. They see not that they suffer their pains in consequence of their sins, nor can they for a moment entertain that thought, for should they do so it would be an active imperfection, and that cannot exist in a state where there is no longer the possibility of sin. At the moment of leaving this life, they see why they are sent to Purgatory, but never again; otherwise they would still retain something private, which has no place there. Being established in charity, they can never deviate therefrom by any defect, and have no will or desire save the pure will of pure love, and can swerve from it in nothing. They can neither commit sin nor merit by refraining from it.

* * * * *

"There is no peace to be compared with that of the souls in Purgatory, save that of the saints in Paradise, and this peace is ever augmented by the inflowing of God into these souls, which increases in proportion as the impediments to it are removed. The rust of sin is the impediment, and this the fire continually consumes, so that the soul in this state is continually opening itself to admit the divine communication. As a covered surface can never reflect the sun, not through any defect in that orb, but simply from the resistance offered by the covering, so, if the covering be gradually removed, the surface will by little and little be opened to the sun and will more and more reflect his light. So it is with

9

the rust of sin, which is the covering of the soul. In Purgatory the flames incessantly consume it, and as it disappears the soul reflects more and more perfectly the true sun, who is God. Its contentment increases as this rust wears away, and the soul is laid bare to the divine ray; and thus one increases and the other decreases until the time is accomplished. The pain never diminishes, although the time does; but, as to the will, so united is it to God by pure charity, and so satisfied to be under His divine appointment, that these souls can never say their pains are pains.

"On the other hand, it is true that they suffer torments which no tongue can describe nor any intelligence comprehend, unless it be revealed by such a special grace as that which God has vouchsafed to me, but which I am unable to explain. And this vision which God revealed to me has never departed from my memory. I will describe it as far as I am able, and they whose intellects our Lord will deign to open will understand me.

* * * * *

"The source of all suffering is either original or actual sin. God created the soul pure, simple, free from every stain, and with a certain beatific instinct towards Himself. It is drawn aside from Him by original sin, and when actual sin is afterwards added this withdraws it still farther, and ever, as it removes from Him, its sinfulness increases because its communication with God grows less and less.

* * * * *

"Since the souls in Purgatory are freed from the guilt of sin, there is no barrier between them and God save only the pains they suffer, which delay the satisfaction of their desire. And when they see how serious is even the slightest hindrance, which the necessity of justice causes to check them, a vehement flame kindles within them, which is like that of hell. They feel no guilt, however, and it is guilt which is the cause of the malignant will of the condemned in hell, to whom God does not communicate His goodness; and thus they remain in despair and with a will forever opposed to the good-will of God.

* * * * *

"The souls in Purgatory are entirely conformed to the will of God; therefore, they correspond with His goodness, are contented with all that He ordains, and are entirely purified from the guilt of their sins. They are pure from sins because they have in this life abhorred them and confessed them with true contrition; and for this reason God remits their guilt, so that only the stains of sin remain, and these must be devoured by the fire. Thus freed from guilt and united to the will of God, they see Him clearly according to that degree of light which He allows them, and comprehend how great a good is the fruition of God, for which all souls were created. Moreover, these souls are in such close conformity to God and are drawn so powerfully toward Him by reason of the natural attraction between Him and the soul, that no illustration or comparison could make this impetuosity understood in the way in which my spirit conceives it by its interior sense. Nevertheless, I will use one which occurs to me.

"Let us suppose that in the whole world there were but one loaf to appease the hunger of every creature, and that the bare sight of it would satisfy them. Now man, when in health, has by nature the instinct for food, but if we can suppose him to abstain from it and neither die, nor yet lose health and strength, his hunger would clearly become increasingly urgent. In this case, if he knew that nothing but this loaf would satisfy him, and that until he reached it his hunger could not be appeased, he would suffer intolerable pain, which would increase as his distance from the loaf diminished; but if he were sure that he would never see it, his hell would be as complete as that of the damned souls, who, hungering after God, have no hope of ever seeing the bread of life. But the souls in Purgatory have an assured hope of seeing Him and of being entirely satisfied; and therefore they endure all hunger and suffer all pain until that moment when they enter into eternal possession of this bread, which is Jesus Christ, our Lord, our Saviour, and our Love.

* * * * *

"I will say, furthermore: I see that as far as God is concerned, Paradise has no gates, but he who will may enter. For God is all mercy, and His open arms are ever extended to receive us into His glory. But I see that the divine essence is so pure—purer than the imagination can conceive—that the soul, finding in itself the slightest imperfection, would rather cast itself into a thousand hells than appear, so stained, in the presence of the divine majesty. Knowing, then, that Purgatory was intended for her cleansing, she throws herself therein, and finds there that great mercy, the removal of her stains.

"The great importance of Purgatory, neither mind can conceive nor tongue describe. I see only that its pains are great as those of hell; and yet I see that a soul, stained with the slightest fault, receiving this mercy, counts the pains as nought in comparison with this hindrance to her love. And I know that the greatest misery of the souls in Purgatory is to behold in themselves aught that displeases God, and to discover that, in spite of His goodness, they had consented to it. And this is because, being in the state of grace, they see the reality and the importance of the impediments which hinder their approach to God.

* * * * *

"From that furnace of divine love I see rays of fire dart like burning lamps towards the soul; and so violent and powerful are they that both soul and body would be utterly destroyed, if that were possible. These rays perform a double office; they purify and they annihilate.

"Consider gold: the oftener it is melted the more pure does it become; continue to melt it and every imperfection is destroyed. This is the effect of fire on all materials. The soul, however, cannot be annihilated in God, but in herself she can, and the longer her purification lasts the more perfectly does she die to herself, until at length she remains purified in God.

"When gold has been completely freed from dross, no fire, however great, has any further action on it, for nothing but its imperfections can be consumed. So it is with the divine fire in the soul. God retains her in these flames until every stain is burned away, and she is brought to the highest perfection of which she is

11

capable, each soul in her own degree. And when this is accomplished, she rests wholly in God. Nothing of herself remains, and God is her entire being. When He has thus led her to Himself and purified her, she is no longer passible, for nothing remains to be consumed. If, when thus refined, she should again approach the fire she would feel no pain, for to her it has become the fire of divine love, which is life eternal and which nothing mars."

* * * * *

And thus this blessed Soul, illuminated by the divine ray, said: "Would that I could utter so strong a cry that it would strike all men with terror, and say to them: O wretched beings! why are you so blinded by this world that you make, as you will find at the hour of death, no provision for the great necessity that will then come upon you?

"You shelter yourselves beneath the hope of the mercy of God, which you unceasingly exalt, not seeing that it is your resistance to His great goodness which will be your condemnation. His goodness should constrain you to His will, not encourage you to persevere in your own. Since His justice is unfailing, it must needs be in some way fully satisfied.

"Have not the boldness to say: 'I will go to confession and gain a plenary indulgence, and thus I shall be saved?' Remember that the full confession and entire contrition which are requisite to gain a plenary indulgence are not easily attained. Did you know how hardly they are come by, you would tremble with fear and be more sure of losing than of gaining them."

EXTRACTS FROM THE FATHERS. [1]

[Footnote 1: These extracts are purposely different from those quoted by the learned author of "Purgatory Surveyed," in that portion of his treatise herein comprised.]

ST. CYPRIAN [1] writes: "Our predecessors prudently advised that no brother, departing this life should nominate any churchman his executor; and should he do it, that no oblation should be made for him, nor sacrifice offered for his repose; of which we have had a late example, when no oblation was made, nor prayer, in his name, offered in the Church." [2]

[Footnote 1: Ep., xlvi., p. 114.]

[Footnote 2: Cardinal Wiseman commenting upon this passage, says: "It was considered, therefore, a severe punishment, that prayers and sacrifices should not be offered up for those who had violated any of the ecclesiastical laws."—*Lectures on the Catholic Church*. Lecture xi., p. 59.]

ORIGEN, who wrote in the same century as Cyprian, and some two hundred years after Christ, speaks as follows, in language the most distinct, upon our doctrine of Purgatory: "When we depart this life, if we take with us virtues or vices, shall we receive reward for our virtues, and shall those trespasses be forgiven to us which we knowingly committed; or shall we be punished for our faults, and not receive the reward of our virtues? Neither is true: because we shall suffer for our sins and receive the reward of our virtues. For if on the foundation of Christ you shall have built not only gold and silver and precious stones, but also wood and hay and stubble, what do you expect when the soul shall be separated from the body? Would you enter into Heaven with your wood, and hay, and stubble, to defile the Kingdom of God; or on account of those encumbrances remain without, and receive no reward for your gold and silver and precious stones? Neither is this just. It remains, then, that you be committed to the fire, which shall consume the light materials; for our God, to those who can comprehend heavenly things, is called a *consuming fire*. But this fire consumes not the creature, but what the creature has himself built—wood, and hay, and stubble. It is manifest that, in the first place, the fire destroys the wood of our transgressions, and then returns to us the reward of our good works." [1]

[Footnote 1: Homil. xvi al. xii. in Jerem. T. iii. p. 231,232.]

ST. BASIL, or a contemporary author, thus writes, commenting on the words of Isaiah: "Through the wrath of the Lord is the land burned; the things which are earthly are made the food of a punishing fire; to the end, that the soul may receive favor and be benefited." He continues: "And the people shall be as the fuel of the fire." (*Ibid.*) This is not a threat of extermination; but it denotes expurgation, [1] according to the expression of the Apostles: "If any man's works burn, he shall suffer loss, but he himself shall be saved, yet so as by fire." (1 Cor. iii. 15.) [2]

[Footnote 1: Cardinal Wiseman in commenting upon this passage, says: "Now, mark well the word purgation here used. For it proves that our very term of Purgatory is not modern in the Church."—*Lectures on the Catholic Church*. Lecture xi., p. 60.]

[Footnote 2: Com. in C., ix. Isai. T. I., p. 554.]

The following is from ST. EPHREM, of Edessa: "My brethren, come to me, and prepare me for my departure, for my strength is wholly gone. Go along with me in psalms and in your prayers; and please constantly to make oblations for me. When the thirtieth day [1] shall be completed, then remember me: for the dead are helped by the offerings of the living. If also the sons of Mathathias, who celebrated their feasts in figures only, could cleanse those from guilt by their offerings who fell in battle, how much more shall the priests of Christ aid the dead by their oblations and prayers?" [2]

[Footnote 1: "The very day," says Cardinal Wiseman, "observed by the Catholic Church with peculiar solemnity, in praying and observing Mass for the dead". Archbishop Corrigan, of New York, in announcing to the clergy of his diocese the death of His Eminence the late Cardinal McCloskey, speaks as follows: "The reverend rectors are also requested to have solemn services for the soul of our late beloved chief pastor, on the *seventh* and *thirtieth* day."]

[Footnote 2: In Testament. T. ii., p. 334. p. 371, Edit. Oxen.]

Thus speaks ST. GREGORY of Nyssa: "In the present life, God allows man to remain subject to what himself has chosen; that, having tasted of the evil which he desired, and learned by experience how bad an exchange has been made, he might feel an ardent wish to lay down the load of those vices and inclinations, which are contrary to reason; and thus, in this life, being renovated by prayers and the pursuit of wisdom, or, in the next, being expiated by the purging fire, he

13

might recover the state of happiness which he had lost.... When he has quitted his body, and the difference between virtue and vice is known, he cannot be admitted to approach the Divinity till the purging fire shall have expiated the stains with which his soul was infected. The same fire, in others, will cancel the corruption of matter and the propensity to evil." [1]

[Footnote 1: Orat. de Defunctis. T. ii., p. 1066, 1067, 1068.]

ST. CYRIL of Jerusalem: "Then" (in the Liturgy of the Church) "we pray for the holy Fathers and Bishops that are dead; and, in short, for all those who are departed this life in our communion; believing that the souls of those, for whom the prayers, are offered, receive very great relief while this holy and tremendous victim lies upon the altar." [1]

[Footnote 1: Catech. Mystag., V. N., ix., x., p. 328.]

ST. EPIPHANIUS writes: "There is nothing more opportune, nothing more to be admired, than the rite which directs the names of the dead to be mentioned. They are aided by the prayer that is offered for them, though it may not cancel all their faults. We mention both the just and sinners, in order that for the latter we may obtain mercy." [1]

[Footnote 1: Haer. IV. Lib. LXXV., T. i., p. 911.]

ST. AUGUSTINE speaks as follows: "The prayers of the Church, or of good persons, are heard in favor of those Christians who departed this life not so bad as to be deemed unworthy of mercy, nor so good as to be entitled to immediate happiness. So also, at the resurrection of the dead, there will some be found, to whom mercy will be imparted, having gone through these pains, to which the spirits of the dead are liable. Otherwise it would not have been said of some with truth, that their sin shall not be forgiven, neither in this world nor in the world to come (Matt. xii., 32) unless some sins were remitted in the next world." [1]

[Footnote 1: De Civit. Dei., Lib. XX, c. xxiv., p. 492.]

In another passage he comments on the words of St. Paul: "If they had built *gold* and *silver* and *precious stones,* they would be secure from both fires; not only from that in which the wicked shall be punished for ever, but likewise from that fire which will purify those who shall be saved by fire. But because it is said *he shall be saved,* that fire is thought lightly of; though the suffering will be more grievous than anything man can undergo in this life."

Let us hear ST. JEROME: [1] "As we believe the torments of the devil, and of those wicked men who said in their hearts *there is no God,* to be eternal, so, in regard to those sinners who have not denied their faith, and whose works will be proved and purged by fire, we conclude that the sentence of the Judge will be tempered by mercy."

[Footnote 1: Comment. in c. xv., Isai., T. ii., p. 492.]

St. Jerome thus speaks in his letter to Paula, concerning the death and burial of her mother, Eustochium: "From henceforward there were no wailings nor lamentations as are usual amongst men of this world, but the swarms of those present resounded with psalms in various tongues. And being removed by the hands of the bishops, and by those placing their shoulders under the bier, while

14

other pontiffs were carrying lamps and wax tapers, and others led the choirs of psalmodists, she was laid in the middle of the church of the cave of the Saviour.... Psalms resounded in the Hebrew, Greek, Latin, and Syriac tongues, not only during the three days intervening until she was laid under the church and near the cave of the Lord, but through the entire week."

ST. AMBROSE has many passages throughout his works, as Dr. Wiseman remarks. Thus he quotes St. Paul's First Epistle to the Corinthians (iii., 5): "'If any man's works burn he shall suffer loss; but he shall be saved, yet so as by fire.' He will be saved, the Apostle said, because his substance shall remain, while his bad doctrine shall perish. Therefore, he said, yet so as by fife, in order that his salvation be not understood to be without pain. He shows that he shall be saved indeed, but he shall undergo the pain of fire, and be thus purified, not like the unbelieving and wicked man who shall be punished in everlasting fire." [1]

[Footnote 1: Comment. in I Ep. ad Cor., T. ii.; in App, p. 122.]

The following is from his funeral oration on the Emperor Theodosius: "Lately we deplored together his death, and now, while Prince Honorius is present before our altars, we celebrate the fortieth day. Some observe the third and the thirtieth, others the seventh and the fortieth. Give, O Lord, rest to Thy servant Theodosius, that rest which Thou hast prepared for Thy Saints. May his soul thither tend, whence it came, where it cannot feel the sting of death, where it will learn that death is the termination, not of nature, but of sin. I loved him, therefore will I follow him to the land of the living; I will not leave him, till, by my prayers and lamentation, he shall be admitted to the holy mount of the Lord to which his deserts call him." [1]

[Footnote 1: De obitu. Theodosii. Ibid., pp. 1197-8; 1207-8.]

He thus concludes his letter to ST. FAUSTINUS on the death of his sister: "Therefore I consider her not so much to be deplored as to be followed by our prayers, nor do I think that her soul should be saddened with tears, but rather commended to the Lord in oblations. For our flesh cannot be perpetual or lasting; it must necessarily fall in order that it may rise again—it must be dissolved in order that it may rest, and that there may be some end of sin." [1]

[Footnote 1: St. Ambr., p. 39, ad Faustini, t. 2, p 944, ed. Ben.]

In his funeral oration upon his brother Satyrus, he cries out: "To Thee now, O omnipotent God, I commend this innocent soul,—to Thee I offer my victim. Accept graciously and serenely the gift of the brother—the sacrifice of the priest."

[Footnote 1: De excessu frateris satyri, No. 80, p. 1135.]

In his discourse on the deceased Emperor Valentinian the Younger, murdered in 392: "Give the holy mysteries to the dead. Let us, with pious earnestness, beg repose for his soul. Lift up your hands with me, O people, that at least by this duty we may make some return for his benefits." [1] Joining him with the Emperor Gratian, his brother, dead some years before, he says: "Both blessed, if my prayers can be of any force! No duty shall pass over you in silence. No prayer of mine shall ever be closed without remembering you. No night shall pass you over without some vows of my supplications. You shall have a share in all my sacrifices. If I forget you let my own right hand be forgotten." [2]

[Footnote 1: St. Ambr. de obitu Valent, No. 56, t. 2, p 1189, ed. Bened.]

[Footnote 2: Ibid., No. 78, p. 1194.]

"It was not in vain," says ST. CHRYSOSTOM, "that the apostles ordained a commemoration of the deceased in the holy and tremendous mysteries. They were sensible of the benefit and advantage which accrues to them from this practice. For, when the congregation stands with open arms as well as the priests, and the tremendous sacrifice is before them, how should our prayers for them not appease God? But this is said of such as have departed in faith." [1]

[Footnote 1: Hom. 3 in Phil., t. n., p. 217 ed. Montfauc.]

ST. AUGUSTINE again says: "Nor is it to be denied that the souls of the departed are relieved by the piety of their living friends, when the sacrifice of the Mediator is offered for them, or alms are given in the Church. But these things are profitable to those who, while they lived, deserved that they might avail them. There is a life so good as not to require them, and there is another so wicked that after death it can receive no benefit from them. When, therefore, the sacrifices of the altar or alms are offered for all Christians, for the very good they are thanksgivings, they are propitiations for those who are not very bad. For the very wicked, they are some kind of comfort to the living."

In another of his works he says that prayer for the dead in the holy mysteries was observed by the whole church. He expounds the thirty- seventh Psalm as having reference to Purgatory. The words: "Rebuke me not in thy fury, neither chastise me in thy wrath," he explains as follows: "That you purify me in this life, and render me such that I may not stand in need of that purging fire."

ARNOBIUS speaks of the public liturgies: "In which peace and pardon are begged of God for kings, magistrates, friends and enemies, both the living and those who are delivered from the body."

To these few extracts, which space permits, might be added innumerable others from St. Clement of Alexandria, St. Athanasius, St. Paulinus, St. Eusebius, Lactantius, Tertullian, St. Caesarius of Arles, St. Bernard, Venerable Bede, St. Thomas Aquinas, and so on down to our own immediate time. Their testimony is most clear not only as regards the custom of praying for the dead, but the actual doctrine of Purgatory, as it is now understood in the Church. They are, in fact, in many cases most explicit upon this point, obviously referring to a middle state of suffering and expiation, and thus refuting by anticipation the objections of those who claim that the primitive Christians prayed indeed for the dead, but knew nothing of Purgatory: a contradiction, it would seem, as prayer for the dead, to be available, supposes a place or state of probation. But, even where the mention made by the Fathers of prayer for the dead does not refer expressly to a place of purgation, it is no more a proof that they did not hold this doctrine than that those modern Catholic authors disbelieve in it, who suppose this middle state of suffering to be admitted by their readers. Or even, which rarely happens, if they be silent altogether upon the subject, it no more infers their ignorance of such a belief than the same silence to be noted in theological and religious works of our own day. It proves no more than that they are at the time engaged in treating of some other subject. The following, which may serve as a conclusion to these extracts, is the solemn decision of the Council of Trent in regard to this doctrine: "The Church, inspired by the Holy Ghost, has always taught, according to the Holy Scriptures and apostolic tradition, that there is a Purgatory, and that the souls there detained receive comfort from the prayers and good works of the faithful, particularly through the sacrifice of the Mass, which is so acceptable to God."

In the thirteenth Canon of the sixth session, it decrees that, "if any one should say that a repentant sinner, after having received the grace of justification, the punishment of eternal pains being remitted, has no temporary punishment to be suffered either in this life or in the next in Purgatory, before he can enter into the Kingdom of God, let him be anathema."

In the third Canon of the twenty-fourth session, it defines "that the sacrifice of the Mass is propitiatory both for the living and the dead for sins, punishments and satisfactions."

VERSES FROM THE IMITATION.
THOMAS A KEMPIS.

Trust not in thy friends and neighbors, and put not oft thy soul's welfare till the future; for men will forget thee sooner than thou thinkest.

It is better to provide now in time and send some good before thee than to trust to the assistance of others after death.

If thou art not solicitous for thyself now, who will be solicitous for thee hereafter.

Did'st thou also well ponder in thy heart the future pains of hell or Purgatory, methinks thou would'st bear willingly labor and sorrow and fear no kind of austerity.

Who will remember thee when thou art dead? and who will pray for thee?

Now thy labor is profitable, thy tears are acceptable, thy groans are heard, thy sorrow is satisfying and purifieth the soul.

The patient man hath a great and wholesome purgatory.

Better is it to purge away our sins, and cut off our vices now, than to keep them for purgation hereafter.

If thou shalt say thou are not able to suffer much, how then wilt thou endure the fire of Purgatory. Of two evils, one ought always to choose the less.

When a Priest celebrateth, he honoreth God, he rejoiceth the Angels, he edifieth the Church, he helpeth the living, he obtaineth rest for the departed, and maketh himself partaker of all good things.

I offer to Thee also all the pious desires of devout persons; the necessities of my parents, friends, brothers, sisters, and all those that are dear to me; ... and all who have desired and besought me to offer up prayers and Masses for themselves and all theirs, whether they are still living in the flesh or are already dead to this

17

world.

ST. AUGUSTINE AND HIS MOTHER, ST. MONICA.

[In the beautiful account given by the great St. Augustine of the last illness and death of his holy mother, St. Monica, we find some touching proofs of the pious belief of mother and son in the existence of a middle state for souls in the after life. The holy doctor had been relating that memorable conversation on heavenly things which took place between his mother and himself on that moonlight night at the window in the inn at Ostia, immortalized by Ary Schaeffer in his beautiful picture.]

To this what answer I made her I do not well remember. But scarce five days, or not many more, had passed after this before she fell into a fever: and one day, being very sick, she swooned away, and was for a little while insensible. We ran in, but she soon came to herself again, and looking upon me and my brother (Navigius), that were standing by her, said to us like one inquiring: "Where have I been?" then, beholding us struck with grief, she said: "Here you shall bury your mother." I held my peace and refrained weeping; but my brother said something by which he signified his wish, as of a thing more happy, that she might not die abroad but in her own country; which she hearing, with a concern in her countenance, and checking him with her eyes that he should have such notions, then looking upon me, said: "Do you hear what he says?" then to us both: "Lay this body anywhere; be not concerned about that; only this I beg of you, that wheresoever you be, you make remembrance of me at the Lord's altar." And when she had expressed to us this, her mind, with such words as she could, she said no more, but lay struggling with her disease that grew stronger upon her.

* * * * *

And now behold the body is carried out to be buried, and I both go and return without tears. Neither in those prayers, which we poured forth to Thee when the sacrifice of our ransom was offered to Thee for her, the body being set down by the grave before the interment of it, as custom is there, neither in those prayers, I say, did I shed any tears.

* * * * *

And now, my heart being healed of that wound in which a carnal affection might have some share, I pour out to Thee, our God, in behalf of that servant of Thine, a far different sort of tears, flowing from a spirit frighted with the consideration of the perils of every soul that dies in Adam. For, although she, being revived in Christ, even before her being set loose from the flesh and lived in such manner, as that Thy name is much praised in her faith and manners; yet I dare not say that from the time Thou didst regenerate her by baptism, no word came out of her mouth against Thy command.... I, therefore, O my Praise and my Life, the God of my heart, setting for a while aside her good deeds, for which with joy I give Thee thanks, entreat Thee at present for the sins of my mother. Hear me, I beseech Thee, through that Cure of our wounds that hung upon the tree, and that, sitting now at Thy right hand, maketh intercession to Thee for us. I know that she did mercifully, and from her heart forgive to her debtors their trespasses: do Thou likewise forgive her her debts, if she hath also contracted some in those many years she lived after the saving water.... And I believe Thou hast already done what I ask, but these free offerings of my mouth approve, O Lord.

For she, when the day of her dissolution was at hand, had no thought for the sumptuous covering of her body, or the embalming of it, nor had she any desire of a fine monument, nor was solicitous about her sepulchre in her own country: none of these things did she recommend to us; but only desired that we should make a remembrance of her at Thy altar, at which she had constantly attended without one day's intermission, from whence she knew was dispensed that Holy Victim by which was cancelled that handwriting that was against us (Coloss. II.), by which that enemy was triumphed over who reckoneth up our sins and seeketh what he may lay to our charge, but findeth nothing in Him through whom we conquer. Who shall refund to Him that innocent blood He shed for us? Who shall repay Him the price with which He bought us, that so he may take us away from Him? To the sacrament of which price of our redemption Thy handmaid bound fast her soul by the bond of faith....

Let her, therefore, rest in peace, together with her husband, before whom and after whom she was known to no man; whom she dutifully served, bringing forth fruit to Thee, in much patience, that she might also gain him to Thee. And do Thou inspire, O Lord, my God, do Thou inspire Thy servants, my brethren, Thy children, my masters, whom I serve with my voice, and my heart, and my writings, that as many as shall read this shall remember, at Thy altar, Thy handmaid Monica with Patricius, formerly her husband. Let them remember, with a pious affection, these who were my parents in this transitory life, my brethren under Thee, our Father, in our Catholic Mother, and my fellow-citizens in the eternal Jerusalem, for which the pilgrimage of Thy people here below continually sigheth from their setting out till their return. That so what my mother made her last request to me may be more plentifully performed for her by the prayers of many, procured by these, my confessions, and my prayers. [1]

[Footnote 1: Conf. B. IX. Chs. XI.-XIII.]

ST. GERTRUDE AND THE HOLY SOULS.

[In the "Life and Revelations of St. Gertrude" we find many instances of the efficacy of prayers for the dead and how pleasing to God is devotion to the souls in Purgatory. From these we select the following.]

Our Blessed Lord once said to the Saint: "If a soul is delivered by prayer from Purgatory I accept it as if I had myself been delivered from captivity, and I will assuredly reward it according to the abundance of my mercy." The religious also beheld many souls meeting before her to testify their gratitude for their deliverance from Purgatory, through the prayers which had been offered for her, and which she had not needed.

* * * * *

As St. Gertrude prayed fervently before matins on the blessed night of the Resurrection, the Lord Jesus appeared to her full of majesty and glory. Then she cast herself at His feet, to adore Him devoutly and humbly, saying: "O glorious Spouse, joy of the angels, Thou who hast shown me the favor of choosing me to be Thy spouse, who am the least of Thy creatures! I ardently desire Thy glory, and my only friends are those who love Thee; therefore I beseech Thee to pardon the souls of Thy special friends [1] by the virtue of Thy most glorious Resurrection. And to obtain this grace from Thy goodness, I offer Thee, in union with Thy Passion, all the sufferings which my continual infirmities have caused me." Then Our Lord, having favored her with many caresses, showed her a great multitude of souls who were freed from their pains, saying: "Behold, I have given them to you as a recompense for your rare affection; and through all eternity they will acknowledge that they have been delivered by your prayers, and you will be honored and glorified for it." She replied: "How many are they?" He answered: "This knowledge belongs to God alone."

As she feared that these souls, though freed from their pains, were not yet admitted to glory, she offered to endure whatever God might please, either in body or soul, to obtain their entrance into that beatitude; and Our Lord, won by her fervor, granted her request immediately.

[Footnote 1: "This seems to refer," says the author of the Saint's life, "to the souls in Purgatory."]

Some time after, as the Saint suffered most acute pain in her side, she made an inclination before a crucifix; and Our Lord freed her from the pain, and granted the merit of it to these souls, recommending them to make her a return by their prayers.

* * * * *

On Wednesday, at the elevation of the Host, she besought Our Lord for the souls of the faithful in Purgatory, that He would free them from their pains by virtue of His, admirable Ascension; and she beheld Our Lord descending into Purgatory with a golden rod in His hand, which had as many hooks as there had been prayers for their souls; by these He appeared to draw them into a place of repose. She understood by this, that whenever any one prays generally, from a motive of charity, for the souls in Purgatory, the greater part of those who, during their lives, have exercised themselves in works of charity, are released.

* * * * *

On another occasion, as she remarked that she had offered all her merits for the dead, she said to Our Lord: "I hope, O Lord, that Thou wilt frequently cast the eyes of Thy mercy on my indigence." He replied: "What can I do more for one who has thus deprived herself of all things through charity, than to cover her immediately with charity?" She answered: "Whatever Thou mayest do, I shall always appear before Thee destitute of all merit, for I have renounced all I have gained or may gain." He replied: "Do you not know that a mother would allow a child who was well clothed to sit at her feet, but she would take one who was barely clad into her arms, and cover her with her own garment?" He added: "And now, what advantages have you, who are seated on the shore of an ocean, over those who sit by a little rivulet?" That is to say, those who keep their good works for themselves, have the rivulet; but those who renounce them in love and humility, possess God, who is an inexhaustible ocean of beatitude.

* * * * *

On one occasion, while Mass was being celebrated for a poor woman who had died lately, St. Gertrude recited five *Pater Nosters*, in honor of Our Lord's five wounds, for the repose of her soul; and, moved by divine inspiration, she offered all her good works for the increase of the beatitude of this person. When she had made this offering, she immediately beheld the soul in heaven, in the place destined for her; and the throne prepared for her was elevated as far above the place where she had been, as the highest throne of the seraphim is above that of the lowest angel. The Saint then asked Our Lord how this soul had been worthy to obtain such advantage from her prayers, and He replied:

"She has merited this grace in three ways: first, because she always had a sincere will and perfect desire of serving Me in religion, if it had been possible; secondly, because she especially loved all religious and all good people; thirdly, because she was always ready to honor Me by performing any service she could for them." He added: "You may judge, by the sublime rank to which she is elevated, how agreeable these practices are to Me."

A certain religious died who had always been accustomed to pray very fervently for the souls of the faithful departed; but she had failed in the perfection of obedience, preferring her own will to that of her superior in her fasts and vigils. After her decease she appeared adorned with rich ornaments, but so weighed down by a heavy burden, which she was obliged to carry, that she could not approach to God, though many persons were endeavoring to lead her to Him.

As Gertrude marvelled at this vision, she was taught that the persons who endeavored to conduct the soul to God were those whom she had released by her prayers; but this heavy burden indicated the faults she had committed against obedience. Then Our Lord said: "Behold how those grateful souls endeavor to free her from the requirements of My justice, and show these ornaments; nevertheless, she must suffer for her faults of disobedience and self-will." ...

Then the Saint beheld her ornament, which appeared like a vessel of boiling water containing a hard stone, which must be completely dissolved therein before she could obtain relief from this torment; but in these sufferings she was much consoled and assisted by those souls, and by the prayers of the faithful. After this Our Lord showed St. Gertrude the path by which the souls ascend to heaven. It resembled a straight plank, a little inclined; so that those who ascended did so with difficulty. They were assisted and supported by hands on either side, which indicated the prayers offered for them.

* * * * *

One day St. Gertrude asked Our Lord how many souls were delivered from Purgatory by her prayers and those of her sisters. "The number," replied Our Lord, "is proportioned to the zeal and fervor of those who pray for them." He added: "My love urges me to release a great number of souls for the prayers of each religious, and at each verse of the psalms which they recite, I release many."

21

* * * * *

When Mass was offered for the deceased Brother Hermann, his soul appeared to St. Gertrude all radiant with light, and transported with joy. Then Gertrude said to Our Lord: "Is this soul now entirely freed from its sufferings?" Our Lord answered: "He is already free from much suffering, and no human being can form an idea of his glory; but he is not yet so perfectly purified as to be worthy to enjoy My presence, though he is approaching nearer and nearer to this purity by the prayers which are offered for him, and is more and more consoled and relieved."

ST. JOSEPH'S INTERCESSION FOR THE FAITHFUL DEPARTED.

(From "Le Propagateur de la Devotion a Saint Joseph.")

ST. FRANCIS DE SALES says: "We do not often enough remember our dead, our faithful departed." Thus the Church, like a good mother, recalls to us the thought of the dead when we have forgotten them, and therefore she consecrates the month of November to the memory of the dead. This pious and salutary practice of praying for an entire month for the dead takes its rise from the earliest ages of the Church. The custom of mourning *thirty days* for the dead existed amongst the Jews. The practice of saying thirty Masses on thirty consecutive days was established by St. Gregory, and Innocent XI. enriched it with indulgences. "God has made known to me," says the venerable sister Marie Denise de Martignat, "that a devotion to the death of St. Joseph obtains many graces for those who are agonizing, and that, as St. Joseph did not at once pass into heaven —because Jesus Christ had not opened its gates—but descended into Limbo, it is a most useful devotion for the agonizing, and for the souls in Purgatory, to offer to God the resignation of St. Joseph when he was dying and about to leave Jesus and Mary in this world, and to honor the holy patience of this great Saint waiting calmly in Limbo until Easter-day, when Jesus Christ, risen and glorious, released him." And if St. Joseph consoles the souls in Purgatory, none will be so dear to him as those who were devout to him in life, and zealous in spreading a devotion to him.

ST. FRANCIS DE SALES ON PURGATORY [1]

[Footnote 1: Consoling Thoughts of St Francis de Sales. Arranged by Rev. Father Huguet. Pp. 336-7.]

The opinion of St. Francis de Sales was that from the thought of Purgatory we should draw more consolation than pain. The greater number of those, he said, who fear Purgatory so much, do so in consideration of their own interests and of the love they bear themselves rather than the interests of God; and this happens because those who treat of this place from the pulpit usually speak of its pains and are silent in regard to the happiness and peace which are found in it....

When any of his friends or acquaintances died, he never grew weary of speaking fondly of them and recommending them to the prayers of others.

His usual expression was: "We do not sufficiently remember our dead, our faithful departed;" and the proof of it is that we do not speak enough of them. We turn away from that discourse as from a sad subject. We leave the dead to bury their dead. Their memory perishes from us with the sound of their funeral-bell.

22

We forget that the friendship which ends even with death, is never true, Holy Scripture assuring us that true love is stronger than death.

He was accustomed to say that in this single work of mercy the thirteen others are assembled.

Is it not, he said, in some manner, to visit the sick, to obtain by our prayers the relief of the poor suffering souls in Purgatory?

Is it not to give drink to those who thirst after the vision of God, and who are enveloped in burning flames, to share with them the dew of our prayers?

Is it not to feed the hungry, to aid in their deliverance by the means which faith suggests?

Is it not truly to ransom prisoners?

Is it not truly to clothe the naked, to procure for them a garment of light, a raiment of glory?

Is it not an admirable degree of hospitality, to procure their admission into the heavenly Jerusalem, and to make them fellow-citizens with the Saints and domestics of God?

Is it not a greater service to place souls in heaven than to bury bodies in the earth?

As to spirituals, is it not a work whose merit may be compared to that of counselling the weak, correcting the wayward, instructing the ignorant, forgiving offenses, enduring injuries? And what consolation, however great, that can be given to the afflicted of this world, is comparable with that which is brought by our prayers to those poor souls which have such bitter need of them?

CARDINAL GIBBONS ON PURGATORY.

The Catholic Church teaches that, besides a place of eternal torments for the wicked and of everlasting rest for the righteous, there exists in the next life a middle state of temporary punishment, allotted for those who have died in venial sin, or who have not satisfied the justice of God for sins already forgiven. She also teaches us that, although the souls consigned to this intermediate state, commonly called Purgatory, cannot help themselves, they may be aided by the suffrages of the faithful on earth. The existence of Purgatory naturally implies the correlative dogma—the utility of praying for the dead; for the souls consigned to this middle state have not reached the term of their journey. They are still exiles from heaven, and are fit subjects for divine clemency.

Is it not strange that this cherished doctrine should be called in question by the levelling innovators of the sixteenth century, when we consider that it is clearly taught in the Old Testament; that it is, at least, insinuated in the New Testament; that it is unanimously proclaimed by the Fathers of the Church; that it is embodied in all the ancient liturgies of the Oriental and Western Church; and that it is alike consonant with our reason and eminently consoling to the human heart?
* * * * *

You now perceive that this devotion is not an invention of modern times, but a doctrine universally enforced in the best and purest ages of the Church.

You see that praying for the dead was not a devotion cautiously recommended by some obscure or visionary writer, but an act of religion preached and inculcated by all the great Doctors and Fathers of the Church, who are the recognized expounders of the Christian religion.

You see them, too, inculcating this doctrine not as a cold and abstract principle, but as an imperative act of daily piety, and embodying it in their ordinary exercises of devotion.

They prayed for the dead in their morning and evening devotions. They prayed for them in their daily office, and in the sacrifice of the Mass. They asked the prayers of the congregation for the souls of the deceased, in the public services of Sunday. And on the monuments which were erected to the dead, some of which are preserved even to this day, epitaphs were inscribed, earnestly invoking for their souls the prayers of the living. How gratifying it is to our Catholic hearts, that a devotion so soothing to afflicted spirits is, at the same time, so firmly grounded on the tradition of ages.

That the practice of praying for the dead has descended from apostolic times is also evident from the *Liturgies* of the Church. A Liturgy is the established form of public worship, containing the authorized prayers of the Church. The Missal, or Mass-book, for instance, which you see on our altars, contains a portion of the Liturgy of the Catholic Church. The principal Liturgies are: The Liturgy of St. James the Apostle, who founded the Church of Jerusalem; the Liturgy of St. Mark the Evangelist, founder of the Church of Alexandria, and the Liturgy of St. Peter, who established the Church in Rome. These Liturgies are called after the Apostles who compiled them. There are, besides, the Liturgies of St. Chrysostom and St. Basil, which are chiefly based on that of St. James.

Now, all these Liturgies, without an exception, have prayers for the dead, and their providential preservation serves as another triumphant vindication of the venerable antiquity of this Catholic doctrine.

The Eastern and the Western churches were happily united until the fourth and fifth centuries, when the heresiarchs Arius, Nestorius and Eutyches withdrew millions of souls from the centre of unity. The followers of these sects were called, after their founders, Arians, Nestorians, and Eutychians, and from that day to the present the two latter bodies have formed distinct communions, being separated from the Catholic Church in the East, just as the Protestant churches are separated from her in the West.

The Greek Schismatic Church, of which the present Russo-Greek Church is the offspring, severed her connection with the See of Rome in the ninth century.

But in leaving the Catholic Church, these Eastern sects retained the old Liturgies, which they use to this day....

During my sojourn in Rome, at the Ecumenical Council, I devoted a great deal of my leisure time to the examination of the various Liturgies of the Schismatic churches of the East. I found in all of them formulas of prayers for the dead almost identical with that of the Roman Missal: "Remember, O Lord, Thy servants who are gone before us with the sign of faith, and sleep in peace. To these, O Lord, and to all who rest in Christ, grant, we beseech Thee, a place of refreshment, light, and peace, through the same Jesus Christ our Lord!"

Not content with studying their books, I called upon the Oriental Patriarchs and Bishops in communion with the See of Rome, who belong to the Armenian, the Chaldean, the Coptic, the Maronite, and Syriac rites. They all assured me that the Schismatic Christians of the East among whom they live have, without exception, prayers and sacrifices for the dead.

Now, I ask, when could those Eastern sects have commenced to adopt the Catholic practice of praying for the dead? They could not have received it from us since the ninth century, because the Greek Church separated from us then, and has had no communion with us since that time, except at intervals, up to the twelfth century. Nor could they have adopted the practice since the fourth or fifth century, inasmuch as the Arians, Nestorians, and Eutychians have had no religious communication with us since that period. Therefore, in common with us, they received this doctrine from the Apostles.... I have already spoken of the devotion of the ancient Jewish Church to the souls of the departed. But perhaps you are not aware that the Jews retain to this day, in their Liturgy, the pious practice of praying for the dead. Yet such in reality is the case.

Amid all their wanderings and vicissitudes of life, though dismembered and dispersed, like sheep without a shepherd, over the surface of the globe, the children of Israel have never forgotten or neglected the sacred duty of praying for their deceased brethren.

Unwilling to make this assertion without the strongest evidence, I procured from a Jewish convert an authorized Prayer-book of the Hebrew Church, from which I extract the following formula of prayers which are prescribed for funerals: "Departed brother! mayest thou find open the gates of heaven, and see the city of peace and the dwellings of safety, and meet the ministering angels hastening joyfully towards thee! And may the High Priest stand to receive thee, and go thou to the end, rest in peace, and rise again *into* life! May the repose established in the celestial abode... be the lot, dwelling, and the resting place of the soul of our deceased brother (whom the spirit of the Lord may guide into Paradise), who departed from this world, according to the will of God, the Lord of heaven and earth. May the Supreme King of Kings, through His infinite mercy, hide him under the shadow of His wings. May He raise him at the end of his days, and cause him to drink of the stream of His delights!"

I am happy to say that the more advanced and enlightened members of the Episcopalian Church are steadily returning to the faith of their forefathers, regarding prayers for the dead. An acquaintance of mine, once a distinguished clergyman of the Episcopal communion, but now a convert, informed me that hundreds of Protestant clergymen in this country, and particularly in England, have a firm belief in the efficacy of prayers for the dead, but for well-known reasons they are reserved in the expression of their faith. He easily convinced me of the truth of his assertion, particularly as far as the Church of England is concerned, by sending me six different works published in London, all bearing on the subject of Purgatory. These books are printed under the auspices of the

Protestant Episcopal Church; they all contain prayers for the dead, and prove, from Catholic grounds, the existence of a middle state after death, and the duty of praying for our deceased brethren. [1]

[Footnote 1: See "Path of Holiness," Rivington's, London: "Treasury of Devotion," Ibid; "Catechism of Theology," Masten, London.]

To sum up: we see the practice of praying for the dead enforced in the ancient Hebrew Church, and in the Jewish synagogue of to-day. We see it proclaimed age after age by all the Fathers of Christendom. We see it incorporated in every one of the ancient Liturgies of the East and of the West. We see it zealously taught by the Russian Church of to-day, and by that immense family of schismatic Christians scattered over the East. We behold it, in fine, a cherished devotion of two hundred millions of Catholics, as well as of a respectable portion of the Episcopal Church.

Would it not, my friend, be the height of rashness and presumption in you to prefer your private opinion to this immense weight of learning, sanctity, and authority? Would it not be impiety in you to stand aside with sealed lips, while the Christian world is sending up an unceasing *De profundis* for departed brethren? Would it not be cold and heartless in you not to pray for your deceased friends, on account of prejudices which have no grounds in Scripture, tradition, or reason itself?

* * * * *

Oh! far from us a religion which would decree an eternal divorce between the living and the dead. How consoling is it to the Catholic, to think that, in praying thus for his departed friend, his prayers are not in violation of, but in accordance with, the voice of the Church; and that as, like Augustine, he watches at the pillow of a dying mother, so, like Augustine, he can continue the same office of piety for her soul after she is dead, by praying for her. How cheering the reflection that the golden link of prayer unites you still to those who "fall asleep in the Lord," and that you can still speak to them and pray for them!....

Oh! it is this thought that robs death of its sting and makes the separation of friends endurable. And if your departed friend needs not your prayers, they are not lost, but, like the rain absorbed by the sun, and descending again in fruitful showers on our fields, they will be gathered by the Sun of Justice, and they will come down in refreshing showers of grace upon your head. "Cast thy bread upon the running waters; for, after a long time, thou shalt find it again." [1]

[Footnote 1: Faith of our Fathers, chap. xvi.]

THE DOCTRINE OF PURGATORY.
ARCHBISHOP HUGHES. [1]

[Footnote 1: Answer to nine objections made.]

The Catholic Church does not believe that God created any to be damned absolutely, notwithstanding their co-operation with the means of salvation which were secured to them by the death of Jesus Christ; nor any to be saved absolutely, unless they co-operate with those means. Hence she has ever taught the doctrine which is inculcated in Scripture, that heaven may be obtained by all who shall apply the means which the Saviour of the World has left in His Church for that end: in a word, that every man shall be judged according to his works. This doctrine is consonant with the justice which must belong to the Deity. She knows God is too pure to admit anything defiled into His heavenly abode (Apoc. xxi. 27); and yet too just and merciful to punish a slight transgression with the same severity as is due to an enormous crime. Now, suppose two men to sin against God at the same time, the one by the deliberate murder of his father—for the case is possible—and the other, by a slight, almost inadvertent, falsehood; and suppose, further, that they are both to appear before God the next moment to answer for the deeds done in the flesh, I ask whether it is consistent with the idea we have of divine justice to think that both will be condemned to the same everlasting punishment? If it be, then there is no more moral turpitude in parricide than in telling a trivial falsehood, which injures no one, but still is offensive and displeasing to God. But if it be not consistent with divine justice, then you must admit the distinction of guilt, and consequently of punishment. Now, that God exacts a temporary punishment for sin, after the guilt and eternal punishment are remitted, appears from the testimony of His Sacred Word. St. Paul teaches that the death of the body is a punishment which the sin of our first parent entailed on his progeny; and yet many who have been regenerated by baptism from that original guilt, nevertheless die before they have committed any actual sin whatever. The children of Israel had to leave their bones in the wilderness, after the forty years' sojournment, as a punishment, inflicted by the Almighty Himself, for sins which He had expressly forgiven them. Num. xiv. 20, 22. David was forgiven his sin—and yet he was punished for it, by the death of his child, whom he loved most tenderly. He sinned by numbering his people; and although it was forgiven him, he had still to choose his punishment—either war, famine, or pestilence. If such be the dispensation of God to His creatures in this world, why may it not be also after death? Will you say it is because the body is the medium of suffering in this life? This is not exactly true—the body, indeed, is the medium, in many instances, through which the soul is made to suffer. But God inflicted no corporal chastisement on David by taking his child—it was the king's soul that was touched, and felt, and suffered. Does not the soul remain susceptible of suffering after death; and may not God, conformably with the examples here laid down, extend to it in a future state the same salutary dispensation, for His own just and merciful purposes? But you will ask what Scripture I can quote to show that He really does so. Now, suppose I were to refer you to the same rule, and demand from you the text by which you feel warranted to profane the Sabbath, and sanctify the Sunday in its stead—what will you have to answer in reply? Surely if the authority of the Catholic Church is sufficient to authorize your *practice* in the one case, it is equally so with regard to my belief in the other. But our situations are very different; because I admit the authority of the Church in both instances, and I shall prove that her doctrine of Purgatory, so far from opposing, is grounded on Scripture. Whereas you reject the Church, you make, as you say, the Scripture the *only rule* of your faith; and yet when the

Scripture says, "Thou shalt keep holy the Sabbath day," you say I will not sanctify the Sabbath, but I will sanctify the day after.... This tenet of belief is proved by every text of Scripture in which it is implied that God will render to every man according to his works.... If the word Purgatory has anything in it peculiarly offensive, you will not be the less a Catholic for rejecting it, and using the Scriptural word *prison*, provided you admit that such a place exists; in which God after having forgiven the guilt and temporal punishment of their sins, causes the souls of the imperfect just to undergo, nevertheless, a temporary chastisement, as David did in this life, before admitting them into the realms of felicity. Now, if this be so, is it not rational to believe that the mercy of God will be moved by the prayers of His faithful servants on earth, who intercede in behalf of their departed brethren?... In a word, the economy of God to His creatures even in this life is consistent with the doctrine of Purgatory.

PURGATORY AND WHAT WE OWE TO THE DEAD.
ARCHBISHOP LYNCH.

The infallible Church, the spouse of the Holy Ghost, the Pillar and Ground of Truth and the true teacher of the doctrine of Christ, has, in the distribution of her feasts and festivals, set apart one day in the year, the second of November, in favor of the suffering souls in Purgatory. She calls on all her children to assemble around her sacred altars, to assist and pray at the Holy Sacrifice of the Mass for the deliverance from Purgatory of the souls of those who, whilst dying in peace with Our Lord, still had debts to pay to His infinite justice.

These debts were contracted by the commission of mortal sin, whose grievous fault, though removed by the Sacrament of Penance, yet left on the soul a debt which was not sufficiently atoned for, or by the commission of venial sin not sufficiently repented of. Purgatory is one of the great consoling doctrines of the Church of Christ. Only the pure and perfect can enter Heaven; and how few persons leave this earth of temptation, sin, and trouble in that state of purity and perfection! If there were not a place of purification, how few could go straight to Heaven! Nearly the whole human race would be deprived forever of the beatific vision of God. God has chosen this way of exhibiting His justice and mercy: His justice, by exacting the last particle of debt; and His mercy, by saving the poor repentant sinner. God rewards every one according to his works. Some are imperfect through want of pure intention, through carelessness, vanity, or other causes, like the hay and stubble adhering to gold and precious stones which dull their lustre.

* * * * *

Oh, how few are perfect, and how few do penance in proportion to their sins! How few, in their dealing with their fellow-men, giving measure for measure, goods equal to the money paid for them, or services equal to the pay received! How many fail in charity, in words and actions! How many prayers said carelessly and without thought, even at the most solemn times! These will have to be repeated, as it were, in Purgatory. How many will suffer from their want of charity and mercy to the poor, and failing to pay their just dues to God's Church for the spiritual favors they receive from it! "If we give you," says St. Paul, "spiritual things, you should administer to us temporal things."...

All spiritual writers agree that the pains of Purgatory are intense, yet the souls are satisfied to suffer till the last debt is paid. They would not wish to enter Heaven with stains on their souls. God, in His great mercy, has permitted some souls suffering in Purgatory to appear to friends on earth to solicit their prayers and Masses, and to pay their debts. This the Lives of the Saints and Ecclesiastical History at all times attest. In these days when faith is fading from some minds, even in the Church, it behooves especially the Bishops to remind the faithful of their duties and obligations to their departed friends. It is thought by some that an expensive funeral, with its many carriages, and a grand monument over the grave, will satisfy all the requirements of decency and of family love. Alas! if the dead could only speak from their graves, they would cry out and say, "All these monuments and this worldly pageantry only crush us. They only satisfy the vanity of the living, but in no way alleviate our sufferings in Purgatory."...

But the Bishops must, from time to time, remind the people of their duty towards God's servants suffering in Purgatory. In olden times, when faith, love, and affection were stronger than now, devotion towards the souls in Purgatory showed itself in numerous foundations in favor of the souls in Purgatory. Churches and canonries where Masses were celebrated every day by canons and monks, benefices for the education of poor students, hospitals for the care of the sick, periodical distribution of alms to the poor, to have rosaries and other prayers said and pilgrimages made for the souls in Purgatory. All these have been swept away by the ruthless hand of the civil power, wishing to reform the Church; and even at the present day, when the Christian soul is about to appear before the judgment-seat, there are legal impediments in the way of his making by will donations for prayers or Masses. Therefore, my dear people, whilst you are well make provision for your own soul. Do not entrust it to the care of others who cannot love you more than you love yourselves.

* * * * *

This doctrine of Purgatory has always been taught in the Church and handed down from bishops and priests to their successors in the sacred ministry, and by the voice of the people. "Stand fast, and hold the tradition you have learned, whether by word or by our epistle." (II. Thess. ii. 14.) Now prayers and Masses for the dead are to be found in every ancient liturgy of the Church. There is no Oriental liturgy without prayers for those who have departed in peace. The Apostolic Constitutions—the most ancient and genuine work—speak largely of prayers for the dead, for the conversion of sinners.

There are religious congregations and pious associations specially devoted to the relief of the souls in Purgatory. St. Vincent de Paul ordered the priests of his congregation never to go to meals without first saying the *De Profundis* for the souls in Purgatory. The Church ends all the prayers of the divine office with: "May the souls of the faithful departed, through the mercy of God, rest in peace." One may turn away with a sad thought from a tomb on which is not engraved: "May he rest in peace," or on which a cross—the emblem of our hope in God and in a happy resurrection—does not figure.

We exhort you, beloved children in Christ, to entertain an earnest charity towards the souls in Purgatory. You loved them during life; do not let it be said: "Out of sight, out of mind." Love them in death or, living, wishing earnestly to go to God. This charity will greatly help yourselves. If a cup of cold water given to a servant of God shall not go without its reward, how much more a cup of celestial grace, that will shorten the time in the flames of Purgatory of a soul that most ardently longs to see God, who desires it Himself with great love, and will reward those who shorten the exile of His dear servants. "Those," says St. Alphonsus Liguori, "who succor the souls in Purgatory will be succored in turn by the gratitude of those whom they have relieved, and who enjoy sooner, by their prayers, the beatific vision of God."

* * * * *

The Council of Trent, under the inspiration of the Holy Ghost, has made decrees on the subject which bind the consciences of the faithful. In the Thirteenth Canon of the Sixth Session it decrees "that if any one should say that a repentant sinner, after having received the grace of justification, the punishment of eternal pains being remitted, has no temporary punishment to be suffered, either in this life or in the next, in Purgatory, before he can enter into the Kingdom of God, let him be anathema."

Though King David was assured, after his sincere repentance, that his sin was forgiven, yet the Prophet told him that he had still to suffer by the death of his child.

In the Twenty-fourth Session and Third Canon the Holy Council defines that the Sacrifice of the Mass is propitiatory, both for the living and the dead, for sins, punishments, satisfactions, and for other necessities, according to Apostolic traditions; and the Bishop, when he ordains, places the patena and chalice, with the bread and wine, in the hands of the young priest and says to him: "Receive the power to offer to God the Sacrifice of the Mass, as well for the living as for the dead, in the name of the Lord. Amen."

The Holy Sacrifice of the Mass is, therefore, the most powerful means of relieving the souls in Purgatory; next is the fervent performance of the Stations of the Cross, to which so many indulgences are attached; then other indulgenced prayers; for example, the Rosary. Alms to the poor is another powerful means. "Blessed are the merciful, for they shall obtain mercy."

There is another means which our ancestors loved—to educate a student for the priesthood. St. Monica rejoiced, on her death-bed, that she had a son to remember her every day at the altar. If you have not a son you can adopt one, or subscribe, according to your means, to the Students' Fund.

It is the custom in many places—and we wish that it should be introduced where it is not—to receive the offerings of the people on All Souls' Day, or the Sunday previous, or subsequent, and the proceeds to be computed and Masses offered up accordingly.

We attach the indulgences of the Way of the Cross to certain crucifixes, and thus enable persons who cannot conveniently visit the Church to make the Stations there, to gain the indulgences of the Stations by reciting fourteen times the "Our Father" and "Hail Mary," with a "Glory be to the Father," etc., for each Station, and five "Our Fathers" and "Hail Marys" in honor of the five Adorable Wounds, with one for the intentions of the Pope.

PURGATORY SURVEYED. [1]

[Footnote 1: Published by Burns & Oates, London.]

FATHER BINET, S. J.

[The following passages are taken from a most excellent and valuable work, "Purgatory Surveyed," edited by the late lamented Dr. Anderdon, S. J., being by him "disposed, abridged, or enlarged," from a treatise by Father Binet, a French Jesuit, published at Paris in 1625, at Douay in 1627, and translated soon after by Father Richard Thimbleby, an English member of the Society of Jesus. Says Dr. Anderdon in his preface: "The alterations ventured upon in this reprint, consist chiefly in the mode of punctuation, which, being probably left to a French compositor, are anomalous, and often perplexing. Some expressions, so obsolete as to prevent the sense being clear, and in the same degree lessening the value of the book to the general reader, have been exchanged for others in more common use.... Let us earnestly hope that, at this moment, on the threshold of the month specially dedicated by the Church to devotion on behalf of the Holy Souls, the joint work of Fathers Binet and Thimbleby may produce an abundant harvest of intercession. If, during their own brief time of trial, they were inspired to put together and to enforce such powerful motives to stir up the faithful to this devotion, will they not now rejoice in the re-production of their act of zeal and charity? During the two hundred and fifty years which have elapsed since the first publication of the French work, many changes and revolutions have taken place in the histories of those spots of earth, known as France and England. But the History of Purgatory is ever the same; "happiness and unhappiness" combined; both unspeakably great; long detention, perhaps, or perhaps swift release, according to the degree of faith and charity animating the Church militant. May we now, and henceforth, realize in act, in habitual practice, and, all the more, from the considerations given in the following pages, the immense privilege of holding, to so great a degree, the keys of Purgatory in our hands."]

Believe it, it is one of the first rudiments, but main principles, of a Christian, to captivate his understanding, and so regulate all his dictamens, that they be sure to run parallel with the sentiments of the Church. And this I take to be the case when the question is started about Purgatory fire, which I shall ever reckon in the class of those truths, which cannot be contradicted without manifest temerity; as being the doctrine generally preached and taught all over Christendom.

You must, then, conceive Purgatory to be a vast, darksome and hideous chaos, full of fire and flames, in which the souls are kept close prisoners, until they have fully satisfied for all their misdemeanors, according to the estimate of Divine justice. For God has made choice of this element of fire wherewith to punish souls, because it is the most active, piercing, sensible, [1] and insupportable of all others. But that which quickens it, indeed, and gives it more life, is this: that it acts as the instrument of God's justice, who, by His omnipotent power, heightens and reinforces its activity as He pleases, and so makes it capable to act upon bodiless spirits. Do not, then, look only upon this fire, though in good earnest it be dreadful enough of itself; but consider the Arm that is stretched out, and the Hand that strikes, and the rigor of God's infinite justice, who, through this element of fire, vents His wrath, and pours out whole tempests of His most severe and yet most just vengeance. So that the fire works as much mischief, [2] as I may say, to the souls, as God commands; and He commands as much as is due; and as much is due as the sentence bears: a sentence irrevocably pronounced at the high tribunal of the severe and rigorous justice of an angry God, and whose anger is so prevalent that the Holy Scripture styles it "a day of fury." Now, you will easily believe that this fire is a most horrible punishment in its own nature; but you may do well to reflect also on that which I have now suggested; that the fury of Almighty God is, as it were, the fire of this fire, and the heat of its heat; and that He serves Himself of it as He pleases, by doubling and redoubling its sharp pointed forces; for this is that which makes it the more grievous and insupportable to the souls that are thus miserably confined and imprisoned.

[Footnote 1: *i.e.*, apprehended by the senses]

[Footnote 2: *i.e.*, Not implying injury, far less injustice; but simply punishment and suffering]

They were not much out of the way, that styled Purgatory a transitory kind of hell, because the principal pains of the damned are to be found there; with this only difference, that in hell they are eternal, and in Purgatory they are only transitory and fleeting: for, otherwise, it is probably the very same fire that burns both the Holy Souls and the damned spirits; and the pain of loss is, in both places, the chief torment.... Now, does not your hair stand on end? does not your heart tremble, when you hear that the poor souls in Purgatory are tormented with the same, or the like flames to those of the damned? Can you refrain from crying out, with the Prophet Isaias: "Who can dwell with such devouring fire, and unquenchable burnings?" Heavens! what a lamentable case is this! Those miserable souls, who of late, when they were wedded to their bodies, were so nice and dainty, forsooth, that they durst scarce venture to enjoy the comfortable heat of a fire, but under the protection of their screens and their fans, for fear of spoiling their complexions, and if, by chance, a spark had been so rude as to light upon them, or a little smoke, it was not to be endured:... —Alas! how will it fare with them, when they shall see themselves tied to unmerciful firebrands, or imbodied, as it were, with flames of fire, surrounded with frightful darkness, broiled and consumed without intermission, and perhaps condemned to the same fire with which the devils are unspeakably tormented? (Pages 4-7.)

* * * * *

Good God! how the great Saints and Doctors astonish me when they treat of this fire, and of the pain of sense, as they call it! For they peremptorily pronounce that the fire that purges those souls, those both happy and unhappy souls, surpasses all the torments that are to be found in this miserable life of man, or are possible to be invented, for so far they go… Thus they discourse: The fire and the pains of the other world are of another nature from those of this life, because God elevates them above their nature to be instruments of His severity. Now, say they, things of an inferior degree can never reach the power of such things as are of a higher rank. For example, the air, let it be ever so inflated, unless it be converted into fire, can never be so hot as fire. Besides, God bridles His rigor in this world; but, in the next, He lets the reins loose and punishes almost equally to the desert. And, since those souls have preferred creatures before their Creator, He seems to be put upon a necessity of punishing them beyond the ordinary strength of creatures; and hence it is that the fire of Purgatory burns more, torments and inflicts more, than all the creatures of this life are able to do. But is it really true that the least pain in Purgatory exceeds the greatest here upon earth? O God! the very statement makes me tremble for fear, and my very heart freezes into ice with astonishment. And yet, who dare oppose St. Augustine, St. Thomas, St. Anselm, St. Gregory the Great? Is there any hope of carrying the negative assertion against such a stream of Doctors, who all maintain the affirmative, and bring so strong reasons for it?…

* * * * *

But for Thy comfort, there are Doctors in the Catholic Church that cannot agree with so much severity; and, namely, St. Bonaventure, who is very peremptory in denying it. "For, what way is there," says this holy Doctor, "to verify so great a paradox, without sounding reason, and destroying the infinite mercy of God? I am easily persuaded there are torments in Purgatory far exceeding any in this mortal life; this is most certain, and it is but reasonable it should be so; but that the least there should be more terrible than the most terrible in the world cannot enter into my belief. May it not often fall out that a man comes to die in a most eminent state of perfection, save only, that in his last agony, out of mere frailty, he commits a venial sin, or carries along with him some relic of his former failings, which might have been easily blotted out with a *Pater Noster*, or washed away with a little holy water; for I am supposing it to be some very small matter. Now, what likelihood is there, I will not say, that the infinite mercy of God, but that the very rigor of His justice, though you conceive it to be ever so severe, should inflict so horrible a punishment upon this holy soul, as not to be equalled by the greatest torments in this life; and all this for some petty fault scarce worth the speaking of? How! would you have God, for a kind of trifle, to punish a soul full of grace and virtue, and so severely to punish her as to exceed all the racks, cauldrons, furnaces, and other hellish inventions, which are scarce inflicted upon the most execrable criminals in the world?" (Pp. 9-11.)

* * * * *

It is not the fire, nor all the brimstone and tortures they endure, which murders them alive. No, no; it is the domestical cause of all these mischiefs that racks their consciences and is their crudest executioner. This, this is the greatest of their evils; for a soul that has shaken off the fetters of flesh and blood, and is full of the love of God, no more disordered with unruly passions, nor blinded with the night of ignorance, sees clearly the vast injury she has done to herself to have offended so good a God, and to have deserved to be thus banished out of His sight and deprived of that Divine fruition. She sees how easily she might have flown up straight to heaven at her first parting with her body, and what trifle it was that impeded her. A moment lost of those inebriating joys, seems to her now worthy to be redeemed with an eternity of pains. Then, reflecting with herself that she was created only for God, and cannot be truly satisfied but by enjoying God, and that, out of Him, all this goodly machine of the world is no better than a direct hell and an abyss of evils. Alas! what worms, what martyrdoms, and what nipping pincers are such pinching thoughts as these. The fire is to her but as smoke in comparison to this vexing remembrance of her own follies, which betrayed her to this disgraceful and unavoidable misfortune. There was a king who, in a humor gave away his crown and his whole estate, for the present refreshment of a cup of cold water; but, returning a little to himself and soberly reflecting what he had done, had like to have run stark mad to see the strange, irreparable folly he had committed. To lose a year, or two years (to say no more), of the beatifical vision for a glass of water, for a handful of earth, for the love of a fading beauty, for a little air of worldly praise, a mere puff of honor—ah! it is the hell of Purgatory to a soul that truly loves God and frames a right conceit of things. (Pp. 14, 15.)

* * * * *

Confusion is one of the most intolerable evils that can befall a soul; and, therefore, St. Paul, speaking of Our blessed Saviour, insists much upon this, that He had the courage and the love for us all to overcome the pain of a horrible confusion, which doubtless is an insupportable evil to a man of intelligence and courage. Tell me, then, if you can, what a burning shame and what a terrible confusion it must be to those noble and generous souls, to behold themselves overwhelmed with a confused chaos of fire, and such a base fire which affords no other light but a sullen glimmering, choked up with a sulphureous and stinking smoke; and in the interim to know that the souls of many country clowns, mere idiots, poor women and simple religious persons, go straight up to heaven, whilst they lie there burning—they that were so knowing, so rich and so wise; they that were counsellors to kings, eminent preachers of God's word, and renowned oracles in the world; they that were so great divines, so great statesmen, so capable of high employments. This confusion is much heightened by their further knowing how easily they might have avoided all this and would not. Sometimes they would have given whole mountains of gold to be rid of a stone in the kidneys or a fit of the gout, colic or burning fever, and for a handful of silver they might have redeemed many years' torments in that fiery furnace; and, alas! they chose rather to give it to their dogs and their horses, and sometimes to men more beasts than they and much more unworthy. Methinks this thought must be more vexing than the fire itself, though never so grievous.

34

And yet there remains one thought more, which certainly has a great share in completing their martyrdom; and that is the remembrance of their children or heirs which they left behind them; who swim in nectar and live jollily on the goods which they purchased with the sweat of their brows, and yet are so ungrateful, so brutish, and so barbarous that they will scarce vouchsafe to say a Pater Noster in a whole month for their souls who brought them into the world, and who, to place them in a terrestrial paradise of all worldly delights, made a hard venture of their own souls and had like to have exchanged a temporal punishment for an eternal. The leavings and superfluities of their lackeys, a throw of dice, and yet less than that, might have set them free from these hellish torments; and these wicked, ungrateful wretches would not so much as think on it. (Pp. 31-33.)

* * * * *

Before I leave off finishing this picture, or put a period to the representation of the pains of Purgatory, I cannot but relate a very remarkable history which will be as a living picture before your eyes. But be sure you take it not to be of the number of those idle stories which pass for old wives' tales, or mere imaginations of cracked brains and simple souls. No; I will tell you nothing but what Venerable Bede, so grave an author, witnesses to have happened in his time, and to have been generally believed all over England without contradiction, and to have been the cause of wonderful effects; and which is so authenticated that Cardinal Bellarmine, a man of such judgment as the world knows, having related it himself, concludes thus: "For my part I firmly believe this history, as very conformable to the Holy Scripture, and whereof I can have no doubt without wronging truth and wounding my own conscience, which ought readily to yield assent unto that which is attested by so many and so credible witnesses and confirmed by such holy and admirable events."

About the year of our Lord 690, a certain Englishman, in the county of Northumberland, by name Brithelmus, being dead for a time, was conducted to the place of Purgatory by a guide, whose countenance and apparel was full of light; you may imagine it was his good Angel. Here he was shown two broad valleys of a vast and infinite length, one full of glowing firebrands and terrible flames, the other as full of hail, ice, and snow; and in both these were innumerable souls, who, as with a whirlwind, were tossed up and down out of the intolerable scorching flames, into the insufferable rigors of cold, and out of these into those again, without a moment of repose or respite. This he took to be hell, so frightful were those torments; but his good Angel told him no, it was Purgatory, where the souls did penance for their sins, and especially such as had deferred their conversion until the hour of death; and that many of them were set free before the Day of Judgment for the good prayers, alms, and fasts of the living, and chiefly by the holy Sacrifice of the Mass. Now this holy man, being raised again from death to life by the power of God, first made a faithful relation of all that he had seen, to the great amazement of the hearers, then retired him self into the church and spent the whole night in prayer; and soon after, gave away his whole estate, partly to his wife and children, partly to the poor, and taking upon him the habit and profession of a monk, led so austere a life that even if his tongue had been silent, yet his life and conversation spake aloud what wonders he had seen in the other world. Sometimes they would see him, old as he was, in freezing water up to his ears, praying and singing with much sweetness and incredible fervor; and if they asked him, "Brother, alas! how can you suffer such sharp and biting cold?" "O my friends," would he say, "I have seen other manner of cold than this." Thus, when he even groaned under the voluntary burden of a world of most cruel mortifications, and was questioned how it was possible for a weak and broken body like his to undergo such austerities, "Alas! my dear brethren," would he still say, "I have seen far greater austerities than these: they are but roses and perfumes in comparison of what I have seen in the subterraneous lakes of Purgatory." And in these kinds of austerities he spent the remainder of his life and made a holy end, and purchased an eternal paradise, for having had but a sight of the pains of Purgatory. And we, dear Christians, if we believed in good earnest, or could but once procure to have a true sight or apprehension of them, should certainly have other thoughts and live in another fashion than we do. (Pp. 44-46.)

* * * * *

Now, would you clearly see how the souls can at the same instant swim in a paradise of delights and yet be overwhelmed with the hellish torments of Purgatory? Cast your eyes upon the holy martyrs of God's Church, and observe their behavior. They were torn, mangled, dismembered, flayed alive, racked, broiled, burnt—and tell me, was not this to live in a kind of hell? And yet, in the very height of their torments their hearts and souls were ready to leap for joy; you would have taken them to be already transported into heaven. Hear them but speak for themselves. "O lovely cross," cried out St. Andrew, "made beautiful by the precious Body of Christ, how long have I desired thee, and with what care have I sought thee! and now, that I have found thee, receive me into thine arms, and lift me up to my dear Redeemer! O death, [1] how amiable art thou in my eyes, and how sweet is thy cruelty!" "Your coals," said St. Cecily, "your flaming firebrands, and all the terrors of death, are to me but as so many fragrant roses and lilies, sent from heaven." "Shower down upon me," cried St. Stephen, "whole deluges of stones, whilst I see the heavens open and Jesus Christ standing at the right side of His Eternal Father, to behold the fidelity of His champion." "Turn," exclaimed St. Lawrence, "oh! turn, the other side, thou cruel tyrant, this is already broiled, and cooked fit for thy palate. Oh, how well am I pleased to suffer this little Purgatory for the love of my Saviour!" "Make haste, O my soul," cried St. Agnes, "to cast thyself upon the bed of flames which thy dear Spouse has prepared for thee!" "Oh," cried St. Felicitas, and the mother of the Machabees, "Oh, that I had a thousand children, or a thousand lives, to sacrifice them all to my God. What a pleasure it is to suffer for so good a cause!" "Welcome tyrants, tigers, lions," writes St. Ignatius the Martyr; "let all the torments that the devils can invent come upon me, so I may enjoy my Saviour. I am the wheat of Christ;

oh, let me be ground with the lions' teeth. Now I begin indeed to be the disciple of Christ." "Oh, the happy stroke of a sword," might St. Paul well exclaim, "that no sooner cuts off my head, but it makes a breach for my soul to enter into heaven. Let it be far from me to glory in anything, but in the Cross of Our Lord Jesus Christ. Let all evils band against me, and let my body be never so overloaded with afflictions, the joy of my heart will be sure to have the mastery, and my soul will be still replenished with such heavenly consolations that no words, nor even thoughts, are able to express it."

[Footnote 1: From the author's text, it seems doubtful whether this sentence is to be attributed to St. Andrew or St. Cecilia.]

You may imagine, then, that the souls, once unfettered from the body, may, together with their torments, be capable of great comforts and divine favors, and break forth into resolute, heroical, and even supercelestial acts.

* * * * *

But there is yet something of a higher nature to be said…. We have all the reason in the world to believe that God, of His infinite goodness, inspires these holy souls with a thousand heavenly lights, and such ravishing thoughts, that they cannot but take themselves to be extremely happy: so happy that St. Catherine of Genoa professed she had learnt of Almighty God that, excepting only the blessed Saints in heaven, there were no joys comparable to those of the souls in Purgatory. "For," said she, "when they consider that they are in the hands of God, in a place deputed for them by His holy providence, and just where God would have them, it is not to be expressed what a sweetness they find in so loving a thought: and certainly they had infinitely rather be in Purgatory, to comply with His divine pleasure, than be in Paradise, with violence to His justice, and a manifest breach of the ordinary laws of the house of God. I will say more," continued she: "it cannot so much as steal into their thoughts to desire to be anywhere else than where they are. Seeing that God has so placed them, they are not at all troubled that others get out before them; and they are so absorbed in this profound meditation, of being at God's disposal, in the bosom of His sweet providence, that they cannot so much as dream of being anywhere else. So that, methinks, those kind expressions of Almighty God, by His prophets, to His chosen people, may be fitly applied to the unhappy and yet happy condition of these holy souls. 'Rejoice, my people,' says the loving God; 'for I swear unto you by Myself, that when you shall pass through flames of fire, they shall not hurt you: I shall be there with you; I shall take off the edge, and blunt the points, of those piercing flames. I will raise the bright Aurora in your darkness; and the darkness of your nights shall outshine the midday. I will pour out My peace into the midst of your hearts, and replenish your souls with the bright shining lights of heaven. You shall be as a paradise of delights, bedewed with a living fountain of heavenly waters. You shall rejoice in your Creator, and I will raise you above the height of mountains, and nourish you with manna and the sweet inheritance of Jacob; for the mouth of the Lord hath spoken it: and it cannot fail, but shall be sure to fall out so, because He hath spoken it'" (Pp. 61, 62).

37

* * * * *

But let not this discourse cool your charity; lest, seeing the souls enjoy so much comfort in Purgatory, your compassion for them grow slack, and so continue not equal to their desert. Remember, then, that notwithstanding all these comforts here rehearsed, the poor creatures cease not to be grievously tormented; and consequently have extreme need of all your favorable assistance and pious endeavors. When Christ Jesus was in His bitter agony, sweating blood and water, the superior part of His soul enjoyed God and His glory, and yet His body was so oppressed with sorrow, that He was ready to die, and was content to be comforted by an Angel. In like manner, these holy souls have indeed great joys; but feel withal such bitter torments, that they stand in great need of our help. So that you will much wrong them, and me, too, to stand musing so long upon their joys, as not to afford them succor. (P. 80.)

* * * * *

In the history of the incomparable order of the great St. Dominic, it is authentically related that one of the first of those holy, religious men was wont to say, that he found himself not so much concerned to pray for the souls in Purgatory, because they are certain of their salvation; and that, upon this account, we ought not, in his judgment, to be very solicitous for them, but ought rather to bend our whole care to help sinner, to convert the wicked, and to secure such souls as are uncertain of their salvation, and probably certain of their damnation, as leading very evil lives. Here it is, said he, that I willingly employ my whole endeavors. It is upon these that I bestow my Masses and prayers, and all that little that is at my disposal; and thus I take it to be well bestowed. But upon souls that have an assurance of eternal happiness, and can never more lose God or offend Him, I believe not, said he, that one ought to be so solicitous. This certainly was but a poor and weak discourse, to give it no severer a censure; and the consequence of it was this, that the good man did not only himself forbear to help these poor souls, but, which was worse, dissuaded others from doing it; and, under color of a greater charity, withdrew that succor which, otherwise, good people would liberally have afforded them. But God took their cause in hand; for, permitting the souls to appear and show themselves in frightful shapes, and to haunt the good man by night and day without respite, still filling his fancy with dreadful imaginations, and his eyes with terrible spectacles, and withal letting him know who they were, and why, with God's permission, they so importuned him with their troublesome visits, you may believe the good Father became so affectionately kind to the souls in Purgatory, bestowed so many Masses and prayers upon them, preached so fervently in their behalf, stirred up so many to the same devotion, that it is a thing incredible to believe, and not to be expressed with eloquence. Never did you see so many and so clear and convincing reasons as he alleged, to demonstrate that it is the most eminent piece of fraternal charity in this life to pray for the souls departed. Love and fear are the two most excellent orators in the world; they can teach all rhetoric in a moment, and infuse a most miraculous eloquence. This good Father, who thought he should have been frightened to death, was grown so fearful of a second assault, that he bent his whole understanding to invent the most pressing and convincing arguments to stir up the world both to pity and to piety, and so persuade souls to help souls; and it is incredible what good ensued thereupon. (Pp. 82- 84.)

* * * * *

Is there anything within the whole circumference of the universe so worthy of compassion, and that may so deservedly claim the greatest share in all your devotions and charities, as to see our fathers, our mothers, our nearest and dearest relations, to lie broiling in cruel flames, and to cry to us for help with tears that are able to move cruelty itself? Whence I conclude there is not upon the earth any object that deserves more commiseration than this, nor where fraternal charity can better employ all her forces. (P. 86.)

* * * * *

St. Thomas tells us there is an order to be observed in our works of charity to our neighbor; that is, we are to see where there is a greater obligation, a greater necessity, a greater merit, and the like circumstances. Now, where is there more necessity, or more obligation, than to run to the fire, and to help those that lie there, and are not able to get out? Where can you have more merit, than to have a hand in raising up Saints and servants of God? Where have you more assurance than where you are sure to lose nothing? Where can you find an object of more compassion, than where there is the greatest misery in the world? Where is there seen more of God's glory, than to send new Saints into heaven to praise God eternally? Lastly, where can you show more charity, and more of the love of God, than to employ your tears, your sighs, your goods, your hands, your heart, your life, and all your devotion, to procure a good that surpasses all other goods; I mean, to make souls happy for all eternity, by translating them into heavenly joys, out of insupportable torments? That glorious Apostle of the Indies, St. Francis Xavier, could run from one end of the world to the other, to convert a soul, and think it no long journey. The dangers by sea and land seemed sweet, the tempests pleasing, the labor easy, and his whole time well employed. Good God! what an advantage have we, that with so little trouble and few prayers, may send a thousand beautiful souls into heaven, without the least hazard of losing anything? St. Francis Xavier could not be certain that the Japanese, for example, whom he baptized, would persevere in their faith; and, though they should persevere in it, he could have as little certainty of their salvation. Now, it is an article of our faith, that the holy souls in Purgatory are in grace, and shall assuredly one day enter into the Kingdom of Heaven. (Pp. 91, 92.)

* * * * *

We read in the life of St. Catherine of Bologna, ... that she had not only a strange tenderness for the souls, but a singular devotion to them, and was wont to recommend herself to them in all her necessities. The reason she alleged for it was this: that she had learned of Almighty God how she had frequently obtained far greater favors by their intercession than by any other means. And the story adds this: that it often happened that what she begged of God, at the intercession of the Saints in heaven, she could never obtain of Him; and yet, as soon as she addressed herself to the souls in Purgatory she had her suit instantly granted. Can there be any question but there are souls in that purging fire who are of a higher pitch of sanctity, and of far greater merit in the sight of God, than a thousand and a thousand Saints who are already glorious in the Court of Heaven. (P. 102.)

* * * * *

Cardinal Baronius, a man of credit beyond exception, relates, in his Ecclesiastical Annals, how a person of rare virtue found himself dangerously assaulted at the hour of his death; and that, in this agony, he saw the heavens open and about eight thousand champions, all covered with white armor, descend, who fell instantly to encourage him by giving him this assurance: that they were come to fight for him and to disengage him from that doubtful combat. And when, with infinite comfort, and tears in his eyes, he besought them to do him the favor to let him know who they were that had so highly obliged him: "We are," said they, "the souls whom you have saved and delivered out of Purgatory; and now, to requite the favor, we are come down to convey you instantly to heaven." And with that, he died.

We read another such story of St. Gertrude; how she was troubled at her death to think what must become of her, since she had given away all the rich treasure of her satisfactions to redeem other poor souls, without reserving anything to herself; but that Our Blessed Saviour gave her the comfort to know that she was not only to have the like favor of being immediately conducted into heaven out of this world, by those innumerable souls whom she had sent thither before her by her fervent prayers, but was there also to receive a hundred-fold of eternal glory in reward of her charity. By which examples we may learn that we cannot make better use of our devotion and charity than this way. (Pp. 104, 105.)

* * * * *

The Church Triumphant, to speak properly, cannot satisfy, because there is no place for penal works in the Court of Heaven, whence all grief and pain are eternally banished.

Wherefore, the Saints may well proceed by way of impetration and prayers; or, at most, represent their former satisfactions, which are carefully laid up in the treasury of the Church, in lieu of those which are due from others; but, as for any new satisfaction or payment derived from any penal act of their own, it is not to be looked for in those happy mansions of eternal glory.

The Church Militant may do either; as having this advantage over the Church Triumphant, that she can help the souls in Purgatory by her prayers and satisfactory works, and by offering up her charitable suffrages, wherewith to pay the debts of those poor souls who are run in arrear in point of satisfaction due for their sins. Had they but fasted, prayed, labored, or suffered a little more in this life, they had gone directly into heaven; what they unhappily neglected we may supply for them, and it will be accepted for good payment, as from their bails and sureties. You know, he that stands surety for another takes the whole debt upon himself. This is our case; for, the living, as it were, entering bond for the dead, become responsible for their debts, and offer up fasts for fasts, tears for tears, in the same measure and proportion as they were liable to them, and so defray the debt of their friends at their own charge, and make all clear. (Pp. 117, 118.)

* * * * *

I am in love with that religious practice of Bologna, where, upon funeral days, they cause hundreds and thousands of Masses to be said for the soul departed, in lieu of other superfluous and vain ostentations. They stay not for the anniversary, nor for any other set day; but instantly do their best to release the poor soul from her torments, who must needs think the year long, if she must stay for help till her anniversary day appears. They do not, for all this, despise the laudable customs of the Church; they bury their friends with honor; they clothe great numbers of poor people; they give liberal alms; but, as there is nothing so certain, nothing so efficacious, nothing so divine, as the Holy Sacrifice of the Mass, they fix their whole affection there, and strive all they can to relieve the souls this way; and are by no means so lavish, as the fashion is, in other idle expenses and inopportune feastings, which are often more troublesome to the living than comfortable to the dead.

But you may not only comfort the afflicted souls by procuring Masses for them, nor yet only by offering up your prayers, fasts, alms-deeds, and such other works of piety; but you may bestow upon them all the good you do, and all the evil you suffer, in this world…. If you offer up unto God all that causes you any grief or affliction, for the present relief of the poor languishing souls, you cannot believe what ease and comfort they will find by it. (Pp. 123-125).

* * * * *

The world has generally a great esteem of Monsieur d'Argenton, Philip Commines; and many worthily admire him for the great wisdom and sincerity he has labored to express in his whole history. But, for my part, I commend him for nothing more than for the prudent care he took here for the welfare of his own soul in the other world. For, having built a goodly chapel at the Augustinians in Paris, and left them a good foundation, he tied them to this perpetual obligation, that they should no sooner rise from table, but they should be sure to pray for the rest of this precious soul. And he ordered it thus, by his express will, that one of the religious should first say aloud: "Let us pray for the soul of Monsieur d'Argenton;" and then all should instantly say the psalm *De Profundis*. Gerson lost not his labor when he took such pains to teach little children to repeat often these words: "My God, my Creator, have pity on Thy poor servant, John Gerson." For these innocent souls, all the while the good man was dying, and after he was dead, went up and down the town with a mournful voice, singing the short lesson he had taught them, and comforting his dear soul with their innocent prayers.

Now, as I must commend their prudence who thus wisely cast about how to provide for their own souls, against they come into Purgatory, so I cannot but more highly magnify their charity, who, less solicitous for themselves, employ their whole care to save others out of that dreadful fire. And sure I am, they can lose nothing by the bargain, who dare thus trust God with their own souls, while they do their uttermost to help others; nay, though they should follow that unparalleled example of Father Hernando de Monsoy, of the Society of Jesus, who, not content to give away all he could from himself to the poor souls, while he lived, made them his heirs after death; and, by express will, bequeathed them all the Masses, rosaries, and whatsoever else should be offered for him by his friends upon earth. (Pp. 131-132.)

* * * * *

It will not be amiss here to resolve you certain pertinent questions. Whether the suffrages we offer up unto God shall really avail them for whom we offer them; and whether they alone, or others also, may receive benefit by them? Whether it be better to pray for a few at once, or for many, or for all the souls together, and for what souls in particular?

To the first I answer: if your intention be to help any one in particular who is really in Purgatory, so your work be good, it is infallibly applied to the person upon whom you bestow it. For, as divines teach, it is the intention of the offerer which governs all; and God, of His infinite goodness, accommodates Himself to the petitioner's request, applying unto each one what has been offered for its relief. If you have nobody in your thoughts for whom you offer up your prayers, they are only beneficial to yourself; and what would be thus lost for want of application, God lays up in the treasury of the Church, as being a kind of spiritual waif or stray, to which nobody can lay any just claim. And, since it is the intention which entitles one to what is offered before all others, what right can others pretend to it; or with what justice can it be parted or divided amongst others, who were never thought of?

And hence I take my starting-point to resolve your other question—that if you regard their best advantage whom you have a mind to favor, you had better pray for a few than for many together; for, since the merit of your devotions is but limited, and often in a very small proportion, the more you divide and subdivide it amongst many, the lesser share comes to every one in particular. As if you should distribute a crown or an angel [1] amongst a thousand poor people, you easily see your alms would be so inconsiderable, they would be little better for it; whereas, if it were all bestowed upon one or two, it were enough to make them think themselves rich.

[Footnote 1: A gold coin of that period so called because it was stamped with the image of an angel.]

Now, to define precisely, whether it be always better done, to help one or two souls efficaciously, than to yield a little comfort to a great many, is a question I leave for you to exercise your wits in. I could fancy it to be your best course to do both; that is, sometimes to single out some particular soul, and to use all your powers to lift her up to heaven; sometimes, again, to parcel out your favors upon many; and, now and then, also to deal out a general alms upon all Purgatory. And you need not fear exceeding in this way of charity, whatsoever you bestow; for you may be sure nothing will be lost by it. And St. Thomas will tell you, for your comfort, that since all the souls in Purgatory are perfectly united in charity, they rejoice exceedingly when they see any of their whole number receive such powerful helps as to dispose her for heaven. They every one take it as done to themselves, whatsoever is bestowed upon any of their fellows, whom they love as themselves; and, out of a heavenly kind of courtesy, and singular love, they joy in her happiness, as if it were their own. So that it may be truly said, that you never pray for one or more of them, but they are all partakers, and receive a particular comfort and satisfaction by it. (Pp. 132-134.)

* * * * *

It would go hard with many, were it true that a person who neglected to make restitution in his life-time, and only charged his heirs to do it for him in his last will and testament, shall not stir out of Purgatory till restitution be really made; let there be never so many Masses said, and never so many satisfactory works offered up for him. And yet St. Bridget, whose revelations are, for the most part, approved by the Church, hesitates not to set this down for a truth which God had revealed unto her. Nor are there wanting grave divines that countenance this rigorous position, and bring for it many strong reasons and examples, which they take to be authentical: and the law itself, which says that if a man do not restore another's goods, there will always stick upon the soul a kind of blemish, or obligation of justice. And since the fault lies wholly at his door, he cannot, say they, have the least reason to complain of the severity of God's justice, but must accuse his own coldness and extreme neglect of his own welfare. Nay, even those that are of the contrary persuasion, yet maintain that it is not only much more secure, but far more meritorious, to satisfy such obligations while we live, than to trust others with it, let them be never so near and dear to us…. (Pp. 140, 141.)

* * * * *

… I have just cause to fear that all I can say to you will hardly suffice to mollify that hard heart of yours; and, therefore, my last refuge shall be to set others on, though I call them out of the other world.

And first, let a damned soul read you a lecture, and teach you the compassion you ought to bear to your afflicted brethren. Remember how the rich glutton in the Gospel, although he was buried in hell-fire, took care for his brothers who survived him; and besought Abraham to send Lazarus back into the world, to preach and convert them, lest they should be so miserable as to come into that place of torments. A strange request for a damned soul! and which may shame you, that are so little concerned for the souls of your brethren, who are in so restless a condition.

In the next place, I will bring in the soul of your dear father, or mother, to make her own just complaints against you. Lend her, then, a dutiful and attentive ear; and let none of her words be lost; for she deserves to be heard out, while she sets forth the state of her most lamentable condition. Peace! it is a holy soul, though clothed in flames, that directs her speech to you after this manner:

"Am I not the most unfortunate and wretched parent that ever lived? I that was so silly as to presume that having ventured my life, and my very soul also, to leave my children at their ease, they would at least have had some pity on me, and

43

endeavor to procure for me some ease and comfort in my torments. Alas! I burn insufferably, I suffer infinitely, and have done so, I know not how long; and yet this is not the only thing that grieves me. Alas, no! it is a greater vexation to me to see myself so soon forgotten by my own children, and so slighted by them, for whom I have in vain taken so much care and pains. Ah, dost thou grudge thy poor mother a Mass, a slight alms, a sigh, or a tear? Thy mother, I say, who would most willingly have kept bread from her own mouth, to make thee swim in an ocean of delights, and to abound with plenty of all worldly goods? ... Who will not refuse me comfort, when my own children, my very bowels, do their best to forget me? What a vexation is it to me, when my companions in misery ask me whether I left no children behind me, and why they are so hard-hearted as to neglect me?.... I was willing to forget my own concerns to be careful of theirs; and those ungrateful ones have now buried me in an eternal oblivion, and clearly left me to shift for myself in these dread tortures, without giving me the least ease or comfort. Oh, what a fool was I! had I given to the poor the thousandth part of those goods which I left these miserable children, I had long before this been joyfully singing the praises of my Creator, in the choir of Angels; whereas now I lie panting and groaning under excessive torments, and am like still to lie, for any relief that is to be looked for from these undutiful, ungracious children whom I made my sole heirs.... But am I not all this while strangely transported, miserable that I am, thus to amuse myself with unprofitable complaints against my children; whereas, indeed, I have but small reason to blame any but myself? since it is I, and only I, that am the cause of all this mischief. For did not I know that in the grand business of saving my soul, I was to have trusted none but myself? did I not know that with the sight of their friends, at their departure, men used to lose all the memory and friendship they had for them?.... Did I not know that God Himself had foretold us, that the only ready way to build ourselves eternal tabernacles in the next world, is not to give all to our children, but to be liberal to the poor?.... I cannot deny, then, but the fault lies at my door, and that I am deservedly thus neglected by my children.... The only comfort I have left me in all my afflictions, is, that others will learn at my cost this clear maxim: not to leave to others a matter of such near concern as the ease and repose of their own souls; but to provide for them carefully themselves. O God! how dearly have I bought this experience; to see my fault irreparable, and my misery without redress!" (Pp. 146-149.)

* * * * *

One must have a heart of steel, or no heart at all, to hear these sad regrets, and not feel some tenderness for the poor souls, and as great an indignation against those who are so little concerned for the souls of their parents and other near relations. I wish, with all my soul, that all those who shall light upon this passage, and hear the soul so bitterly deplore her misfortune, may but benefit themselves half as much by it as a good prelate did when the soul of Pope Benedict VIII, by God's permission, revealed unto him her lamentable state in Purgatory. [1] For so the story goes, which is not to be questioned: This Pope Benedict appears to the

Bishop of Capua, and conjures him to go to his brother, Pope John, who succeeded him in the Chair of St. Peter, and to beseech him, for God's sake, to give great store of alms to poor people, to allay the fury of the fire of Purgatory, with which he found himself highly tormented. He further charges him to let the Pope know withal, that he did acknowledge liberal alms had already been distributed for that purpose; but had found no ease at all by it because all the money that had been then bestowed was acquired unjustly, and so had no power to prevail before the just tribunal of God for the obtaining of the least mercy. The good Bishop, upon this, makes haste to the Pope, and faithfully relates the whole conference that had passed between him and the soul of his predecessor; and with a grave voice and lively accent enforces the necessity and importance of the business; that, in truth, when a soul lies a burning, it is in vain to dispute idle questions; the best course, then, is to run instantly for water, and to throw it on with both hands, calling for all the help and assistance we can, to relieve her; and that His Holiness should soon see the truth of the vision by the wonderful effects which were like to follow. All this he delivers so gravely, and so to the purpose, that the Pope resolves out of hand to give in charity vast sums out of his own certain and unquestionable revenue; whereby the soul of Pope Benedict was not only wonderfully comforted, but, questionless, soon released of her torments. In conclusion, the good Bishop, having well reflected with himself in what a miserable condition he had seen the soul of a Pope who had the repute of a Saint, and was really so, worked so powerfully with him, that, quitting his mitre, crosier, bishopric, and all worldly greatness, he shut himself up in a monastery, and there made a holy end; choosing rather to have his Purgatory in the austerity of a cloister than in the flames of the Church suffering. (Pp. 150, 151.)

[Footnote 1: Baronius, *An.* 1024.]

* * * * *

I wish, again, they would in this but follow the example of King Louis of France, who was son to Louis the Emperor, surnamed the Pious. For they tell us [1] that this Emperor, after he had been thirty-three years in Purgatory, not so much for any personal crimes or misdemeanors of his own as for permitting certain disorders in his empire, which he ought to have prevented, was at length permitted to show himself to King Louis, his son, and to beg his favorable assistance; and that the king did not only most readily grant him his request, procuring Masses to be said in all the monasteries of his realm for the soul of his deceased father, but drew thence many good reflections and profitable instructions, which served him all his life-time after. Do you the same; and believe it, though Purgatory fire is a kind of baptism, and is so styled by some of the holy Fathers, because it cleanses a soul from all the dross of sin, and makes it worthy to see God, yet is it your sweetest course, here to baptize yourself frequently in the tears of contrition, which have a mighty power to cleanse away all the blemishes of sin; and so prevent in your own person, and extinguish in others, those baptismal flames of Purgatory fire, which are so dreadful. (Pp. 151, 152.)

[Footnote 1: Baronius, *An.* 874.]

45

* * * * *

What shall I say of those other nations, whose natural piety led them to place burning lamps at the sepulchres of the dead, and strew them over with sweet flowers and odoriferous perfumes. [1] Do they not put Christians in mind to remember the dead, and to cast after them the sweet incense of their devout sighs and prayers, and the perfumes of their alms-deeds, and other good works?

[Footnote 1: Herod lib. 2.]

It was very usual with the old Romans to shed whole floods of tears, to reserve them in phial-glasses, and to bury them with the urns, in which the ashes of their dead friends were carefully laid up; and by them to set lamps, so artificially composed as to burn without end. By which symbols they would give us to understand, that neither their love nor their grief should ever die; but that they would always be sure to have tears in their eyes, love in their hearts, and a constant memory in their souls for their deceased friends....

They had another custom, not only in Rome but elsewhere, to walk about the burning pile where the corpse lay, and, with their mournful lamentations, to keep time with the doleful sound of their trumpets; and still, every turn, to cast into the fire some precious pledge of their friendship. The women themselves would not stick to throw in their rings, bracelets, and other costly attires, nay, their very hair also, the chief ornament of their sex; and they would have been sometimes willing to have thrown in both their eyes, and their hearts too. Nor were there some wanting, that in earnest threw themselves into the fire, to be consumed with their dear spouses; so that it was found necessary to make a severe law against it; such was the tenderness that they had for their deceased friends, such was the excess of a mere natural affection. Now, our love is infused from Heaven; it is supernatural, and consequently ought to be more active and powerful to stir up our compassion for the souls departed; and yet we see the coldness of Christians in this particular; how few there are who make it their business to help poor souls out of their tormenting flames. It is not necessary to make laws to hinder any excess in this article; it were rather to be wished that a law were provided to punish all such ungrateful persons as forgot the duty they owe to their dead parents, and all the obligations they have to the rest of their friends. (Pp. 156-158.)

* * * * *

It is a pleasure to observe the constant devotion of the Church of Christ in all ages, to pray for the dead. And first, to take my rise from the Apostles' time, there are many learned interpreters, who hold that baptism for the dead, of which the Apostle speaks, [1] to be meant only of the much fasting, prayer, alms-deeds, and other voluntary afflictions, which the first Christians undertook for the relief of their deceased friends. But I need not fetch in obscure places to prove so clear an Apostolical and early custom in God's Church.

[Footnote 1: Cor. xv 29.]

You may see a set form of prayer for the dead prescribed in all the ancient liturgies of the Apostles. [1] Besides, St. Clement [2] tells us, it was one of the chief heads of St. Peter's sermons, to be daily inculcating to the people this devotion of praying for the dead; and St. Denis [3] sets down at large the solemn ceremonies and prayers, which were then used at funerals; and receives them no otherwise than as Apostolical traditions, grounded upon the Word of God. And certainly, it would have done you good to have seen with what gravity and devotion that venerable prelate performed the divine office and prayer for the dead, and what an ocean of tears he drew from the eyes of all that were present.

[Footnote 1: Liturgia utrinque, S. Jacobi, S. Math., S. Marci, S. Clem.]

[Footnote 2: Epist. I.]

[Footnote 3: S Dion. *Eccles. Hier.* C. 7.]

Let Tertullian [1] speak for the next age. He tells us how carefully devout people in his time kept the anniversaries of the dead, and made their constant oblations for the sweet rest of their souls. "Here it is," says this grave author, "that the widow makes it appear whether or no she had any true love for her husband; if she continue yearly to do her best for the comfort of his soul." ... Let your first care be, to ransom him out of Purgatory, and when you have once placed him in the empyrean heaven, he will be sure to take care for you and yours. I know your excuse is, that having procured for him the accustomed services of the Church, you need do no more for him; for you verily believe he is already in a blessed state. But this is rather a poor shift to excuse your own sloth and laziness, than that you believe it to be so in good earnest. For there is no man, says Origen, but the Son of God, can guess how long, or how many ages, a soul may stand in need of the purgation of fire. Mark the word *ages*; he seems to believe that a soul may, for whole ages—that is, for so many hundred years—be confined to this fiery lake, if she be wholly left to herself and her own sufferings.

[Footnote 1: Tertull. _De cor. mil. c 3; _De monogam, c. 10.]

It was not without confidence, says Eusebius, of reaping more fruit from the prayers of the faithful, that the honor of our nation, and the first Christian Emperor, Constantine the Great, took such care to be buried in the Church of the Apostles, whither all sorts of devout people resorting to perform their devotions to God and His Saints, would be sure to remember so good an emperor. Nor did he fail of his expectation; for it is incredible, as the same author observes, what a world of sighs and prayers were offered up for him upon this occasion.

St. Athanasius [1] brings an elegant comparison to express the incomparable benefit which accrues to the souls in Purgatory by our prayers. As the wine, says he, which is locked up in the cellar, yet is so recreated with the sweet odor of the flourishing vines which are growing in the fields, as to flower afresh, and leap, as it were, for joy, so the souls that are shut up in the centre of the earth feel the sweet incense of our prayers, and are exceedingly comforted and refreshed by it.

[Footnote 1: St. Augustine's views on this subject may be seen from the extract elsewhere given, from his "Confessions," on the occasion of the death of his mother, St. Monica.]

We do not busy ourselves, says St. Cyril, with placing crowns or strewing flowers at the sepulchres of the dead; but we lay hold on Christ, the very Son of God, who was sacrificed upon the Cross for our sins: and we offer Him up again to His Eternal Father in the dread Sacrifice of the Mass, as the most efficacious means to reconcile Him, not only to ourselves, but to them also.

St. Epiphanius stuck not to condemn Arius for this damnable heresy amongst others, that he held it in vain to pray for the dead: as if our prayers could not avail them.

St. Ambrose prayed heartily for the good Emperor Theodosius as soon as he was dead, and made open profession that he would never give over praying for him till he had, by his prayers and tears, conveyed him safe to the holy mountain of Our Lord, whither he was called by his merits, and where there is true life everlasting. He had the same kindness for the soul of the Emperor Valentinian, the same for Gratian, the same for his brother Satyrus and others. He promised them Masses, tears, prayers, and that he would never forget them, never give over doing charitable offices for them.

"Will you honor your dead?" says St. John Chrysostom; "do not spend yourselves in unprofitable lamentations; choose rather to sing psalms, to give alms, and to lead holy lives. Do for them that which they would willingly do for themselves, were they to return again into the world, and God will accept it at your hands, as if it came from them." (Pp. 162-166.)

St. Paulinus, that charitable prelate who sold himself to redeem others, could not but have a great proportion of charity for captive souls in the other world. No; he was not only ready to become a slave himself to purchase their freedom, but he became an earnest solicitor to others in their behalf; for, in a letter to Delphinus, alluding to the story of Lazarus, he beseeches him to have at least so much compassion as to convey, now and then, a drop of water wherewith to cool the tongues of poor souls that lie burning in the Church which is all a-fire.

I am astonished when I call to mind the sad regrets of the people of Africa when they saw some of their priests dragged away to martyrdom. The author says they flocked about them in great numbers and cried out: "Alas! if you leave us so, what will become of us? Who must give us absolution for our sins? Who must bury us with the wonted ceremonies of the Church when we are dead? and who will take care to pray for our souls?" Such a general belief they had in those days, that nothing is more to be desired in this world than to leave those behind us who will do their best to help us out of our torments. (Pp. 167-8.)

* * * * *

Almighty God has often miraculously made it appear how well He is pleased to be importuned by us in the souls' behalf, and what comfort they receive by our prayers. St. John Climacus writes, [1] that while the monks were at service, praying for their good father, Mennas, the third day after his departure, they felt a marvellous sweet smell to rise out of his grave, which they took for a good omen that his sweet soul, after three days' purgation, had taken her flight into heaven. For what else could be meant by that sweet perfume but the odor of his holy and innocent conversation, or the incense of their sacrifices and prayers, or the

48

primitial fruits of his happy soul, which was now flown up to the holy mountain of eternal glory, there enjoying the odoriferous and never-fading delights of Paradise?

[Footnote 1: In 4, gradu scalæ.]

Not unlike unto this is that story which the great St. Gregory relates of one Justus, a monk. [1] He had given him up at first for a lost creature; but, upon second thoughts, having ordered Mass to be said for him for thirty days together, the last day he appeared to his brother and assured him of the happy exchange he was now going to make of his torments for the joys of heaven.

[Footnote 1: Dial. c. 55, lib. 4.]

Pope Symmachus and his Council [1] had reason to thunder out anathemas against those sacrilegious persons who were so frontless as to turn pious legacies into profane uses, to the great prejudice of the souls for whose repose they were particularly deputed by the founders. And, certainly, it is a much fouler crime to defraud souls of their due relief than to disturb dead men's ashes and to plunder their graves. (Pp. 168-9.)

[Footnote 1: 6 Synod., Rom.]

St. Isidore delivers it as an apostolic tradition and general practice of the Catholic Church in his time, to offer up sacrifices and prayers, and to distribute alms for the dead; and this, not for any increase of their merit, but either to mitigate their pains or to shorten the time of their durance.

Venerable Bede is a sure witness for the following century; whose learned works are full of wonderful stories, which he brings in confirmation of this Catholic doctrine and practice.

St. John Damascene made an elegant oration on purpose to stir up this devotion; where, amongst other things, he says it is impossible to number up all the stories in this kind which bear witness that the souls departed are relieved by our prayers; and that, otherwise, God would not have appointed a commemoration of the dead to be daily made in the unbloody Sacrifice of the Mass, nor would the Church have so religiously observed anniversaries and other days set apart for the service of the dead.

Were it but a dog, says Simon Metaphrastes, that by chance were fallen into the fire, we should have so much compassion for him as to help him out; and what shall we do for souls who are fallen into Purgatory fire? I say, souls of our parents and dearest friends; souls that are predestinate to eternal glory, and extremely precious in the sight of God? And what did not the Saints of God's Church for them in those days? Some armed themselves from head to foot in coarse hair-cloth; others tore off their flesh with chains and rude disciplines; some, again, pined themselves with rigorous fasts; others dissolved themselves into tears; some passed whole nights in contemplation; others gave liberal alms or procured great store of Masses; in fine, they did what they were able, and were not well pleased that they were able to do no more, to relieve the poor souls in Purgatory. Amongst others, Queen Melchtild [1] is reported to have purchased immortal fame for her discreet behavior at the death of the king, her husband; for whose soul she caused a world of Masses to be said, and a world of alms to be distributed, in lieu of other idle expenses and fruitless lamentations.

[Footnote 1: Luitprand, c. 4, c. 7.]

There is one in the world, to whom I bear an immortal envy, and such an envy as I never mean to repent of. It is the holy Abbot Odilo, who was the author of an invention which I would wittingly have found out, though with the loss of my very heart's blood.

Reader, take the story as it passed, thus: [1] A devout religious man, in his return from Jerusalem, meets with a holy hermit in Sicily; he assures him that he often heard the devils complain that souls were so soon discharged of their torments by the devout prayers of the monks of Cluny, who never ceased to pour out their prayers for them. This the good man carries to Odilo, then Abbot of Cluny; he praises God for His great mercy in vouchsafing to hear the innocent prayers of his monks; and presently takes occasion to command all the monasteries of his Order, to keep yearly the commemoration of All Souls, next after the feast of All Saints, a custom which, by degrees, grew into such credit, that the Catholic Church thought fit to establish it all over the Christian world; to the incredible benefit of poor souls, and singular increase of God's glory. For who can sum up the infinite number of souls who have been freed out of Purgatory by this invention? or who can express the glory which accrued to this good Abbot, who thus fortunately made himself procurator-general of the suffering Church, and furnished her people with such a considerable supply of necessary relief, to alleviate the insupportable burthen of their sufferings?

[Footnote 1: Sigeb. in *Chron.* An. 998.]

St. Bernard would triumph when he had to deal with heretics that denied this privilege of communicating our suffrages and prayers to the souls in Purgatory. And with what fervor he would apply himself to this charitable employment of relieving poor souls, may appear by the care he took for good Humbertus, though he knew him to have lived and died in his monastery so like a Saint, that he could scarce find out the fault in him which might deserve the least punishment in the other world; unless it were to have been too rigorous to himself, and too careless of his health: which in a less spiritual eye than that of St. Bernard, might have passed for a great virtue. But it is worth your hearing, that which he relates of blessed St. Malachy, who died in his very bosom. This holy Bishop, as he lay asleep, hears a sister of his, lately dead, making lamentable moan, that for thirty days together she had not eaten so much as a bit of bread. He starts up out of his sleep; and, taking it to be more than a dream, he concludes the meaning of the vision was to tell him, that just thirty days were now past since he had said Mass for her; as probably believing she was already where she had no need of his prayers.... Howsoever, this worthy prelate so plied his prayers after this, that he soon sent his sister out of Purgatory; and it pleased God to let him see, by the daily change of her habit, how his prayers had purged her by degrees, and made her fit company for the Angels and Saints in heaven. For, the first day, she was covered all over with black cypress; the next, she appeared in a mantle something whitish, but a dusky color; but the third day, she was seen all clad in white, which is the proper livery of the Saints....

This for St. Bernard. But I cannot let pass in silence one very remarkable passage, which happened to these two great servants of God. St. Malachy had passionately desired to die at Clarvallis, [1] in the hands of the devout St. Bernard; and this, on the day immediately before All Souls' Day; and it pleased God to grant him his request. It fell out, then, that while St. Bernard was saying Mass for him, in the middle of Mass it was revealed to him that St. Malachy was already glorious in heaven; whether he had gone straight out of this world, or whether that part of St. Bernard's Mass had freed him out of Purgatory, is uncertain; but St. Bernard, hereupon, changed his note; for, having begun with a Requiem, he went on with the Mass of a bishop and confessor, to the great astonishment of all the standers-by.

[Footnote 1: Clairvaux.]

St. Thomas of Aquin, that great champion of Purgatory, gave God particular thanks at his death, for not only delivering a soul out of Purgatory, at the instance of his prayers, but also permitting the same soul to be the messenger of so good news. (Pp. 169-174.)

* * * * *

And now, we are come down to the fifteenth age, where the Fathers of the Council of Florence, both Greeks and. Latins, with one consent, declare the same faith and constant practice of the Church, thus handed down to them from age to age, since Christ and His Apostles' time, as we have seen; viz., that the souls in Purgatory are not only relieved, but translated into heaven, by the prayers, sacrifices, alms, and other charitable works, which are offered up for them according to the custom of the Catholic Church. Nor did their posterity degenerate, or vary the least, from this received doctrine, until Luther's time; when the holy Council of Trent thought fit again to lay down the sound doctrine of the Church, in opposition to all our late sectaries. And I wish all Catholics were but as forward to lend their helping hands to lift souls out of Purgatory, as they are to believe they have the power to do it; and that we had not often more reason than the Roman Emperor to pronounce the day lost; since we let so many days pass over our heads, and so many fair occasions slip out of our hands, without easing, or releasing, any souls out of Purgatory, when we might do it with so much ease. (P. 175.)

ON DEVOTION TO THE HOLY SOULS.
FATHER FABER.

Although we are mercifully freed from the necessity of descending into hell to seek and promote the interests of Jesus, it is far from being so with Purgatory. If heaven and earth are full of the glory of God, so also is that most melancholy, yet most interesting land, where the prisoners of hope are detained by their Saviour's loving justice, from the Beatific Vision; and if we can advance the interests of Jesus on earth and in heaven, I may almost venture to say that we can do still more in Purgatory. And what I am endeavoring to show you in this treatise is,

51

how you may help God by prayer, and the practices of devotion, whatever your occupation and calling may be: and all these practices apply especially to Purgatory. For although some theologians say that in spite of the Holy Souls placing no obstacle in the way, still the effect of prayer for them is not infallible; nevertheless, it is much more certain than the effect of prayer for the conversion of sinners upon earth, where it is so often frustrated by their perversity and evil dispositions. Anyhow, what I have wanted to show has been this: that each of us, without aiming beyond our grace, without austerities for which we have not courage, without supernatural gifts to which we lay no claim, may, by simple affectionateness and the practices of sound Catholic devotion, do great things, things so great that they seem incredible, for the glory of God, the interests of Jesus, and the good of souls. I should, therefore, be leaving my subject very incomplete if I did not consider at some length devotion to the Holy Souls in Purgatory; and I will treat, not so much of particular practices of it, which are to be found in the ordinary manuals, as of the spirit of the devotion itself.

* * * * *

By the doctrine of the Communion of Saints and of the unity of Christ's mystical body, we have most intimate relations both of duty and affection with the Church Triumphant and Suffering; and Catholic devotion furnishes us with many appointed and approved ways of discharging these duties toward them.... For the present it is enough to say that God has given us such power over the dead that they seem, as I have said before, to depend almost more on earth than on heaven; and surely that He has given us this power, and supernatural methods of exercising it, is not the least touching proof that His Blessed Majesty has contrived all things for love. Can we not conceive the joy of the Blessed in Heaven, looking down from the bosom of God and the calmness of their eternal repose upon this scene of dimness, disquietude, doubt and fear, and rejoicing in the plenitude of their charity, in their vast power with the Sacred Heart of Jesus, to obtain grace and blessing day and night for the poor dwellers upon earth? It does not distract them from God, it does not interfere with the Vision, or make it waver and grow misty; it does not trouble their glory or their peace. On the contrary, it is with them as with our Guardian Angels—the affectionate ministries of their charity increase their own accidental glory. The same joy in its measure may be ours even upon earth. If we are fully possessed with this Catholic devotion for the Holy Souls, we shall never be without the grateful consciousness of the immense powers which Jesus has given us on their behalf. We are never so like Him, or so nearly imitate His tender offices, as when we are devoutly exercising these powers.... Oh! what thoughts, what feelings, what love should be ours, as we, like choirs of terrestrial angels, gaze down on the wide, silent, sinless kingdom of suffering, and then with our own venturous touch wave the sceptred hand of Jesus over its broad regions all richly dropping with the balsam of His saving Blood!

* * * * *

Oh! how solemn and subduing is the thought of that holy kingdom, that realm of pain! There is no cry, no murmur; all is silent, silent as Jesus before His enemies. We shall never know how we really love Mary till we look up to her out of those deeps, those vales of dread mysterious fire. O beautiful region of the Church of God. O lovely troop of the flock of Mary! What a scene is presented to our eyes when we gaze upon that consecrated empire of sinlessness and yet of keenest suffering! There is the beauty of those immaculate souls, and then the loveliness, yea, the worshipfulness of their patience, the majesty of their gifts, the dignity of their solemn and chaste sufferings, the eloquence of their silence; the moonlight of Mary's throne lighting up their land of pain and unspeechful expectation; the silver-winged angels voyaging through the deeps of that mysterious realm; and above all, that unseen Face of Jesus which is so well remembered that it seems to be almost seen! Oh! what a sinless purity of worship is here in this liturgy of hallowed pain! O world! O weary, clamorous, sinful world! Who would not break away if he could, like an uncaged dove, from thy perilous toils and unsafe pilgrimage, and fly with joy to the lowest place in that most pure, most safe, most holy land of suffering and of sinless love!

* * * * *

But some persons turn in anger from the thought of Purgatory, as if it were not to be endured, that after trying all our lives long to serve God, we should accomplish the tremendous feat of a good death, only to pass from the agonies of the death-bed into fire—long, keen, searching, triumphant, incomparable fire. Alas! my dear friends; your anger will not help you nor alter facts. But have you thought sufficiently about God? Have you tried to realize His holiness and purity in assiduous meditation? Is there a real divorce between you and the world, which you know is God's enemy? Do you take God's side? Have you wedded His interests? Do you long for His glory? Have you put sin alongside of our dear Saviour's Passion, and measured the one by the other? Oh! if you had, Purgatory would but seem to you the last, unexpected, and inexpressibly tender invention of an obstinate love which was mercifully determined to save you in spite of yourself! It would be a perpetual wonder to you, a joyous wonder, fresh every, morning—a wonder that would be meat and drink to your soul; that you, being what you are, what you know yourself to be, what you may conceive God knows you to be, should be saved eternally! Remember what the suffering soul said so simply, yet with such force, to Sister Francesca: "Ah! those on that side the grave little reckon how dearly they will pay on this side for the lives they live!" To be angry because you are told you will go to Purgatory! Silly, silly people! Most likely it is a great false flattery, and that you will never be good enough to go there at all. Why, positively, you do not recognize your own good fortune when you are told of it. And none but the humble go there. I remember Maria Crocifissa was told that although many of the Saints while on earth loved God more than some do even in heaven, yet that the greatest saint on earth was not so *humble* as are the souls in Purgatory. I do not think I ever read anything in the lives of the Saints which struck me so much as that....

But we not only learn lessons for our own good, but for the good of the Holy

Souls. We see that our charitable attentions toward them must be far more vigorous and persevering than they have been; for that men go to Purgatory for very little matters, and remain there an unexpectedly long time. But their most touching appeal to us lies in their helplessness; and our dear Lord, with His usual loving arrangement, has made the extent of our power to help them more than commensurate with their inability to help themselves.... St. Thomas has taught us that prayer for the dead is more readily accepted with God than prayer for the living. We can offer and apply for them all the satisfactions of our Blessed Lord. We can do vicarious penance for them. We can give to them all the satisfaction of our ordinary actions, and of our sufferings. We can make over to them by way of suffrage, the indulgences we gain, provided the Church has made them applicable to the dead. We can limit and direct upon them, or any one of them, the intention of the Adorable Sacrifice. The Church, which has no jurisdiction over them, can yet make indulgences applicable or inapplicable to them by way of suffrage; and by means of liturgy, commemoration, incense, holy water, and the like, can reach efficaciously to them, and most of all by her device of privileged altars. .... All that I have said hitherto has been, indirectly, at least, a plea for this devotion; but I must come now to a more direct recommendation of it.

* * * * *

It is not saying too much to call devotion to the Holy Souls, a kind of centre in which all Catholic devotions meet, and which satisfies more than any other single devotion our duties in that way; because it is a devotion all of love, and of disinterested love. If we cast an eye over the chief Catholic devotions, we shall see the truth of this. Take the devotion of St. Ignatius to the glory of God. This, if I may dare to use such an expression of Him, was the special and favorite devotion of Jesus. Now, Purgatory is simply a field white for the harvest of God's glory. Not a prayer can be said for the Holy Souls, but God is at once glorified, both by the faith and the charity of the mere prayer. Not an alleviation, however trifling, can befall any one of the souls, but He is forthwith glorified by the honor of His Son's Precious Blood, and the approach of the soul to bliss. Not a soul is delivered from its trial but God is immensely glorified.

* * * * *

Again, what devotion is more justly dear to Christians than the devotion to the Sacred Humanity of Jesus? It is rather a family of various and beautiful devotions, than a devotion by itself. Yet see how they are all, as it were, fulfilled, affectionately fulfilled, in devotion to the Holy Souls. The quicker the souls are liberated from Purgatory, the more is the beautiful harvest of His Blessed Passion multiplied and accelerated. An early harvest is a blessing, as well as a plentiful one; for all delay of a soul's ingress into the praise of heaven is an eternal and irremediable loss of honor and glory to the Sacred Humanity of Jesus. How strangely things sound in the language of the Sanctuary! yet so it is. Can the Sacred Humanity be honored more than by the Adorable Sacrifice of the Mass? And here is our chief action upon Purgatory....

Devotion to our dearest Mother is equally comprehended in this devotion to the

Holy Souls, whether we look at her as the Mother of Jesus, and so sharing the honors of His Sacred Humanity, or as Mother of mercy, and so specially honored by works of mercy, or, lastly, as, in a particular sense, the Queen of Purgatory, and so having all manner of dear interests to be promoted in the welfare and deliverance of those suffering souls.

Next to this we may rank devotion to the Holy Angels, and this also is satisfied in devotion to the Holy Souls. For it keeps filling the vacant thrones in the angelic choirs, those unsightly gaps which the fall of Lucifer and one-third of the heavenly host occasioned. It multiplies the companions of the blessed spirits. They may be supposed also to look with an especial interest on that part of the Church which lies in Purgatory, because it is already crowned with their own dear gift and ornament of final perseverance, and yet it has not entered at once into its inheritance as they did. Many of them also have a tender personal interest in Purgatory. Thousands, perhaps millions of them, are guardians to those souls, and their office is not over yet. Thousands have clients there who were especially devoted to them in life. Will St. Raphael, who was so faithful to Tobias, be less faithful to his clients there? Whole choirs are interested about others, either because they are finally to be aggregated to that choir, or because in life-time they had a special devotion to it. Marie Denise, of the Visitation, used to congratulate her angel every day on the grace he had received to stand when so many around him were falling. It was the only thing she could know for certain of his past life. Could he neglect her, if by the will of God she went to Purgatory? Again, St. Michael, as prince of Purgatory, and Our Lady's regent, in fulfilment of the dear office attributed to him by the Church in the Mass for the Dead, takes as homage to himself all charity to the Holy Souls; and if it be true, that a zealous heart is always a proof of a grateful one, that bold and magnificent spirit will recompense us one day in his own princely style, and perhaps within the limits of that his special jurisdiction.

Neither is devotion to the Saints without its interests in this devotion for the dead. It fills them with the delights of charity as it swells their numbers and beautifies their ranks and orders. Numberless patron saints are personally interested in multitudes of souls. The affectionate relation between their clients and themselves not only subsists, but a deeper tenderness has entered into it, because of the fearful suffering, and a livelier interest, because of the accomplished victory. They see in the Holy Souls their own handiwork, the fruit of their example, the answer to their prayers, the success of their patronage, the beautiful and finished crown of their affectionate intercession.

* * * * *

Another point of view from which we may look at this devotion for the dead, is as a specially complete and beautiful exercise of the three theological virtues of faith, hope, and charity, which are the supernatural fountains of our whole spiritual life. It exercises faith, because it leads men not only to dwell in the unseen world, but to work for it with as much energy and conviction as if it was before their very eyes. Unthoughtful or ill-read persons almost start sometimes at the minuteness, familiarity, and assurance with which men talk of the unseen world, as if it were the banks of the Rhine, or the olive-yards of Provence, the Campagna of Rome, or the crescent shores of Naples, some place which they have seen in their travels, and whose geographical features are ever in their memory, as vividly as if before their eyes. It all comes of faith, of prayer, of spiritual reading, of knowledge of the lives of the Saints, and of the study of theology. It would be strange and sad if it were not so. For, what to us, either in interest or importance, is the world we see, to the world we do not see? This devotion exercises our faith also in the effects of the sacrifice and sacraments, which are things we do not see, but which we daily talk of in reference to the dead as undoubted and accomplished facts. It exercises our faith in the communion of Saints to a degree which would make it seem impossible to a heretic that he ever could believe so wild and extravagant a creed. It acts with regard to indulgences as if they were the most inevitable material transactions of this world. It knows of the unseen treasure out of which they come, of the unseen keys which open the treasury, of the indefinite jurisdiction which places them infallibly at its disposal, of God's unrevealed acceptance of them, and of the invisible work they do, just as it knows of trees and clouds, of streets and churches—that is, just as certainly and undoubtingly; though it often can give others no proof of these things, nor account for them to itself…. It exhibits the same quiet faith in all those Catholic devotions which I mentioned before as centering themselves in this devotion for the dead.

* * * * *

Neither is this devotion a less heroic exercise of the theological virtue of hope, the virtue so sadly wanting in the spiritual life of these times. For, look what a mighty edifice this devotion raises; lofty, intricate, and of magnificent proportions, into which somehow or other all creation is drawn, from the little headache we suffer up to the Sacred Humanity of Jesus, and which has to do even with God Himself. And upon what does all this rest, except on a simple, child-like trust in God's fidelity, which is the supernatural motive of hope? We hope for the souls we help, and unbounded are the benedictions which we hope for in their regard. We hope to find mercy ourselves, because of our mercy; and this hope quickens our merits without detracting from the merit of our charity…. For the state of the dead is no dream, nor our power to help them a dream, any more than the purity of God is a dream, or the Precious Blood a dream.

* * * * *

As to the charity of this devotion, it dares to imitate even the charity of God Himself. What is there in heaven or on earth which it does not embrace, and with so much facility, with so much gracefulness, as if there were scarcely an effort in it, or as if self was charmed away, and might not mingle to distract it? It is an exercise of the love of God, for it is loving those whom He loves, and loving them because He loves them, and to augment His glory and multiply His praise…. To ourselves also it is an exercise of charity, for it gains us friends in heaven; it earns mercy for us when we ourselves shall be in Purgatory, tranquil victims, yet, oh! in what distress! and it augments our merits in the sight of God, and so, if only we persevere, our eternal recompense hereafter. Now if this tenderness for the dead is such an exercise of these three theological virtues, and if, again, even heroic sanctity consists principally in their exercise, what store ought we not to set upon this touching and beautiful devotion?

* * * * *

Look at that vast kingdom of Purgatory, with its empress-mother, Mary! All those countless throngs of souls are the dear and faithful spouses of Jesus. Yet in what a strange abandonment of supernatural suffering has His love left them! He longs for their deliverance; He yearns for them to be transferred from that land, perpetually overclouded with pain, to the bright sunshine of their heavenly home. Yet He has tied His own hands, or nearly so. He gives them no more grace; He allows them no more time for penance; He prevents them from meriting; nay, some have thought they could not pray. How, then, stands the case with the souls in the suffering Church? Why, it is a thing to be meditated on when we have said it—they depend almost more on earth than they do on heaven, almost more on us than on Him; so He has willed it on whom all depend, and without whom there is no dependence. It is clear, then, that Jesus has His interests there. He wants His captives released. Those whom He has redeemed He now bids us redeem, us whom, if there be life at all in us, He has already Himself redeemed. Every satisfaction offered up to God for these suffering souls, every oblation of the Precious Blood to the Eternal Father, every Mass heard, every communion received, every voluntary penance undergone; the scourge, the hair- shirt, the prickly chain, every indulgence gained, every jubilee whose conditions we have fulfilled, every *De Profundis* whispered, every little alms doled out to the poor who are poorer than ourselves, and, if they be offered for the intention of these dear prisoners, the interests of Jesus are hourly forwarded in Mary's Kingdom of Purgatory…. There is no fear of overworking the glorious secretary of that wide realm, the blessed Michael, Mary's subject. See how men work at the pumps on ship-board when they are fighting for their lives with an ugly leak. Oh! that we had the charity so to work, with the sweet instrumentality of indulgence, for the Holy Souls in Purgatory! The infinite satisfactions of Jesus are at our command, and Mary's sorrows, and the Martyr's pangs, and the Confessor's weary perseverance in well- doing! Jesus will not help Himself here, because He loves to see us helping Him, and because He thinks our love will rejoice that He still leaves us something we can do for Him. There have been Saints who have devoted their whole lives to this one work, mining in Purgatory; and, to those who reflect in faith, it does not seem, after all, so strange. It is a foolish comparison, simply because it is so much below the mark; but on all principles of reckoning, it is a much less work to have won the battle of Waterloo, or to have invented the steam-engine, than to have freed one soul from Purgatory.

WHY THE SOULS IS PURGATORY ARE CALLED "POOR" SOULS. FATHER MULLER, C.S.S.R. [1]

[Footnote 1: Charity to the Holy Souls in Purgatory]

We have just seen that the Jews believed in the doctrine of Purgatory; we have seen that their charity for the dead was so great that the Holy Ghost could not help praising them for it. Yet for all that, we may assert in truth that the people of God under the Old Law were not so well instructed in this doctrine as we are, nor had they such powerful means to relieve the souls—in Purgatory as we have. Our faith, therefore, should be more lively, and our charity for the souls in Purgatory more ardent and generous.

A short time ago a fervent young priest of this country had the following conversation with a holy Bishop on his way to Rome. The Bishop said to him: "You make mementoes now and then, for friends of yours that are dead—do you not?" The young priest answered: "Certainly, I do so very often." The Bishop rejoined: "So did I, when I was a young priest. But one time I was grievously ill. I was given up as about to die. I received Extreme Unction and the Viaticum. It was then that my whole past life, with all its failings and all its sins, came before me with startling vividness. I saw how much I had to atone for; and I reflected on how few Masses would be said for me, and how few prayers. Ever since my recovery I have most fervently offered the Holy Sacrifice for the repose of the pious and patient souls in Purgatory; and I am always glad when I can, as my own offering, make the 'intention' of my Masses for the relief of their pains."

Indeed, dear reader, no one is more deserving of Christian charity and sympathy than the poor souls in Purgatory. They are *really* POOR *souls*. No one is sooner forgotten than they are.

How soon their friends persuade themselves that they are in perfect peace! How little they do for their relief when their bodies are buried! There is a lavish expense for the funeral. A hundred dollars are spent where the means of the family hardly justify the half of it. Where there is more wealth, sometimes five hundred or a thousand, and even more, dollars are expended on the poor dead body. But let me ask you what is done for the *poor living soul?* Perhaps the poor soul is suffering the most frightful tortures in Purgatory, whilst the lifeless body is laid out in state, and borne pompously to the graveyard. You must not misunderstand me: it is right and just to show all due respect even to the body of your deceased friend, for that body was once the dwelling-place of his soul. But tell me candidly, what joy has the departed, and, perhaps, suffering soul, in the fine music of the choir, even should the choir be composed of the best singers in the country? What consolation does the poor suffering soul find in the superb coffin, in the splendid funeral? What pleasure does the soul derive from the costly marble monument, from all the honors that are so freely lavished on the body? All this may satisfy, or at least seem to satisfy, the living, but it is of no avail whatever to the dead.

Poor unhappy souls! how the diminution of true Catholic faith is visited upon you while you suffer, and those that loved you in life might help you, and do not, for want of knowledge or of faith!

Poor unhappy souls! your friends go to their business, to their eating and drinking, with the foolish assurance that the case cannot be hard on one they knew to be so good! Oh, how much and how long this *false charity* of your friends makes you suffer!

The venerable Sister, Catherine Paluzzi, offered up, for a long time, and with the utmost fervor, prayers and pious works for the soul of her deceased father. At last she thought she had good reason to believe that her father was already enjoying the bliss of Paradise. But how great was her consternation and grief when Our Lord, in company with St. Catherine, her patroness, led her one day, in spirit, to Purgatory. There she beheld her father in an abyss of torments, imploring her assistance. At the sight of the pitiful state the soul of her father was in, she melted into tears; she cast herself at the feet of her Heavenly Spouse, and begged Him, through His precious Blood, to free her father from his excruciating sufferings. She also begged St. Catherine to intercede for him, and then turning to Our Lord, she said: "Charge me, O Lord, with my father's indebtedness to Thy justice. In expiation of it, I am ready to take upon myself all the afflictions Thou art pleased to bestow upon me." Our Lord graciously accepted this act of heroic charity, and released at once her father's soul from Purgatory. But how heavy were the crosses which she, from that time, had to suffer, may be more easily imagined than described. This pious sister seemed to have good reason to believe that her father's soul was in Paradise. Yet she was mistaken. Alas! how many are there who resemble her! How many are there whose hope as to the condition of their deceased friends is far more vain and false than that of this religious, because they pray much less for the souls of their departed friends than she did for her father.

* * * * *

It is related in the life of St. Mary Magdalen of Pazzi, that one day she saw the soul of one of her deceased sisters kneeling in adoration before the Blessed Sacrament, in the church, wrapped up in a mantle of fire, and suffering great pains, in expiation of her neglecting to go to Holy Communion on one day, when she had her confessor's permission to communicate.

The Venerable Bede relates that it was revealed to Drithelm, a great servant of God, that the souls of those who spend their whole lives in the state of mortal sin, and are converted only on their death-bed, are doomed to suffer the pains of Purgatory to the day of the last judgment.

In the life and revelations of St. Gertrude we read that those who have committed many grievous sins, and who die without having done due penance, are not assisted by the ordinary suffrages of the Church until they are partly purified by Divine Justice in Purgatory.

After St. Vincent Ferrer had learned the death of his sister Frances, he at once began to offer up many fervent prayers and works of penance for the repose of her soul. He also said thirty Masses for her, at the last of which it was revealed to him that, had it not been for his prayers and good works, the soul of his sister would have suffered in Purgatory to the end of the world.

From these examples you may draw your own conclusion as to the state of your deceased friends and relatives. Rest assured that the judgments of God are very different from the judgments of men.

59

* * * * *

In heaven, love for God is the happiness of the elect; but in Purgatory it is the source of the most excruciating pains. It is principally for this reason that the souls in Purgatory are called "poor souls," they being, as they are, in the most dreadful state of poverty—that of the privation of the beatific vision of God.

After Anthony Corso, a Capuchin Brother, a man of great piety and perfection, had departed this life, he appeared to one of his brethren in religion, asking him to recommend him to the charitable prayers of the community, in order that he might receive relief in his pains. "For I do not know," said he, "how I can bear any longer the pain of being deprived of the sight of my God. I shall be the most unhappy of creatures as long as I must live in this state. Would to God that all men might understand what it is to be without God, in order that they might firmly resolve to suffer anything during their life on earth rather than expose themselves to the danger of being damned, and deprived forever of the sight of God." [1]

[Footnote 1: 1 Aunal. Pp. Capuc., A.D. 1548.]

* * * * *

The souls in Purgatory are *poor* souls, because they suffer the greatest pain of the senses, which is that of *fire*. Who can be in a poorer or more pitiful condition than those who are buried in fire? Now, this is the condition of these poor souls. They are buried under waves of fire. It is from the smallest spark of this purgatorial fire that they suffer more intense pains than all the fires of this world put together could produce....

Could these poor souls leave the fire of Purgatory for the most frightful earthly fire they would, as it were, take it for a pleasure- garden; they would find a fifty years' stay in the hottest earthly fire more endurable than an hour's stay in the fire of Purgatory. Our terrestrial fire was not created by God to torment men, but rather to benefit them; but the fire of Purgatory was created by God for no other purpose than to be an instrument of His justice; and for this reason it is possessed of a burning quality so intense and penetrating that it is impossible for us to conceive even the faintest idea of it.

* * * * *

In the year 1150 it happened that, on the Vigil of St. Cecilia, a very old monk, one hundred years of age, at Marchiennes, in Flanders, fell asleep while sacred lessons were being read, and saw, in a dream, a monk all clad in armor, shining like red-hot iron in a furnace. The old man asked him who he was. He was told that he was one of the monks of the convent; that he was in Purgatory, and had yet to endure this fiery armor for ten years more, for having injured the reputation of another.

* * * * *

Another reason why these holy prisoners and debtors to the divine justice are really *poor* is because they are not able, in the least, to assist themselves. A sick man afflicted in all his limbs, and a beggar in the most painful and most destitute of conditions, has a tongue left to ask for relief. At least they can implore Heaven;

it is never deaf to their prayer. But the souls in Purgatory are so poor that they cannot even do this. Those cases in which some of them were permitted to appear to their friends and ask assistance are but exceptions. To whom is it they should have recourse? Is it, perhaps, to the mercy of God? Alas! they send forth their sighs in plaintive voices.... But the Lord does not regard their tears, nor heed their moans and cries, but answers them that His justice must be satisfied to the last farthing.

* * * * *

Oh, what cruelty! A sick man weeps on his bed and his friend consoles him; a baby cries in his cradle and his mother at once caresses him; a beggar knocks at the door for an alms and receives it; a malefactor laments in his prison, and comfort is given him; even a dog that whines at the door is taken in; but these poor, helpless souls cry day and night from the depths of the fire in Purgatory: "Have pity on me, have pity on me, at least you, my friends, because the hand of the Lord hath smitten me;" and there is none to listen! Oh, what great cruelty, my brethren!

But it seems to me that I hear these poor souls exclaim: "Priest of the Lord, speak no longer of our sufferings and pitiable condition. Let your description of it be ever so touching, it will not afford us the least relief. When a man has fallen into the fire, instead of considering his pains, you try at once to draw him out or quench the fire with water. This is true charity. Now, tell Christians to do the same for us. Tell them to give us their feet, by going to hear Mass for us; to give us their eyes, by seeking an occasion to perform a good work for us; to give us their hands, by giving an alms for us, or by often making an offering for the 'intention' of Masses in our behalf; to give us their lips, by praying for us; to give us their tongue, by requesting others to be charitable to us; to give us their memory, by remembering us constantly in their devotions; to give us their body, by offering up for us to the Almighty all its labors, fatigues, and penance."...

We read in the Acts of the Apostles, that the faithful prayed unceasingly for St. Peter when he was imprisoned, and that an Angel came and broke his chains and released him. "We, too, should be good angels to the poor souls in Purgatory, and free them from their painful captivity by every means in our power."

* * * * *

In the time of St. Bernard, a monk of Clairvaux appeared after his death to his brethren in religion, to thank them for having delivered him from Purgatory. On being asked what had most contributed to free him from his torments, he led the inquirer to the church, where a priest was saying Mass. "Look!" said he; "this is the means by which my deliverance has been effected; this is the power of God's mercy; this is the saving Sacrifice which taketh away the sins of the world." Indeed, so great is the efficacy of this Sacrifice in obtaining relief for the souls in Purgatory, that the application of all the good works which have been performed from the beginning of the world, would not afford so much assistance to one of these souls as is imparted by a single Mass. To illustrate: The blessed Henry Suso made an agreement with one of his brethren in religion that, as soon as either of

61

them died, the survivor should say two Masses every week for one year, for the repose of his soul. It came to pass that the religious with whom Henry had made this contract, died first. Henry prayed every day for his deliverance from Purgatory, but forgot to say the Masses which he had promised; whereupon the deceased religious appeared to him with a sad countenance, and sharply rebuked him for his unfaithfulness to his engagement. Henry excused himself by saying that he had often prayed for him with great fervor, and had even offered up for him many penitential works. "Oh, brother!" exclaimed the soul, "blood, blood is necessary to give me some relief and refreshment in my excruciating torments. Your penitential works, severe as they are, cannot deliver me. Nothing can do this but the blood of Jesus Christ, which is offered up in the Sacrifice of the Mass. Masses, Masses—these are what I need!"

* * * * *

Another means to relieve the souls in Purgatory is to gain indulgences for them. A very pious nun had just died in the convent in which St. Mary Magdalen of Pazzi lived. Whilst her corpse was exposed in the church, the Saint looked lovingly upon it, and prayed fervently that the soul of her sister might soon enter into eternal rest. Whilst she was thus wrapt in prayer her sister appeared to her, surrounded by great splendor and radiance, in the act of ascending into heaven. The Saint, on seeing this, could not refrain from calling out to her: "Farewell, dear sister! When you meet your Heavenly Spouse, remember us who are still sighing for Him in this vale of tears!" At these words our Lord Himself appeared, and revealed to her that this sister had entered heaven so soon on account of the indulgences gained for her. [1]

[Footnote 1: Vita S. Magd. de Pazzi, L. I., chap, xxxix.]

Very many plenary indulgences can be gained for the souls in Purgatory, if you make the Stations of the Cross. The merit of this exercise, if applied to these souls, obtains great relief for them. We read in the life of Catherine Emmerich, a very pious Augustinian nun, that the souls in Purgatory often came to her during the night, and requested her to rise and make the Stations for their relief. It is also related in the life of the venerable Mary of Antigua, that a deceased sister of her convent appeared to her and said: "Why do you not make the Stations of the Way of the Cross for me?" Whilst the servant of the Lord felt surprised and astonished at these words, Jesus Christ Himself spoke to her, thus: "The exercise of the Stations is of the greatest advantage to the souls in Purgatory; so much so that this soul has been permitted by Me, to ask of you its performance in behalf of them all. Your frequent performance of this exercise to procure relief for these souls has induced them to hold intercourse with you, and you shall have them for so many intercessors and protectors before My justice. Tell your sisters to rejoice at these treasures, and the splendid capital which they have in them, that they may grow rich upon it."

* * * * *

After St. Ludgarde had offered up many fervent prayers for the repose of the soul of her deceased friend Simeon, Abbot of the monastery of Toniac, Our

Lord appeared to her, saying: "Be consoled, My daughter; on account of thy prayers, I will soon release this soul from Purgatory." "O Jesus, Lord and Master of my heart!" she rejoined, "I cannot feel consoled so long as I know that the soul of my friend is suffering so much in the Purgatorial fire. Oh! I cannot help shedding most bitter tears until Thou hast released this soul from its sufferings." Touched and overcome by this fervent prayer, Our Lord released the soul of Simeon, who appeared to Ludgarde all radiant with heavenly glory, and thanked her for the many fervent prayers which she had offered up for his delivery. He also told the Saint that, had it not been for her fervent prayers, he should have been obliged to stay in Purgatory for eleven years....

Peter, the venerable Abbot of Cluny, relates an event somewhat similar. There was a monk at Cluny, named Bernard Savinellus. One night as he was returning to the dormitory, he met Stephen, commonly called Blancus, Abbot of St. Giles, who had departed this life a few days before. At first, not knowing him, he was passing on, till he spoke, and asked him whither he was hastening. Bernard, astonished and angry that a monk should speak, contrary to the rules, in the nocturnal hours, and in a place where it was not permitted, made signs to him to hold his peace; but as the dead abbot replied, and urged him to speak, the other, raising his head, asked in amazement who he might be. He was answered, "I am Stephen, the Abbot of St. Giles, who have formerly committed many faults in the Abbey, for which I now suffer pains; and I beseech you to implore the lord Abbot, and other brethren, to pray for me, that by the ineffable mercy of God, I may be delivered." Bernard replied that he would do so, but added that he thought no one would believe his report; to which the dead man answered, "In order, then, that no one may doubt, you may assure them that within eight days you will die;" he then disappeared. The monk, returning to the church, spent the remainder of the night in prayer and meditation. When it was day, he related his vision to St. Hugo, who was then abbot. As is natural, some believed his account, and others thought it was some delusion. The next day the monk fell sick, and continued growing worse, constantly affirming the truth of what he had related, till his death, which occurred within the time specified.

* * * * *

Besides prayer and other acts of devotion we can offer up for the poor souls, we may especially reckon *alms-deeds*; for since this is a work of mercy, it is more especially apt to obtain mercy for the poor souls. But not the rich alone can give alms, but the poor also, since it does not so much depend on the greatness of the gift. Of the poor widow who gave but one penny, Our Lord said; that she had given more than all the rich who had offered gold and silver, because these offered only of their abundance, whilst the poor widow gave what she saved from her daily sustenance....

The venerable servant of God, Father Clement Hoffbauer, of the Congregation of the Most Holy Redeemer, who died in Vienna in the year 1820, and whose cause of beatification has already been introduced, once assisted a man of distinction in death. A short time afterwards the same man appeared to his wife in

63

a dream, in a very pitiable condition, his clothes in rags and quite haggard, and shivering with cold. He begged her to have pity on him, because he could scarcely endure the extreme hunger and cold which he suffered. His wife went without delay to Father Hoffbauer, related her dream, and asked his advice on this point. The confessor, enlightened by God, immediately understood what this dream meant, and what kind of assistance was especially needed and asked for by this poor soul. He accordingly advised her to clothe a poor beggar. The woman followed the advice, and soon after her husband again appeared to her, dressed in a white garment, and his countenance beaming with joy, thanking her for the help which she had given to him.

* * * * *

We can assist the poor souls not only by prayers, devotions, exterior works of penance, alms-deeds, and other works of charity, but we can also aid them by *interior mortifications*. Everything which appears to us difficult, and which costs us a sacrifice, the pains of sickness, and all the sufferings and troubles of this life, may be offered up for these poor souls...

The only son of a rich widow of Bologna had been murdered by a stranger. The culprit fell into her hands, but the pious widow was far from taking revenge by delivering him up to the hands of justice. She thought of the infinite love of our Saviour when He died for us upon the cross, and how He prayed for His executioners when dying. She, therefore, thought that she could in no way honor the memory of her dear son better, and that she could do nothing more efficient for the repose of his soul, than by granting pardon to the culprit, by protecting him, and by even adopting him as her son and heir to all her riches. This heroic self-denial, and the sacrifice which she thereby offered to Our Lord in memory of His bitter Passion, was so pleasing to God, that, in reward thereof, He remitted to her son all the pains of Purgatory. The happy son then appeared to his mother in a glorified state, at the very moment when he was entering heaven. He thanked her for having thus delivered him from the sufferings of Purgatory much sooner than any other good work could have effected it.

* * * * *

Those who give themselves up to immoderate grief at the loss of beloved friends, should bear this in mind also: instead of injuring their health by a grief which is of no avail to the dead, they should endeavor to deliver their souls from Purgatory by Masses, prayers, and good works; nay, the very thought that they thus render to the souls of their beloved friends the greatest possible act of charity, will console them and mitigate their sorrow. For this reason St. Paul exhorts the Thessalonians not to be afflicted on account of the departed, after the manner of heathens who have no hope.

* * * * *

Thomas Cantipratensis relates of a certain mother, that she wept day and night over the death of her darling son, so much so that she forgot to assist his soul in Purgatory. To convince her of her folly, God one day permitted her to be rapt in spirit, and see a long procession of youths hastening towards a city of indescribable beauty. Having looked for her son in vain for some time, she at last discovered him walking slowly along at the end of the procession. At once her son turned towards her, and said: "Ah, mother, cease your useless tears! and if you truly love me, offer up for my soul Masses, prayers, alms-deeds, and such like good works." Then he disappeared, and his mother, instead of any longer wasting her strength by foolish grief, began henceforth to give her son proofs of a true Christian and motherly love, by complying with his request. (L. II. Appar., 5, 17.)

Among the appointments to the Italian Episcopate made by our Holy Father Pope Pius IX. was that of an humble and holy monk, hidden away in a poor monastery of Tuscany. When he received his Bulls he was thrown into the greatest affliction. He had gone into religion to be done with the world outside; and here he was to be thrown again into its whirlpool. He made a novena to Our Blessed Lady, invoking her help to rid him of the burden and the danger. Meantime, he wrote a letter to the See of Rome setting forth reasons why he ought not to be asked to accept, and also sending back the Bulls, with a positive *noluit*, but Rome would not excuse him. Then he went in person to see the Pope, and to implore leave to decline, which he did, even with tears. Among other reasons, the good monk said that of late he had a most miserable memory. "That is unfortunate," said the Holy Father, "for after your death, if you continue so, no one will ever refer to you as Monsignor ———, *of happy memory*! but that will be no great loss to you." Then, seeing the intense grief of the nominated Bishop, the Holy Father changed his tone and said: "At one time of my life I, also, was threatened with the loss of my memory. But I found a remedy, used it, and it has not failed me. *For the special intention of preserving this faculty of memory I have said every day a 'De Profundis' for the souls in Purgatory.* I give you this receipt for your use; and now, do not resist the will of him who gives you and the people of your diocese his blessing."

It is a new revelation that our Holy Father Pius IX. was ever threatened with loss of memory. Of all his faculties of mind there was not one that excited such general astonishment as his wonderful memory.

* * * * *

The following incident took place at Dole, in France: One day, in the year 1629, long after her death, Leonarda Colin, niece to Hugueta Roy, appeared to her, and spoke as follows: "I am saved by the mercy of God. It is now seventeen years since I was struck down by a sudden death. My poor soul was in mortal sin, but, thanks to Mary, whose devoted servant I had ever striven to be, I obtained grace, in the last extremity, to make an act of perfect contrition, and thus I was rescued from hell- fire, but by no means from Purgatory. My sufferings in those purifying flames are beyond description. At last Almighty God has permitted my guardian angel to conduct me to you in order that you may make three pilgrimages to three Churches of our Blessed Lady in Burgundy. Upon the fulfillment of said condition, my deliverance from Purgatory is promised." Hugueta did as she was requested; whereupon the same soul appeared in a glorified state, thanking her benefactress, and promising to pray for her, and admonishing her always to remember the four last things.

The Greek Emperor Theophilus was, after his death, condemned to the pains of Purgatory, because he had been unable to perform the penances which, towards the end of his life, he had wished to perform. His wife, the pious Empress Theodora, was not satisfied with pouring forth fervent prayers and sighs for the repose of his soul, but she also had prayers and Masses said in all the convents of the city of Constantinople. Besides this, she besought the Patriarch St. Methodius, that for this end he would order prayers to be said by both the clergy and the people of the city. Divine mercy could not resist so many fervent prayers. On a certain day, when public prayers were again offered up in the church of St. Sophia, an Angel appeared to St. Methodius, and said to him: "Thy prayers, O Bishop, have been heard, and Theophilus has obtained pardon." Theodora, the Empress, had, at the same time, a vision, in which our Lord Himself announced to her that her husband had been delivered from Purgatory. "For your sake," He said, "and on account of the prayers of the priests, I pardon your husband."

* * * * *

In the life of Blessed Margaret Mary Alacoque it is related that the soul of one of her departed sisters appeared to her, and said: "There you are, lying comfortably in your bed; but think of the bed on which I am lying, and suffering the most excruciating pains." "I saw this bed," says the Saint, "and I still tremble in all my limbs at the mere thought of it. The upper and lower part of it was full of red-hot sharp iron points, penetrating into the flesh. She told me that she had to endure this pain for her carelessness in the observance of her rules. 'My heart is lacerated,' she added, 'and this is the hardest of my pains. I suffer it for those fault-finding and murmuring thoughts which I entertained in my heart against my superiors. My tongue is eaten up by moths, and tormented, on account of uncharitable words, and for having unnecessarily spoken in the time of silence. Would to God that all souls consecrated to the service of the Lord could see me in these frightful pains! Would to God I could show them what punishments are inflicted upon those who live negligently in their vocation! They would indeed change their manner of living, observing most punctually the smallest point of their rules, and guarding against those faults for which I am now so much tormented.'"

APPEAL TO ALL CLASSES FOR THE SOULS IN PURGATORY.
BY A PAULIST FATHER.

"My daughter is just now dead; but come, lay thy hand upon her, and she shall live."—St. Matt. ix. 18.

Such was the entreaty made by the ruler to our Lord in the Gospel, and such are the words that the Lord says to us during the month of November, in behalf of the poor souls in Purgatory. These souls have been saved by the Precious Blood, they have been judged by Jesus Christ with a favorable judgment, they are His spouses, His sons and daughters—His children. He cries to us: "My children are even now dead; but come, lay your hands upon them, and they shall live." What hand is that which our Lord wants us to lay upon His dead children? Brethren, it is the hand of prayer. Now, it seems to me that there are three classes of persons who ought to be in an especial manner the friends of God's dead children; three classes who ought always to be extending a helping hand to the souls in Purgatory. First, the poor, because the holy souls are poor like yourselves. They have no work— that is to say, the day for them is past in which they could work and gain indulgences and merit, the money with which the debt of temporal punishment is paid; for them the "night has come when no man can work." They are willing to work, they are willing to pay for themselves, but they cannot; they are out of work, they are poor, they cannot help themselves. They are suffering, as the poor suffer in this world from the heats of summer and the frosts of winter. They have no food; they are hungry and thirsty; they are longing for the sweets of heaven. They are in exile; they have no home; they know there is abundance of food and raiment around them which they cannot themselves buy. It seems to them that the winter will never pass, that the spring will never come; in a word they *are poor*. They are poor as many of you are poor. They are in worse need than the most destitute among you. Oh! then, ye that are poor, help the holy souls by your prayers. Secondly, the rich ought to be the special friends of those who are in Purgatory, and among the rich we wish to include those who are what people call "comfortably off." God has given you charge of the poor; you can help them by your alms in this world, so you can in the next. You can have Masses said for them; you can say lots of prayers for them, because you have plenty of time on your hands. Again remember, many of those who were your equals in this world, who, like yourselves, had a good supply of this world's goods, have gone to Purgatory because those riches were a snare to them. Riches, my dear friends, have sent many a soul to the place of purification. Oh! then, those of you who are well off, have pity upon the poor souls in Purgatory. Offer up a good share of your wealth to have Masses said for them. Do some act of charity, and offer the merit of it for some soul who was ensnared by riches, and who is now paying the penalty in suffering; and spend some considerable portion of your spare time in praying for the souls of the faithful departed.

And lastly, sinners and those who have been converted from a very sinful life ought to be the friends of God's dead children. Why? Because, although the souls in Purgatory cannot pray for themselves, they can pray for others, and these prayers are most acceptable to God. Because, too, they are full of gratitude, and they will not forget those who helped them when they shall come before the throne of God. Because sinners, having saddened the Sacred Heart of Jesus by their sins, cannot make a better reparation to it than to hasten the time when He shall embrace these souls whom He loves so dearly, and has wished for so long. Because sinners have almost always been the means of the sins of others. They have, by their bad example, sent others to Purgatory. Ah! then, if they have helped them in, they should help them out.

You, then, that are poor, you that are rich, you that have been great sinners, listen to the voice of Jesus; listen to the plaint of Mary during this month of November; "My children are now dead; come lay thy prayers up for them, and they shall live." Hear Mass for the poor souls; say your beads for them; supplicate Jesus and Mary and Joseph in their behalf. Fly to St. Catherine of Genoa and beg her to help them, and many and many a time during the month say with great fervor: "May the souls of the faithful departed through the mercy of God rest in peace."—*Five-Minute Sermons for Low Masses.*

THE SOULS IN PURGATORY. [1]

[Footnote 1: From the "Original, Short and Practical Sermons for every Feast of the Ecclesiastical Year."]

REV. F. H. WENINGER, S.J., D.D.

On the Feast of All Souls, and whenever we are reminded of Purgatory, we cannot help thinking of the dreadful pains which the souls in Purgatory have to suffer, in order to be purified from every stain of sin; of the excruciating torments they have to undergo for their faults and imperfections, and how thoroughly they have to atone for the least offences committed against the infinite holiness and justice of God. It is but just, therefore, that we should condole with them, and do all that we can to deliver them from the flames of Purgatory, or, at least, to soothe their pains…. The fire of Purgatory, as the doctors of the Church declare, is as intense as that of the abode of hell; with this difference, that it has an end. Yea! it may be that to-day a soul in Purgatory is undergoing more agony, more excruciating suffering than a damned soul, which is tormented in hell for a few mortal sins; while the poor soul in Purgatory must satisfy for millions of venial sins.

All the pains which afflict the sick upon earth, added to all that the martyrs have ever suffered, cannot be compared with those in Purgatory, so great is the punishment of those poor souls.

We read, how once a sick person who was very impatient in his sufferings, exclaimed; "O God, take me from this world!" Thereupon the Angel Guardian appeared to him, and told him to remember that, by patiently bearing his afflictions upon his sick-bed, he could satisfy for his sins, and shorten his Purgatory. But the sick man replied that he chose rather to satisfy for his sins in Purgatory. The poor sufferer died; and behold, his Guardian Angel appeared to him again, and asked him if he did not repent of the choice he had made of satisfying for his sins in Purgatory, by tortures, rather than upon earth by afflictions. Thereupon the poor soul asked the angel: "How many years am I now here in these terrible flames?" The Angel replied: "How many years? Thy body upon earth is not yet buried; nay, it is not yet cold and still thou believest already thou art here for many years!" Oh, how that soul lamented upon hearing this. Great indeed was its grief for not having chosen patiently to undergo upon earth the sufferings of sickness, and thereby shorten its Purgatory.

* * * * *

Upon earth, persons who anxiously seek another abode or another state of life, often know not whether, perhaps, they may not fall into a more wretched condition. How many have forsaken the shores of Europe, with the bright hope of a better future awaiting them in America? All has been disappointment! They have repented a thousand times of having deserted their native country. Now does this disappointment await the souls in Purgatory upon their deliverance? Ah! by no means. They *know* too well that when they are released heaven will be their home. Once there, no more pains, no more fire for them; but the enjoyment of an *everlasting bliss*, which no eye hath seen nor ear heard; nor hath it entered into the heart of man to conceive. Such will be their future happy state. Oh! how great is their desire to be there already. Another circumstance which especially intensifies hope in the breast of man, is *intercourse*—union with those who are near and dear to him.

How many, indeed, have bid a last farewell to Europe, where they would have prospered; but oh, there are awaiting them in another land their beloved ones—those who are so dear, and in whose midst they long to be! Oh, what a great source of desire is not this, for the poor souls in Purgatory to go to heaven! In heaven they shall find again those whom they have loved and cherished upon earth, but who have already preceded them on their way to the heavenly mansion.... There is still another feature, another circumstance which presents itself in the condition of the poor souls in Purgatory: I mean the irresistible force or tendency with which they are drawn towards *God*; their intense longing after Him, their last aim and end.... Oh, with what intense anxiety and longing is not a poor soul in Purgatory consumed, to behold the splendor of its Lord and Creator! But, also! with what marks of *gratitude* does not every soul whom we have assisted to enter heaven pray for us upon its entrance!

Therefore, let us hasten to the relief of the poor suffering souls in Purgatory. Let us help them to the best of our power, so that they may supplicate for us before the throne of the Most High; that they may remember us when we, too, shall one day be afflicted in that prison house of suffering, and may procure for us a speedy release and an early enjoyment of a blissful eternity.

* * * * *

When it will be your turn one day to dwell in those flames, and be separated from God, how happy will you not be, if others alleviate and shorten your pains! Do you desire this assistance for your own soul? Then begin in this life, while you have time, to render aid to the poor souls in Purgatory.... He who does not assist others, unto him shall no mercy be shown; for this is what even-handed justice requires. Hence, let us not be deaf to the pitiful cries of the departed ones.... What afflicts those poor, helpless souls still more, is the circumstance that, despite their patience in *suffering*, they can earn nothing for heaven. With us, however, such is not the case. We, by our patience under affliction, may merit much, very much indeed, for Paradise.... I well remember a certain sick person who was sorely pressed with great sufferings. Wishing to console him in his distress, I said: "Friend, such severe pains will not last long. You will either recover from your illness and become well and strong again, or God will soon call you to himself." Thereupon the sick man, turning his eyes upon a crucifix which had been placed for him at the foot of his bed, replied: "Father, I desire no alleviation in my suffering, no relief in my pains. I cheerfully endure all as long as it is God's good pleasure, but I hope that I now undergo my Purgatory." Then, stretching forth his hands towards his crucifix he thus addressed it, filled with the most lively hope in God's mercy: "Is it not so, dear Jesus? Thou wilt only take me from my bed of pain to receive me straightway into heaven!"

* * * * *

We find in the lives of all the saints a most ardent zeal in the cause of these poor afflicted ones. For their relief they offered to God not only prayers, but also Masses, penances, the most severe sicknesses, and the most painful trials, and all this as a recognition and a practical display of the belief which they cherished— that they who have slept in Christ are finally to repose with him in glory.... Because all that we perform for the help and delivery of the poor souls in Purgatory, are works of Christian faith and piety. Such are prayer, the august sacrifice of the Mass, the reception of the holy sacraments, alms-deeds, and acts of penance and self-denial....

Remember, dear Christians, that we, too, shall be poor, helpless, and suffering souls in Purgatory, and what shall we carry with us of all our earthly goods and treasures? Not a single farthing.

* * * * *

We read, in the life of St. Gertrude, that God once allowed her to behold Purgatory. And, lo! she saw a soul that was about issuing from Purgatory, and Christ, who, followed by a band of holy virgins, was approaching, and stretching forth his hands towards it. Thereupon the soul, which was almost out of Purgatory, drew back, and of its own accord sank again into the fire. "What dost thou?" said St. Gertrude to the soul. "Dost thou not see that Christ wishes to release thee from thy terrible abode?" To this the soul replied: "O Gertrude, thou beholdest me not as I am. I am not yet immaculate. There is yet another stain upon me. I will not hasten thus to the arms of Jesus."

A POPULAR VIEW OF PURGATORY.
REV. J. J. MORIARTY, LL.D.

Purgatory is a state of suffering for such souls as have left this life in the friendship of God, but who are not sufficiently purified to enter the kingdom of heaven—having to undergo some temporal punishment for their lighter sins and imperfections, or for their grievous sins, the eternal guilt of which has been remitted. In other words, we believe that the souls of all who departed this life— not wicked enough to be condemned to hell, nor yet pure enough to enjoy the Beatific Vision of God—are sent to a place of purgation, where, in the crucible of suffering, the lighter stains of their souls are thoroughly removed, and they themselves are gradually prepared to enter the Holy of Holies —where nothing defiled is permitted to approach.

* * * * *

——There are many venial faults which the majority of persons commit, and for which they have little or no sorrow—sins which do not deprive the soul of God's friendship, and yet are displeasing to His infinite holiness. For all these we must suffer either in this life or the next. Divine justice weighs everything in a strict balance, and there is no sin that we commit but for which we shall have to make due reparation. Faults which we deem of little or no account the Almighty will not pass unnoticed or unpunished. Our Blessed Saviour warns us that even for "every idle word that man shall say he shall render an account in the day of judgment."

We know full well that no man will be sent to hell merely for an "idle word," or for any venial fault he may commit; consequently there must be a place where such sins are punished. If they be not satisfied for here upon earth by suffering, affliction, or voluntary penance, there must be a place in the other life where proper satisfaction is to be made. That place cannot be either heaven or hell. It cannot be heaven, for no sufferings, no pain, no torment is to be found there, where "God shall wipe away all tears from their eyes, where death shall be no more, nor mourning nor weeping." It cannot be hell, where only the souls of those who have died enemies of God are condemned to eternal misery, for "out of hell there is no redemption."

There must be, then, a Middle Place where lighter faults are cleansed from the soul, and proper satisfaction is rendered for the temporal punishment that still remains due. The punishment of every one will vary according to his desert.

* * * * *

Our Divine Lord warns us to make necessary reparation whilst we have the time and opportunity.

"Make an agreement with thy adversary quickly whilst thou art in the way with him; lest, perhaps, the adversary deliver thee to the judge, and the judge deliver thee to the officer, and thou be cast into prison. Amen I say to thee, thou shalt not go out from thence till thou pay the last farthing." (St. Matthew, v., 25, 26.)

This expresses the doctrine of Purgatory most admirably. The Scriptures always describe our life as a pilgrimage. We are only on our way. We have to meet the claims of Divine justice here before being called to the tribunal of the everlasting Judge; otherwise, even should we die in His friendship and yet have left these claims not entirely satisfied, we shall be cast into the prison of Purgatory; and "Amen, I say unto thee that thou shalt not go out from thence until thou pay the last farthing."

* * * * *

Our Saviour declares (St. Matthew, xii. 32,) that "whoever shall speak a word against the Son of Man, it shall be forgiven him; but he that shall speak against the Holy Ghost, it shall not be forgiven him, either in this life or in the world to come;" which shows, as St. Augustine says in the twenty-first book of his work, "The City of God," that there are some sins (venial of course) which shall be forgiven in the next world, and that, consequently, there is a middle state, or place of purgation in the other life, since no one can enter heaven having any stain of sin, and surely no one can obtain forgiveness in hell.

The testimony of St. Paul is very clear on this point of doctrine: "For no man can lay another foundation but that which is laid; which is Jesus Christ. Now if any man build on that foundation, gold, silver, precious stones, wood, hay, stubble: every man's work shall be made manifest; for the day of the Lord shall declare it, because it shall be revealed by fire; and the fire shall try every man's work, of what sort it is. If any man's work abide, which he had built thereupon, he shall receive a reward. If any man's work burn, he shall suffer loss; *but he himself shall be saved, yet so as by fire.*"

* * * * *

In the First Epistle of St. Peter (Chap. iii. 18, 19), we learn that Christ "being put to death, indeed, in the flesh, but brought to life by the spirit, in which also He came and preached to those spirits who were in prison."

Our Blessed Saviour, immediately after death, descended into that part of hell called Limbo, and, as St. Peter informs us, "preached to the spirits who were in prison." This most certainly shows the existence of a middle state. The spirits to whom our Lord preached were certainly not in the hell of the damned, where His preaching could not possibly bear any fruit; they were not already in heaven, where no preaching is necessary, since there they see God face to face. Therefore they must have been in some middle state—call it by whatever name you please—where they were anxiously awaiting their deliverance at the hands of their Lord and Redeemer.

Belief in Purgatory is more ancient than Christianity itself. It was the belief among the Jews of old, and of this we have clear proof in the Second Book of Machabees, xii., 43. After a great victory gained by that valiant chieftain, Judas Machabeus, about two hundred years before the coming of Christ, "Judas making a gathering, he sent twelve thousand drachmas of silver to Jerusalem for sacrifice to be offered for the sins of the dead, thinking well and justly concerning the resurrection…. It is, therefore, a holy and wholesome thought to pray for the dead, that they may be loosed from their sins."

It is customary, even in our days, in Jewish synagogues, to erect tablets reminding those present of the lately deceased, in order that they may remember them in their prayers. Surely, if there did not exist a place of purgation, no prayers nor sacrifices would be of any avail to the departed. We find the custom of praying, of offering the Holy Sacrifice of the Mass for their spiritual benefit, more especially on their anniversaries, an universal practice among the primitive Christians of the Eastern and Western Churches, of the Greek, Latin, and Oriental Rites.

Even if we did not find strong warrant, as we do, in the Scriptures, the authority of Apostolic Tradition would be amply sufficient for us; for, remember, we Catholics hold the traditions, handed down from the Apostles, to be of as much weight as their own writings.

… Hence it is that we have recourse to sacred tradition as well as to Scripture for the proof of our teaching. With reference, then, to the doctrine of "Purgatory," we are guided by the belief that prevailed among the primitive Christians.

That the custom of praying for the dead was sanctioned by the Apostles themselves, we have the declaration of St. John Chrysostom: "It was not in vain instituted by the Apostles that in the celebration of the tremendous mysteries a remembrance should be made of the departed. They knew that much profit and advantage would be thereby derived."

Tertullian—the most ancient of the Latin Fathers, who flourished in the age immediately following that of the Apostles—speaks of the duty of a widow with regard to her deceased husband: "Wherefore also does she pray for his soul, and begs for him, in the interim, refreshment, and in the first resurrection, companionship, and makes offerings for him on the anniversary day of his falling asleep in the Lord. For unless she has done these things, she has truly repudiated him so far as is in her power." All this supposes a Purgatory.

"The measure of the pain," says St. Gregory Nyssa, "is the quantity of evil to be found in each one…. Being either purified during the present life by means of prayer and the pursuit of wisdom, or, after departure from this life, by means of the furnace of the fire of purgatory."

* * * * *

Not only deeply instructive, but also eminently consoling is the doctrine of Purgatory. We need not "mourn as those who have no hope," for those nearest and dearest who have gone hence and departed this life in the friendship of God.

How beautifully our Holy Mother the Church bridges over the terrible chasm of the grave! How faithfully and tenderly she comes to our aid in the saddest of our griefs and sorrows! She leaves us not to mourn uncomforted, unsustained. She chides us not for shedding tears over our dear lost ones—a beloved parent, a darling child, a loving brother, affectionate sister, or deeply-cherished friend or spouse. She bids us let our tears flow, for our Saviour wept at the grave of Lazarus.

She whispers words of comfort—not unmeaning words, but words of divine hope and strength—to our breaking hearts. She pours the oil of heavenly consolation into our deepest wounds. She bids us cast off all unseemly grief, assuring us that not even death itself can sever the bond that unites us; that we can be of service to those dear departed ones whom we loved better than life itself; that we can aid them by our prayers and good works, and especially by, the Holy Sacrifice of the Mass. Thus may we shorten their time of banishment, assuage their pains, and continue to storm Heaven itself with our piteous appeals until the Lord deign to look down in mercy, open their prison doors, and admit them to the full light of His holy presence, and to the everlasting embrace of their Redeemer and their God.

EXTRACTS FROM "CATHOLIC BELIEF."
VERY REV. FAÁ DI BRUNO. [1]

[Footnote 1: Catholic Belief, or, A Short and Simple Exposition of Catholic Doctrine, by Very Rev. Joseph Faá Di Bruno. D. D., Rector-General of the Pious Society of Missions of the Church of San Salvatore in Onde, Ponte Sisto, Rome, and St. Peter's Italian Church in London. American Edition, edited by Father Lambert, author of Notes on Ingersoll, &c.]

As works of penance have no value in themselves except through the merits of Jesus Christ, so the pains of Purgatory have no power in themselves to purify the soul from sin, but only in virtue of Christ's Redemption, or, to speak more exactly, the souls in Purgatory are able to discharge the debt of temporal punishment demanded by God's justice, and to have their venial sins remitted only through the merits of Jesus Christ, "yet so as by fire."

The Catholic belief in Purgatory rests on the authority of the Church and her apostolic traditions recorded in ancient Liturgies, and in the writings of the ancient Fathers: Tertullian, St. Cyprian, Origen, Eusebius of Cæsarea, Arnobius, St. Basil, St. Ephrem of Edessa, St. Cyril of Jerusalem, St. Gregory of Nyssa, St. Ambrose, St. Epiphanius, St. John Chrysostom, St. Jerome, St. Augustine. It rests also on the Fourth Council of Carthage, and on many other authorities of antiquity.

That this tradition is derived from the Apostles, St. John Chrysostom plainly testified in a passage quoted at the end of this chapter, in which he speaks of suffrages or help for the departed.

St. Augustine tells us that Arius was the first who dared to teach that it was of no use to offer up prayers and sacrifices for the dead; and this doctrine of Arius he reckoned among heresies. (Book of Heresies, Heresy 53d.)

There are also passages in Holy Scripture from which the Fathers have confirmed the Catholic belief on this point.

St. Paul, in his first epistle to the Corinthians, chap. iii. 11-15, writes: "For other foundations no one can lay, but that which is laid; which is Christ Jesus. Now, if any man build upon this foundation, gold, silver, precious stones, wood, hay, stubble; every man's work shall be manifest; for the day of the Lord shall declare it, because it shall be revealed in fire; and the fire shall try every man's work of what sort it is. If any man's work abide, which he hath built thereupon, he shall receive a reward. If any man's work burn, he shall suffer loss; but he himself shall be saved, yet so as by fire."

The ancient Fathers, Origen in the third century, St. Ambrose and St. Jerome in the fourth, and St. Augustine in the fifth, have interpreted this text of St. Paul as relating to venial sins committed by Christians which St. Paul compares to "wood, hay, stubble," and thus with this text they confirm the Catholic belief in Purgatory, well known and believed in their time, as it is by Catholics in the present time. In St. Matthew (chap. v. 25, 26) we read, "Be at agreement with thy adversary betimes, whilst thou art in the way with him; lest, perhaps, the adversary deliver thee to the judge, and the judge deliver thee to the officer, and thou be cast into prison. Amen, I say to thee, thou shalt not go out from thence till thou repay the last farthing."

On this passage, St. Cyprian, Bishop of Carthage, a Father of the third century, says: "It is one thing to be cast into prison, and not go out from thence till the last farthing be paid, and another to receive at once the reward of faith and virtue: one thing in punishment of sin to be purified by long-suffering and purged by long fire, and another to have expiated all sins of suffering (in this life); one in

74

fire, at the day of Judgment to wait the sentence of the Lord, another to receive an immediate crown from Him." (Epist. iii.)

Our Saviour said: "He that shall speak against the Holy Ghost, it shall not be forgiven him in this world, nor in the world to come." (St. Matt. xii. 32.)

From this text St. Augustine argues, that "It would not have been said with truth that their sin shall not be forgiven, neither in this world, nor in the world to come, unless some sins were remitted in the next world." (*De Civitate Dei*, Book xxi. chap. 24.)

On the other hand, we read in several places in Holy Scripture that God will render to every one (that is, will reward or punish) according as each deserves. See, for example, in Matthew xvi. 27. But as we cannot think that God will punish everlastingly a person who dies burdened with the guilt of venial sin only, it may be an "*idle word*," it is reasonable to infer that the punishment rendered to that person in the next world will be only temporary.

The Catholic belief in Purgatory does not clash with the following declarations of Holy Scripture, which every Catholic firmly believes, namely, that it is Jesus who cleanseth us from all sin, that Jesus bore "the iniquity of us all," that "by His bruises we are healed," (Isaias iii., 5); for it is through the blood of Jesus and His copious Redemption that those pains of Purgatory have power to cleanse the souls therein detained.

Again, the Catholic belief in Purgatory is not in opposition to those texts of Scripture in which it is said that a man when he is justified is "translated from death to life;" that he is no longer judged: that there is no condemnation in him. For these passages do not refer to souls taken to Heaven when natural death occurs, but to persons in this world, who from the death of sin pass to the life of grace. Nor does it follow that dying in that state of grace, that is, in a state of spiritual life, they must go at once to Heaven. A soul may be justified, entirely exempt from eternal *condemnation*, and yet have something to suffer for a time; thus, also, in this world, many are justified, and yet are not exempt from suffering.

Again, it is not fair to bring forward against the Catholic doctrine on Purgatory that text of the Apocalypse, Rev. xix. 13: "Blessed are the dead, who die in the Lord. From henceforth now, saith the Spirit, that they may rest from their labors: for their works follow them," for this text applies only to those souls who die perfectly in the Lord, that is, entirely free from every kind of sin, and from the *stain*, the *guilt*, and the *debt of temporal punishment* of every sin. Catholics believe that these souls have no pain to suffer in Purgatory, as is the case with the martyrs and saints who die in a perfect state of grace.

It is usual to bring forward against the Catholic belief in Purgatory that text which says: "If the tree fall to the south, or to the north, in what place soever it shall fall, there shall it be." (Eccles. xi. 3.)

This text confirms and illustrates the truth that, when death comes, the *final doom* of every one is fixed, and that there is no possibility of changing it; so that one dying in a state of mortal sin will always remain in a state of mortal sin, and consequently be rejected forever; and one dying in a state of grace and friendship with God, will forever remain accepted by God and in a state of grace, and in friendship with Him.

But this text proves nothing against the existence of Purgatory; for a soul, although in a state of grace, and destined to heaven, may still have to suffer for a time before being perfectly fit to enter upon the eternal bliss, to enjoy the vision of God.

Some might be disposed, notwithstanding, to regard this text as opposed to the Catholic doctrine of Purgatory by saying that the two places alluded to in the texts are heaven and hell. But this interpretation Catholics readily admit, for at death either heaven or hell is the final place to which all men are allotted, Purgatory being only a passage to heaven. This text surely does not tell against those just ones under the Old Law who died in a state of grace and salvation, and who, though sure of heaven, had yet to wait in a middle state until after the Ascension of Jesus Christ; neither, therefore, does it tell against Purgatory.

Christ's Redemption is abundant, "*plentiful*" as Holy Scripture, says (Ps. cxxix. 7), and Catholics do not believe that those Christians who die guilty only of _venial the practice of the Catholic Church to offer prayers and other pious works in suffrage for the dead, as is amply testified by the Latin Fathers; for instance, Tertullian, St. Cyprian, St. Augustine, St. Gregory; and amongst the Greek Fathers, by St. Ephrem of Edessa, St. Basil and St. John Chrysostom. St. Chrysostom says: "It was not without good reason ordained by the Apostles that mention should be made of the dead in the tremendous mysteries, because they knew well that, these would receive great benefit from it" (on the First Epistle to Philippians, Homily iii.) By the expression "tremendous mysteries," is meant the Holy Sacrifice of the Mass.

St. Augustine says: "It is not to be doubted that the dead are aided by the prayers of Holy Church and by the salutary sacrifice, and by the alms which are offered for their spirits, that the Lord may deal with them more mercifully than their sins have deserved. For this, which has been handed down by the Fathers, the universal Church observes." (*Enchirid*, Vol. v., Ser. 172.)

The same pious custom is proved also from the ancient Liturgies of the Greek and other Eastern Churches, both Catholic and Schismatic, in which the Priest is directed to pray for the repose of the dead during the celebration of the Holy Mysteries.

PURGATORY AND THE FEAST OF ALL SOULS.
ALBAN BUTLER.

By Purgatory no more is meant by Catholics than a middle state of souls; namely of purgation from sin by temporary chastisements, or a punishment of some sin inflicted after death, which is not eternal. As to the place, manner or kind of these sufferings nothing has been defined by the Church; and all who with Dr. Deacon except against this doctrine, on account of the circumstance of a material fire, quarrel about a mere scholastic question, in which a person is at liberty to choose either side…. Certainly some sins are venial, which deserve not eternal death. Yet if not effaced by condign punishment in this world must be punished in the next. The Scriptures frequently mention those venial sins, from which ordinarily the just are not exempt, who certainly would not be just if these lesser sins into which men easily fall by surprise, destroyed grace in them, or if they fell from charity. Yet the smallest sin excludes a soul from heaven so long as it is not blotted out.... Who is there who keeps, so constant a guard upon his heart and whole conduct as to avoid all sensible self-deceptions? Who is there upon whose heart no inordinate attachments steal; into whose actions no sloth, remissness, or other irregularity ever insinuates itself?... The Blessed Virgin was preserved by an extraordinary grace from the least sin in the whole tenor of her life and actions; but, without such a singular privilege, even the saints are obliged to say that they sin daily.... The Church of Christ is composed of three different parts: the Triumphant in Heaven, the Militant on earth, and the Patient or Suffering in Purgatory. Our charity embraces all the members of Christ.... The Communion of Saints which we profess in our Creed, implies a communication of certain good works and offices, and a mutual intercourse among all the members of Christ. This we maintain with the Saints in heaven by thanking and praising God for their triumphs and crowns, imploring their intercession, and receiving the succors of their charitable solicitude for us: likewise with the souls in Purgatory by soliciting the divine mercy in their favor. Nor does it seem to be doubted but they, as they are in a state of grace and charity, pray for us; though the Church never address public suffrages to them, not being warranted by primitive practice and tradition so to do.

... St. Odilo, abbot of Cluni, in 998, instituted the commemoration of all the faithful departed in all the monasteries of his congregation on the 1st of November, which was soon adopted by the whole Western Church. The Council of Oxford, in 1222, declared it a holiday of the second class, on which certain necessary and important kinds of work were allowed. Some dioceses kept it a holiday of precept till noon; only those of Vienne and Tours, and the order of Cluni, the whole day: in most places it is only a day of devotion. The Greeks have long kept on Saturday sevennight before Lent, and on Saturday before Whitsunday, the solemn commemoration of all the faithful departed; but offer up Mass every Saturday for them.... The dignity of these souls most strongly recommends them to our compassion, and at the same time to our veneration. Though they lie at present at a distance from God, buried in frightful dungeons under waves of fire, they belong to the happy number of the elect. They are united to God by His grace; they love Him above all things, and amidst their torments never cease to bless and praise Him, adoring the severity of His justice with perfect resignation and love.... They are illustrious conquerors of the devil, the world and hell; holy spirits loaded with merits and graces, and bearing the precious badge of their dignity and honor by the nuptial robe of the Lamb with which by an indefeasible right they are clothed. Yet they are now in a state of suffering, and endure greater torments than it is possible for any one to suffer, or for our imagination to represent to itself in this mortal life.... St. Cæsarius of Aries writes: "A person," says he, "may say, I am not much concerned how long I remain in Purgatory, provided I may come to eternal life. Let no one reason thus. Purgatory fire will be more dreadful than whatever torments can be seen, imagined, or endured in this world. And how does any one know whether he will stay days, months, or years? He who is afraid now to put his finger into the fire, does he not fear lest he be then all buried in torments for a long time.... The Church approves perpetual anniversaries for the dead; for some souls may be detained in pains to the end of the world, though after the day of judgment no third state can exist.... If we have lost any dear friends in Christ, while we confide in His mercy, and rejoice in their passage from the region of death to that of life, light, and eternal joy, we have reason to fear some lesser stains may retard their bliss. In this uncertainty let us earnestly recommend them to the divine clemency.... Perhaps, the souls of some dear friends may be suffering on our account; perhaps, for their fondness for us, or for sins of which we were the occasion, by scandal, provocation, or otherwise, in which case motives not only of charity, but of justice, call upon us to endeavor to procure them all the relief in our power.... Souls delivered and brought to glory by our endeavors will amply repay our kindness by obtaining divine graces for us. God Himself will be inclined by our charity to show us also mercy, and to shower down upon us His most precious favors. 'Blessed are the merciful, for they shall obtain mercy.' By having shown this mercy to the suffering souls in Purgatory, we shall be particularly entitled to be treated with mercy at our departure hence, and to share more abundantly in the general suffrages of the Church, continually offered for all that have slept in Christ."

PART II

ANECDOTES AND INCIDENTS.

We know them not, nor hear the sound
They make in treading all around:
Their office sweet and mighty prayer
Float without echo through the air;
Yet sometimes, in unworldly places,
Soft sorrow's twilight vales,
We meet them with uncovered faces,
Outside their golden pales,
Though dim, as they must ever be,
Like ships far-off and out at sea,
With the sun upon their sails.—FABER.

THE FRUIT OF A MASS.

The incident we are about to relate and which, in some way, only the price of the first Mass paid for, reminds us of another which seems to be also the fruit of a single Mass given under the inspiration of faith. This fact is found in the life of St. Peter Damian, and we are happy to reproduce it here, in order to tell over again the marvels of God in those He loves, and to make manifest that charity for the poor souls brings ever and always its own reward.

Peter, surnamed Damian, was born in 988, at Ravenna, in Italy. His family was poor, and he was the youngest of several children. He lost his father and mother while still very young, and was taken by one of his brothers to his home. But Damian was treated there in a very inhuman manner. He was regarded rather as a slave, or, at least, as a base menial, than as the brother of the master of the house. He was deprived of the very necessaries of life, and, after being made to work like a hired servant, he was loaded with blows. When he was older, they gave him charge of the swine.

Nevertheless, Peter Damian, being endowed with rare virtue, received all with patience as coming from God. This sweet resignation on the part of a child was most pleasing to the Lord, and He rewarded him by inspiring him to a good action.

One day the little Damian, leading his flocks to the pasture, found on the way a small piece of money. Oh! how rejoiced he was! How his heart swelled within him!

He clapped his hands joyfully, thinking himself quite rich, and already he began to calculate all he could do with his money. Suggestions were not wanting, for he was in need of everything.

Nevertheless, the noble child took time to reflect; a sudden shadow fell on the fair heaven of his happy thoughts. He all at once remembered that his father, his poor mother who had so loved him, might be still suffering cruel torments in the place of expiation. And despising his own great necessities, and generously making the sacrifice of what was for him a treasure, Damian, raised above himself and his wants by the thought of his beloved parents, brought his money to a priest, to have the Holy Sacrifice offered for them.

That generous child had obeyed a holy inspiration, and this good deed of his was quickly rewarded. Fortune suddenly changed with him. He was taken by another of his brothers, who took all possible care of him. Seeing that the child had such excellent dispositions, he made him begin to study. He sent him first to Florence, then to a famous school in Parma, where he had for his master the celebrated Ivo. The brilliant qualities of Damian were rapidly developed, and soon he became professor where he had been a pupil. He afterwards gave up the world and became a religious, and was, in course of time, not only a remarkable man, but a great saint. He was charged by the Holy See with affairs the most important, and died clothed in the Roman purple. He is still a great light in the Church, and his writings are always full of piety and erudition.

The little Damian, then, might well think that he possessed a treasure in his little coin, since with it he purchased earthly honors and heavenly bliss. We all of us have often had in our hand Damian's little piece of money, but have we known how to make a treasure of it? *Almanac of the Souls in Purgatory*, 1877.

THE FAITH OF A PIOUS LADY.

"In the course of the month of July of last year," said a zealous member of our Association for the Souls in Purgatory, "I was accosted by one of our associates who told me, with an exuberance of joy, 'Ah! we have great reason to thank the souls in Purgatory; I beg you to unite with us in thanking them for the favor they have just done us.' 'Indeed? Well! I am very happy to hear it. Has anything extraordinary happened to you? Tell me, if you please, what seems to cause you so much joy?'

"Then our fervent associate—a young man of a mild and pleasing aspect, usually somewhat reserved, but of gentlemanly bearing—said, in a tone of deep emotion:

"'I am rejoiced to tell you, in the first place, that I have the happiness of still having my good mother. God seems to leave her on the earth to complete the work of her purification, for she is always sick and suffering, and, as she says herself, there is neither rest nor peace for her here below; nevertheless, she resigns herself so patiently to the sufferings and tribulations which weigh so heavily upon her that it does me a twofold good every time I see her, for I love her as my mother, I venerate her as a saint.

"'One day, then, last week, finding herself a little stronger, she thought she would take a short drive, being in the country for her health. The drive seemed really to do her good; the beauty of the country, and still more, the fresh, pure air, appeared to revive her, and altogether she enjoyed her drive immensely. Her heart, as well as her mind, was changed, for you know there is often a sickness of the head, as of the body. She already began to flatter herself with the hope of a speedy recovery, when, in the midst of the drive which was having so beneficial an effect, the horse, from some unknown cause, suddenly took fright, and, taking the bit between his teeth, started off at a fearful pace.

"'Imagine the terror of my poor mother! On either side the road was a broad, deep ditch, and the rough, uneven soil caused the carriage to jolt fearfully, which was another great danger; and, as it so often happens in the country, the road was deserted, and no one to be seen who might give any assistance.

"'To crown all, it happened that the servant who drove my mother, in his efforts to restrain the horse in his headlong flight, had the misfortune to break the reins, which were their only chance of guiding the animal in his mad career.

"'Ah! how can I describe the feelings of my poor dear mother, already so sick and so feeble; in fact, she was almost dead with fright. She thought every moment that she was going to be thrown into the ditch, or dashed against the stake paling which bordered the road on either side. She was nearly in despair, when all at once the thought occurred to her to promise a Mass for the Souls in Purgatory, if the horse stopped.

"'And what do you think?—Ah! I am still so agitated myself, that I can hardly tell it!—But, wonderful to relate, that horse, in the wild excitement of his flight, without so much as a thread to restrain him, who could not have been stopped by any natural cause whatsoever,—that horse stopped immediately, and one might say, suddenly, as though a barrier were placed before him!

"'It were utterly impossible to express my mother's joy and gratitude. Her life will henceforth be but one long act of thanksgiving; for, without that unlooked-for help it had certainly been all over with her. Oh, I beseech you help me to thank Heaven for so great a favor.'"

This example will serve to show still more clearly that God is pleased to manifest His power, even for the slightest service rendered to those whom He deigns to call His "Beloved" of Purgatory.—*Almanac of the Souls in Purgatory*. 1877.

PAY WHAT THOU OWEST.

When the fathers of the Society of Jesus first established their order in Kentucky, a wealthy and respected Catholic citizen of Bardstown, Mr. S——, sought admission among them,—although his age and lack of a thorough preparatory education offered obstacles to his success. He entered the Novitiate, only to be convinced that it was too late for him to become a priest, as had been prudently represented to him at the outset. However, his love for the Society had been strengthened by his short stay in the sanctuary of the community, and he resolved to devote himself to the service of the Fathers in another way. He determined to secure a suitable residence, and found a college, which, as soon as it was in a flourishing condition, he would turn over to the Society.

With this object in view, Mr. S—— made diligent inquiries, and advertised in various county newspapers for a suitable residence in which to begin his good work. One of his advertisements received a prompt reply from the executors of an estate in C—— County. The property offered for sale was unencumbered, its broad lands under high cultivation, the mansion in good repair, etc. Accompanied by a friend, Mr. S—— hastened to visit the plantation. He found one wing of the house occupied by the overseer and his family, and observed with pleasure that the advertisement seemed not to have exaggerated the value of the estate.

Mr. S—— and his friend tarried over night, and were assigned separate apartments, which the administrators had ordered to be kept in readiness for the reception of prospective purchasers. Although greatly fatigued by a long ride on horseback over ill-kept roads, neither of the gentlemen could sleep, on account of a wearisome, incessant knocking in an adjoining room. Each believing the other to be sound asleep, forbore to awake his tired companion, but when they met at an early breakfast, they both, as in one breath, inquired of the farmer's wife the cause of the continuous tapping in the adjoining apartment. Mrs. F—— exchanged a significant glance with her husband, and a sort of grim smile overspread the face of the latter. After a moment's hesitation, he declared that he and his wife, and the servants on the estate, had in vain tried to find out the cause. All who slept in those two rooms heard the noise, and could not sleep. Both husband and wife assured their guests that the knocking took place in the apartment always occupied, during her lifetime, by Mrs. G——, the late owner of the estate; furthermore, that the disturbance was unknown before her death. Mr. S —— and his companion naturally became more and more interested, and after suggesting all the ordinary causes of unusual and mysterious knocks, such as rats, cats, chipmunks, creaking doors, broken shutters, and the like, rode off with Mr. F —— to make a thorough examination of the estate.

The two gentlemen rode all over the plantation, conferred with the executors and some lawyers, and after inspecting the house thoroughly, sat down to a dinner that was highly creditable to the hostess, who seemed anxious concerning the

81

disclosures of the morning. When night came on, the visitors were shown to the same rooms they had previously occupied. In the morning each spoke again of his inability to get any refreshing sleep, and as they rode back to B——, talking over dreams, visions, and other supernatural occurrences, they asked themselves, might not this knocking have a supernatural cause? Concluding it might have, they considered it would be well to lay the case before the Rev. Father Q——; at least, they could go, and tell him of their journey into C—— County, and also of the mysterious knocking, if it seemed to come in naturally; for each felt a little dread of being laughed at as too credulous. In the course of their conversation with the Father, the full details of what they had learned and had personally experienced were related. Father Q—— seemed to consider the occurrence quite easily accounted for by some physical cause; but when the gentlemen recalled to his attention the circumstance of Mrs. G——'s death, he appeared to take another view of the matter.

Finally, it was decided that Father Q—— and a brother priest should accompany Mr. S—— and his friend to the plantation, for a personal investigation. Soon after their arrival at the mansion the priests, preceded by the servants of the family, Mr. and Mrs. F——, and the two visitors, repaired to the mysterious chamber. When a little Holy Water had been sprinkled about the room, there was a cessation of the knocking, and after reciting some prayers, Father Q—— inquired, in Latin, of whatever spirit might be there the cause of the disturbance. He was distinctly answered in the same tongue that the soul of Mrs. G—— could not rest in peace, because of an uncancelled debt to the shoemaker, Mr. ——. The interlocutor was assured that the matter should be attended to at once. Thereupon the knocking re-commenced and continued.

All were painfully surprised, but thanked God that it would be so easy a matter to settle the debt. The Rosary was then recited by the assembly, most of whom had supposed that the priests were present to bless the house. Without delay, Mr. S. and Father Q—— repaired to the shop of the village shoemaker, and begged him to present any bill that he might have against the estate of the late Mrs. G ——. The shoemaker said that he did not believe there was anything due to him, for payments had always been made very punctually. However, he ran over his account-book, and declared that he found nothing. In sorrowful surprise, the two friends then took their departure, telling the shoe dealer that if, at any time, he should find aught against the property, to inform them without delay.

On his return home, the shoemaker related to his mother what had happened in the shop. After reflection, she asked if he had looked over his father's accounts. "Certainly not," he said. She then remarked that the request was only half complied with, for Mrs. G—— had long been his father's customer. After dinner, they repaired to the attic, and, searching out the old ledgers, went over them carefully. To their surprise they found a bill of twelve dollars and a half, for a pair of white satin slippers (probably Mrs. G——'s wedding shoes), which, in the midst of various affairs, had remained unsettled. A messenger was sent with all speed to the mansion. On the way he chanced to meet Father Q—— and Mr. S

82

——. The bill, with interest, was paid on the spot, and, returning to the house, they learned from the astonished and delighted tenants that the rappings had suddenly and entirely ceased.

Shortly after, Mr. S—— became the owner of the estate, the heirs of which, preferring to live in Europe, had permitted its sale, in order to divide and enjoy the proceeds. As Mr. S—— had planned, a college was there founded, and before long it was under the control of the Society of his aspirations and his enthusiastic love.—*Ave Maria*, Nov. 15, 1884.

THE VIA CRUCIS

In November, 1849, Prince Charles Löwenstein Wertheim Rosenberg died. A lady who filled a subordinate office in his family as governess, communicated to the author the incidents which follow. At the prince's deathbed, which she was permitted to visit, she made a vow to say certain prayers daily for the repose of his soul, in accordance with a wish which he had expressed. When the family was residing at the castle of Henbach on the Maine, it was this lady's habit to spend a short time every evening in the private chapel. After one of those visits, about three months after the prince's death, she retired to rest, and in the course of the night had a singular dream. She was in the chapel, kneeling in a tribune; opposite to her was the high altar. She had spent some time in prayer, when suddenly, on the steps of the altar, she saw the tall figure of the deceased prince, kneeling with great apparent devotion. Presently he turned towards her, and in his usual manner of addressing her, said: "Dear child, come down to me here in the chapel; I want to speak to you." She replied that she would gladly, but that the doors were all locked. He assured her that they were all open. She went down to him, taking her candle with her. When she came near him, the prince rose to meet her, took her hand, and, without speaking, led her to the altar, and they both knelt down together. They prayed for some time in silence, then he rose once more, and standing at the foot of the altar, said: "Tell my children, my dear child, that their prayers and yours are heard. Tell them that God has accepted the *Via Crucis* [1] which they have daily made for me, and your prayers also. I am with God in His glory, and I will pray for all those who have so faithfully prayed for me." As he spoke, his face seemed lighted up as with the glory usually painted round the head of a saint. With a farewell look he vanished, and she awoke.

[Footnote 1: Way of the Cross, more commonly called the Stations of the Cross.]

At breakfast she appeared agitated. She sat beside the prince's granddaughter, Princess Adelaide Löwenstein, afterwards married to Don Miguel of Portugal. This lady asked her what was the matter. She related her dream, and then begged to know what prayers the princesses had offered for the repose of his Highnesses' soul. They were the *Via Crucis.—Footsteps of Spirits.* [1]

[Footnote 1: Published by Burns & Lambert of London.]

STRANGE INCIDENTS.

When the Benedictine College at Ampleforth, in Yorkshire, was building, a few years ago, one of the masons attracted the attention of the community by the interest which he took in the incidents of their daily life. He had to walk from a village three miles off, so as to be at the college every morning by six o'clock. He was first much pleased with the regularity of the community, whom he always found in the church, singing the Hours before Mass, on his arrival in the morning. By degrees he was taught the whole of the Catholic doctrine, and was received into the Church. None of his family, however, would follow his example. Exposure to cold and wet brought on an illness, of which he died, in a very pious manner. A short time after his death, his wife was one morning sweeping about the open door of her house, when her husband walked in, and sat down on a seat by the fire, and began to ask her how she did. She answered that she was well, and hoped he was happy where he was. He replied that he was, at that time; that, at first, he had passed through Purgatory, and had undergone a brief purification; but that, when this was ended, he had been taken to the enjoyment of the bliss of God in heaven. He remained talking to her some little time longer, then he bade her farewell, and disappeared.

The woman applied to a Catholic priest for instruction; and it was found that, although she had never in her life read a Catholic book, nor conversed about the Catholic religion with any one, she had acquired a complete knowledge of the doctrine of Purgatory from that short interview with her husband. She, too, became a Catholic. The author was told this story by one who was a member of the community of Ampleforth at the time.

A missionary priest at B—— (in England), a very few years ago, promised to say Mass for a woman in his congregation who had died. Among other engagements of the same kind, he unconsciously overlooked her claim upon him. By and by her husband came to him, and begged him to remember his promise. The missionary thought that he had already done so. "Oh! no, sir," the man replied; "I can assure you that you have not; my poor wife has been to me to tell me so, and to get you to do this act of charity for her." The priest was satisfied of his omission, and immediately supplied it. Soon after, the poor man returned to thank him, at the woman's desire. She had told her husband that now she was perfectly happy in heaven; her face, which had appeared much disfigured at her first visit, was surrounded with a halo of light when she came again. This anecdote reached the author through a common friend of his own and of the missionary.

A similar anecdote is told of a nun in the English convent of Bruges, between thirty and forty years ago. A relation of Canon Schmidt had died in the house, and Miss L——, another nun, much attached to her, saw her friend one night in a dream. She seemed to come with a serious countenance, and pointed to the Office for the Dead in an office-book, which she appeared to hold in her hand. Her friend was much perplexed, and consulted Miss N——, a third nun, who suggested that perhaps Miss L—— had not said the Office three times, as usual, for her deceased sister. Miss L—— was nearly sure that she had; but as she had a habit of marking off this obligation as it was discharged, it could be easily ascertained. On examining her private note-book, it turned out that she had not

84

said the three Offices. Miss N——'s sister, who was educated in the same convent, told the author this little story, and afterwards was good enough to revise his narrative of it. So that this account is virtually her own. Though seeming to have passed through two channels on its way to this book, that is, through the author's memory and his friend's, yet having, submitted to the latter a written memorandum of the narrative, and received and adopted his friend's corrections, the story is as authentic as if it had passed through only one intermediate channel. For there is no doubt that the value of a story diminishes rapidly with every additional hand through which it passes.— *Footsteps of Spirits*, 113-14.

A TRUE STORY OF THE "DE PROFUNDIS."

One evening in the month of July, 184—, a happy group were gathered in the wide porch of a well-known mansion in Prince George's County, Maryland. A little Catholic church had been recently built in the village of L—— by the zealous and wealthy proprietor of "Monticello," and as the means of the newly-formed congregation were too limited to support a resident pastor, one of the Reverend Fathers from Georgetown kindly came out once a fortnight to celebrate Mass and administer the Sacraments. On the eve of the favored Sunday, Doctor J —— took his carriage to the railway station and brought back the Reverend Father named for that week's services; and his visit was always looked for with delight by all the household at Monticello, domestics and children, but by none so much as by three recent converts to our holy faith, who often took occasion to propound to their amiable and learned guest any doubts on religious questions that had arisen during the course of the intervening weeks.

On the evening above mentioned, the priest who came was an Italian Jesuit, the Reverend Father G——. He held his little audience entranced with a fund of edifying stories and interesting replies to the questions asked. The calm serenity of the night, the gentle, refreshing breeze that came from a neighboring wood of pine-trees, the beautiful glitter of the flitting glow-worm, and the rich perfume wafted from the purple magnolia *grandiflora*—all added to the enchantment. The doctor broke the charm by saying: "Reverend Father, we shall be obliged to leave early to-morrow morning. The carriage will be ready for you at 6 o'clock."

"Is it a long drive to the church?" asked Father G——.

"No; only four miles," answered the doctor; "but there will be many confessions to hear and, perhaps, some baptisms to administer; hence, unless the work is begun early, Mass will not be over before 12 o'clock."

"I hope, then," replied the Father, smiling, "that you will not fail to awake betimes."

"As to that," rejoined the doctor, "when I have to arise at any particular time, I recite a *De Profundis* for the relief of the suffering souls, and I am sure of awaking promptly at he right hour."

"I can easily credit that," said Father G——.

"It is a pious practice which was recommended to me by the late Dr. Ryder, of Georgetown, when I was at the College," said the host; "and I have never found that any one to whom I taught the practice failed to find it truly efficacious."

85

"If it would not detain you too long beyond your customary hours," said Father G——, "I would add to my long list of anecdotes one more on the *De Profundis*."

All present besought the priest to favor them; in truth, the worthy household never wearied of pious conversation.

"It happened," began the good priest, with religious modesty, "that about twenty years ago I accompanied a number of prominent members of our Society who had been summoned to the Mother House, in Rome, on business of importance. The Fathers carried with them precious documents from their several provinces; and, besides the purse necessary to meet their current travelling expenses, certain contributions from churches as Peter's Pence, and donations for the General of the Society. Our way lay across the Apennines, and we were numerous enough to fill a large coach. We knew that the fastnesses of the mountains were infested by outlawed bands, and we had been careful to select an honest driver. Before setting out, it was agreed that we should place ourselves under the protection of the Holy Souls by reciting a *De Profundis* every hour. At a given signal, mental or vocal prayer, reading or recreation, would be suspended, and the psalm recited in unison.

"Luigi, the driver, had been instructed, in case of any apparent danger, to make three distinct taps on the roof of our vehicle with the heavy end of his whip. We travelled the whole day undisturbed, without other interruptions than those called for by the observance of our itinerary. Just as the evening twilight began, we reached the summit of a lofty mountain. The air was cool, the scenery wild and majestic, and each of us seemed absorbed in the pleasant glimpses of the receding landscapes, when we were startled by three ominous knocks on the roof of our coach. Before we could ask any questions, Luigi had given his horses such blows as nearly made them throw us out of the vehicle, and sent the animals running at a break-neck speed. We looked, we listened, and, to our amazement and horror, beheld about a dozen bandits on either side of the road, with arms uplifted, and holding deadly weapons, as if ready and determined to strike with well-aimed precision. But, strange to say, they all remained as motionless as statues, until we had gone on so far as to leave them a mere speck on the descending horizon.

"Each one of our party had kept exterior silence, but inwardly put his trust in the Most High. At last, Luigi halted. His horses were white with foam, and panting as if they would never breathe naturally again.

"A miracle!" cried Luigi, signing himself with the mystic Sign; "may God and Our Lady be praised! I tell you, Fathers, it is a miracle that we are not dead men!" "'Indeed, a very special protection of Divine Providence said the superior *pro tem.*; 'and we must all thank God with our whole hearts.'

"'I tell you,' broke in Luigi, 'those were horrible men; I never saw any look fiercer.'

"'Then, as soon as your horses are able, we had better move on. Shall you be obliged to change them before we get to our proposed stopping- place?' asked the superior.

"'Oh, we must not stop to change! we should be tracked by some of their spies. We had better go on; and, as the road descends gently, I think this team will make the remainder of the route.'

"'Well,' said our superior, as we re-entered the coach, 'we must all offer a Mass in thanksgiving to-morrow;' to which we all heartily assented, and found subject for conversation the rest of the way in recalling the particulars of our wondrous escape.

"Holy obedience afterwards stationed me," continued the Reverend Father, "at the Gesú. About two years later, I was called upon to instruct a prisoner condemned to capital punishment. 'He appears to have been a desperate man,' said the jailer, as he drew aside the enormous bolts of iron that held fast the door of a corridor leading to a dismal dungeon; 'now, however, he is a little subdued; he even seems contrite at times, and I hope he will die penitent.'

"I visited the prisoner several times; he was always glad to see me, but it cost him a great effort to open his heart, and make a full confession. His birth and parentage, and advantages for a liberal education, should have brought him to a widely-different destiny. He had loved adventure naturally, but had taken a wrong direction. He might have become a famous military man, whereas he was only a rough, desperate highwayman. To win him to God, I began to listen to narratives of his wild brigand exploits. I affected to be interested in these daring adventures, and then succeeded in pointing out to him the sin that abounded in each and every act. One day, as he was speaking of the latest years of his life, I was greatly surprised to hear him recount the identical incident with which I began my story. He described to me in the most graphic terms the wonderful manner in which his hands and those of his comrades had been held by an invisible, irresistible power, saying that they had returned to their mountain haunts perfectly dismayed; that some of them appeared to have a vague and conscientious alarm, though revelry and song soon banished such misgivings. He told me that they knew the carriage was full of Jesuit priests, and that they had been promised a great pecuniary reward by a prominent member of the Freemason Society if they should succeed in seizing our luggage.

"I then made known to my penitent my share in that providential escape; he at once fell on his knees, wept long and bitterly, and finally asked my forgiveness. I prepared him for his dreadful end, and believe he died at peace with God, so great is the mercy of Jesus to the contrite soul, 'even though his sins be as scarlet.' I asked his permission to narrate the particulars of his portion of the story, and he gladly gave it, hoping to merit something for his sin-burdened soul by that act of humility."

We were all much impressed by the Reverend Father's narrative, and as we bade one another good-night, the doctor remarked that a kind deed performed for others was sure to merit a blessing in return, even though it were so small a favor as that gained by his favorite practice of saying the *De Profundis*.

"Yes," said Father G——, "charity never fails."—*Ave Maria*, Nov. 24th, 1883.

CONFIDENCE REWARDED.

The following fact took place in Montreal, Canada, some three or four years since. We shall leave the zealous member of our association who related it to us to tell his own story:

"One morning," said he, "coming back from Mass, I saw Mr. C——, who was also coming out of the church. He was a worthy man, fearing God and fulfilling his duties faithfully and conscientiously. I said to myself: 'There is a man who deserves to belong to our association.' For is it not always a favor when God deems us worthy to do something for Him?

"I approached and asked him if he would not like to become a member of our association. 'What association?' 'The Association of the Way of the Cross and Masses. It is to relieve the dead by prayer and alms, two powerful means.' 'Ah! I knew nothing of it. What has to be done?' 'It suffices to make the Way of the Cross once a week and pay for a Mass once a month.' 'I love the souls in Purgatory,' he said, 'and I do all I can to relieve them. But, you see, things are not going well with me just now. I have been a long time sick, and am hardly able yet to discharge my ordinary duties.'

"At these words I cast my eyes on the speaker, and saw what I had not before noticed, that he looked pale and worn. He went on: 'As for paying anything, it would be impossible for me to do it; I have contracted debts, and if my ill health should continue,' he added, in a faltering voice, 'I shall be obliged to sell my little house.' Then he stopped, his heart evidently full, and tears in his eyes. 'But Providence watches over you, and nothing happens without God's good leave. If a single hair of our head cannot fall unless He will it, what have you to fear? Do something for God whilst you can. If you are liberal to Him, He will be more so towards you. Do you remember the promise Our Lord made to St. Gertrude? 'I will give an hundred-fold,' said He, 'for all thou shalt do for my beloved ones in Purgatory.' This promise was not for St. Gertrude alone; it was likewise for you. For one dollar that you give, you will gain ten; and if you are resolved to help the poor souls all you can, they will get you health to do it.' 'Ah! what you say touches me much, and truly I know not what to do.' After a moment's hesitation, he quickly resumed: 'Well, sir, although I am actually in distress, I am going to try; it may be the best means of getting out of it.' 'Yes, try; we run no risk when we make the Holy Souls our debtors.'

"At these words, he drew from his pocket a small purse which contained only half a dollar. 'There is all my wealth, and I am happy to share it with you,' and he gave me the stipend for a Mass. 'I will perhaps put myself to some inconvenience in giving you that sum, trifling though it be; but, blessed be God! I will bear with the inconvenience, thinking that those who suffer much more than I will obtain some relief in their cruel torments. I will also pray for them, and that they may obtain for me the resignation which is so pleasing to God.'

"When I saw the noble sentiments of this man, I shook him by the hand, warmly thanked him, and reminded him that God was always touched by such acts, and that He knew how to reward them.

88

"From that moment, strange to say, that frail, delicate man began to recover his strength, work came back to his shop, and everything grew brighter around him. And, as an additional reward from Heaven, he was animated by a new zeal for the Holy Souls, for he not only paid his own little contribution regularly, but he also collected the money for as many Masses as he could on one side and another.

"Six or seven months thus passed away amid ever increasing prosperity, when one day he said to me in presence of several persons: 'Last autumn, before I gave my name to the Association for the Souls in Purgatory, I was so sick and so discouraged that I thought I should die; but when I had paid for my first Mass, from that moment, as all may see, my health began to return, and with it my courage. To-day, as you see, I am perfectly well. Moreover, I have found means to pay off one hundred and fifty dollars of debt, and to have fifty dollars' worth of repairs made to my little house. How has all that been done? I know not: for you will admit that, by a poor shoemaker such as I, who works at his bench and without even an apprentice, after such a hard winter, and without any advance before me, to find means, despite all that, to provide for the support of his family and pay two hundred dollars over and above, is something extraordinary.

"'But I know well to whom I owe it all; hence,' he added, with a smile, 'that has given me new zeal. Now, I work not only for myself; every evening I go out collecting for our good Souls in Purgatory, and, blessed be God! I have got one hundred and fifty dollars for the Association of Masses. Have I not, sir?' he added, addressing the treasurer, who was present.

"'Yes, you have, indeed, collected one hundred and fifty dollars, perhaps something more, by twenty-five cents here and twenty-five cents there, with a perseverance and a zeal beyond all praise, and well deserving of the favors you have received.'

"'Ah!' said this worthy man, so admirable in his simplicity and the fervor of his conviction, 'it is that I still desire something; I now expect that they will make me better,' and he sighed.

"Thus was this good man rewarded for his confidence in the Souls in Purgatory, and such was his gratitude to them."—*Almanac of the Souls in Purgatory, 1877.*

ANECDOTE OF THE "DE PROFUNDIS."

I once heard an anecdote of a good priest who was in the habit of saying the De Profundis every day for the Souls in Purgatory, but, happening one day to omit it, either through inadvertence or press of occupation, he was passing through a cemetery about the close of day, when he suddenly heard, through the hushed silence of the lonely place and the solemn evening's hour, a mournful voice repeating the first words of the beautiful psalm—*De Profundis clamavit Domini*—then it stopped, but the priest, as soon as he had recovered from the first shock, and remembering with bitter self-reproach his omission, took up the words where the supernatural voice had left off, and finished the recitation of the *De Profundis*, resolving, as he did so, that, for the time to come, nothing should prevent him from reciting it every day, and more than once in the day, for the benefit of the dear suffering Souls.

89

A STRANGE OCCURRENCE IN A PERSIAN PRISON.

There is a very strange story concerning Purgatory related by St. John the Almoner, Patriarch of Alexandria, in the end of the sixth and the beginning of the seventh century. A little before a great mortality which took place in that city, several inhabitants of the Island of Cyprus were carried off to Persia and cast into a prison so severe that it was called the *Oblivion*. Some of them, however, succeeded in making their escape and returned to their own country. A father and mother, whose son had been carried off with the others, asked them for tidings of their son. "Alas!" said they, "your son died on such a day; we ourselves had the sad consolation of giving him burial." The poor parents hastened then to have a solemn service performed for the repose of his soul; this they had done three times every year, continuing in prayer for the same intention. But, marvellous to relate! one day this son, so much regretted, so fondly remembered, came knocking at their door and threw himself into their arms. He had been supposed dead for four years, yet was really alive, he whom the other prisoners had buried having had a great resemblance to him, that is all. "How! is it really thou, dear son? Oh! how we mourned for thee! Three times every year we had a solemn service for thee." "On what days?" eagerly demanded the son. "On the holy days of Christmas, Easter, and Pentecost." "Precisely!" he exclaimed; "on those very days I saw, each time, an officer radiant with light, who came to me and taking off my chains, opened the doors of my prison. I went forth into the city, walked wherever I wished, without any one appearing to notice me; only, in the evening, I always found myself miraculously chained in my dungeon. It was the fruit of your good prayers, and if I had been in Purgatory, they would have served at the same time to relieve me; I beseech you not to forget me when the good God shall see fit to call me to Himself."—*Leontius, Life of St. John the Almoner.*

A SWISS PROTESTANT CONVERTED BY THE DOCTRINE OF PURGATORY.

I have somewhere read, says a Catholic writer, that a Swiss Protestant was converted to the true religion solely on account of our having the consoling doctrine of Purgatory, whereas Protestants will not admit of it. He was a Lutheran somewhat advanced in age, and he had a brother who passed for a worthy man, as the world goes, but had also the misfortune of being a Protestant. He fell sick, and notwithstanding the care of several physicians, died, and was buried by a Protestant minister of Berne. His death was a terrible blow to the brother of whom I speak. Hoping to dissipate his grief he tried travelling, but the thought of his brother's eternal destiny pursued him everywhere. He one day, on board a steamer, made the acquaintance of a Catholic priest, with whom he entered into conversation. Confidence was soon established between them; they spoke of death, and the afflicted traveller asked the priest what he thought of it. "What I think is this," replied the priest: "When a man has perfectly discharged all his duties to God, his neighbor and himself, he goes straight to heaven; if he have not discharged them, or have neglected any of those which are essential, he goes straight to hell; but if he have only to reproach himself with those trifling faults which are inseparable from our frail nature, he spends some time in Purgatory." At these words the listener smiled with evident relief and satisfaction; he felt consoled. "Sir," cried he, "I will become a Catholic, and for this reason: Protestants only admit of heaven and hell; but, in order to get to Paradise, one must have nothing wherewith to reproach himself. Now, although my brother was a good man, he was by no means free from those slight faults of which you spoke just now. He will not be damned for these faults, but they will prevent him from going to heaven; there must, therefore, be an intermediate place wherein to expiate them; hence, there must be a Purgatory. I will be a Catholic, so as to have the consolation of praying for my brother."—*The Catechism in Examples*, pp. 141-2.

THE DEAD HAND.

SISTER TERESA MARGARET GESTA was struck by apoplexy on the 4th of November, 1859, without any premonitory symptoms to forewarn her of her danger; and, without recovering consciousness, she breathed her last at four o'clock in the afternoon of the same day. Her companions were plunged into the deepest sorrow, for the Sister was a general favorite; but they resigned themselves to the will of God. Whilst lamenting the death of one who had been to them a model, comforter, and mother, they consoled themselves by the remembrance of the virtues of which she was a splendid example, and of which they never tired speaking.

Twelve days had passed since her death. Some of the Sisters felt a certain kind of dread of going alone to the places frequented by the departed one; but Sister Anna Felix Menghini, a person of a lively and pleasant disposition, often rallied them, good-humoredly, on their fears.

About ten o'clock in the forenoon, this same Sister Anna, having charge of the clothing, was proceeding to the work-room. Having gone up- stairs, she heard a mournful voice, which at first she thought might be that of a cat shut up in the clothes-press. She opened and examined it carefully, but found nothing. A sudden and unaccountable feeling of terror came over her, and she cried out: "Jesus, Mary, what can it be?" She had hardly uttered these words when she heard the same mournful voice as at first, which exclaimed in a gasping sob: "O my God, how I suffer!" The religious, though surprised and trembling, recognized distinctly the voice of Sister Teresa; she plucked up courage and asked her "Why?"

"On account of poverty," answered the voice.

"What!" replied Sister Anna, "and you were so poor!"

"Not for me," was answered, "but for the nuns…. If one is enough, why two? and if two are sufficient, why three?… And you—beware for yourself."

At the same time the whole room was darkened by a thick smoke, and the shadow of Sister Teresa, moving towards the exit, went up the steps, talking as it moved. Sister Anna was so frightened that she could not make out what the spirit said. Having reached the door, the apparition spoke again: "This is a mercy of God!" And in proof of the reality, with its open hand it struck the upper panel of the door near the frame, leaving the impression of the hand more perfect than it could have been made by the most skillful artist with a hot iron.

91

Sister Anna was like Balthasar: "Then was the King's countenance changed, and his thoughts troubled him; and the joints of his loins were loosed, and his knees struck one against the other." (Dan., v. 6). She could not stir for a considerable time; she did not even dare to turn her head. But at last she tottered out and called one of her companions, who, hearing her feeble, broken words, ran to her with another Sister; and presently the whole community was gathered round in alarm. They learned in a confused manner what had taken place, perceived the smell of burnt wood, and noticed a whitish cloud or mist that filled the room and made it almost dark. They examined the door carefully though tremblingly, and recognized the fac-simile of Sister Teresa's hand; and, filled with terror, they fled to the choir.

There the Sisters, forgetting the need of food and rest, remained in prayer till after sunset, abandoning everything in their anxiety to procure relief for their beloved Sister Teresa. The zealous Minorite Fathers, who have the spiritual direction of the convent, learning what had happened, were equally earnest in offering prayers and sacrifice, and in singing the psalms for the dead. Many of the faithful likewise assembling, not through idle curiosity, but out of genuine piety, joined in the recitation of the Rosary and other prayers, though the deceased Sister was almost entirely unknown to the people. Her observance of the rule was very strict, and she scrupulously avoided all intercourse with people outside her convent. But still large numbers crowded to join in those devotions for her.

Sister Anna, who was more worn out by excitement than the other religious, was directed to retire early the following night. She herself confesses that she was fully resolved next day to remove, at any cost, the obnoxious marks of the hand. But Sister Teresa appeared to her in a dream, saying: "You intend to remove the sign which I have left. Know that it is not in your power to do so, even with the aid of others; for it is there by the command of God, for the instruction of the people. By His just and inexorable judgment I was condemned to the dreadful fires of Purgatory for forty years on account of my condescension to the will of some of the nuns. I thank you and those who joined in so many prayers to the Lord for me; all of which He was pleased in His mercy to accept as suffrages for me, and especially the Seven Penitential Psalms, which were such a relief!" And then, with a smiling countenance, she added: "Oh! blessed rags, that are rewarded with such rich garments! Oh! happy poverty, that brings such glory to those who truly observe it! Alas! how many suffer irreparable loss, and are in torments, because, under the cloak of necessity, poverty is known and valued by few!"

Finally, Sister Anna, lying down as usual on the night of the 19th, heard her name distinctly pronounced by Sister Teresa. She awoke, all in a tremor, and sat up, unable to answer. Her astonishment was great when, near the foot of the bed, she saw a globe of light that made the cell as bright as noonday, and she heard the spirit say in a joyful voice: "On the day of the Passion I died (on Friday), and on the day of the Passion I go to glory.... Strength in the Cross!... Courage to suffer!..." Then, saying three times "Adieu!" the globe was transformed into a thin, white, shining cloud, rose towards heaven, and disappeared.

The zealous Bishop of the diocese having heard of these events, instituted the process of examination on the 23d of the same month. The grave was opened in presence of a large number of persons assembled for the occasion; the impression of the hand on the door was compared with the hand of the dead, and both were found to correspond exactly. The door itself was set apart in a safe place and guarded. Many persons being anxious to see the impression, it was allowed to be visited, after a certain lapse of time, and with due precautions, by such as had secured the necessary permission.—*Ave Maria*, Nov. 17, 1883.

A BEAUTIFUL EXAMPLE.

The following fact is related by the Treasurer of the Association for the Souls in Purgatory. He himself was personally cognizant of the circumstances of the case. We leave him to speak:

"Mr.——," said he, "was one of our first and most fervent associates. His devotedness for good works is well known, so that he is everywhere regarded as an acquisition in all pious enterprises. His exemplary conduct rendered him, moreover, one of the most precious auxiliaries of the work. Hence his zeal, instead of slackening, did but go on increasing; and whereas, in the beginning, his collection amounted only to some dollars, after a while he often brought me forty or fifty dollars for the suffering souls. May Heaven bless that fervent associate, and may his example serve as a lesson to the indifferent!

"During eighteen months, or two years, this pious and zealous member brought me every six months,—with other moneys,—the sum of fifteen dollars which was thus periodically sent him; and each time that I asked him whence this money came, he answered that he knew nothing of it himself; that it was sent him by a worthy man without further information, and so he brought it to me without asking, or knowing anything more.

"Desirous of getting to the bottom of this mystery, I resolved to try and find out what it meant. I, one day, asked Mr.——. to tell me the name of this generous protector of the poor souls, for I was going to hunt him up.—'Oh!' said he, 'it is Such-a-one; he lives a long way off, towards Hochelaga, [1] but, indeed, I cannot tell you the exact place.'

[Footnote 1: A suburban town or village of Montreal, situated, like the city, on the banks of the St. Lawrence.]

"Such vague information embarrassed me no little. I, nevertheless, took the City Directory, but, alas! there were fully twenty-five persons of the same name. Resolved, however, to put an end to this uncertainty, I proceeded, with the little information I had, to the place indicated to me; I arrive at a house bearing the name of the new benefactor of our work. I go in at a venture; it was a little shoe-store, scarcely fifteen feet square, somewhat gloomy and not over-clean, owing, probably, to the nature of the business carried on there; the whole appearance of the place was, indeed, very unlike one where much money could be made. Going in, I perceived sitting in the farther end of the store, a man whose face was so expressive of goodness, so open and so calm, that only a good conscience could leave so gracious an imprint on the features, and I said to myself: 'That is he.'—

93

Then I asked aloud: 'You are Mr. Such-a-one?'—'That is my name,' he answered, with a pleasant smile.—'But is it you who has sent us every six months for two years, the sum of fifteen dollars,—thirty dollars a year,—for the Souls in Purgatory, apart from your regular contribution?'—'Yes,' said he, quietly, and still with the same smile on his lips.—'Ah!' said I, 'we are very grateful to you, and the Holy Souls will surely be mindful of you. I suppose you have a great compassion for those poor souls who suffer so much, and that that inspires you with zeal, and so you make up this sum amongst your friends and neighbors;—or they, perhaps, bring it to your house, quarter by quarter, as is done elsewhere?'—'No!' said he, still very quietly, 'no, it is my own little share.'—'How! your own little share?' and instinctively I cast a glance around the little store, which seemed hardly to justify the giving of such a sum. 'How! your little share? but we find it a very large and generous one, and we are happy that your zeal and charity make it seem to you so small. Heaven will bless you for it. Still there must be something hidden under these gifts, so often repeated; the Holy Souls must have done you some favor. Please tell me, then, what induces you to give so handsome a sum every year, without being asked?'

"'Well, I will not conceal from you that the Souls in Purgatory have visibly protected me; and to make known to you, in a few words, all my little history, I must tell you that, two or three years ago, I heard people speak so favorably of the Association for the Souls in Purgatory—I heard so much about it, indeed, that from that day forward, I placed all my little business under the care of the Suffering Souls, and ever since, I am happy to tell you, to the credit of those holy Souls, that my affairs go, as if they were on wheels!" (These are his own words.) "I give my thirty-three dollars a year without any injury to myself; on the contrary, all goes the better for it. My store is not much to look at, but it is well filled, and all that is in it is my own. Apart from that, and what is still better, I have not a penny of debt.'

"He then added, in a lower tone: 'I have, moreover, the happiness of honoring in that way the thirty-three years of labors and sufferings which Our Divine Lord spent on earth. That thought does my poor heart good.

"'Ah, sir,' said he, with an impulse of true faith which made my heart thrill —'Ah, sir, if men believed more, they would do wonders, and the word of Our Lord never fails, and He has said that the more one gives the more they receive, for charity never makes any one poor; only we must give without distrust, and without speculation.'

"I warmly shook hands with this admirable man, and returned home as charmed with my visit as delighted with so much faith. Then I said to myself: 'There is a fine example to follow. How many others might have no debts, if they knew how to make sacrifices for the dear Suffering Souls!'"—*Almanac of the Souls in Purgatory, 1877*

HOW TO PAY ONE'S DEBTS.

Speaking just now of that generous man who had no debts, we called to mind an example that teaches a pretty way of paying debts. We are about to furnish the receipt, so that no one may complain, giving to each the chance of making use of it. In divulging this secret we shall certainly pass for the least selfish man in the world; for, to furnish every one with the means of paying their debts, is it not to procure for each the opportunity of enriching himself? But, dear reader, laying aside all thanks, hasten only to profit by the receipt, and we shall, each of us, have obtained our object.

We take this secret from the Chronicles of the good Friars Minors, an authority to which no one can take exception.

The Blessed Berthold belonged to the great Franciscan family. His fine talents and rare virtues had caused him to be appointed a preacher of the Order. The Sovereign Pontiff, seeing all the good that Berthold was destined to do by his eloquent sermons, had given him power to grant to each of his hearers, an indulgence of ten days; which was a great privilege for the faithful, as well as a mark of esteem and distinction for himself.

Friar Berthold, then, had preached a most moving sermon on alms-giving, and had granted the ten days' indulgence to all who were present. Amongst the audience was a lady of quality who, owing to a reverse of fortune, was in great distress and loaded with debt. She had hitherto been content to suffer in silence, being prevented by a false shame from making her condition known; but overcome by the enthusiastic charity of the good father, she went privately to him to explain how she was situated, giving him thus an opportunity of putting in practice what he had so eloquently preached. But Friar Berthold, who, like his father St. Francis, had chosen poverty for his lady and mistress, could not come to her relief. Nevertheless, as poverty, in the man who suffers and endures it voluntarily for the love of God, becomes strength and even riches, Berthold, strong in his sacrifice and rich in his poverty—Berthold, inspired by the Holy Ghost, repeated to her what Peter of old, inspired by God, said to the lame man at the gate of the Temple who had asked him for alms: "Silver and gold have I none, but that which I have I will give unto thee." He then assured the lady that she had gained ten days' indulgence by being present at his preaching, and he added: "Go to such a banker in the city. Hitherto he has busied himself much more about temporal riches than spiritual treasures, but offer him in return for the donation he will give you, to make over to him the merit of this indulgence, so that the pains awaiting him in Purgatory may be diminished. I have every reason to think," continued the good Father, "that he will give you some assistance."

The poor woman, full of that faith which is so powerful, went as she was told, in all simplicity. God touched the heart of the rich man, who received her kindly. He asked her how much she expected to receive in exchange for her ten days' indulgence. Feeling herself animated by an interior strength, she replied: "As much as it weighs in the balance." —"Well!" said the banker, "here is the balance. Write down your ten days' indulgence, and put the paper in one scale; I will place a piece of money in the other." O prodigy! the scale with the paper in it does not rise, but the other does. The banker, much amazed, puts in another piece of money, but the weight is not changed; he puts in another, then another; but the

95

result is still the same, the paper on which the indulgence is written is still the heaviest. The Banker puts down then five, ten, thirty pieces, till there was as much as the whole amount which the lady required for her present needs. Then only did the two scales become equal.

The banker, struck with astonishment, saw in this marvel a precious lesson for him; he was at length made sensible of the value of the things of heaven.

The poor Souls understand it still better, as, for the slightest earthly indulgence they would give all the gold in the world.

You, then, who have no money to give for the Souls in Purgatory—you, too, who have financial difficulties on your shoulders, offer up indulgences for the poor Souls, and they will make themselves your bankers; they will pay you double, nay, a hundred-fold for whatever you have put in the scale of the balance of mercy. They will pay you not only in spiritual treasures, but even in temporal wealth, which will procure for you the double advantage of paying your debts here below, and those of the other world.—*Almanac of the Souls in Purgatory*, 1877.

FAITH REWARDED.

"One day, in the month of July," relates a zelator of the Association, [1] "I met one of our members. He was a man of an amiable disposition, and remarkable for his piety and his devotion to good works. He was a merchant of good standing, engaged in a respectable business. Like many others, however, he had seen bad days; and to the commonplace question, 'How goes business?' he replied: 'Ah! badly enough; I can hardly pay expenses, and I am doubly unfortunate. I had a house which brought me in two or three hundred dollars a year, and I have had the misfortune of being unable to rent it this year, so that, losing on all sides, I find myself a good deal embarrassed.'—'Will you allow me,' said I, 'to give you a little advice? Promise some Masses for the Souls in Purgatory in case you have the good fortune to rent your house. It will be, as it were, the tithe of your rent. We too often forget that we owe to Our Lord a part of what He gives us so freely. It is, nevertheless, only an offering that we make Him of His own goods; and, at the same time, an act of gratitude for that He has deigned to give it to us. Furthermore, it is an act of homage, an acknowledgment of His supremacy. And we shall derive the more profit from it according as we do it with a good heart. Besides all that, you have the additional happiness of assisting your relatives and friends who are suffering in the flames of Purgatory.'

[Footnote 1: For the Relief of the Souls in Purgatory.]

"This little exhortation seemed to strike him to whom it was addressed, and, as if awaking from a long lethargy, he suddenly said: 'Why did I not think of that before? I promise,' added he, 'five dollars for the Souls in Purgatory, if I find a tenant.'

"This eagerness to do good, this species of regret for not having done it sooner, this pious disposition which makes us desire to relieve those who are in affliction, must have been very pleasing to God, for, within the week, the gentleman came to me with his five dollars, and said, smiling: 'I lose no time, you see, in keeping my promise.'—'Why, have you already rented your house?'—'Yes, a manufacturer from the country who had just had the misfortune of being burned out, saw my house by chance, came to ask my terms, and we agreed at once. He is to take possession next week.'

"A week passed, even a month, then two, and no tenant, when I happened again to meet my friend, whom I almost suspected of having forgotten his promise. 'Ah!' said he, 'I am worse off than ever, and I was so sure of having rented my house.'—' How! did that person not come back, then?'—' No, and I thought him such an honest man! The disappointment has been a great loss to me.'—'Write to him, then, threatening to make him responsible for the whole rent. But, better than that, wait still, and have confidence; the Holy Souls cannot fail to bring the matter to a favorable issue. It is, perhaps, a want of faith on your part which has delayed the fulfillment of the contract.'

"Three days had scarcely passed when I again saw our Associate. 'This time,' said he, 'I come to pay; my tenant has arrived.'—'But he has made you lose five or six weeks' rent.'—'Not so; he is, just as I thought, an honorable, upright man. He arrived two days ago. It was I that hired your house,' said he, 'and I come to take possession of it.'—'Mr.——,' said I, 'I am very glad, but I expected you sooner.'— 'It is true I was to have come before now, but was prevented from doing so by important business. How long is it since I rented your house?'— 'Just nine weeks.'—'It is only right, then, that I should pay you for the time I have made you lose;' then handing me a sum of money, 'there,' said he, 'is the amount coming to you; and now, my family arrive to-morrow, so we take possession at once of your house, and your rent shall be paid regularly.'

"So there is an end to my anxiety, and you cannot believe how happy I am in bringing you the trifling sum I promised; but while keeping my promise, I thank you very sincerely for the confidence wherewith you inspired me in the Holy Souls. May God bless you for it!"—*Almanac of the Souls in Purgatory*, 1881.

APPARITION OF A CITIZEN OF ARIES.

LECOYER, in his "Tales of Ghosts and Apparitions," [1] relates a historical occurrence which had great publicity. In the reign of King Charles IV. of France, surnamed the Fair, the last king of the first branch of the Capets, who died in 1323, the soul of a citizen, some years dead and abandoned by his relations, who neglected to pray for him, appeared suddenly in the public square at Aries, relating marvellous things of the other world, and asking for help. Those who had seen him in his lifetime at once recognized him. The Prior of the Jacobins, a man of saintly life, being told of this apparition, hastened to go and see the soul. Supposing at first that it might be a spirit that had taken the form of this citizen, he took, with lighted tapers, a consecrated host, which he held out to it. But the soul immediately showed that it was really there itself, for it prostrated itself and adored Our Lord, asking naught else but prayers which might deliver it from Purgatory, to the end that it might enter purified into heaven.

[Footnote 1: "Histoires des Spectres et des Apparitions."]

THE COUNTESS OF STRAFFORD.

The Countess of Strafford, before her conversion to the Catholic faith, went often to see Monseigneur de la Mothe, Bishop of Amiens, and her conversations with him always made the deepest impression on her mind. But what touched her more than all was a sermon which he preached on the feast of St. John the Baptist, in the chapel of the Ursulines in Amiens. After hearing this discourse, she felt within her a lively desire to believe as did the preacher who had so much edified her. She still had some doubts, however, on the Sacrifice of the Mass and Purgatory. She went to propose them to the holy Bishop, who, without disputing with her or openly attacking her prejudices, deemed it his duty to speak thus to her, in order to undeceive her: "Madam, you know the Bishop of London and have confidence in him? Well, I beg you to ask him what I am going to tell you: The Bishop of Amiens has told me a thing that surprised me; he says that if you can deny that St. Augustine said Mass and prayed for the dead, and particularly for his mother, he himself will become a Protestant." This advice was followed. The Bishop of London made no reply, but contented himself with saying to the bearer of the letter that Lady Strafford had been breathing a contagious atmosphere which had carried her away, and that anything he could write to her would probably not remedy the evil. This silence on the part of a man whom she had trusted implicitly, finished opening the eyes of Lady Strafford, and she soon after made her abjuration at the hands of the Bishop of Amiens.—*Vie de Monsgr. de la Mothe.*

THE MARQUIS BE CIVRAC. *(From une Commune Vendéenne.)*

The belief that the living friends may be of use to their friends in the grave, has in it I know not what instructive and natural which one meets in hearts the most simple and unsophisticated. A pious peasant woman of La Vendée kneeling on the coffin of her good master, the Marquis de Civrac, cried out: "O my God, repay to him all the good he has done to us!" Does not this fervent cry of grateful affection signify: "My God, some rays are perchance wanting in the crown of our benefactor; supply them, we beseech Thee, in consideration of our prayer and all he has done for us?" and this is precisely the consoling doctrine of Purgatory.

GRATITUDE OF THE HOLY SOULS.

[Rev. James Mumford, S.J., born in England in 1605, and who labored for forty years for the cause of the Catholic Church in his native country, wrote a remarkable work on Purgatory; and he mentions that the following incident was written to him by William Freysson, a publisher, of Cologne. May it move many in their difficulties to have recourse to the Holy Souls.]

One festival day, when my place of business was closed, I was occupying myself in reading a book which you had lent me, and which was on "The Souls in Purgatory." I was absorbed in my subject when a messenger came and told me that my youngest child, aged four years, showed the first symptoms of a very grave disease. The child rapidly grew worse, and the physicians at length declared that there was no hope. The thought then occurred to me that perhaps I could save my child by making a vow to assist the Suffering Souls in Purgatory. I accordingly repaired at once to a chapel, and, with all fervor, supplicated God to have pity on me; and I vowed I would distribute gratuitously a hundred copies of the book that had moved me in behalf of the suffering souls, and give them to ecclesiastics and to religious to increase devotion to the Holy Souls. I had, I acknowledge, hardly any hope. As soon as I returned to the house I found the child much better. He asked for food, although for several days he had not been able to swallow anything but liquids. The next day he was perfectly well, got up, went out for a walk, and ate as if he had never had anything the matter with him. Filled with gratitude, I was only anxious to fulfill my promise. I went to the College of the Jesuit Fathers and begged them to accept as many copies of the work as they pleased, and to distribute them amongst themselves and other communities and ecclesiastics as they thought fit, so that the suffering souls, my benefactors, should be assisted by further prayers.

Three weeks had not slipped away, however, when another accident not less serious befell me. My wife, on entering the house one day, was suddenly seized with a trembling in all her limbs, which threw her to the ground, and she remained insensible. Little by little the illness increased, until she was deprived of the power of speech. Remedies seemed to be in vain. The malady at length assumed such aggravated proportions that every one was of opinion she had no chance of recovery. The priest who assisted her had already addressed words of consolation to me, exhorting me to Christian resignation. I turned again with confidence to the souls in Purgatory, who had assisted me once before, and I went to the same church. There, prostrate before the Blessed Sacrament, I renewed my supplication with all the ardor with which affection for my family inspired me. "O my God!" I exclaimed, "Thy mercy is not exhausted: in the name of Thy infinite bounty, do not permit that the recovery of my son should be paid by the death of his mother." I made a vow this time, to distribute two hundred copies of the holy book, in order that a greater number of persons might be moved to intercede for the suffering souls. I besought those who had already been delivered from Purgatory to unite with me on this occasion. After this prayer, as I was returning to the house, I saw my servants running towards me. They told me with delight that my wife had undergone a great change for the better; that the delirium had ceased, and she had recovered her power of speech. I at once ran on to assure myself of the fact: all was true. Very soon my wife was so perfectly recovered that she came with me into the holy place to make an act of thanksgiving to God for all His mercies.—*Ave Maria.*

A STRANGE INCIDENT.

A young German lady of rank, still alive to tell the story, arriving with her friends at one of the most noted hotels in Paris, an apartment of unusual magnificence on the first floor was apportioned to her use. After retiring to rest she lay awake a long while, contemplating, by the dim light of a night-lamp, the costly ornaments in the room, when suddenly the folding-doors opposite the bed, which she had locked, were thrown open, and, amid a flood of unearthly light, there entered a young man in the garb of the French navy, having his hair dressed in the peculiar mode *à la Titus*. Taking a chair and placing it in the middle of the room, he sat down, and drew from his pocket a pistol of an uncommon make, which he deliberately put to his forehead, fired, and fell back as if dead. At the moment of the explosion the room became dark and still, and a low voice said softly: "Say an *Ave Maria* for his soul."

The young lady, though not insensible, became paralyzed with horror, and remained in a kind of cataleptic trance, fully conscious, but unable to move or speak, until, at nine o'clock next day, no answer having been given to repeated calls of her maid, the doors were forced open. At the same moment the power of speech returned, and the poor young lady shrieked out to her attendants that a man had shot himself in the night, and was lying dead on the floor. Nothing, however, was to be seen, and they concluded that she was suffering from the effects of a dream. Not being a Catholic, she could not, of course, understand the meaning of the mysterious command.

A short time afterwards, however, the proprietor of the hotel informed a gentleman of the party that the terrible scene witnessed by the young lady had in reality been enacted only three nights previously in that very room, when a young French officer put an end to his life with a pistol of a peculiar description, which, together with the body, was then lying at the Morgue awaiting identification. The gentleman examined them both, and found them to correspond exactly with the description of the man and the pistol seen in the apparition.

Whether the young officer was insane, or lived long enough to repent of his crime, is not known; however, the then Archbishop of Paris, Monseigneur Sibour, was exceedingly impressed by the incident. He called upon the young lady, and directing her attention to the words spoken by the mysterious voice, urged her to embrace the Catholic faith, to whose teaching it pointed so clearly.—*Ave Maria*, August 15, 1885.

PART III.

HISTORICAL

All the ages, every clime
Strike the silver harp of time,
Chant the endless, holy story,
Souls retained in Purgatory.
Freed by Mass and holy rite,
Requiem, dirge and wondrous might,
A prayer which hut and palace send,
Where king and serf, where lord and hireling blend.
The vast cathedral and the village shrine
Unite in mercy's choral strain divine.

HISTORICAL.

THE DOCTRINE OF PURGATORY, OR A MIDDLE STATE, AMONG THE PAGAN NATIONS OF ANTIQUITY.

BY THE REV. A. A LAMBING, A.M.

[This very interesting article was originally published in the "Ave Maria."]

The attentive student of the mythology of the nations of antiquity cannot fail to discover many vestiges of a primitive revelation of some of the principal truths of religion, although in the lapse of time they have been so distorted and mingled with fiction that it requires careful study to sift the few remaining grains of truth from the great mass of superstition and error in which they are all but lost. Among these truths may be reckoned monotheism, or the belief in, and the worship of, one only God, which the learned Jesuit, the Rev. Aug. Thebaud, in his "Gentilism," has proved to have been the primitive belief of all nations. It may not, however, be so generally known that the doctrine of Purgatory, or a future state of purification, was also held and taught in all the religious systems in the beginning. While a knowledge of this fact cannot add anything to the grounds of our faith as Catholics, it will not be wholly without interest, and it will, besides, better enable us to give a reason for the faith that is in us. It was left to Martin Luther to found an ephemeral religious system that should deny this dogma, founded no less on revelation than on right reason; but, then, logic has never been one of the strong points of Protestants.

Before turning my attention to the nations of the pagan world, I shall briefly give the Jewish belief on this point. It may not generally be known that the doctrine of a middle state is not explicitly proposed to the belief of the Jews in any of the writings of the Old Testament, although it was firmly held by the people. We depend for our knowledge of this fact mainly on the celebrated passage of the Second Book of Machabees (xii. 43-46). The occasion on which the doctrine was stated was this: Some of the soldiers of Judas Machabeus, the leader of the Jewish armies, fell in a certain battle; and when their fellow-soldiers came to bury them, they discovered secreted in the folds of their garments some parts of the spoils of one of the pagan shrines, which it was not permitted them to keep. After praying devoutly, the sacred writer goes on to say that Judas, "Making a gathering, sent twelve thousand drachms of silver to Jerusalem for sacrifices to be offered for the sins of the dead, thinking well and religiously concerning the resurrection [for if he had not hoped that they who were slain should rise again, it would have seemed superfluous and vain to pray for the dead]. And because he considered that they who had fallen asleep with godliness had great grace laid up for them. It is, therefore, a holy and wholesome thought to pray for the dead, that they may be loosed from sins."

The Catholic doctrine is thus briefly laid down in the Catechism: "Purgatory is a place of punishment in the other life where some souls suffer for a time before they can go to heaven;" or, in the words of the Catechism of the Council of Trent, there is "the fire of Purgatory, in which the souls of just men are cleansed by a temporary punishment in order to be admitted into their eternal country, 'into which nothing defiled entereth.'"

How far the pagan notions of a middle state harmonize with the Christian doctrine the reader will be able to determine as we proceed.

I must premise by stating that almost all, if not all, the forms of paganism were two-fold, containing a popular form of religion, believed and practiced by the mass of the people, and a more recondite form that was known only to the initiated, whether this was the priestly caste, as was generally the case, or whether they were designated by some other name. It should also be observed that the forms of religion were constantly undergoing changes of greater or less importance. Nor must we lose sight of the fact that different nations embodied the same idea under different terms. The conception of the phlegmatic Norseman would be different from that of the imaginative Oriental, and the language of the refined Greek would be far other than that of the rude American savage. But yet the same truth may be found to underlie all, the outward garb alone differing.

Turning first to Egypt, which is, rightly or wrongly, commonly considered the cradle of civilization, we may sum up its teaching with regard to the lot of the dead, and the middle state, in these interesting remarks of a learned author: "The continuance of the soul after its death, its judgment in another world, and its sentence according to its deserts, either to happiness or suffering, were undoubted parts both of the popular and of the more recondite religion. It was the universal belief that immediately after death the soul descended into a lower world, and was conducted to the Hall of Truth (or, 'of the Two Truths'), where it was judged in the presence of Osiris and the forty-two demons, the 'Lords of Truth' and judges of the dead. Anubis, 'the director of the weight,' brought forth a pair of scales, and, placing on one scale a figure or emblem of Truth, set on the other a vase containing the good actions of the deceased; Thoth standing by the while, with a tablet in his hand, whereon to record the result. According to the side on which the balance inclined, Osiris delivered the sentence. If the good deeds preponderated, the blessed soul was allowed to enter the 'boat of the sun,' and was conducted by good spirits to Aahlu (Elysium), to the 'pools of peace,' and the dwelling place of Osiris.... The good soul, having first been freed from its infirmities by passing through the basin of purgatorial fire, guarded by the four ape-faced genii, and then made the companion of Osiris three thousand years, returned from Amenti, re-entered its former body, rose from the dead, and lived once more a human life upon earth. This process was reiterated until a certain mystic cycle of years became complete, when finally the good and blessed attained the crowning joy of union with God, being absorbed into the Divine Essence, and thus attaining the true end and full perfection of their being." [1]

[Footnote 1: "History of Ancient Egypt," George Rawlinson, Vol. I., pp. 327-329.]

It may be remarked that all systems of religion which held the doctrine of metempsychosis, or the transmigration of souls, should be considered as believing in a middle state of purgation, since they maintained the necessity of the soul's further purification, after death, before it was permitted to enter into its final rest.

In the ever-varying phases through which Buddhism, the religion of all South-eastern Asia, has passed in its protracted existence, it is difficult to determine with any degree of certainty, precisely what its disciples hold; but the belief in metempsychosis, which is one of its fundamental doctrines, must permit us to range it on the side of those who hold to the idea of a middle state. Certain it is, they believe that the soul, by a series of new births, becomes, in process of time, better fitted for the final state in which it is destined for ever to remain. The same may be said of the religion of the great body of the Chinese; for, although they have their law-giver Confucius, their religion at present, as far as it merits the name, appears to be no more than a certain form of Buddhism.

Coming to the more western nations of Asia, we may remark that, as their religions were evidently a corruption of primitive revelation, less removed in point of time, they must, although they had already become idolatrous, have embodied the idea of a future state of purgation, notwithstanding that it is impossible to determine at this distant day, the exact nature of their doctrines. If, however, we turn from these to the doctrine of Zoroaster, our means of forming an opinion are more ample.

Zoroaster, or, more correctly, Zarathustra, the founder of the Persian religion, was born, according to some accounts, in the sixth century before our era, while others claim for him an antiquity dating at least from the thirteenth century before Christ. Be that as it may—and it does not concern us to inquire into it—this much is certain: he was a firm believer in a middle state, and he transmitted the same to his followers. But, going a step further than some, he taught that the souls undergoing purification are helped by the prayers of their friends upon earth. "The Zoroastrians," says Mr. Rawlinson, "were devout believers in the immortality of the soul and a conscious future existence. They taught that immediately after death the souls of men, both good and bad, proceeded together along an appointed path, to 'the bridge of the gatherer.' This was a narrow road conducting to heaven or paradise, over which the souls of the pious alone could pass, while the wicked fell from it into the gulf below, where they found themselves in the place of punishment. The good soul was assisted across the bridge by the Angel Serosh—'the happy, well-formed, swift, tall Serosh'—who met the weary wayfarer, and sustained his steps as he effected the difficult passage. The prayers of his friends in this world were of much avail to the deceased, and greatly helped him on his journey." [1]

[Footnote 1: "Ancient Monarchies." Vol. II, p 339.]

With regard to the opinions held by the Greeks,—and the same may, in general terms, be applied to the Romans, whose religious views coincided more or less closely with those of their more polished neighbors,—it is difficult to form a correct idea. Not that the classic writers and philosophers have permitted the subject to sink into oblivion,—on the contrary, they have treated it at considerable length, as all classic scholars well know,—but while, on the one hand, as I remarked above, there is a difference between the popular ideas and those of the learned, there is also here a great difference of opinion between the various schools of philosophy. Not only so, but it is difficult to determine how far the philosophers themselves were in earnest in the opinions they expressed; and how far, too, we understand them. The opinions of the people, and much more, those of the learned, vary with the principal periods of Grecian and Roman history. This much, however, may be safely held, that, while they drew their origin from Central or Western Asia, their religion must, in the beginning, have been that of

103

the countries from which they came. But truth only is immutable; error is ever changing.

I shall not tax the patience of the reader by asking him to pass in review the more striking periods of the history of these famous nations, but shall content myself with giving the views of a celebrated writer on a part, at least, of the question. Speaking of the opinions held by the Greek philosophers regarding the future state of the soul, Dr. Dollinger says, "The old and universal tradition admitted, in general, that man continued to exist after death; but the Greeks of the Homeric age did not dream of a retribution appointed to all after death, or of purifying and penitential punishments. It is only some conspicuous offenders against the gods who, in Homer, are tormented in distant Erebus. In Hesiod, the earlier races of man continue to live on, sometimes as good demons, sometimes as souls of men in bliss, or as heroes; yet, though inculcating moral obligations, he does not point to a reward to be looked for beyond the grave, but only to the justice that dominates in this economy…. Plato expressly ascribes to the Orphic writers the dogma of the soul's finding herself in the body as in a sepulchre or prison, on the score of previously contracted guilt; a dogma indubitably ascending to a very high antiquity.

"… It is from this source that Pindar drew, who, of the old Greeks, generally has expressed notions the most precise and minutely distinct of trial and tribulation after death, and the circuits and lustrations of the soul. He assigns the island of the blest as for the everlasting enjoyment of those who, in a triple existence in the upper and lower world, have been able to keep their souls perfectly pure from all sin. On the other hand, the souls of sinners appear after death before the judgment seat of a judge of the nether world, by whom they are sentenced to a heavy doom, and are ceaselessly dragged the world over, suffering bloody torments. But as for those whom Persephone has released from the old guilt of sin, their souls she sends in the ninth year back again to the upper sun; of them are born mighty kings, and men of power and wisdom, who come to be styled saintly heroes by their posterity." And, again: "Plato was the first of the Greeks to throw himself, in all sincerity, and with the whole depth of his intellect, upon the solution of the great question of immortality…. He was, in truth, the prophet of the doctrine of immortality for his time, and for the Greek nation…. The metempsychosis which he taught under Orphic and Pythagorean inspiration is an essential ingredient of his theory of the world, and is, therefore, perpetually recurring in his more important works. He connects it with an idea sifted and taken from popular belief of a state of penance in Hades, though it can hardly be ascertained how large a portion of mystical ornament or poetical conjecture he throws into the particular delineation of 'the last things,' and of transmigration. He adopts ten grades of migration, each of a thousand years; so that the soul, in each migration, makes a selection of its life-destiny, and renews its penance ten times, until it is enabled to return to an incorporeal existence with God, and to the pure contemplation of Him and the ideal world. Philosophic souls only escape after a three-fold migration, in each of which they choose again their first mode

104

of life. All other souls are judged in the nether world after their first life, and there do penance for their guilt in different quarters; the incurable only are thrust down forever into Tartarus. He attaches eternal punishment to certain particularly abominable sins, while such as have lived justly repose blissfully in the dwelling of a kindred star until their entrance into a second life. Plato was clearly acquainted with the fact of the necessity of an intermediate state between eternal happiness and misery, a state of penance and purification after death." [1]

[Footnote 1: "The Gentile and the Jew," Vol. I. pp. 301-320.]

The popular notion of Charon, the ferryman of the lower world, refusing to carry over the river Acheron the souls of such as had not been buried, but leaving them to wander on the shores for a century before he would consent, or rather before he was permitted by the rulers of the Hades to do so, contains a vestige of the belief in a middle state, where some souls had to suffer for a time before they could enter into the abode of the blest. But when it is said that the friends of the deceased could, by interring his remains, secure his entry into the desired repose, we see a more striking resemblance to the doctrine that friends on earth are able to assist the souls undergoing purgation. A remarkable instance of the popular belief in this doctrine is furnished in Grecian history, where the soldiers were encouraged on a certain occasion to risk their lives in the service of their country by their being told to write their names on their arms, so that if any fell his friends could have him properly interred, and thus secure him against all fear of having to wander for a century on the bleak shores of the dividing river. Nothing could better show the hold which this idea had on the minds of the people.

Roman mythological ideas were, as has been said, nearly related to those of Greece; they underwent as great modifications, while the opinions of her philosophers were equally abstruse, varied, and difficult to understand. The author above quoted, treating of the notion of the soul and a future state entertained by the Roman philosophers, proves their ideas to have been extremely vague and ill-defined. Still, there were not wanting those who held to the belief of an existence after this life. Plutarch, a Greek, "has left us a view of the state of the departed. The souls of the dead, ascending through the air, and in part reaching the highest heaven, are either luminous and transparent or dark and spotted, on account of sins adhering to them, and some have even scars upon them. The soul of man, he says elsewhere, comes from the moon; his mind, intellect,—from the sun; the separation of the two is only completely effected after death. The soul wanders awhile between the moon and earth for purposes of punishment—or, if it be good, of purification, until it rises to the moon, where the νοῦς [1] leaves it and returns to its home, the sun; while the soul is buried in the moon. Lucian, on the other hand, whose writings for the most part are a pretty faithful mirror of the notions in vogue among his contemporaries, bears testimony to a continuance of the old tradition of the good reaching the Elysian fields, and the great transgressors finding themselves given up to the Erinnys in a place of torment, where they are torn by vultures, crushed on the wheel, or otherwise tormented; while such as are neither great sinners nor distinguished by their virtues stray about in meadows as bodiless shadows, and are fed on the libations and mortuary sacrifices offered at their sepulchres. An obolus for Charon was still placed in the mouth of every dead body." [2] Here, again, we have both the belief in the existence of a middle state and of the assistance afforded to those detained there.

[Footnote 1: Mind]

[Footnote 2: "The Gentile and the Jew," Vol. II., p. 146.]

The religion of the Druids is so wrapped in mystery that it is difficult to determine what they believed on any point, and much more on that of the future lot of the soul; but as they held the doctrine of metempsychosis, it is fair to class them among the adherents to the notion of a period of purgation between death and the soul's entrance into its final rest. Of the views of the sturdy Norsemen, on the contrary, there can be no two opinions; in their mythology the idea of a middle state is expressed in the clearest language. The following passage from Mr. Anderson, places the matter beyond question. I may first remark, for the information of the general reader, that by Gimle is meant the abode of the righteous after the day of judgment; by Naastrand, the place of punishment after the same dread sentence; by Ragnarok, the last day; Valhal, the temporary place of happiness to which the god Odin invites those who have been slain in battle; and Hel, the goddess of death, whose abode is termed Helheim. With these explanations the reader will be able to understand the subjoined passage, which expresses the Norse idea of the future purgation of the soul.

After speaking of the lot of the departed, the writer says: "But it must be remembered that Gimle and Naastrand have reference to the state of things after Ragnarok, the Twilight of the gods; while Valhal and Hel have reference to the state of things between death and Ragnarok;— a time of existence corresponding somewhat to what is called *Purgatory* by the Catholic Church." [1]

[Footnote 1: "Norse Mythology," p. 393.]

It would appear to be no exaggeration to claim the same belief in a middle state for the American Indians, in as far as it is possible for us to draw anything definite from their crude notions of religion. A good authority on subjects connected with Indian customs and beliefs says: "The belief respecting the land of souls varied greatly in different tribes and different individuals." And, again: "An endless variety of incoherent fancies is connected with the Indian idea of a future life…. At intervals of ten or twelve years, the Hurons, the Neutrals, and other kindred tribes, were accustomed to collect the bones of their dead, and deposit them, with great ceremony, in a common place of burial. The whole nation was sometimes assembled at this solemnity; and hundreds of corpses, brought from their temporary resting-places, were inhumed in one common pit. From this hour the immortality of their souls began." This evidently implies a period during which the souls were wandering at a distance from the place of their eternal repose. Does the following passage throw any light upon it? The reader must decide the point for himself. "Most of the traditions," continues the same writer, "agree, however, that the spirits, on their journey heavenward, were beset with difficulties and perils. There was a swift river which must be crossed on a log that shook beneath their feet, while a ferocious dog opposed their passage, and drove many into the abyss. This river was full of sturgeons and other fish, which the ghosts speared for their subsistence. Beyond was a narrow path between moving rocks which each instant crushed together, grinding to atoms the less nimble of the pilgrims who essayed to pass." [1] A vestige of the same belief seems to crop out in a custom of some of the tribes of Central Africa, as appears from the remarks of a recent traveller. "When a death occurs," says Major Serpa Pinto, "the body is shrouded in a white cloth, and, being covered with an ox-hide, is carried to the grave, dug in a place selected for the purpose. The days following on an interment are days of high festival in the hut of the deceased. The native kings are buried with some ceremony, and their bodies, being arrayed in their best clothes, are conveyed to the tomb in a dressed hide. There is a great feasting on these occasions, and an enormous sacrifice of cattle; for the heir of the deceased is bound to sacrifice his whole herd in order to regale his people, and give peace to the soul of the departed." [2]

[Footnote 1: "The Jesuits in North America," Francis Parkman. Introduction, pp. 81, 92.]

[Footnote 2: "How I Crossed Africa," Vol. I., p. 63.]

Such a unity of sentiment on the part of so many nations differing in every other respect can only be attributed either to a natural feeling inherent in man, or to a primitive revelation, which, amid the vicissitudes of time, has left its impress on the minds of all nations. That the doctrine of a middle state of purification was a part of the primitive revelation cannot, I think, admit of reasonable doubt. To the true servant of God, this unanimity is another proof of the faith once revealed to the Saints, and, at the same time, an additional motive for thanking God for the light vouchsafed him, while so many others are left to grope in the darkness of error.—*Ave Maria,* Nov. 17, 1883.

DEVOTION TO THE DEAD AMONGST THE AMERICAN INDIANS OF THE EARLY JESUIT MISSIONS.

In the "*Rélations des Jésuites,*" on their early missions in New France, now Canada, we find many examples, told in the quaint old French of the seventeenth century, and with true apostolic simplicity, of the tender devotion for the souls in Purgatory cherished by all the Indians of every tribe who had embraced Christianity from the teaching of those zealous missionaries. The few extracts we give below from the "*Rélations*" will serve to show how deeply this touching devotion to the departed is implanted in our nature, seeing that the doctrine of a place of purgation in the after life finds so ready a response in the heart and soul of the untutored children of the forest:

"The devotion which they have for the souls of the departed is another mark of their faith. Not far from this assembly there is a cemetery, in the midst of which is seen a fine cross; sepulchres four or five feet wide and six or seven feet long, rise about four feet from the ground, carefully covered with bark. At the head and feet of the dead are two crosses, and on one side a sword, if the dead were a man, or some domestic article, if a woman. Having arrived there, I was asked to pray to

107

God for the souls of those who were buried in that place. A good Christian gave me a beaver skin by the hands of her daughter, about seven years of age, and said to me, when her daughter presented it: 'Father, this present is to ask you to pray to God for the souls of her sister and her grandmother.' Many others made the same request; I promised to comply with their wishes, but, as for their presents, I could not accept them.

"Some time ago, when the Christians of this place died, their beads were buried with them; this custom was last year changed for a holier one, by means of a good Christian who, when dying, gave her chaplet to another, begging her to keep it and say it for her, at least on feast days. This charity was done to her, and the custom was introduced from that time: so it was that when any one died, his or her rosary was given, with a little present, to some one chosen from the company present, who is bound to take it, and say it for the departed soul, at least on Sundays and Festivals."—*Journal of Father Jacques Buteux in "Rélations," Vol. II.*

* * * * *

In one of the Huron missions, an Indian named Joachim Annicouton, converted after many years of evil courses and, later, of hypocritical pretense of conversion, was murdered by three drunken savages of his own tribe, but lived long enough to edify all around him by his pious resignation, his admirable patience in the most cruel sufferings, and his generous forgiveness of his enemies. Having given a touching account of his death, the good Father Claude Dablon goes on to say:

"A very singular circumstance took place at his burial, which was attended by all the families of the village, with many of the French residents of the neighborhood. Before the body was laid in the earth, the widow inquired if the authors of his death were present; being told that they were not, she begged that they might be sent for. These poor creatures having come, they drew near to the corpse, with downcast eyes, sorrow and confusion in their faces. The widow, looking upon them, said: 'Well! behold poor Joachim Annicouton, you know what brought him to the state in which you now see him; I ask of you no other satisfaction but that you pray to God for the repose of his soul.' ..."

* * * * *

"It is customary amongst the Indians to give all the goods of the dead to their relatives and friends, to mourn their death; but the husband of Catherine, in his quality of first captain, assembled the Council of the Ancients, and told them that they must no longer keep to their former customs, which profited nothing to the dead; that, as for him, his thought was to dress up the body of the deceased in her best garments, as she might rise some day,—and to employ the rest of what belonged to her in giving alms to the poor. This thought was approved of by all, and it became a law which was ever after strictly observed.

"The body of his wife was then arrayed in her best clothes, and he distributed amongst the poor all that remained of her little furniture, charging them to pray for the dead. The whole might have amounted to three hundred francs, which is a great deal for an Indian."— *Rélations,* 1673-4.

* * * * *

"They [1] have established amongst them a somewhat singular practice to help the souls in Purgatory. Besides the offerings they make for that to the Church, and the alms they give to the poor,—besides the devotion of the four Sundays of the month, to which is attached an indulgence for the souls in Purgatory, so great that these days are like Easter; as soon as any one is dead, his or her nearest relations make a spiritual collection of communions in every family, begging them to offer all they can for the repose, of the dead."—*Relations*, 1677-8.

[Footnote 1: The Hurons of Loretto, near Quebec.]

SUPERSTITIOUS BELIEF AMONGST SOME OF THE NORTH AMERICAN INDIANS.

CABRAL.

When they are asked what they think of the soul, they answer that it is the shadow "or living image" of the body; and it is as a consequence of this principle that they believe all animated in the universe. It is by tradition that they suppose the soul immortal. They pretend that, separated from the body, it retains the inclinations it had during life; and hence comes the custom of burying with the dead all that had served to satisfy their wants or their tastes. They are even persuaded that the soul remains a long time near the body after their separation, and that it afterwards passes on into a country which they know not, or, as some will have it, transformed into a turtle. Others give all men two souls, one such as we have mentioned, the other which never leaves the body, and goes from one but to pass into another.

For this reason it is that they bury children on the roadside, so that women passing by may pick up these second souls, which, not having long enjoyed life, are more eager to begin it anew. They must also be fed; and for that purpose it is that divers sorts of food are placed on the graves, but that is only done for a little while, as it is supposed that in time the souls get accustomed to fasting. The difficulty they find in supporting the living makes them forget the care for the nourishment of the dead. It is also customary to bury with them all that had belonged to them, presents being even added thereto; hence it is a grievous scandal amongst all those nations when they see Europeans open graves to take out the beaver robes they have placed therein. The burial-grounds are places so respected that their profanation is accounted the most atrocious outrage that can be offered to an Indian village.

Is there not in all this a semblance of belief in our doctrine of Purgatory?

REMEMBRANCE OF THE DEAD AMONGST THE EGYPTIANS.

In Egypt, as all over the East, the lives of women amongst the wealthier classes are for the most part spent within the privacy of their homes, as it were in close confinement: they are born, live, and die in the bosom of that impenetrable sanctuary. It is only on Thursday that they go forth, with their slaves carrying refreshments and followed by hired weepers. It is a sacred duty that calls them to the public cemetery. There they have funeral hymns chanted, their own plaintive

109

cries mingling with the sorrowful lamentations of the mourners. They shed tears and flowers on the graves of their kindred, which they afterwards cover with the meats brought by their servants, and all the crowd, after inviting the souls of the dead, partake of a religious repast, in the persuasion that those beloved shades taste of the same food and are present at the sympathetic banquet. Is there not in this superstition a distorted tradition of the dogma by which we are commanded not to forget the souls of our brethren beyond the grave?— *Annals of the Propagation of the Faith*, Vol. XVII.

REMEMBRANCE OF THE DEAD THROUGHOUT EUROPE.

PART I.

ANNA T. SADLIER.

"Hark! the whirlwind is in the wood, a low murmur in the vale; it is the mighty army of the dead returning from the air." These beautiful words occur in one of the ancient Celtic poems quoted by Macpherson and dating some thousand years later than Ossian. For the Celts held to the doctrine of the immortality of souls, and believed that their ethereal substance was wafted from place to place by the wind on the clouds of heaven. Amongst the Highlanders a belief prevailed that there were certain hills to which the spirits of their departed friends had a peculiar attachment. Thus the hill of Ore was regarded by the house of Crubin as their place of meeting in the future life, and its summit was supposed to be supernaturally illumined when any member of the family died. It was likewise a popular belief that the spirits of the departed haunted places beloved in life, hovered about their friends, and appeared at times on the occasion of any important family event. In the calm of a new existence,

"Side by side they sit who once mixed in battle their steel."

There is a poetic beauty in many of these ancient beliefs concerning the dead, but they are far surpassed in grandeur and sublimity, as well as in deep tenderness, by the Christian conception of a state of purgation after death, when the souls of the departed are still bound to, their dear ones upon earth by a strong spiritual bond of mutual help. They dwell, then, in an abode of peace, although of intense suffering, and calmly await the eternal decree which summons them to heaven; while the time of their probation is shortened day by day, month by month, year by year by the Masses, prayers, alms-deeds and other suffrages of their friends who are still dwellers on earth, living the old life; and in its rush of cares and duties, of pleasures and of pains, forgetting them too often in all save prayer. That is the reminder. The dead who have died in the bosom of the Holy Church can never be quite forgotten. "The mighty army of the dead returning from the air" might in our Catholic conception be that host of delivered souls who, after the Feast of All Souls, or some such season of special prayer for them, are arising upwards into everlasting bliss. But it is our purpose in the present chapters to gather up from the byways of history occasions when the belief in prayer for the dead is made manifest, whether it be in some noted individual, in a people, or in a country. It is "the low murmur of the vale" going up constantly from all peoples, from all times, under all conditions.

110

In Russia not only is prayer for the dead most sedulously observed by the Catholic Church, but also in a most particular manner by the Schismatic Greeks. The following details under this head will be, no doubt, of interest to our readers:

"As soon as the spirit has departed, the body is dressed and placed in an open coffin in a room decorated for the purpose. Numerous lights are kept burning day and night; and while the relations take turns to watch and pray by the coffin, the friends come to pay the last visit to the deceased.... On the decease of extraordinary persons, the Emperor and his successor are accustomed to visit the corpse, while the poor, on the other hand, never fail to lament at the door the loss of their benefactor, and to be dismissed with handsome donations. Total strangers, too, come of their own accord to offer a prayer for the deceased; for the image of a saint hung up before the door indicates to every passenger the house of mourning.... The time of showing the corpse lasts in general only three or four days, and then follow the blessing of the deceased, and the granting of the pass. The latter is to be taken literally. The corpse is carried to the Church, and the priest lays upon the breast a long paper, which the common people call 'a pass for heaven.' On this paper is written the Christian name of the deceased, the date of his birth and that of his death. It then states that he was baptized as a Christian, that he lived as such, and before his death, received the Sacrament—in short, the whole course of life which he led as a Greek Russian Christian.... All who meet a funeral take off their hats, and offer a prayer to Heaven for the deceased, and such is the outward respect paid on such occasions, that it is not until they have entirely lost sight of the procession that they put on their hats again. This honor is paid to every corpse, whether of the Russian, Protestant, or Catholic Communions.... After the corpse is duly prepared, the priests sing a funeral Mass, called in Russian clerical language, *panichide*.... On the anniversary of the death of a beloved relative, they assemble in the Church, and have a *panichide* read for his soul.... Persons of distinction found a lamp to burn forever at the tombs of their dead, and have these *panichides* repeated every week, for, perhaps, a long series of years. Lastly, every year, on a particular day, Easter Monday, a service and a repast are held for all the dead."

The history of France, like that of all Catholic nations, abounds in instances of public intercession for the dead, the pomp and splendor of royal obsequies, the solemn utterances of public individuals; the celebrations at Père la Chaise, the magnificent requiems. In a nation so purely Catholic as it was and is, though the scum of evil men have arisen like a foul miasma to its surface, it does not surprise us. We shall therefore select from its history an incident or two, somewhat at random. That beautiful one, far back at the era of the Crusades, where St. Louis, King of France, absent in the East, received intelligence of the death of Queen Blanche, his mother. The grief of the Papal Legate, who had come to announce the news, was apparent in his face, and Louis, fearing some new blow, led the prelate into his chapel, which, according to an ancient chronicler, was "his arsenal against all the crosses of the world." Louis, overcome with sorrow, quickly changed his tears and lamentations into the language of resignation, and desiring to be left alone with his confessor, Geoffrey de Beaulieu, recited the office of the dead. "He was present every day at a funeral service celebrated in memory of his mother; and sent into the West a great number of jewels and precious stones to be distributed among the principal churches of France; at the same time exhorting the clergy to put up prayers for the repose of his mother. In proportion with his endeavors," continues the historian, "to procure prayers for his mother, his grief yielded to the hope of seeing her again in heaven; and his mind, when calmed by resignation, found its most effectual consolation in that mysterious tie which still unites us with those we have lost, in that religious sentiment which mingles with our affections to purify them, and with our regrets to mitigate them." [1]

[Footnote 1: "Michaud's Hist. of the Crusades," Vol. II., pp. 477-8.]

In the Instructions which St. Louis addressed on his death-bed to his son, Philip the Bold, is to be found the following paragraph:

"Dear Son, I pray thee, if it shall please our Lord that I should quit this life before thee, that thou wilt help me with Masses and prayers, and that thou wilt send to the congregations of the kingdom of France, to make them put up prayers for my soul, and that thou wilt desire that our Lord may give me part in all the good deeds thou shalt perform." [1]

[Footnote 1: These instructions were preserved in a register of the Chamber of Accounts. See Appendix to "Michaud's History of Crusades," Vol. II., p. 471.]

Philip, on the death of his father, in a letter which was read aloud in all the churches, begs of the clergy and faithful, "to put up to the King of kings their prayers and their offerings for that prince; with whose zeal for religion and tender solicitude for the kingdom of France, which he loved as the apple of his eye, they were so well acquainted." In the Chronicles of Froissart, as well as in the Grande Chronique of St. Denis, we read that the body of King John, who died a prisoner in England, was brought home with great pomp and circumstance, on the first day of May, 1364. It was at first placed in the Abbey of St. Anthony, thence removed to Notre Dame, and finally to St. Denis, the resting-place of royalty, where solemn Mass was said. On the day of his interment, the Archbishop of Sens sang the requiem. Thus did Holy Mother Church welcome the exile home.

A pretty anecdote is that of Marie Lecsinska, Queen of Louis XV., who, on hearing of the death of Marshal Saxe, a Lutheran by profession, and but an indifferent observer of the maxims of any creed, cried out: "Alas! what a pity that we cannot sing a *De Profundis* for a man who has made us sing so many *Te Deums*."

We cannot take our leave of France, without noticing here the beautiful prayer offered up by the saintly Princess Louise de Bourbon Condé, in religion *Sur Marie Joseph de la Miséricorde*, on hearing of the death of her nephew, the Duc d'Enghien, so cruelly put to death by the first Napoleon. Falling, face downwards, on the earth, she prayed: "Mercy, my God, have mercy upon him! Have mercy, Lord, on the soul of Louis Antoine! Pardon the faults of his youth, remembering the precious Blood, which Jesus Christ shed for all men, and have regard to the cruel manner in which his blood was shed. Glory and misfortune have attended his life. But what we call glory, has it any claims in Thy eyes? However, Lord, it is not a demerit before Thee, when it is based on true honor, which is always inseparable from devotion to our duties. Thou knowest, Lord, those that he has fulfilled, and for those in which he has failed, let the misfortunes of which he has been at last the victim, be a repararation and an expiation. Again, Lord, I ask for mercy for his soul." On the death of Napoleon, the murderer of this beloved nephew, the same holy religious wrote to the Bishop of St. Flour: "Bonaparte is dead; he was your enemy, for he persecuted you. I think you will say a Mass for him; I beg also that you say a Mass on my behalf for this unfortunate man."

Turning to the History of Rome, it will be of interest to take a glance at the pious Confraternity *della Morte* which was instituted in 1551, and regularly established in 1560, by His Holiness, Pius IV. It was chiefly composed of citizens of high rank. Its object was to provide burial for the dead. Solemnly broke upon the balmy stillness of the Roman nights, all these years and centuries since its foundation, its chanting of holy psalmody, and its audible praying for the dead, borne along in its religious keeping. The glare of the waxen torches fell upon the bier, the voices of the associates joined in the *Miserere,* and the Church reached, the corpse was laid there, till the fitting hour, when the Requiem Mass should be sung, and the final absolution given, preparatory to interment.

Florence supplies us with a brilliant picture of that sixth day of July, 1439, the feast of Saint Romolo the Martyr, in the ninth year of the Pontificate of Pope Eugenius IV., when long-standing differences between the Greek and Latin Churches were brought to an end in a most amicable manner. Alas! for the Greeks, that they did not accept the decisions of that day as final. On the 22d of January, 1439, Cosmo de Medici, then Gonfaloniere of Florence, received the Pope and his cardinals, with a pomp and splendor unknown to the history of modern Europe. On the 12th of the following month came the Patriarch, Joseph of Constantinople, and his bishops and theologians. On the 15th arrived the Greek Emperor, John Paleologus, who was received at the Porto San Gallo by the Pope and all his cardinals, the Florentine Signory, and a long procession of the members of the monastic orders. "A rare and very remarkable assemblage," says a chronicler [1] "of the most learned men of Europe, and, indeed, of those extra European seats of a past culture, which were even now giving forth the last flashes from a once brilliant light on the point of being quenched in utter darkness, were thus assembled at Florence."

[Footnote 1: T. A. Trollope, in "History of the Commonwealth of Florence," Vol. III., pp. 137-8.]

This was the inauguration of the far-famed Council of Florence, which had the result of settling the points at issue between the Eastern and Western Churches. "The Greeks confessed that the Roman faith proceeded rightly (*prociedere bene*), and united themselves with it by the grace of God." Proclamation was accordingly made in the Cathedral, then called Santa Reparata, that the Greeks had agreed to hold and to believe the five disputed articles of which the fifth was,

"That he who dies in sin for which penance has been done, but from which he has not been purged, goes to Purgatory, and that the divine offices, Masses, prayers, and alms are useful for the purging of him."

In the history of Ireland, as might be expected, we come upon many instances wherein the dead are solemnly remembered from that period, when still pagan, and one of the ancient manuscripts gives us an account of certain races, it calls them, which were held for "the souls of the foreigners slain in battle." This was back in the night of antiquity, and was no doubt some relic of the Christian tradition which had remained amid the darkness of paganism. But to come to the Christian period. The famous Hugues de Lasci, or Hugo de Lacy, Lord of Meath, and one of the most distinguished men in early Irish annals, founded many abbeys and priories, one at Colpe, near the mouth of the Boyne, one at Duleek, one at Dublin, and one at Kells. The Canons of St. Augustine, as we read, "in return for this gift, covenanted that one of them should be constantly retained as a chaplain to celebrate Mass for his soul and for those of his ancestors and successors." We also read how Marguerite, wife of Gualtier de Lasci, brother of the above, gave a large tract in the royal forest of Acornebury, in Herefordshire, for the erection of a nunnery for the benefit of the souls of her parents, Guillaume and Mathilda de Braose, who with their son, her brother, had been famished in the dungeon at Windsor. In the account of the death in Spain of Red Hugh O'Donnell, who holds a high place among the chivalry of Ireland, it is mentioned that on his death-bed, "after lamenting his crimes and transgressions; after a rigid penance for his sins and iniquities; after making his confession without reserve to his confessors, and receiving the body and blood of Christ; after being duly anointed by the hands of his own confessors and ecclesiastical attendants," he expired after seventeen days' illness at the king's palace in Simancas. "His body," says the ancient chronicler, "was conveyed to the king's palace at Valladolid in a four-wheeled hearse, surrounded by countless numbers of the king's State officers, council and guards, with luminous torches and bright flambeaux of wax lights burning on either side. He was afterwards interred in the monastery of St. Francis, in the Chapter, precisely, with veneration and honor, and in the most solemn manner that any of the Gaels had been ever interred in before. Masses and many hymns, chants and melodious canticles were celebrated for the welfare of his soul; and his requiem was sung with becoming solemnity."

On the death of the celebrated Brian Boroihme, historians relate how his body was conveyed by the clergy to the Abbey of Swords, whence it was brought by other portions of the clergy and taken successively to two monasteries. It was then met by the Archbishop of Armagh, at the head of his priesthood, and conveyed to Armagh, where the obsequies were celebrated with a pomp and a fervor worthy the greatness and the piety of the deceased monarch.

In view of the arguments which are sometimes adduced to prove that the early Irish Church did not teach this doctrine of prayer for the dead, it is curious to observe how in St. Patrick's second Council he expressly forbids the holy sacrifice being offered up after death for those who in life had made themselves unworthy of such suffrages. At the Synod of Cashel, held just after the Norman conquest, the claim of each dead man's soul to a certain part of his chattels after death was asserted. To steal a page from the time-worn chronicles of Scotland, it is told by Theodoric that when Queen Margaret of Scotland, that gentle and noble character upon whom the Church has placed the crown of canonization, was dying, she said to him: "Two things I have to desire of thee;" and one of these was thus worded, "that as long as thou livest thou wilt remember my poor soul in thy Masses and prayers." It had been her custom in life to recite the office of the dead every day during Lent and Advent. Sir Walter Scott mentions in his Minstrelsy of the Scottish Border "a curious league or treaty of peace between two hostile clans, by which the heads of each became bound to make the four pilgrimages of Scotland for the benefit of those souls who had fallen in the feud." In the Bond of Alliance or Field Staunching Betwixt the Clans of Scott and Ker this agreement is thus worded: "That it is appointed, agreed and finally accorded betwixt honorable men," the names are here mentioned, "Walter Ker of Cessford, Andrew Ker of Fairnieherst," etc., etc., "for themselves, kin, friends, maintenants, assisters, allies, adherents, and partakers, on the one part; and Walter Scott of Branxholm," etc., etc., etc. For the staunching of all discord and variance between them and so on, amongst other provisions, that "the said Walter Scott of Branxholm shall gang, or cause gang, at the will of the party, to the four head pilgrimages of Scotland, and shall say a Mass for the unquhile Andrew Ker of Cessford and them that were slain in his company in the field of Melrose; and, upon his expence, shall cause a chaplain to say a Mass daily, when he is disposed, in what place the said Walter Ker and his friend pleases, for the weil of the said souls, for the space of five years next to come. Mark Ker of Dolphinston, Andrew Ker of Graden, shall gang at the will of the party to the four head pilgrimages of Scotland, and shall gar say a Mass for the souls of the unquhile James Scott of Eskirk and other Scots, their friends, slain in the field of Melrose; and, upon their expence, shall gar a chaplain say a Mass daily, when he is disposed, for the heal of their souls, where the said Walter Scott and his friend pleases, for the space of the next three years to come." We may mention that the four pilgrimages are Scoon, Dundee, Paisley, and Melrose. This devotion of praying for the dead seems, indeed, to have taken strong hold upon these rude borderers, who, Sir Walter Scott informs us, "remained attached to the Roman Catholic faith rather longer than the rest of Scotland." In many of their ancient ballads, at some of which we have already glanced, this belief is prominent. The dying man, or as in the case of Clerk Saunders, the ghost begs of his survivors to "wish my soul good rest." This belief is intermingled with their superstitions as in that one attached to Macduff's Cross. This cross is situated near Lindores, on the marsh dividing Fife from Strathern. Around the pedestal of this cross are tumuli, said to be the graves of those who, having claimed the privilege of the law, failed in proving their consanguinity to the Thane of Fife. Such persons were instantly executed. The people of Newburgh believe that the spectres of these criminals still haunt the ruined cross, and claim that mercy for their souls which they had failed to obtain for their mortal existence.

Thus does the historian [1] mention the burial of St. Ninian, one of the favorite Saints of the Scots: "He was buried in the Church of St. Martin, which he had himself built from the foundation, and placed in a stone coffin near the altar, the clergy and people standing by and lifting up their heavenly hymns with heart and voice, with sighs and tears."

[Footnote 1: Walsh's Hist, of the Cath. Church in Scotland.]

In the treasurer's books which relate to the reign of James IV. of Scotland, there is the following entry for April, 1503: "The king went again to Whethorn." (A place of pilgrimage.) "While there he heard of the death of his brother, John, Earl of Mar, and charged the priests to perform a 'dirge and soul Mass' for his brother, and paid them for their pains."

In Montalembert's beautiful description of Iona, he mentions the tradition which declares that eight Norwegian kings or princes, four kings of Ireland, and forty-eight Scottish kings were buried there, as also one king of France, whose name is not mentioned, and Egfrid, the Saxon King of Northumbria. There is the tomb of Robert Bruce, the tombs of many bishops, abbots, and of the great chiefs and nobles, the Macdougalls, Lords of Lorn; the Macdonalds, Lords of the Isles; the Macleods, and the Macleans. Nowhere, perhaps, has death placed his seal on a more imposing assemblage, of truly royal stateliness, of astonishingly cosmopolitan variety. In the midst of it all, in the very centre of the burying-ground, stands a ruined chapel, under the invocation of St. Oran, the first Irish monk who died in this region. The church was built by the sainted Margaret, the wife of Malcolm Canmore, and the mother of St. David. Its mission there was obvious. From its altar arose to the Most High, the solemn celebration of the dread mysteries, the psalm and the prayer, for prince and for prelate, for the great alike in the spiritual and temporal hierarchy.

The Duke of Argyle, in his work on Iona, seems astonished to find that St. Columba believed in all the principal truths of Catholic faith, amongst others, prayers for the dead, and yet he considers that he could not be called a Catholic. The process of reasoning is a curious one.

Mention is made in the history of Scotland of a famous bell, preserved at Glasgow until the Reformation. It was supposed to have been brought from Rome by St. Kentigern, and was popularly called "St. Mungo's Bell." It was tolled through the city to invite the citizens to pray for the repose of departed souls.

In the great cathedrals of Scotland, before the Reformation, private chapels and altars were endowed for the relief of the dead, while in the cities and large towns, each trade or corporation had an altar in the principal churches and supported a chaplain to offer up Masses and prayers as well for the dead as for the living. The following incident is related in the life of the lovely and so sadly maligned Mary Queen of Scots. In the early days of her reign, when still struggling with the intolerant fury of Knox and his followers,—it was in the December of 1561— Mary desired to have solemn Mass offered up for the repose of the soul of her deceased husband, the youthful Francis. This so aroused the fury of the fanatics

116

about her, that they threatened to take the life of the priests who had officiated. "Immediately after the Requiem was over, she caused a proclamation to be made by a Herald at the Market Cross, that no man on pain of his life should do any injury, or give offense or trouble to her chaplains."

The poet Campbell in his dirge for Wallace, makes the Lady of Elderslie, the hero's wife, cry out in the first intensity of her sorrow;

"Now   sing   you   the   death-song   and   loudly   pray
For the soul of my knight 'so dear.'"

We shall now leave the wild poetic region of Scotland, and with it conclude Part First, taking up again in Part Second the thread of our narrative, which will wind in and out through various countries of Europe, ending at last with a glance at our own America.

REMEMBRANCE OF THE DEAD THROUGHOUT EUROPE.
PART II.

In Austria we find an example of devotion to the dead, in the saintly Empress Eleanor, who, after the death of her husband, the Emperor Leopold, in 1705, was wont to pray two hours every day for the eternal repose of his soul. Not less touching is an account given by a Protestant traveller of an humble pair, whom he encountered at Prague during his wanderings there. They were father and daughter, and attached, the one as bell-ringer, the other as laundress, to the Church on the Visschrad. He found them in their little dwelling. It was on the festival of St. Anne, when all Prague was making merry. The girl said to him: "Father and I were just sitting together, and this being St. Anne's Day, we were thinking of my mother, whose name was also Anne." The father then said, addressing his daughter: "Thou shalt go down to St. Jacob's to-morrow, and have a Mass read for thy mother, Anne." For the mother who had been long years slumbering in the little cemetery hard by. There is, something touching to me in this little incident, for it tells how the pious memory of the beloved dead dwelt in these simple hearts, dwells in the hearts of the people everywhere, as in that of the pious empress, whose inconsolable sorrow found vent in long hours of prayer for the departed.

In the will of Christopher Columbus there is special mention made of the church which he desired should be erected at Concepcion, one of his favorite places in the New World, so named by himself. In this church he arranged that three Masses should be celebrated daily—the first in honor of the Blessed Trinity; the second, in honor of the Immaculate Conception; and the third for the faithful departed. This will was made in May, 1506. The body of the great discoverer was laid in the earth, to the lasting shame of the Spaniards, with but little other remembrance than that which the Church gives to the meanest of her children. The Franciscans, his first friends, as now his last, accompanied his remains to the Cathedral Church of Valladolid, where a Requiem Mass was sung, and his body laid in the vault of the Observantines with but little pomp. Later on, however, the king, in remorse for past neglect, or from whatever cause, had the body taken up and transported with great pomp to Seville. There a Mass was sung, and a solemn

117

funeral service took place at the cathedral, whence the corpse of the Admiral was conveyed beyond the Guadalquivir to St. Mary of the Grottoes (Santa Maria de las Grutas). But the remains of this most wonderful of men were snatched from the silence of the Carthusian cloister some ten years later, and taken thence to Castile, thence again to San Domingo, where they were laid in the sanctuary of the cathedral to the right of the main altar. Again they were disturbed and taken on board the brigantine Discovery to the Island of Cuba, where solemnly, once more, the Requiem for the Dead swelled out, filling with awe the immense assembly, comprising, as we are told, all the civil and military notables of the island.

In the annals of the Knight Hospitallers of St. John, it is recorded that after a great and providential victory won by them over the Moslem foe, and by the fruits of which Rhodes was saved from falling into the hands of the enemy, the Grand Master D'Aubusson proceeded to the Church of St. John to return thanks. And that he also caused the erection of three churches in honor of Our Blessed Lady, and the Patron Saints of the city. These three churches were endowed for prayers and Masses to be offered in perpetuity for the souls of those who had fallen in battle. This D'Aubusson was in all respects one of the most splendid knights that Christendom has produced. A model of Christian knighthood, he is unquestionably one of the greatest of the renowned Grand Masters of St. John. There is a touching incident told in these same annals of two knights, the Chevalier de Servieux, counted the most accomplished gentleman of his day, and La Roche Pichelle. Both of them were not only the flower of Christian knighthood, but model religious as well. They died of wounds received in a sea fight off Saragossa in 1630, and on their death-beds lay side by side in the same room, consoling and exhorting each other, it being arranged between them, that whoever survived the longest should offer all his pains for the relief of his companion's soul.

We have now reached a part of our work, upon which we shall have occasion to dwell at some length, and notwithstanding the fact that it has already formed the subject of two preceding articles. It is that which relates to England, and which is doubly interesting to Catholics, as being the early record of what is now the chief Protestant nation of Europe. To go back to those Anglo-Saxon days, which might be called in some measure the golden age of Catholic faith in England, we shall see what was the custom which prevailed at the moment of dissolution. In the regulations which follow there is not question of a monarch nor a public individual, nor of priest nor prelate, but simply of an ordinary Christian just dead. "The moment he expired the bell was tolled. Its solemn voice announced to the neighborhood that a Christian brother was departed, and called on those who heard it to recommend his soul to the mercy of his Creator. All were expected to join, privately, at least, in this charitable office; and in monasteries, even if it were in the dead of night, the inmates hastened from their beds to the church, and sang a solemn dirge. The only persons excluded from the benefit of these prayers were those who died avowedly in despair, or under the sentence of

118

excommunication.

"... Till the hour of burial, which was often delayed for some days to allow time for the arrival of strangers from a distance, small parties of monks or clergymen attended in rotation, either watching in silent prayer by the corpse or chanting with subdued voice the funeral service.... When the necessary preparations were completed, the body of the deceased was placed on a bier or in a hearse. On it lay the book of the Gospels, the code of his belief, and the cross, the emblem of his hope. A pall of linen or silk was thrown over it till it reached the place of interment. The friends were invited, strangers often deemed it a duty to attend. The clergy walked in procession before, or divided into two bodies, one on each side, singing a portion of the psalter and generally bearing lights in their hands. As soon as they entered the church the service for the dead was performed; a Mass of requiem followed; the body was deposited in the grave, the sawlshot paid, and a liberal donation distributed to the poor." [1]

[Footnote 1: "Lingard's Antiquities of the Anglo Saxon Church," Vol. II, pp. 46-47.]

In the northern portico of the Cathedral of Canterbury was erected an altar in honor of St. Gregory, where a Mass was offered every Saturday for the souls of departed archbishops. We read that Oidilwald, King of the Deiri, and son of King Oswald, founded a monastery that it might be the place of his sepulture, because "he was confident of deriving great benefit from the prayers of those who should serve the Lord in that house." Dunwald the Thane, on his departure for Rome to carry thither the alms of his dead master, King Ethelwald, A.D. 762, bequeathed a dwelling in the market in Queengate to the Church of SS. Peter and Paul for the benefit of the king's soul and his own soul.

As far back as the days of the good King Arthur, whose existence has been so enshrouded in fable that many have come to believe him a myth, we read that Queen Guenever II., of unhappy memory, having spent her last years in repentance, was buried in Ambreabury, Wiltshire. The place of her interment was a monastery erected by Aurelius Ambrose, the uncle of King Arthur, "for the maintenance of three hundred monks to pray for the souls of the British noblemen slain by Hengist." Upon her tomb was inscribed, "in rude letters of massy gold," to quote the ancient chronicler, the initials R. G. and the date 600 A.D.

In the Saxon annals Enfleda, the wife of Oswy, King of Northumbria, plays a conspicuous part. Soon after her marriage, Oswin, her husband's brother, consequently her cousin and brother-in-law, was slain. The queen caused a monastery to be erected on the spot where he fell as a reparation for her husband's fratricide, and as a propitiation for the soul of the departed. This circumstance is alluded to by more than one English poet, as also the monastery which Enfleda, for the same purpose, caused to be erected at Tynemouth. Thus Harding:

"Queen Enfled, that was King Oswy's wife,
King Edwin, his daughter, full of goodnesse,

For Oswyn's soule a minster, in her life,
Made at Tynemouth, and for Oswy causeless
That hym so bee slaine and killed helpeless;
For she was kin to Oswy and Oswin,
As Bede in chronicle dooeth determyn."

The most eminent Catholic poet of our own day, Sir Aubrey de Vere, in his Saxon legends, likewise refers to it. He describes first what

"Gentlest form kneels on the rain-washed ground,
From Giling's Keep a stone's throw. Whose those hands
Now pressed in anguish on a bursting heart.
… What purest mouth
"Presses a new-made grave, and through the blades
Of grass wind shaken, breathes her piteous prayer?
… Oswin's grave it is,
And she that o'er it kneels is Eanfleda,
Kinswoman of the noble dead, and wife
To Oswin's murderer—Oswy."

Again, describing the repentance of Oswy:

"One Winter night
From distant chase belated he returned,
And passed by Oswin's grave. The snow, new fallen,
Whitened the precinct. In the blast she knelt,
She heard him not draw nigh. She only beat
Her breast, and, praying, wept. Our sin! our sin!
"So came to him those words. They dragged him down:
He knelt beside his wife, and beat his breast,
And said, 'My sin! my sin!' Till earliest morn
Glimmered through sleet that twain wept on, prayed on:—
Was it the rising sun that lit at last
The fair face upward lifted?
……. Aloud she cried,
'Our prayer is heard: our penitence finds grace.'
Then added: 'Let it deepen till we die.
A monastery build we on this grave:
So from this grave, while fleet the years, that prayer
Shall rise both day and night, till Christ returns
To judge the world,—a prayer for him who died;
A prayer for one who sinned, but sins no more!'"

In the grant preserved in the Bodleian Collection, wherein Editha the Good, the widow of Edward the Confessor, confers certain lands upon the Church of St. Mary at Sarum, occurs the following:

"I, Editha, relict of King Edward, give to the support of the Canons of St. Mary's Church, in Sarum, the lands of Secorstan, in Wiltshire, and those of Forinanburn, to the Monastery of Wherwell, for the support of the nuns serving

120

God there, with the rights thereto belonging, for the soul of King Edward." [1]

[Footnote 1: "Phillips' Account of Old Sarum."]

This queen was buried in Westminster Abbey, her remains being removed from the north to the south side of St. Edward's shrine, on the rebuilding of that edifice, and it is recorded that Henry III. ordered a lamp to be kept burning perpetually at the tomb of Editha the Good.

It is related of the celebrated Lady Godiva of Coventry, the wife of the wealthy and powerful Leofric, that on her death-bed she "bequeathed a precious circlet of gems, which she wore round her neck, valued at one hundred marks of silver (about two thousand pounds sterling) to the Image of the Virgin in Coventry Abbey, praying that all who came thither would say as many prayers as there were gems in it." [1]

[Footnote 1: Saxon Chronicle, Strickland's "Queens of England Before the Conquest, etc."]

The following is an ancient verse, occurring in an old French treatise, on the manner of behaving at table, wherein one is warned never to arise from a meal without praying for the dead. This treatise was translated by William Caxton.

"Priez Dieu pour les trepassés,
Et te souveigne en pitié
Qui de ce monde sont passez,
Ainsi que tu es obligez,
Priez Dieu pour les trepassés!"

[We subjoin a rough translation of the verse.

To God, for the departed, pray
And of those in pity think
Who have passed from this world away,
As, indeed, thou art bound to do,
To God, for the departed pray.]

Speaking of his early education, Caxton says:

"Whereof I humbly and heartily thank God, and am bounden to pray for my father and mother's souls, who in my youth set me to school." [1]

[Footnote 1: "Christian Schools and Scholars."]

In 1067, William the Conqueror founded what was known as Battle Abbey, which he gave to the Benedictine Monks, that they might pray for the souls of those who fell in the Battle of Hastings. Speaking of William the. Conqueror, it is not out of place to quote here these lines from the pen of Mrs. Hemans:

"Lowly upon his bier
The royal Conqueror lay,
Baron and chief stood near,
Silent in war's array.
Down the long minster's aisle
Crowds mutely gazing stream'd,
Altar and tomb the while
Through mists of incense gleamed.

"They lowered him with the sound
Of requiems to repose."

These stanzas on the Burial of William the Conqueror lead us naturally to others from the pen of the same gifted authoress on "Coeur de Lion at the Bier of his Father."

"Torches were blazing clear,
Hymns pealing deep and slow,
Where a king lay stately on his bier,
In the Church of Fontevraud.
　* * * * *

"The marble floor was swept
By many a long dark stole
As the kneeling priests, round him that slept,
Sang mass for the parted soul.
And solemn were the strains they pour'd
Through the stillness of the night,
With the cross above, and the crown and sword,
And the silent king in sight."

We forgive the ignorance of the gentle poetess with regard to the Mass, for the beauty and solemnity of the verse, which is quite in keeping with the nature of the subject.

We read, again, of tapers being lit at the tomb of Henry V., the noble and chivalrous Henry of Monmouth, for one hundred years after his death. The Reformation extinguished that gentle flame with many another holy fire, both in England and throughout Christendom.

We shall now pass on to another period—a far different and most troublous one of English history, that of the Reformation.

In the Church of St. Lawrence at Iswich is an entry of an offering made to "pray for the souls of Robert Wolsey and his wife Joan, the father and mother of the Dean of Lincoln," thereafter to be Cardinal and Chancellor of the Kingdom. An argument urged to show the Protestantism of Collet, one of the ante-Reformation worthies, is that he "did not make a Popish will, having left no monies for Masses for his soul; which shows that he did not believe in Purgatory." The dying prayer of Sir Thomas More concludes with these words: "Give me a longing to be with Thee; not for avoiding the calamities of this wicked world, nor so much the pains of Purgatory or of hell; nor so much for the attaining of the choice of heaven, in respect of mine own commodity, as even for a very love of Thee." The unfortunate Anne Boleyn, who during her imprisonment had repented and received the last sacraments from the hands of Father Thirlwall, begs on the scaffold that the people may pray for her. In her address to her ladies before leaving the Tower, she concludes it by begging them to forget her not after death. "In your prayers to the Lord Jesus forget not to pray for my soul." In the account of the death of another of King Henry's wives, the Lady Jane Seymour, who died, as Miss Strickland says, after having all the rites of the Catholic Church administered to her, we read that Sir Richard Gresham thus writes to Lord Cromwell:

"I have caused twelve hundred Masses to be offered up for the soul of our most gracious Queen…. I think it right that there should also be a solemn dirge and high Mass, and that the mayor and aldermen should pray and offer up divers prayers for Her Grace's soul."

Anne of Cleves some two years before her death likewise embraced the Catholic faith. At her funeral Mass was sung by Bonner, Bishop of London, and many monks and seculars attended her obsequies. The infamous Thomas Cromwell, converted, as it seems evident from contemporary witnesses, on his death-bed, left what might be called truly a "Popish will." After bequeathing money or effects to various relatives and friends, he speaks of charity "works for the health of my soul." "I will," he says, "that my executors shall sell said farm (Carberry), and the money thereof to be employed in deeds of charity, to prayer for my soul and all Christian souls." Item. "I will mine executors shall conduct and hire a priest, being an honest person of continent and good living, to sing (pray) for my soul for the space of seven years next after my death." Item. "I give and bequeath to every one of the five orders of Friars within the Citie of London, to pray for my soul, twenty shillings. …" He further bequeaths £20 to be distributed amongst "poor householders, to pray for his soul."

In this he closely resembled his royal master, Henry VIII., who ordained that Masses should be said "for his soul's health while the world shall endure." And after his death it was agreed that the obsequies should be conducted according to the observance of the Catholic Church. Church-bells tolled and Masses were celebrated daily throughout London. In the Privy Chamber, where the corpse was laid, "lights and Divine service were said about him, with Masses, obsequies, etc." After the body was removed to the chapel it was kept there twelve days, with "Masses and dirges sung and said everyday." Norroy, king at arms, stood each day at the choir door, saying: "Of your charity pray for the soul of the high and mighty prince, our late sovereign lord and king, Henry VIII." When the body was lowered into the grave we read of a *De Profundis* being read over it. God grant it was not all a solemn mockery, this praying for the soul of him who was styled "the first Protestant King of England," and who by his crimes separated England from the unity of Christendom! May these "Popish practices," which were amongst those he in his ordinances condemned, have availed him in that life beyond the grave, whither he went to give an account of his stewardship!

The Catholic Queen, Mary, after her accession to the throne, caused a requiem Mass to be sung in Tower Chapel for her brother, Edward the Sixth. Elizabeth, in her turn, had Mary buried with funeral hymn and Mass, and caused a solemn dirge and Mass of Requiem to be chanted for the soul of the Emperor Charles V.

With this period of spiritual anarchy and desolation we shall take our leave of England, passing on to pause for an instant to observe the peculiar *cultus* of the dead in Corsica. It is represented by some writers as being similar to that which prevailed amongst the Romans. But as a traveller remarks, "it is a curious relic of

123

paganism, combined with Christian usages." Thus the dirge sung by women, their wild lamenting, their impassioned apostrophizing of the dead, their rhetorical declamation of his virtues, finds its analogy among many of the customs of pagan nations, while the prayer for the dead, "the relatives standing about the bed of death reciting the Rosary," the Confraternity of the Brothers of the Dead coming to convey the corpse to the church, where Mass is sung and the final absolution given, is eminently Christian and Catholic. In the Norwegian annals we read how Olaf the Saint, on the occasion of one of his battles, gave many marks of silver for the souls of his enemies who should fall in battle.

A traveller in Mexico relates the following: "I remember to have seen," he says, "on the high altar of the dismantled church of Yanhuitlan a skull as polished as ivory, which bore on the forehead the following inscription in Spanish:

'Io soy Jesus Pedro Sandoval; un Ave Maria y un Padre Nuestro, por Dios, hermanos!' [1]

[Footnote 1: Ferdinand Gregorovius, "Wanderings in Corsica," translated by Alexander Muir.]

'I am Jesus Pedro Sandoval; a Hail Mary and an Our Father for the love of God, my brother.'

"I cannot conceive," he continues, "anything more heart-rending than the great silent orbs of this dead man staring me fixedly in the face, whilst his head, bared by contact with the grave, sadly implored my prayers." [1]

[Footnote 1: "Deux Ans au Mexique," Faucher de St. Maurice.]

It would be impossible to conclude our *olla podrida*, if I may venture on the expression, of historical lore, relating to the dead, without referring, however briefly, to the two great deaths, and consequently the magnificent obsequies which have marked this very year of 1885, in which we write. Those of Archbishop Bourget, of Montreal, and of His Eminence, Cardinal McCloskey, of New York. They were both expressions of national sorrow, and the homage paid by sorrowing multitudes to true greatness. On the 10th of June, 1885, the venerable Archbishop Bourget died at Sault-au-Recollet, and was brought on the following morning to the Church of Notre Dame, Montreal. The days that ensued were all days of Requiem. Psalms were sung, and the office of the dead chanted by priests of all the religious orders in succession, by the various choirs of the city, by the secular clergy, and by lay societies. Archbishops and bishops sang high Mass with all the pomp of our holy ritual, and the prayers of the poor for him who had been their benefactor, mingled with those of the highest in the land, and followed the beloved remains from the bed of death whence they were taken down into the funeral vault. On the 10th of October, 1885, His Eminence the Cardinal Archbishop of New York passed peacefully away, amidst the grief of the whole community, both Protestant and Catholic. Again, there was a very ovation of prayer. The obsequies were marked by a splendor such as, according to a contemporary journal, had never before attended any ecclesiastical demonstration on this side of the water. The clergy, secular and religious, formed one vast assemblage, while layman vied with layman in showing honor to the dead, and in

124

praying for the soul's repose. "All that man could do," says a prominent Catholic journal, "to bring honor to his bier was done, and in honor and remembrance his memory remains. All that Mother Church could offer as suffrage for his soul has been offered."

That is wherein the real beauty of it all consists. Honor to the great dead may, it is true, be the splendid expression of national sentiment. But in the eyes of faith it is meaningless. Other great men, deservedly honored by the nations, have passed away during this same year, but where was the prayer, accompanying them to the judgment-seat, assisting them in that other life, repairing their faults, purging away sins or imperfections? The grandeur that attended Mgr. Bourget's burial and Cardinal McCloskey's obsequies consisted chiefly in that vast symphony of prayer, which arose so harmoniously, and during so many days, for their soul's welfare.

Devotion to the dead, as we have seen, exists everywhere, is everywhere dear to the hearts of the people, from those first early worshippers, who, in the dawn of Christianity, in the dimness of the Catacombs prayed for the souls of their brethren in Christ, begging that they might "live in God," that God might refresh them, down through the ages to our own day, increasing as it goes in fervor and intensity. We meet with its records, written boldly, so to say, on the brow of nations, or in out-of-the-way corners, down among the people, in the littleness and obscurity of humble domestic annals. In the earliest liturgies, in the most ancient sacramentaries, there is the prayer for "refreshment, light, and peace," as it is now found in the missals used at the daily sacrifice, on the lips of the priest, in the prayers of the humblest and most unlettered petitioner. It is the "low murmur of the vale," changing, indeed, at times into the thunder on the mountain tops, amazing the unbelieving world which stands aloof and stares, as in the instances but lately quoted, or existing forgotten, and overlooked by them, but no less deep and solemn. It is a *Requiem Æternam* pervading all time, and ceasing only with time itself, when the Eternity of rest for the Church Militant has begun.

PRAYER FOR THE DEAD IN THE ANGLO-SAXON CHURCH.
DR. LINGARD.

The Anglo-Saxons had inherited from their teachers the practice of prayer for the dead—a practice common to every Christian Church which dates its origin from any period before the Reformation. It was not that they pretended to benefit by their prayers the blessed in heaven, or the reprobate in hell; but they had never heard of the doctrine which teaches that "every soul of man, passing out of the body, goeth immediately to one or other of those places" (Book of Homilies. Hom. VII. On Prayer). And therefore assuming that God will render to all according to their works, they believed that the souls of men dying in a state of less perfect virtue, though they might not be immediately admitted to the supreme felicity of the saints, would not, at least, be visited with the everlasting punishment of the wicked. [1] It was for such as these that they prayed, that if they were in a state of imperfect happiness, that happiness might be augmented; if in a state of temporary punishment, the severity of that punishment might be

125

mitigated; and this they hoped to obtain from the mercy of God, in consideration of their prayers, fasts, and alms, and especially of the "oblation of the most Holy Victim in the Sacrifice of the Mass."

[Footnote 1: "Some souls proceed to rest after their departure; some go to punishment for that which they have done, and are often released by alms-deeds, but chiefly through the Mass, if it be offered for them; others are condemned to hell with the devil." (Serm. ad. Pop. in Oct. Pent.) "There be many places of punishment, in which souls suffer in proportion to their guilt before the general judgment, so that some of them are fully cleansed, and have nothing to suffer in that fire of the last day." (Hom. apud. Whelock, p. 386.)]

This was a favorite form of devotion with our ancestors. It came to them recommended by the practice of all antiquity; it was considered an act of the purest charity on behalf of those who could no longer pray for themselves; it enlisted in its favor the feelings of the survivor, who was thus enabled to intercede with God for his nearest and dearest friends, and it opened at the same time to the mourner a source of real consolation in the hour of bereavement and distress. It is true, indeed, that the petitioners knew not the state of the departed soul; he might be incapable of receiving any benefit from their prayers, but they reasoned, with St. Augustine, that, even so, the piety of their intentions would prove acceptable to God. When Alcuin heard that Edilthryde, a noble Saxon lady, lamented most bitterly the death of her son, he wrote to her from his retreat at Tours, in the following terms:—"Mourn not for him whom you cannot recall. If he be of God, instead of grieving that you have lost him, rejoice that he is gone to rest before you. Where there are two friends, I hold the death of the first preferable to that of the second, because the first leaves behind him one whose brotherly love will intercede for him daily, and whose tears will wash away the frailties of his life in this world. Be assured that your pious solicitude for the soul of your son will not be thrown away. It will benefit both you and him—you, because you exercise acts of hope and charity; him, because such acts will tend either to mitigate his sufferings, or to add to his happiness."

[Footnote 1: Ep. Cli Tom. I, p. 212.]

But they did not only pray for others, they were careful to secure for themselves, after their departure, the prayers of their friends. This they frequently solicited as a favor or recompense, and for this they entered into mutual compacts by which the survivor was bound to perform certain works of piety or charity for the soul of the deceased. Thus Beda begs of the monks of Lindisfarne that, at his death, they will offer prayers and Masses for him as one of their own body; thus Alcuin calls upon his former scholars at York to remember him in their prayers when it shall please God to withdraw him from this world; and thus in the multifarious correspondence of St. Boniface, the apostle of Germany, and of Lullus, his successor in the See of Mentz, both of them Anglo-Saxons, with their countrymen, prelates, abbots, thanes, and princes, we meet with letters the only object of which is to renew their previous engagements, and to transmit the names of their defunct associates. It is "our earnest wish," say the King of Kent and the Bishop of Rochester in their common letter to Lullus, "to recommend ourselves and our dearest relatives to your piety, that by your prayers we may be protected till we come to that life which knows no end. For what have we to do on earth but faithfully to exercise charity towards each other? Let us then agree, that when any among us enter the path which leads to another life (may it be a life of happiness), the survivors shall, by their alms and sacrifices, endeavor to assist him in his journey. We have sent you the names of our deceased relations, Irmige, Vorththry, and Dulicha, virgins dedicated to God, and beg that you will remember them in your prayers and oblations. On a similar occasion we will prove our gratitude by imitating your charity."

Such covenants were not confined to the clergy, or to persons in the higher ranks of life. England, at this period, was covered with "gilds," or associations of townsmen and neighbors, not directly for religious purposes, but having a variety of secular objects in view,— such as the promotion of trade and commerce, the preservation of property and the prosecution of thieves, the legal defence of the members against oppression, and the recovery of bots, or penalties, to which they were entitled; but whatever might be their chief object, all imposed one common obligation, that of accompanying the bodies of f the deceased members to the grave, of paying the soul-shot for them at their interment, and of distributing alms for the repose of their souls. As a specimen of such engagements, I may here translate a portion of the laws established in the gild at Abbotsbury. "If," says the legislator, "any one belonging to this association chance to die, each member shall pay one penny for the good of the soul, before the body be laid in the grave. If he neglect, he shall be fined in a triple sum. If any of us fall sick within sixty miles, we engage to find fifteen men, who may bring him home; but if he die first, we will send thirty to convey him to the place in which he desired to be buried. If he die in the neighborhood, the steward shall inquire where he is to be interred, and shall summon as many members as he can to assemble, attend the corpse in an honorable manner, carry it to the minster, and pray devoutly for the soul. Let us act in this manner, and we shall truly perform the duty of our confraternity. This will be honorable to us both before God and man. For we know not who among us may die first; but we believe that, with the assistance of God, this agreement will profit us all if it be rightly observed."

But the clerical and monastic bodies inhabiting the more celebrated monasteries offered guildships of a superior description. Among them the service for the dead was performed with greater solemnity; the rules of the institute insured the faithful performance of the duty; and additional value was ascribed to their prayers on account of the sanctity of the place and the virtue of its inmates. Hence it became an object with many to obtain admission among the brotherhood in quality of honorary associates; an admission which gave them the right to the same spiritual benefits after death to which the professed members were entitled. Such associates were of two classes. To some the favor was conceded on account of their reputation for piety or learning; to others it was due on account of their benefactions. Instances of both abound in the Anglo-Saxon records. Beda, though a monk at Jarrow, procured his name to be entered for this purpose on the bead-roll of the monks at Lindisfarne; and Alcuin, though a canon at Tours, in France, had obtained a similar favor from the monks at Jarrow. It belonged, of right, to the founders of churches, to those who had made to them valuable benefactions, [1] or had rendered to them important services, or had bequeathed to them a yearly rent charge [2] for that purpose.

[Footnote 1: When Osulf, ealdorman, by the grace of God, gave the land at Stanhamstede to Christ Church, he most humbly prayed that he and his wife, Beornthrythe, might be admitted "into the fellowship of God's servants there, and of their lords who had been, and of those who had given lands to the Church."—Cod. Dipl. I. 292. The following is an instance of a rent charge given by Ealburge and Eadwald to Christ Church for themselves, and for Ealred and Ealwyne forty ambres of malt, two hundred loaves, one wey, &c, &c.; "and I, Ealburge," she adds, "command my son Ealwyne, in the name of God, and of all the saints, that he perform this duty in his day, and then command his heirs to perform it as long as Christendom shall endure."]

[Footnote 2: I Monast. Ang. i. 278. A similar regulation is found among the laws of the gild in London. "And ye have ordained respecting every man who has given his 'wed' in our gildships, if he should die, that each gild brother shall give a 'genuine loaf' for his soul, and sing a ditty, or get it sung, within thirty days."—Thorpe's Laws of London Gilds.]

Of all these individuals an exact catalogue was kept; the days of their decease [1] were carefully noted, and on their anniversaries a solemn service of Masses and psalmody was yearly performed. [2] It may be easily conceived that to men of timorous and penitent minds this custom would afford much consolation. However great might be their deficiencies, yet they hoped that their good works would survive them; they had provided for the service of the Almighty a race of men, whose virtues they might in one respect call their own, and who were bound, by the strongest ties, to be their daily advocate at the throne of divine mercy. [3] Such were the sentiments of Alwyn, the caldorman of East Anglia, and one of the founders of Ramsey. Warned by frequent infirmities of his approaching death, he repaired, attended by his sons Edwin and Ethelward, to the abbey. The monks were speedily assembled. "My beloved," said he, "you will soon lose your friend and protector. My strength is gone: I am stolen from myself. But I am not afraid to die. When life grows tedious death is welcome. To-day I shall confess before you the many errors of my life. Think not that I wish to solicit a prolongation of my existence. My request is that you protect my departure by your prayers, and place your merits in the balance against my defects. When my soul shall have quitted my body, honor your father's corpse with a decent funeral, grant him a constant share in your prayers, and recommend his memory to the charity and gratitude of your successors." At the conclusion of his address the aged thane threw himself on the pavement before the altar, and, with a voice interrupted by frequent sighs, publicly confessed the sins of his past years, and earnestly implored the mercies of his Redeemer.... He exhorted the brethren to a punctual observance of their rule, and forbade his sons, under their father's malediction, to molest them in possession of the lands which he had bestowed on the abbey.... Within a few weeks he died, his body was interred with proper solemnity in the Church; and his memory was long cherished with gratitude by the monks of Ramsey. [4]

[Footnote 1: According to Wanly there is in the Cotton Library (Dom. A. 7) of the reign of Athelstan, in which the names of the chief benefactors of the Church of Lindisfarne are written in letters of gold and silver, which catalogue was afterwards continued, but not in the same manner (Wanly, 249). This is probably the same book which was published in 1841 by the Surtees Society, under the name of *Liber Vitæ Ecclesiæ Dunelmensis*. It contains the names of all the benefactors of St. Cuthbert's Church from its foundation, and lay constantly on the altar for upwards of six centuries.]

[Footnote 2: According to Wanly there is in the Cotton Library (Dom. A. 7) of the reign of Athelstan, in which the names of the chief benefactors of the Church of Lindisfarne are written in letters of gold and silver, which catalogue was afterwards continued, but not in the same manner (Wanly, 249). This is probably the same book which was published in 1841 by the Surtees Society, under the name of *Liber Vitæ Ecclesiæ Dunelmensis*. It contains the names of all the benefactors of St. Cuthbert's Church from its foundation, and lay constantly on the altar for upwards of six centuries.]

[Footnote 3: Thus when Leofric established canons in the Church of Exeter, he made them several valuable presents, on condition that, in their prayers and Masses, they should always remember his soul, "that it might be the more pleasing to God." Monas. Ang. tom i. p. 222.]

[Footnote 4: Hist. Rames, p. 427.]

There were three kinds of good works usually performed for the benefit of the dead: One consisted in the distribution of charity. To the money, which the deceased, if he were in opulent or in easy circumstances, bequeathed for that purpose, an addition was often made by the contributions of his relatives and friends. Large sums were often distributed in this manner. King Alfred the Great says in his will: "Let there be given for me, and for my father, and for the friends that he prayed for, and that I pray for, two hundred pounds; fifty among the Mass-priests throughout my kingdom; fifty among the servants of God that are in need, fifty among lay paupers, and fifty to the church in which my body shall rest." [1] Archbishop Wulfred in his will, (an. 831) made provision for the permanent support and clothing of twenty-seven paupers, out of the income from certain manors which, at his own cost and labor, he had recovered for the Church of Canterbury. Frequently the testator bequeathed a yearly dole of money and provisions to the poor on the anniversary of his death. Thus the clergy of Christ-church gave away one hundred and twenty suffles, or cakes of fine flour, on the anniversaries of each of their lords, by which word we are probably to understand archbishops; but Wulfred was not content with his accustomed charity; he augmented it tenfold on his own anniversary, having bequeathed a loaf, a certain quantity of cheese, and a silver penny to be delivered to twelve hundred poor persons on that day. Of such dole some vestiges still remain in certain parts of the kingdom.

[Footnote 1: Cod Diplom (double S?) i. 115.]

Another species of charity, at the death of the upper ranks, was the grant of freedom to a certain number of slaves, whose poverty, to render the gift more valuable, was relieved with a handsome present. In the Council of Calcuith, it was unanimously agreed that each prelate at his death should bequeath the tenth part of his personal property to the poor, and set at liberty all bondmen of English descent, whom the Church had acquired during his administration; and that each bishop and abbot who survived him, should manumit three of his slaves, and give three shillings to each, for the benefit of the soul of the deceased prelate.

The devotions in behalf of the dead consisted in the frequent repetition of the Lord's Prayer, technically called a belt of Paternosters, which was in use with private individuals, ignorant of the Latin tongue; 2d, in the chanting of a certain number of psalms, generally fifty, terminating with the collect for the dead, during which collect all knelt down, and then repeated the anthem in Latin or English: "According to Thy great mercy give rest to his soul, O Lord, and of Thine infinite bounty grant to him eternal light in the company of the saints;" [1] 3d, in the sacrifice of the Mass, which was offered as soon as might be after death, again on the third day, and afterwards as often as was required by the solicitude of the relatives or friends of the deceased. No sooner had St. Wilfred expired than Talbert, to whom he had intrusted the government of his monastery at Ripon, ordered a Mass to be celebrated, and alms to be distributed daily for his soul. On his anniversary the abbots of all the monasteries founded by Wilfred were summoned to attend; they spent the preceding night in watching and prayer, on the following morning a solemn Mass was performed, and then the tenth part of the cattle belonging to the monastery was distributed among the neighboring poor.

[Footnote 1: On the death of St. Guthlade, his sister Pega recommended his soul to God, and sang psalms for that purpose during three days.]

In like manner we find the ealdorman Osulf, "for the redemption and health of his own soul, and of his wife, Beornthrythe," giving certain lands to the Church of Liming, in Kent, under the express condition that "every twelve months afterwards, the day of their departure out of this life should be kept with fasting and prayer to God, in psalmody and the celebration of Masses."

It would appear that some doubt existed with respect to the exact meaning of this condition; and a few years later the archbishop, to set the question at rest, pronounced the following decree: "Wherefore I order that the godly deeds following be performed for their souls at the tide of their anniversary; that every Mass priest celebrate two Masses for the soul of Osulf, and two for Beornthrythe's soul; that every deacon read two passions (the narratives of our Lord's sufferings in the gospels) for his soul, and two for hers; and each of God's servants (the inferior members of the brotherhood) two fifties" (fifty psalms) "for his soul, two for hers; that as you in the world are blessed with worldly goods through them, so they may be blessed with godly goods through you."

It should, however, be observed, that such devotions were not confined to the anniversaries of the dead. In many, perhaps in all, of these religious establishments, the whole community on certain days walked, at the conclusion of the matin service, in procession to the cemetery, and there chanted the dirge over the graves of their deceased brethren and benefactors.

Respecting these practices some most extraordinary opinions have occasionally been hazarded. We have been told that the custom of praying for the dead was no part of the religious system originally taught to the Anglo-Saxons, that it was not generally received for two centuries after their conversion, and that it probably took its rise "from a mistaken charity, continuing to do for the departed what it was only lawful to do for the living." To this supposition it may be sufficient to reply, that it is supported by no reference to ancient authority, but contradicted in every page of Anglo-Saxon history. Others have admitted the universal prevalence of the practice, but have discovered that it originated in the interested views of the clergy, who employed it as a constant source of emolument, and laughed among themselves at the easy faith of their disciples. But this opinion is subject to equal difficulties with the former. It rests on no ancient testimony: it is refuted by the conduct of the ancient clergy. No instance is to be found of any one of these conspirators as they are represented, who in an unguarded moment, or of any false brother who, in the peevishness of discontent, revealed the secret to the ears of their dupes. On the contrary, we see them in their private correspondence holding to each other the same language which they held to their disciples; requesting from each other those prayers which we are told that they mutually despised, and making pecuniary sacrifices during life to purchase what, if their accusers be correct, they deemed an illusory assistence after death.

A SINGULAR FRENCH CUSTOM.

Vernon is perhaps the only town in France wherein the ancient custom of which we are about to speak still exists. When a death occurs, an individual, robed in a mortuary tunic, adorned with cross-bones and tear-drops, goes through the streets with a small bell in either hand, the sound of which is sharp and penetrating; at every place where the streets cross each other, he rings his bells three times, crying out in a doleful voice: "Such-a-one, belonging to the Confraternity of St. Roch, or the Confraternity of St. Sebastian, &c., &c., is recommended to your prayers. He is dead. The funeral will take place at such-an-hour." Then he rings again three times. The first Sunday of each month arrives. Then, at the dawn of day the same individual goes again through the town, ringing continuously, knocking thrice at the door of each member of the confraternity, and stopping at the corners of the streets, he sings: "Good people," or "good souls, who sleep, awake! awake! pray for the dead! &c."—*Voix de la Verité*, July 22, 1846.

131

DEVOTION TO THE HOLY SOULS AMONGST THE EARLY ENGLISH.

ANNA T. SADLIER.

An English writer, the gifted author of the Knights of St. John, makes the following assertion as regards the people of her own nationality: "Our Catholic ancestors," she says, "are said to have been distinguished above all other nations for their devotion towards the dead; and it harmonizes with one feature in our national character, namely, that gravity and attraction to things of solemn and pathetic interest which, uncontrolled by the influence of faith, degenerates even into melancholy." In view of this assertion, it will be interesting to spend a few moments in gathering up the links of this most ancient and most touching devotion, amongst a people who have collectively, as it were, fallen away from grace. It is therefore our purpose to look backwards into that solemn and beautiful past of which heretical England can boast, and behold her, as Carlyle beheld her in his "Past and Present," offering to the world the sublime spectacle of a people devout and faithful, undisturbed by doubt, tranquilized by the harmonious influence of religion, and unharassed by the spirit of so called philosophic inquiry, which, misdirected, is the true bane of English society at the present day.

This retrospection, as we shall have occasion later on to recur to the subject of devotion to the dead in England, must necessarily be both brief and cursory. But even the merest outlines are of interest, for they prove that prayer for the departed was no less the favorite devotion of the learned than of the simple, and that it had its home in those ancient seats of learning, Oxford and Cambridge and their dependencies, from the very hour of their foundation. Of the Founder of Oxford, it is said, that prayer for the dead was one of his devotions of predilection. It is not necessary here for us to follow him, the great and good William of Wykeham, Bishop of Winchester, and subsequently Lord Chancellor of England, in the gradual unfoldings of that project of founding a University, so dear to him from almost the moment of his elevation to the episcopate. Suffice that in the March of 1379, he laid the corner-stone of "St. Marie's College of Winchester, Oxenford." It is with his great charity towards the Holy Souls that we are at present concerned, and of this we have ample proof in the testimonies of his biographers. Here is one of them, in the paragraph which follows:

"There was another devotion which was most dearly cherished by Wykeham, and which is an equal indication of the singular *spirituality* of his mind,—we mean, that for the suffering souls in Purgatory. It may be safely affirmed, that this devotion, so unselfish and unearthly in its tendencies, carrying us beyond the grave, and making us familiar with the secrets of the unseen world, could never find a place in the heart of one who was engrossed by secular cares, or the love of money. Its existence in any marked and special degree argues in the soul of its possessor a profound sense of sin, a deep compassion for the sufferings of others, and a habit of dwelling on the thoughts of death, judgment, and eternity. Moreover, it is utterly opposed to anything of that mercenary or commercial spirit which exists among men of the world, who like to see some large practical result even in matters of devotion. We pray, and are sensible of no return; we spend our money in a Requiem Mass, and there is nothing but trust in God's word, and God's fidelity, to assure us that the money is not thrown away. Every *De Profundis* that we say is as much an act of faith as it is an act of charity; and it has its reward. We do not speak merely of the benefit reaped by the souls of the faithful departed; but who can measure the effect of this devotion on a man's own soul, bringing him (as it does) into communion with the world of spirits, and realizing to him the worth of Christian suffering, and the awful purity of God?"...

Wykeham's heart was full of compassion for suffering, and the dead shared his charity with the living. Never did he offer the Holy Sacrifice for the departed without abundant tears. His reverence for the Holy Mysteries, and the singular devotion with which he celebrated, are often referred to by those who have written his life; one of whom, after speaking of his various charities, thus continues: "Not only did he, as we have said, offer his goods, but also his very self, as a lively sacrifice to God, and hence, in the solemn celebration of Mass, and chiefly at that part where there is made a special memorial of the living and the dead, he was wont to shed many tears out of the humility of his heart, reputing himself unworthy, as he was wont to express it in speaking to his secretary, to perform such an office, or to handle the most sublime mysteries of the Church."

From the same biographer we add to the foregoing a further testimony as to what a hold this devotion of predilection had taken upon the soul of the Founder of Oxford:

"Among his charities we accordingly find a great many which were solely directed to the relief of the suffering souls. Wykeham's benevolence had in it one admirable feature: it was not left to be carried out after his death by his executors, but all his great acts of munificence were performed in his own lifetime. One of his first cares, after his accession to the See of Winchester, was to found a chantry in the Priory of Southwyke, near Wykeham, for the repose of the souls of his father and mother and sister, who were buried within the priory church; and in all his after foundations provisions were made for the continual remembrance of the dead; and (ever grateful to his early friends) King Edward III., the Black Prince, and King Richard II. were all commended to the charity of those who, as they prayed for Wykeham, were charged at the same time to pray for the souls of his benefactors."

In Winchester we read, also, of the College of the Holy Trinity, endowed as a "carnarie," or charnel-house, of the city. The chief duties of the priests belonging to the chantry attached thereto were to bury the dead, and keep up perpetual Masses for the souls of the departed.

Those Colleges of Winchester, with their simple beauty and grandeur of design, with their conventional rule of life, the singing of Matins, and the daily chanting of the divine office by chaplains and fellows, offer to us a very fair picture, indeed. But we observe that in the Masses sung with "note and chant," there is one specially mentioned for the souls of the founder's parents, and of all the faithful departed; a second for the souls of King Edward III., Queen Philippa, the Black Prince, Richard II., Queen Anne, and certain benefactors.

On the 24th of July, 1403, the saintly Wykeham made his will. He directed that his body should be laid in a chantry which he had himself founded, and at the altar of which he was wont to offer up the Holy Sacrifice. He desired that on the day of his burial, "to every poor person coming to Winchester, and asking alms, for the love of God, and for the health of his soul, there should be given fourpence." Alms were likewise to be distributed in every place through which his body was to pass, and large provision was made for Masses and prayers for the repose of his soul. He had, besides, made an agreement with the monks of St. Swithin's, by which they were to offer three Masses daily for his parents and benefactors in the chantry chapel; the first of these was a Mass of Our Lady, to be said very early. The boys attached to the College were, moreover, to sing every night in perpetuity, either the *Salve Regina* or *Ave Regina*, with a *De Profundis* for his soul's repose. So, as the hour of his death drew near, he who had concerned himself through life with the souls of the departed, essayed to make provision for his own. Since that hour when he proceeded to the high altar of Winchester Cathedral, escorted by the Lord Prior of Winchester and the Abbot Hyde, to celebrate his first Pontifical Mass, the same constant memory of the dead had been with him, as when kneeling he prayed aloud for the soul of his predecessor, William de Edyndon, and bade the choir chant the *De Profundis*, while he himself recited the *Fidelium omnium conditor*.

But leaving Oxford and its pious founder, we turn our gaze upon that ancient foundation of Eton, which was to serve as a preparatory school for the new establishment of King's College of Cambridge, which Henry had in contemplation. Henry, in his famous Eton charter, makes mention of his desire that this college shall be, as it were, a memorial of him, and be composed of clerks, "who," he says, "shall pray for our welfare whilst we live, and for our soul when we shall have departed this life." The Pope, Eugenius IV., afterwards granted a plenary indulgence to all who should visit the College Chapel of Our Lady of Eton, after Confession and Communion. Henry having visited the Colleges of Winchester, first met there with William Wayneflete, with whom he was to be united in so warm and beautiful a friendship. The "Master of Winton," as Wayneflete then was, is described as "simple, devout, and full of learning." But a short time after he was removed to Eton, and presently raised to the Provostship. Among many beautiful and pious customs, the memory of the dead was carefully preserved among the Eton scholars, and their verses on All Souls' Day were on the blessedness of those who die in the Lord. But Wayneflete is, of course, chiefly identified with Magdalen College, Oxford, said to be "the finest collegiate building in England," and of which he was the founder. It was, in truth, his dream, and one which he was destined to see realized. Here is neither the place nor time to dwell upon its beauties. The first stone was laid by the venerable Tybarte, its first president. He was buried in the middle of the inner chapel, and upon a cope, preserved among the ancient church vestments, is one upon which is worked the inscription, "*Orate pro anima Magistri Tybarte.*" [1]

[Footnote 1: Pray for the soul of Master Tybarte.]

Among the rules and regulations of this new foundation was one which obliged the president, fellows, and scholars to recite, while dressing, certain prayers in honor of the Blessed Trinity, and a suffrage for the founder. Daily prayers were offered up for the repose of the souls of the founder's father and mother, "those of benefactors of the college, and for all the souls of the faithful departed." These suffrages were to be made by every one, at whatever hour of the day was most convenient.

There were many foundations of Masses attached to this College of Magdalen. Of these daily Masses, offered at the six altars of the chapel, the early "Morrow Mass" was always said in the Arundel Chapel, for the soul of Lord Arundel, the chief benefactor of the institute. Another Mass was to be said every day for "souls of good memory," including, besides the two kings, Henry III. and Edward III., his dear and never forgotten friends, Henry VI., Lord Cromwell, and Sir John Fastolfe, as well as King Edward IV. Other Masses and prayers were said for other intentions. The founder was to be especially remembered every quarter. Every day, after High Mass, one of the demys was to say aloud in the chapel, "*Anima fundatoris nostri Willielmi, et animae omnium fidelium defunctorum, per misericordiam Dei in pace requiescat.*" [1] The same prayer was to be repeated in the hall after dinner and supper.

[Footnote 1: "May the soul of our founder, William, and the souls of all the faithful departed, through the mercy of God, rest in peace."]

But the life of the Founder of Magdalen, the great Bishop, was drawing to a close. We shall see by his will how firm his faith in that most Catholic of all doctrines—Purgatory. After various bequests, he left a certain portion of his property for Masses and alms-deeds for his own soul and the souls of his parents and friends. On the day of his burial, and on the thirtieth day from the time of his decease, and on other appointed days, his executors are charged to have 5,000 Masses said in honor of the Five Wounds of Christ, and the Five Joys of Mary— his favorite devotions—for the same intention. His remains were buried at Winchester, in a tomb which he had prepared as a place of burial during his lifetime. His was, indeed, the third chantry chapel in Winchester, the others being those of his predecessor. This custom was common to all the great prelates of the time. They prepared a place of sepulture during their life, and there where they officiated at all solemn offices, and so frequently celebrated requiems for the departed, they knew that their remains were one day to be laid, and prayers and the Holy Sacrifice of the Mass to be offered for themselves. It was thus a constant reminder of death.

A ceremony connected with Magdalen Tower seems likewise to have had its origin in this pious custom of remembrance of the dead. "On the 1st of May," says Anthony Wood, "the choral ministers of this house do, according to ancient custom, salute Flora from the top of the tower, at four in the morning, with vocal music of several parts." Of course, as a chronicler remarks, it was not to salute

Flora that any Catholic choristers thus made vocal the sweet air of May. "The sweet music of Magdalen Tower," remarks the author of the Knights of St. John, "had a directly religious origin. On the 1st of May the society was wont annually to celebrate the obit or Requiem Mass of King Henry VII., who proved a generous benefactor to the College, and who is still commemorated as such upon that day. The requiem was not, indeed, celebrated *on the top of the tower*, as Mr. Chalmers, in his history of the university, affirms, in total ignorance that a *requiem* is a Mass, and that a Mass must be said upon an altar; but it is probable that the choral service chanted on the 1st of May consisted originally of the *De Profundis*, or some other psalm, for the repose of Henry's soul, and as a special mark of gratitude." Some semblance of the old custom is still kept up, as ten pounds is still annually paid by the rectory of Slimbridge, in Gloucestershire, for the purpose of keeping up this ceremony.

Such are a few brief glimpses of this belief in Purgatory, which was so dear to the hearts of Englishmen, in those centuries before the blight of heresy had fallen upon the Island of the Saints. These hints upon the subject are given very much at random, and will simply serve to show how prayer for the dead was a part of all Christian lives in those ages of faith. It was incorporated in the rules of every collegiate institute, and more especially those two most notable ones of Oxford and Cambridge. It entered into every man's calculations, and was provided for in every Will and Testament. Had it been in our power to go backwards, into a still more remote antiquity, it would have been our pleasant task to find this belief in suffrage for the dead taking so vigorous root in every heart. Do we not find the Venerable Bede, "the Father of English Learning," who was born in 673 and died in 734, asking that his name may be enrolled amongst the monks of the monastery founded by St. Aidan, in order that his soul after death might have a share in the Masses and prayers of that numerous community, as he tells us himself in his Preface to the Life of St. Cuthbert. "This pious anxiety," says Montalembert, "to assure himself of the help of prayer for his soul after death is apparent at every step in his letters. It imprints the last seal of humble and true Christianity on the character of the great philosopher, whose life was so full of interest, and whose last days have been revealed to us in minute detail by an eye-witness." [1]

[Footnote 1: "Monks of the West," Vol v, p 89.]

The passionate entreaties of Anselm, another of the shining lights of early Anglo-Saxon days, that the soul of his young disciple Osbern be remembered in prayers and Masses, proves what value he attached to suffrages for the departed:

"I beg of you," he writes to his friend Gondulph, "of you and of all my friends, to pray for Osbern. His soul is my soul. All that you do for him during my life, I shall accept as if you had done it for me after my death. ... I conjure you for the third time, remember me, and forget not the soul of my well-beloved Osbern. And if I ask too much of you, then forget me and remember him.... The soul of my Osbern, ah! I beseech thee, give it no other place than in my bosom."

And do we not read of those "prayers for souls," incessant and obligatory, which were identified with all the monastic habits—thanks to that devotion for the dead which received in a monastery its final and perpetual sanction. "They were not content," says Montalembert, "even with common and permanent prayer for the dead of each isolated monastery. By degrees, vast spiritual associations were formed among communities of the same order and the same country, with the aim of relieving by their reciprocal prayers the defunct members of each house. Rolls of parchment, transmitted by special messengers from cloister to cloister, received the names of those who had 'emigrated,' according to the consecrated expression, 'from this terrestrial light to Christ,' and served the purpose of a check and register to prevent defalcation in that voluntary impost of prayer which our fervent cenobites solicited in advance for themselves or for their friends." And, of course, this was many years, even centuries, before the Feast of All Souls was instituted by the Abbot Odilo and the monks of Cluny in 998. English history, like every other history, furnishes us, indeed, with innumerable traits of this pious devotion to the Holy Souls. Obviously, our space must prevent us from entering more deeply into the subject. May the few scattered hints we have been enabled to throw out be of interest and profit to our readers!

DOCTRINE OF PURGATORY IN THE EARLY IRISH CHURCH. WALSH. [1]

[Footnote 1: "Ecclesiastical History of Ireland." Rev J. Walsh.]

Coerced by the unvarying as well as unequivocal testimony of our writers, our liturgies, our canons, Usher was obliged to admit that the ancient Irish had been in the constant practice of offering up the eucharistic sacrifice, and that Masses, termed *Requiem Masses*, used to be celebrated daily. So interwoven is the doctrine of the eucharistic sacrifice with the records of the nation, that the antiquarian himself should reject the antiquities of Ireland if he had ventured on the denial of this practice …. Admitting the practice of the ancient Irish Church, Usher strives to escape from the difficulty, as well as attempts to deceive his readers, by pretending that it had been only a sacrifice of thanksgiving, offered as such for those souls who were in possession of eternal happiness, and that it had not been believed or practiced in the ancient Irish Church as a propitiatory sacrifice. …. The ancient canons of the Irish Church as clearly point out as the firmament demonstrates the glory of God, the doctrine of our Church regarding the eucharistic sacrifice, as one of thanksgiving, and also one of propitiation. In an ancient canon contained in D'Achery's collection (lib. 2, cap. 20), the synod says: "The Church offers for the souls of the deceased in four ways—for the very good, the oblations are simply thanksgiving; for the very bad, they become consolations to the living; for such as were not very good, the oblations are made in order to obtain full remission; and for those who were not very bad, that their punishment may be rendered more tolerable." Here, then, is enunciated in plain terms, the doctrine of the eucharistic oblation being a propitiatory sacrifice. When offered for the first class of happy souls, it is an offering of thanksgiving. When offered for those whose lives were bad in the sight of Heaven, its oblation is a comfort to the faithful. When offered for those who were not very good or very bad, the object of its oblation was to render their state more tolerable, and that full pardon would be at length accorded. The framers of this canon give us also the doctrine of a middle state, as a tenet also believed by the Church of Ireland.

Another canon, still more ancient, and which is reckoned among those of St. Patrick, is entitled "Of the Oblation for the Dead." This canon is couched in the following words: "There is a sin unto death, I do not say that for it any do pray." This sin is final impenitence.

The ancient Irish Missal, "the *Cursus Scotorum*" contains an oration for the dead: "Grant, O Lord, to him, Thy servant, deceased, the pardon of all his sins, in that secret abode where there is no longer room for penance. Do Thou, O Christ, receive the soul of Thy servant, which Thou hast given, and forgive him his trespasses more abundantly than he has forgiven those who have trespassed against him." An oration is also given for the living and the dead: "Propitiously grant that this sacred oblation may be profitable to the dead in obtaining pardon, and to the living, in obtaining salvation; grant to them (living and dead) the full remission of all their sins, and that indulgence they have always deserved."

The liturgy usually called *"Cursus Scotorum"* was that which had been first brought to Ireland by St,. Patrick, and was the only one that had been used, until about the close of the sixth century. About this period the Gallican liturgy, *"Cursus Gallorum"* was, it is probable, introduced into Ireland. The *"Cursus Scotorum"* is supposed to have been the liturgy originally drawn up and used by St. Mark the evangelist; it was afterwards followed by St. Gregory Nazianzen, St. Basil, and other Greek Fathers; then by Cassian, Honoratus, St. Cassarius of Aries, St. Lupus of Troyes, and St. Germaine of Auxerre, from whom St. Patrick received it, when setting out on his mission to Ireland. A copy of the *"Cursus Scotorum"* was found by Mabillon, in the ancient monastery of Bobbio, of which St. Columbanus was founder, and which missal that learned writer believes to have been written at least one thousand years before his time. ... It contains two Masses for the dead; one a general Mass, and the other *"Missa Sacerdotis defuncti"* (Mass for a deceased priest).

PRINCE NAPOLEON'S PRAYER.

This prayer, in the handwriting of the Prince Imperial, was found among the papers in his desk at Camden Palace. In publishing it the Morning Post adds: "The elucidation of his character alone justifies the publication of such a sacred document, which will prove to the world how intimately he was penetrated with all the feelings which most become a Christian, and which give higher hopes than are afforded by the pains and merits of this transitory life." The following is a translation: "O God, I give to Thee my heart, but give me faith. Without faith there is no strong prayer, and to pray is a longing of my soul. I pray, not that Thou shouldst take away the obstacles on my path, but that Thou mayst permit me to overcome them. I pray, not that Thou shouldst disarm my enemies, but that Thou shouldst aid me to conquer myself. Hear, O God, my prayer. Preserve to my affection those who are dear to me. Grant them happy days. If Thou only givest on this earth a certain sum of joy, take, O God, my share, and bestow it on the most worthy, and, may the most worthy be my friends. If thou seekest vengeance on man, strike me. Misfortune is converted into happiness by the sweet thought that those whom we love are happy. Happiness is poisoned by the bitter thought: while I rejoice, those whom I love a thousand times better than myself are suffering. For me, O God, no more happiness. Take it from my path. I can only find joy in forgetting the past. *If I forget those who are no more, I shall be forgotten in my turn*, and how sad the thought that makes me say, 'Time effaces all.' The only satisfaction I seek is that which lasts forever, that which is given by a tranquil conscience. O, my God! show me where my duty lies, and give me strength to accomplish it always. Arrived at the term of my life, I shall turn my looks fearlessly to the past. Remember it will not be for me a long remorse. I shall be happy. Grant, O God, that my heart may be penetrated with the conviction that those whom I love and who are dead shall see all my actions. My life shall be worthy of this witness, and my innermost thoughts shall never make them blush."

That single line, "If I forget those who are no more, I shall be forgotten in my turn," is an epitome of what is taught us, and what our own hearts feel in relation to the dead. May the noble young heart that poured forth this beautiful prayer be remembered by Christian charity now that he is amongst the departed!

THE HELPERS OF THE HOLY SOULS. BY LADY GEORGIANA ILLERTON.

It has always seemed to me a particularly interesting subject of thought to trace as far back as possible the origin of great and good works,—to ascertain what were the tendencies or the circumstances which concurred in awakening the first ideas, or giving the first impulses, which have eventually led to results the magnitude of which was little foreseen by those destined to bring them about; how much of natural character, and what peculiar gifts, united with God's grace in the formation of some of those grand developments of religion which have been the joy and the glory of the Church.

What would we not give to know, for instance, at what page, at what sentence, of the volume of the "Lives of the Saints" which St. Ignatius was reading on his sick couch at the Castle of Loyola, the thought came into his mind the ultimate development of which was the foundation of the Society of Jesus? or when the blessed Father Clavers' soul was for the first time moved by a casual mention, perhaps, of the sufferings of the negro race? or the particular disappointment at some Parisian lady going out of town in the midst of her works of charity, or at another being detained at home by the sickness of some relative, which suggested to St. Vincent de Paul the first idea of gathering together a few servant girls from the country, to do with greater regularity, if not more zeal, the visiting amongst the poor which the ladies had undertaken, and thus founding the Order of the Sisters of Charity? I suppose that every one who has done anything worth doing in the course of their lives could call to mind the moment when a book, a sermon, a conversation, a casual word, perhaps,—or, if they have been so favored, a direct inspiration from God in the hour of prayer,—has given the impulse—set fire, as it were, to the train lying ready in their hearts. But long

139

before this decisive time has come, indications have existed, thoughts have arisen, feelings have been awakened, which, like the cloud big as a man's hand, have foreshadowed the deluge of graces and mercies about to inundate their souls.

As an instance of these indications of a particular bias, I was struck with the mention of a childish fancy in the early years of the foundress of the Order of Helpers of the Souls in Purgatory,—a new community, which has sprung up during the last ten years, and has a history well worth relating. To many this fresh manifestation of the spirit of the Church on earth, and of its close affinity with the suffering Church in Purgatory, has come as a wonderful blessing and consolation, and inspired them with a grateful regard for these new oblates and victims of charity to the dead.

About thirty years ago a little girl in the town of N—, in France, had been much struck with the mention of Purgatory. It made a very great impression upon her. She used to picture it to herself as a dark closet, in which a little friend of hers who had lately died was perhaps shut up, whilst she herself was playing in the garden and running after butterflies; and she kept longing to open the door and let her out. This little girl was subsequently educated in one of the Convents of the Sacred Heart, and learnt in that school lessons of self-devotion and ardent zeal for souls which were hereafter to bear fruit. She has retained to this day an enthusiastic affection for the religious teachers of her childhood; and devotion to the Sacred Heart of Jesus is one of the principal devotions of the order she has founded.

The thought which had occurred to her almost in infancy continued to haunt her in another form as she grew older. She kept asking herself," How could I help God? He is our helper: how can we help Him? He gives me everything: how could I give Him everything?" And the answer which grace put into her heart to these oft-repeated questions was always, "By paying the debts of the souls in Purgatory."

The inevitable result of this thought was the desire to have wherewith to pay these debts. For this object the necessity of a perfect life, of a daily sanctification, of an ever-increasing store of merits and satisfactions, was obvious. Hence naturally arose the idea of the community-life, of the practice of the evangelical counsels, and of a meritorious, arduous, self-sacrificing charity towards the poor, in order worthily to pray, to act, and to suffer for the souls in Purgatory—to become, as it were, a co-operator with our Lord, by aiding His designs of mercy towards them, whilst satisfying His justice by voluntary expiation. This lady was not led by one of those startling bereavements which close a person's prospects of earthly happiness, and leave them no object to live for but the hope of winning mercy at God's hands for some dear departed one; or by the terrible anxiety about the state of some beloved soul which forces on the survivor the practice of a continual appeal to His compassionate goodness. Her zeal for the souls in Purgatory was perfectly free from any earthly attachment; it was as disinterested as possible, and sprung up in her heart before she had known what it is to lose a friend or a relative, before she had experienced the keen anguish of bereavement.

140

She was a happy, contented girl, living in a cheerful and comfortable home, beloved by her family, enjoying all innocent pleasures, going occasionally into society, and amusing herself like other young people; devoted, indeed, to good works, and taking the lead in the numerous charities existing in her native town. But this was not to be her eventual mode of life. It was good as far as it went; but she had been chosen for the accomplishment of a special work, and grace was continually urging her to its fulfilment.

On the 1st of November, 1853, Mdlle. —— was hearing vespers with her father and her mother in a church dedicated to Our Lady. Whilst the Blessed Sacrament was being exposed on the altar, she felt a strong internal inspiration prompting her to form an association of prayers and offerings for the dead; but, afraid of being misled by her imagination, she prayed earnestly that God would give her a sign that this was indeed His will. As she was coming out of the church, a friend of hers stopped her in the porch, and of her own accord proposed that they should offer up jointly, during the month set apart for special devotion to the souls in Purgatory, all their prayers and works for their relief. This seemed to her a token that her inspiration had been a true one, and that very evening an association was begun which by this time numbers not less than fifteen thousand members. On the following day, the 2d of November, during her thanksgiving after Communion, Mdlle. —— was strongly impressed with the thought that there existed orders intended to supply every need in the Church militant, but none exclusively devoted to the relief of the suffering portion of the Church, and it appeared to her that she was called upon to fill up this void. This idea seemed at the outset too bold a one. She felt startled, almost alarmed, at its magnitude, and earnestly entreated our Lord to make known to her if such was indeed to be her mission. She begged of Him, by His Five Sacred Wounds, to give her five indications of His will in this respect. Her prayers were heard, and during the course of the years 1854 and 1855 these tokens were successively vouchsafed to her. What she had asked for was, 1st, that the Holy Father should approve of in writing, and give his blessing to, the association of prayers set on foot on All Saints' Day (on the 7th of July, 1854, Pius IX. wrote, with his own hand, at the bottom of the petition presented to him, "*Benedicat vos Deus benedictione perpetua*"— may God bless you with an everlasting blessing); 2d, that a great number of Bishops should approve of this association; 3d, that it should extend rapidly; 4th, that a few pious persons should co- operate in the scheme, and devote themselves to works of charity in behalf of the souls in Purgatory; 5th, that a priest might be met with who had previously formed a similar project.

In the month of July, 1855, Mdlle. —— thought of consulting the Curé d'Ars, whom she had for the first time heard of a little while before. The sanctity of this extraordinary man was beginning to be much spoken of, not only in France, but all over Europe. Pilgrims flocked to the insignificant little town of Ars, seeking the advice and help of the poor *curé*—whose ascetic mode of life, spiritual discernment, heroic virtues, and even miraculous gifts, were gradually becoming known, in spite of the desperate efforts he made to conceal them. We can hardly imagine, when reading his Life, that in the neighboring country of France, and in our own day, a man was actually living that we might have seen and spoken and gone to confession to, the details of whose supernatural existence are like the marvels that we read of in the "Lives of the Saints." Mdlle. —— felt persuaded that this holy priest was the instrument appointed by God to make her acquainted with His will, and earnestly longed in some way or other to communicate with him. She did not think of obtaining leave from her parents to go to Ars. It seemed to her that his answer to her question, after he had considered the subject before God in prayer, would be more unbiassed, and carry greater weight with it, than if she had spoken of it to him herself. She did not wish to be influenced by any human considerations, or to be tempted to say more than, "Such is my thought and desire; does it come from God?" With this view she began a novena, and on the day it ended one of her friends called to tell her she was going to Ars, and to inquire if she could do anything for her. On the 5th of August this friend sent her M. Vianney's answer: "Tell her that she can establish, as soon as she likes, an order for the souls in Purgatory."

The future foundress never had any personal communication with the Curé d'Ars, and yet he always used to say, "I know her." On the 30th of October Mdlle. —— entreated him to pray on All Souls' Day for her intention, and on the 11th of November the Abbé T—, his assistant in his extensive correspondence, wrote to her as follows:

"Your edifying letter reached me at Pont d'Ain, where our worthy Bishop, Monseigneur Chalandon, was preaching a retreat. This seemed expressly arranged by Providence, in order that I should speak to him of you and your pious projects. On my return to Ars, on All Souls' Day, I mentioned your wishes to my holy *curé*, begging him to meditate on the subject in prayer before he gave me an answer. Three or four times since I have put to him the same question, and always received the same answer. 'He thinks that it is God who has inspired you with the thought of a heroic self-devotion, and that you will do well to found an order in behalf of the souls in Purgatory.' Whether the good *curé* speaks in consequence of a divine enlightenment, or whether he only expresses his own opinion and his own wishes, which his tender devotion to the souls in Purgatory would naturally incline in favor of your design, neither I nor any of those most intimately acquainted with him can presume to say. But you can remain certain of two things,—that he quite approves of your vocation to the religious life, and of the foundation of this new order, which he thinks will increase rapidly. This is surely enough to confirm you in your intention, which you will carry into effect whenever and wherever it will please God to open a way to it, and you will then be the faithful instrument of His Divine Providence."

On the 25th of the same month M. Vianney sent a message to Mdlle. —— in answer to a letter in which she had spoken of the obstacles which she foresaw on the part of her family. The Abbé T—— writes:

"If I have not written to you before, it is because you particularly wished to have an answer *after special prayer*. And now here is this much-wished-for answer.

The good *cure* has expressed himself as explicitly as possible. I told him that you were troubled at the thought of a separation from your family more on their account than your own, and also at relinquishing the many charitable works which you carry on in your parish. To my great surprise, he who generally very strongly recommends young people not to act against their parents' wishes, but patiently to await their consent, did not hesitate in advising you to proceed. He says that the tears your parents are now shedding will soon be dried up. Do not, then, be afraid to let your heart burn with the love of Jesus. He will find a way of removing all the obstacles in your path, and of making you an angel of consolation to His holy spouses, the souls in Purgatory. The moon has no light in herself, and only reflects that of the sun. This is truly my case with regard to our saintly priest. I will constantly remind him to pray for you, and will unite my unworthy prayers to his, that, in the terrible struggle in your heart between nature and grace, grace may remain victorious."

When this letter reached Mdlle. ———, the principal difficulty she foresaw was already removed. On the 21st of November, the Feast of the Presentation of the Blessed Virgin, her mother, seeing that her heart was ready to break with the wish and the fear of broaching the subject so painfully interesting to them both, had the pious courage to speak first, and to give her full consent to her child's vocation.

Both mother and daughter were struck some time afterwards at finding in a little prayer-book they had not seen before, called "The Month of November Consecrated to the Souls in Purgatory," the following prayer, appointed to be said on the 21st of November, the very day on which they had made their sacrifice, and uttered for the first time the bitter word *separation.*

"O Holy Spirit! who at divers times has raised up religious orders for the needs of the Church Militant; O Father of Light! full of compassion and zeal for the dead; we implore Thee to raise up also in behalf of the suffering Church a new order, the object of which will be to work day and night for the relief and the deliverance of the souls in Purgatory; whose intentions, invariably dedicated to the dead, will apply to them the merits of all their prayers, fastings, vigils, and good works. Thou alone, Creating Spirit, canst achieve a work which will procure so much glory to God, and for which we shall never cease to sigh and pray."

Other difficulties failed not to arise. Some persons were of opinion that Mdlle. ——— ought to remain in the world for the very sake of the objects she had in view, whereas her whole heart and soul were bent on consecrating herself without any reserve to our Lord. She was warned that her parents, who had never been separated from their children, would suffer terribly if she left them; and finally, her own health began to fail. But whilst the world and the devil were multiplying the obstacles in her way, the venerable Curé d'Ars spared neither advice nor encouragement to support her in her arduous struggle. On the 23d of December his coadjutor writes:

"Divine Providence always acts with sweetness and with power. The consent of your good mother is an important step gained. The good *cure* advises you not to go to Paris until you have some means wherewith to begin your work. You will do well to avail yourself of the interest you possess in your diocese to obtain some aid towards it. The *curé* entirely approves of your becoming a religious. It is quite possible that God may restore your health; and he advises you to make a novena to St. Philomena.

"The very day I received your letter, Monseigneur Chalandon, our worthy Bishop, came to Ars, to call on my holy *curé*. I mentioned you to him. He told me he had written to you. He also says that you must not begin without some means and better health. Pray very hard that God may give you both. I think the souls in Purgatory ought to take this opportunity to prove that they have influence with God. Their interests are at stake in the removal of these obstacles." Mdlle. ⸺ had asked to make this novena conjointly with M. Vianney; and she soon received the following letter:

"It is to-day, the 9th of January, that our much-wished-for novena is to begin. The souls in Purgatory are interested in the re-establishment of your health. I am, you know, but the echo of our good and holy *curé*. Your director gives you excellent advice. You might, indeed, as soon as you have means enough of support for one year, go to Paris for a while, and come back again to forward the work in the same way you are doing now. You say, 'St. Vincent de Paul used to begin his works with nothing.' So he did. But then, as my good *curé* observes, 'St. Vincent de Paul was a great saint!'"

According to M. Vianney's advice, on the 19th of January, 1856, the foundress went to Paris, where she met some persons who had, like her, resolved to devote themselves to the service of the souls in Purgatory; but who were quite at a loss how to proceed, and had no means of support. All sorts of crosses awaited this little band of Helpers of the Holy Souls, for such was the name they had taken. Not only were funds wanting for their establishment, but they did not know where to apply for work, and sufferings of every kind assailed them. Mdlle. ⸺ experienced what always happens to generous souls at the outset of their enterprises, when they have unreservedly devoted themselves to the service of God, and are being tried like gold in the furnace. Blame and neglect became her portion. Nobody thought it worth their while to assist a little band of women, whose heroic project had seemed admirable, indeed, in theory, but was now declared to be impracticable. They were considered as mere enthusiasts; and, indeed, as was said by M. Desgenettes, the venerable Curé of Notre Dame des Victoires, they were truly possessed with the holy folly of the Cross.

Meantime they had to work for their bread, and did work with all their might. But it was not always that work could be obtained; and trials without end beset the infant community, lodged in an attic in the Rue St. Martin. Every day, as they asked their Heavenly Father for their daily bread, they prepared themselves to receive with it their habitual portion of sufferings and privations—a fit noviceship for souls undertaking a work of heroic expiation. Mdlle. ⸺, who, for the first time in her life quitted a home where she had known all the comforts of affluence, had to undergo numberless privations. Illness combined with poverty to heighten their trials. Their Divine Master made them experience the kind of suffering which it was hereafter to be their special vocation to relieve. The Curé d'Ars fully understood the nature of that training, and never offered them any help but that of his advice and prayers. "He does not give you anything," says a letter written on the 16th of March, "but *he* will ask St. Philomena, his heavenly treasurer, to put it into the hearts of those who could assist you to do so." And, indeed, help used to come whenever the distress of the holy society became too urgent. One day the foundress had not a single penny left, and was, to use a common expression, at her wits' end. But, thank God, there is something better than human wits or human ingenuity in such extremities; and that is prayer. The Sister who acted as housekeeper placed her bills before the Superioress, and asked for money to buy food for the day. Mdlle. —— told her to wait a little, and went out, not knowing very well what to do next. She entered a church, threw herself on her knees before the Blessed Sacrament, and prayed long and fervently. As she was coming away she stopped before an image of our Holy Mother, and clasping her hands, exclaimed: "My Blessed Mother, you *must* get me 100 francs to-day. I will take no refusal. You *cannot*, you never do forsake your children." She went straight home, and up the dingy stairs into the little room inhabited by the infant community. The instant she opened the door her eyes fell on a letter lying on the table. She opened it with a beating heart, and found in it a note of 100 francs. There was no name; not a word written on the cover. The postman had just left it, and to this day the donor of this sum, or the place it came from, has not been discovered. Another time eight sous was all that remained in the purse of the associates. They agreed to lay out this money to advantage, and accordingly employed it in purchasing a little statue of St. Joseph, whom they instituted their treasurer. The Saint has fulfilled ever since the trust reposed in him; but he often waits till the very last moment to supply the necessities of his clients. I have seen this little image in their convents. It is, of course, very dear to them.

One day, when no needle-work was to be had, and distress was threatening them, a little girl came to their room, and asked if they had finished the bracelets she had been told to call for. Finding she had mistaken the direction, the child said: "You could have some of that work to do if you liked."

Upon inquiry they found that the employment consisted in threading rows of pearls for foreign exportation; that it was less fatiguing and better paid than needle-work, and proved for some months a valuable resource. On another occasion the sum of 500 francs was required for some pressing necessity. This time the foundress had recourse to our Lady of Victories. Having placed the matter in her hands, she went to call on a person whom she thought might lend her this money, but met with a decided negative. She did not know any one else in Paris to whom she could apply; but on leaving the house she met a gentleman, with whom she had no previous acquaintance, who came up to her and said: "I think you are Mdlle. ——, and that you have a special devotion for the souls in Purgatory. Will you allow me to place this 500 francs at your disposal, and to recommend my intentions to your prayers?" Meanwhile illnesses and trials continued to affect the little community. The Abbé T—— writes from Ars: "Do not ask for miraculous cures. *M. le Curé* complains that St. Philomena sends us too many people." The next letter is full of kind encouragement: "*M. le Curé* only smiles when I tell him all you have to go through, and he bids me repeat the same thing to you, which he desired me to write to a good Sister, devoted to all sorts of good works and suffering cruel persecution. 'Tell her that these crosses are flowers which will soon bear fruit.' You have thought, prayed, taken advice, and thoroughly weighed the sacrifices you will have to make, and you have every reason to believe that in doing this work you are doing God's will. The energy which He alone can give will enable you to accomplish what you have begun."..."*M. le Curé* has said to me several times, in a tone of the strongest conviction, 'Their enterprise cannot fail to succeed; but the foundress will have to experience what anxiety and what labor, what efforts and what sufferings, have to be endured ere such a work can be consolidated; but,' he adds, 'if God is with them, who shall be against them?'"

On the 20th of June the Superioress received another letter from the same good priest:

"I feel deeply affected," he writes, "at the thought of the many and severe trials which beset you. Tell your friend that the holy *curé* bids her not to look back, but obey with courage the sacred call she has received. The souls in Purgatory must be enabled to say of you, 'We have advocates on earth who can feel for us, because they know themselves what it is to suffer.' And mind you go on praying to St. Philomena, and begging of her to obtain for you the means necessary for the accomplishment of your holy projects."

The associates continued to pray, to work, and to suffer with patience and cheerfulness. They received at last some unexpected assistance. New members proposed to join them; but it became then absolutely necessary to hire a house. The Superioress searched in every direction for a suitable one, but without success. It seems as if the words, "there was no room for them," were destined to prove applicable to all religious foundations during their periods of probationary trial. After having exerted herself, and employed others in vain for a long time, the Superioress received a message from a holy man whose prayers she had asked, desiring her to go to a particular part of the town, and to await there some providential indication as to the abode she was seeking. For several hours she paced up and down the streets of that part of Paris, praying interiorly, but totally at a loss where to apply. At last she accidentally turned into the Rue de la Barouillière, and saw a house and garden with a bill upon it indicating that it was to be let or sold. She immediately asked to go over it. All sorts of difficulties, apparently insurmountable ones, stood in the way of the purchase. They were overcome in a strangely unaccountable manner, and the money which had to be paid in advance was actually forthcoming on the appointed day, to the astonishment of all concerned. The history of this negotiation, and the wonderful answers to prayer vouchsafed in the course of it, are very striking; only the more we study the manifestations of God's Providence with regard to works carried on in faith and simple reliance on His assistance, the more *accustomed* we get to these miracles of mercy. The Helpers of the Souls in Purgatory took possession of their new home on the 1st of July, 1856, and not long after began their labors amongst the poor. An act of kindness solicited at their hands towards a sick and destitute neighbor soon after their arrival, was the primary cause of their choosing as their particular line of charity attendance on the sick poor in their own destitute homes by day and by night also. This, together with their prayers, their fasts, and their watches, is the continual sacrifice they offer up for the souls in Purgatory.

* * * * *

Before I go on with the history of the Helpers of the Holy Souls in Purgatory, I must describe to you their house,—No. 16 Rue de la Barouillière,—a very small and inconvenient one at the time of their installation, but which has since been re-modelled according to the wants of the increasing community, and an adjoining one added to it. I have often visited this convent, which soon becomes dear to those who would fain help the many beloved ones removed from their sight, but feel the impotency of their own efforts, their want of holiness, of courage, and of perseverance in this blessed work. The sight of this religious house is very touching; the inscriptions on the walls, which are taken from the Holy Scriptures and the writings of the Saints, all bear reference to the state of departed souls, and our duty towards them; the quiet chapel where the Office for the Dead is daily said, and a number of Masses offered up. The memorials of the saintly Curé d'Ars, whose spirit seems to hover over the place, gives a peculiar character to its aspect. The nuns do not wear the religious dress, but are simply dressed in black, like persons in mourning.

* * * * *

On the 18th of August, 1856, Monseigneur Sibour, the Archbishop of Paris, came to visit and bless the new community. "It is a grain of mustard-seed," he said, "which will become a great tree, and spread its branches far and wide." He approved of all that had been done since the house had been opened, and allowed Mass to be said every day in the chapel as soon as it could be properly fitted up, which was the case on the ensuing 5th of November. On the 8th of the same month the house was solemnly consecrated to the Blessed Virgin; the keys were laid at the feet of her image, and she was entreated to become herself the Superioress of the congregation.

It was on the 27th of December, the feast of the disciple whom Jesus loved, the great apostle of charity, that the foundress and five other Sisters made their first vows. A few days afterwards, Monseigneur Sibour was about to sign a grant of indulgences for the work of the religious; someone standing beside him said, "Monseigneur, the souls in Purgatory are guiding your pen." He smiled, and made haste to write his name. He little thought how soon he would be himself numbered with the dead. It was on the 3d of January, 1857, that his tragical death took place.

* * * * *

147

On the 4th of August, 1859, the holy Curé of Ars died; but he lives in the hearts and in the memories of the community which owes so much to his prayers and his advice. His name is frequently on their lips; often has his intercession obtained for them miraculous cures. Every memorial of him is carefully preserved and venerated.

* * * * *

In the course of the year 1859, on the Feast of St. Benedict, Cardinal Morlot sanctioned the institution of a third order of Helpers of the Souls in Purgatory, and the affiliation to it of honorary members. The ladies of the third order engage to lead a practically Christian life in the world, to perform exactly all their religious duties, and those of their state of life. They promise, in their measure, to suffer, act, and pray for the dead, and offer up their good works, the sacrifices they may be inspired to make, and the devotions prescribed by a simple and easy rule adapted to their condition, for this object.... On the day of the institution of the third order, twenty-eight ladies joined it, received the cross, and made their act of consecration in presence of the Archbishop. The honorary members have been continually and rapidly increasing in number.

* * * * *

The new order has a special devotion to St. Joseph, the great minister of God's mercy to all religious, the particular protector of the souls in Purgatory, the foster-father of Christ's poor, and the helper of the dying. He was himself once in limbo, and knows what it is to wait. It is scarcely necessary to speak of their devotion to the Blessed Virgin, whom they have crowned as the Queen of Purgatory, and invoke under the title of Our Lady of Providence. They specially keep the Feast of the Sacred Heart, those of St. Ignatius and St. Gertrude; but All Souls is of course the day of their most particular devotion. The Holy Sacrament is exposed during the whole time of the Octave.

* * * * *

And now, to use words of Père Blot, of the Society of Jesus: "How consoling a thought it is that as the Holy Souls in Purgatory, in all probability, and according to the opinion of the greatest theologians, know what we do for them, and pray for us, they see these acts of charity; they see these devoted women making themselves the slaves of the poor, and sowing in tears, that they themselves may reap in joy. We cannot also but believe that the prayers of the Holy Souls, and perhaps their influence, contribute to the success of the mission carried on for their sakes and in their name amidst the poor and suffering. Several times when they have been invoked by the community, wonderful cures have been vouchsafed and favors obtained. Instances of this kind have excited the astonishment of physicians, and confirmed a pious belief in the efficacy of those prayers. St. Catherine, of Bologna, used to say, 'When I wish to obtain some favor from the Eternal Father, I invoke the souls in the place of expiation, and charge them with the petition I have to make to Him, and I feel I am heard through their means.' Let us, then, if we feel inspired to do so, ask the prayers of the souls in Purgatory; but, above all things, let us pray for them, and, like these religious, join to our

148

prayers acts of self-denying charity towards the poor. Let us always remember, that to the Eternal Lord of all things everything is present—the future as well as the past. We call Him the King of Ages, because the order of events depends wholly on His will, and nothing in their course or succession can alter or change the effects of that will. He looks upon what is to come as if it were present or already past. In consideration of the prayers, the suffrages, and the good works of the Church, which He foresees, He grants proportionate graces, even as if those prayers and good works had been already offered up.... Amongst the Helpers of the Holy Souls several have made great sacrifices to God in order to obtain mercy for souls long ago called away from this world. We can all imitate their example. 'Oh! if it was not too late!' is the cry of many a heart tortured by anxiety for the fate of some loved one who has died apparently out of the Church, or not in a state of grace. We answer, 'It is never too late. Pray; act; suffer. The Lord foresaw your efforts. The Lord knew what was to come, and may have given to that soul at its last hour some extraordinary graces, which snatched it from destruction, and placed it in safety where your love may still reach it, your prayers relieve, your sacrifices avail.'"

I could not resist closing this letter with these sentences, which have raised the hopes and stimulated the courage of many mourners. I only wish this imperfect sketch of the Order of Helpers of the Holy Souls, and of the nature of their work, might prove a first though feeble step towards the introduction amongst us at some future day of a Sisterhood which, in the words used on his death-bed by Father Faber, the great advocate amongst us of devotion to the Holy Souls in Purgatory, "procures such immense glory to God."

THE MASS IN RELATION TO THE DEAD.
O'BRIEN [1]

[Footnote 1: Rev. John O'Brien, A.M., Prof. of Sacred Liturgy at Mt. St. Mary's, Emmittsburg. "History of the Mass and its Ceremonies in the Eastern and Western Churches."]

The Mass of Requiem is one celebrated in behalf of the dead.... If the body of the deceased be present during its celebration, it enjoys privileges that it otherwise would not, for it cannot be celebrated unless within certain restrictions. Masses of this kind are accustomed to be said in memory of the departed faithful, *first*, when the person dies—or, as the Latin phrase has it, *dies obitus seu deposifionis*, which means any day that intervenes from the day of one's demise to his burial; *secondly*, on the third day after death, in memory of Our Divine Lord's resurrection after three days' interval; *thirdly*, on the seventh day, in memory of the mourning of the Israelites seven days for Joseph (Gen. i. 10); *fourthly*, on the thirtieth day, in memory of Moses and Aaron, whom the Israelites lamented this length of time (Numb. xx.; Deut. xxxiv.); and, finally, at the end of the year, or on the anniversary day itself (Gavant., Thesaur. Rit. 62). This custom also prevails with the Orientals.

During the early days it was entirely at the discretion of every priest whether he said daily a plurality of Masses or not (Gavant., Thesaur. Rit. p. 19). It was quite

149

usual to say two Masses, one of the occurring feast, the other for the benefit of the faithful departed. This practice, however, kept gradually falling into desuetude until the time of Pope Alexander II. (A. D. 1061-1073), when that pontiff decreed that no priest should say more than one Mass on the same day.

* * * * *

Throughout the kingdom of Aragon, in Spain (including Aragon, Valentia, and Catalonia), also in the kingdom of Majorca (a dependency of Aragon), it is allowed each secular priest to say two Masses on the 2d of November, the Commemoration of all the Faithful Departed, and each regular priest three Masses. This privilege is also enjoyed by the Dominicans of the Monastery of St. James at Pampeluna (Benedict XIV., *De Sacrif. Missal Romae, ex. Congr. de Prof. Fide*, an. 1859 editio, p. 139). This grant, it is said, was first made either by Pope Julius or Pope Paul III., and though often asked for afterwards by persons of note, was never granted to any other country, or to any place in Spain except those mentioned. For want of any very recent information upon the subject, I am unable to say how far the privilege extends at the present day. A movement is on foot, however, to petition the Holy See for an extension of this privilege to the Universal Church, in order that as much aid as possible may be given to the suffering souls in Purgatory.

* * * * *

In case of a death occurring (amongst the Armenians) Mass is never omitted. The Armenians say one on the day of burial and one on the seventh, fifteenth, and fortieth after death; also one on the anniversary day. This holy practice of praying for the dead and saying Mass in their behalf is very common throughout the entire East, with schismatics as well as Catholics.

* * * * *

As late as the sixteenth century, a very singular custom prevailed in England— viz.: that of presenting at the altar during a Mass of Requiem all the armor and military equipments of deceased knights and noblemen, as well as their chargers. Dr. Kock (Church of our Fathers, II. 507), tells us that as many as eight horses, fully caparisoned, used to be brought into the church for this purpose at the burial of some of the higher nobility. At the funeral of Henry VII., in Westminster Abbey, after the royal arms had first been presented at the foot of the altar, we are told that Sir Edward Howard rode into Church upon "a goodlie courser," with the arms of England embroidered upon his trappings, and delivered him to the abbots of the monastery (*ibid*). Something similar happened at the Mass of Requiem for the repose of the soul of Lord Bray in A. D. 1557, and at that celebrated for Prince Arthur, son of Henry VII. (*ibid*).

* * * * *

As the priest begins to recite the memento for the dead, he moves his hands slowly before his face, so as to have them united at the words "*in somno pacis*." This gentle motion of the hands is aptly suggestive here of the slow, lingering motion of a soul preparing to leave the body, and the final union of the hands forcibly recalls to mind the laying down of the body in its quiet slumber in the earth. As this prayer is very beautiful, we transcribe it in full. It is thus worded: "Remember, also, O Lord! Thy servants, male and female, who have gone before us with the sign of faith and sleep in the sleep of peace, N. N.; to them, O Lord! and to all who rest in Christ, we beseech Thee to grant a place of refreshment, light, and peace; through the same Christ our Lord. Amen." At the letters N. N. the names of the particular persons to be prayed for among the departed were read out from the diptychs in ancient times. When the priest comes to them now he does not stop, but pauses awhile at "*in, somno pacis*" to make his private memento of those whom he wishes to pray for in particular, in which he is to be guided by the same rules that directed him in making his memento for the living, only that here he cannot pray for the conversion of any one, as he could there, for this solely relates to the dead who are detained in Purgatory. Should the Holy Sacrifice be offered for any soul among the departed which could not be benefited by it, either because of the loss of its eternal salvation or its attainment of the everlasting joys of heaven, theologians commonly teach that in that case the fruit of the Mass would enter the treasury of the Church, and be applied afterwards in such indulgences and the like as Almighty God might suggest to the dispensers of his gift (Suarez, *Disp.*, xxxviii, sec. 8). We beg to direct particular attention here to the expression "sleep of peace." That harsh word *death*, which we now use, was seldom or never heard among the early Christians when talking of their departed brethren. Death to them was nothing else but a sleep until the great day of resurrection, when all would rise up again at the sound of the angel's trumpet; and this bright idea animated their minds and enlivened all their hopes when conversing with their absent friends in prayer. So, too, with the place of interment; it was not called by that hard name that distinguishes it too often now, viz., the *grave-yard*, but was called by the milder term of *cemetery*, which, from its Greek derivation, means a dormitory, or sleeping-place. Nor was the word *bury* employed to signify the consigning the body to the earth. No, this sounded too profane in the ears of the primitive Christians; they rather chose the word *depose*, as suggestive of the treasure that was put away until it pleased God to turn it to better use on the final reckoning day. The old Teutonic expression for cemetery was, to say the least of it, very beautiful. The blessed place was called in this tongue *gottes-acker*—that is, God's field—for the reason that the dead were, so to speak, the seed sown in the ground from which would spring the harvest reaped on the day of general resurrection in the shape of glorified bodies. According to this beautiful notion, the stone which told who the departed person was that lay at rest beneath, was likened to the label that was hung upon a post by the farmer or gardener to tell the passer-by the name of the flower that was deposited beneath. This happy application of the word *sleep* to death runs also through Holy Scripture, where we frequently find such expressions as "He slept with his fathers," "I have slept and I am refreshed," applied from the third Psalm to our Divine Lord's time in the sepulchre; the "sleep of peace," "he was gathered to his fathers," etc.

The prayers of the Orientals for the faithful departed are singularly touching. In the Coptic Liturgy of St. Basil the memento is worded thus: "In like manner, O Lord! remember also all those who have already fallen asleep in the priesthood and amidst the laity; vouchsafe to give rest to their souls in the bosoms of our holy fathers, Abraham, Isaac, and Jacob; bring them into a place of greenness by the waters of comfort, in the paradise of pleasure where grief and misery and sighing are banished, in the brightness of the saints." The Orientals are very much attached to ancient phraseology, and hence their frequent application of "the bosom of Abraham" to that middle state of purification in the next life which we universally designate by the name of Purgatory. In the Syro-Jacobite Liturgy of John Bar Maadan, part of the memento is thus worded: "Reckon them among the number of Thine elect; cover them with the bright cloud of Thy saints; set them with the lambs on Thy right hand, and bring them into Thy habitation." The following extract is taken from the Liturgy of St. Chrysostom, which, as we have said already, all the Catholic and schismatic Greeks of the East follow: "Remember all those that are departed in the hope of the resurrection to eternal life, and give them rest where the light of Thy countenance shines upon them." But of all the Orientals, the place of honor in this respect must be yielded to the Nestorians; for, heretics as they are, too much praise cannot be given them for the singular reverence they show towards their departed brethren. From a work of theirs called the "Sinhados," which Badger quotes in his "Nestorians and their Rituals," we take the following extract: "The service of third day of the dead is kept up, because Christ rose on the third day. On the ninth day, also, there should be a commemoration, and again on the thirtieth day, after the example of the Old Testament, since the people mourned for Moses that length of time. A year after, also, there should be a particular commemoration of the dead, and some of the property of the deceased should be given to the poor in remembrance of him. We say this of believers; for, as to unbelievers, should all the wealth of the world be given to the poor in their behalf, it would profit them nothing." The Armenians call Purgatory by the name *Goyan*—that is, a mansion. The Chaldeans style it *Matthar*, the exact equivalent of our term. By some of the other Oriental Churches it is called *Kavaran*, or place of penance; and *Makraran*, a place of purification (Smith and Dwight, I. p. 169).

We could multiply examples at pleasure to prove that there is no church in the East to which the name of Christian can be given that does not look upon praying for the faithful departed, and offering the Holy Mass for the repose of their souls, as a sacred and solemn obligation. Protestants who would fain believe otherwise, and who not unfrequently record differently in their writings about the Oriental Christians, can verify our statements by referring to any Eastern Liturgy and examining for themselves. We conclude our remarks on this head by a strong argument in point from a very unbiased Anglican minister—the Rev. Dr. John Mason Neale. Speaking of prayers for the dead in his work entitled "A History of the Holy Eastern Church," general introduction, Vol. I. p. 509, this candid-speaking man uses the following language: "I am not now going to prove, what nothing but the blindest prejudice can deny, that the Church, east, west, and south, has, with one consentient and universal voice, even from Apostolic times, prayed in the Holy Eucharist for the departed faithful."

FUNERAL ORATION ON DANIEL O'CONNELL.
REV. THOMAS BURKE, O. P.

["Wisdom conducted the just man through the right ways, and showed him the kingdom of God, made him honorable in his labors, and accomplished his works. She kept him safe from his enemies, and gave him a strong conflict that he might overcome; and in bondage she left him not till she brought him the sceptre of the kingdom, and power against those that oppressed him, and gave him everlasting glory."—Wisdom x. [1]]

[Footnote 1: From the funeral oration preached at Glassaevin Cemetery, in May, 1869, on the occasion of the removal of the remains of the Liberator to their final resting place.]

Nor was Ireland forgotten in the designs of God. Centuries of patient endurance brought at length the dawn of a better day. God's hour came, and it brought with it Ireland's greatest son, Daniel O'Connell. We surround his grave to-day to pay him a last tribute of love, to speak words of praise, of suffrage, and prayer. For two and twenty years has he silently slept in the midst of us. His generation is passing away, and the light of history already dawns upon his grave, and she speaks his name with cold, unimpassioned voice. In this age of ours a few years are as a century of times gone by. Great changes and startling events follow each other in such quick succession that the greatest names are forgotten almost as soon as those who bore them disappear, and the world itself is surprised to find how short-lived is the fame which promised to be immortal. The Church alone is the true shrine of immortality—the temple of fame which perisheth not; and that man only whose name and memory is preserved in her sanctuaries receives on this earth a reflection of that glory which is eternal in heaven. But before the Church will crown any one of her children, she carefully examines his claims to the immortality of her gratitude and praise. She asks, "What has he done for God and for man?" This great question am I come here to answer to-day for him whose tongue, once so eloquent, is now stilled in the silence of the grave, and over whose tomb a grateful country has raised a monument of its ancient faith and a record of its past glories; and I claim for him the need of our gratitude and love, in that he was a man of faith, whom wisdom guided in "the right ways," who loved and sought "the kingdom of God," who was "most honorable in his labors," and who accomplished his "great works;" the liberator of his race, the father of his people, the conqueror in "the undented conflict" of principle, truth and justice....

....Before him stretched, full and broad, the two ways of life, and he must choose between them: the way which led to all that the world prized—wealth, power, distinction, title, glory, and fame; the way of genius, the noble rivalry of intellect, the association with all that was most refined and refining—the way which led up to the council chambers of the nation, to all places of jurisdiction and of honor, to the temples wherein were enshrined historic names and glorious

153

memories, to a share in all blessings of privilege and freedom.... Before him opened another way. No gleam of sunshine illumined this way; it was wet with tears—it was overshadowed by misfortune—*it was pointed out to the young traveller of life by the sign of the cross*, and he who entered it was bidden to leave all hope behind him, for it led through the valley of humiliation, into the heart of a fallen race, and an enslaved and afflicted people. I claim for O'Connell the glory of having chosen this latter path, and this claim no man can gainsay, for it is the argument of the Apostle in favor of the great lawgiver of old—"By faith Moses" denied himself to be the son of Pharoah's daughter.

....Into this way was he led by his love for his religion and his country. He firmly believed in that religion in which He was born. He had that faith which is common to all Catholics, and which is not merely a strong opinion nor even a conviction, but an absolute and most certain knowledge that the Catholic Church is the one and the only true messenger and witness of God upon earth; and that to belong to her communion and to possess her faith is the first and greatest of all endowments and privileges, before which everything else sinks into absolute nothing ... He was Irish of the Irish and Catholic of the Catholic. His love for religion and country was as the breath of his nostrils, the blood of his veins, and when he brought to the service of both the strength of his faith and the power of his genius, with the instinct of a true Irishman, his first thought was to lift up the nation by striking the chains off the National Church. And here again, two ways opened before him. One was a way of danger and of blood, and the history of his country told him that it ever ended in defeat and in great evil.... He saw that the effort to walk in it had swept away the last vestige of Ireland's national legislature and independence. But another path was still open to him, and wisdom pointed it out as "the right way." Another battle-field lay before him on which he could "fight the good fight" and vindicate all the rights of his religion and of his country. The armory was furnished by the inspired Apostle when he said: ... "Having your loins girt about with truth, and having on the breast-plate of justice, and your feet shod with the preparation of the Gospel of Peace, in all things taking the shield of faith.... And take unto you the sword of the Spirit, which is the Word." O'Connell knew well that such weapons in such a hand as his were irresistible— that girt around with the truth and justice of his cause, he was clad in the armor of the Eternal God, that with words of peace and order on his lips, with the strong shield of faith before him and the sword of eloquent speech in his hand, with the war-cry of obedience, principle, and law, no power on earth could resist him, for it is the battle of God, and nothing can resist the Most High.

* * * * *

... He who was the Church's liberator and most true son, was also the first of Ireland's statesmen and patriots. Our people remember well, as their future historian will faithfully record, the many trials borne for them, the many victories gained in their cause, the great life devoted to them by O'Connell. Lying, however, at the foot of the altar, as he is to-day, whilst the Church hallows his grave with prayer and sacrifice, it is more especially as the Catholic Emancipator of his

154

people that we place a garland on his tomb. It is as the child of the Church that we honor him, and recall with tears of sorrow our recollections of the aged man, revered, beloved, whom all the glory of the world's admiration and the nation's love had never lifted up in soul out of the holy atmosphere of Christian humility and simplicity. Obedience to the Church's laws, quick zeal for her honor and the dignity of her worship, a spirit of penance refining whilst it expiated, chastening while it ennobled all that was natural in the man; constant and frequent use of the Church's holy sacraments which shed the halo of grace around his venerated head,—these were the last grand lessons which he left to his people, and thus did the sun of his life set in the glory of Christian holiness.

.... In the triumph of Catholic Emancipation, he pointed out to the Irish people the true secret of their strength, the true way of progress, and the sure road to victory.... Time, which buries in utter oblivion so many names and so many memories, will exalt him in his work. The day has already dawned and is ripening into its perfect noon, when Irishmen of every creed will remember O'Connell, and celebrate him as the common friend, and the greatest benefactor of their country. What man is there, even of those whom our age has called great, whose name, so many years after his death, could summon so many loving hearts around his tomb? We, to-day, are the representatives not only of a nation but of a race.... Where is the land that has not seen the face of our people and heard their voice? And wherever, even to the ends of the earth, an Irishman is found to-day, his spirit and his sympathy are here. The millions of America are with us—the Irish Catholic soldier on India's plains is present amongst us by the magic of love—the Irish sailor standing by the wheel this moment in far-off silent seas, where it is night, and the Southern stars are shining, joins his prayer with ours, and recalls the glorious image and the venerated name of O'Connell. ... He is gone, but his fame shall live forever on the earth, as a lover of God and of His people. Adversities, political and religious, he had many, and like a

"Tower of strength
Which stood full square to all the winds that blew,"

the Hercules of justice and of liberty stood up against them. Time, which touches all things with mellowing hand, has softened the recollections of past contests, and they who once looked upon him as a foe, now only remember the glory of the fight, and the mighty genius of him who stood forth the representative man of his race, and the champion of his people. They acknowledge his greatness, and they join hands with us to weave the garland of his fame.

But far other, higher and holier are the feelings of Irish Catholics all the world over to-day. They recognize in the dust which we are assembled to honor, the powerful arm which promoted them, the eloquent tongue which proclaimed their rights and asserted their freedom, the strong hand which, like that of the Maccabees of old, first struck off their chains and then built up their holy altars. They, mingling the supplication of prayer and the gratitude of suffrage with their tears, recall—oh! with how much love—the memory of him who was a Joseph to

Israel—their tower of strength, their buckler, and their shield—who shed around their homes, their altars, and their graves the sacred light of religious liberty, and the glory of unfettered worship. "His praise is in the Church," and this is the pledge of the immortality of his glory. "A people's voice" may be "the proof and echo of all Human fame," but the voice of the undying Church, is the echo of "everlasting glory," and, when those who surround his grave to-day shall have passed away, all future generations of Irishmen to the end of time will be reminded of his name and glory.

THE INDULGENCE OF PORTIUNCULA.

Towards the middle of the fourth century, four pilgrims from Palestine came to settle in the neighborhood of Assisi, and built a chapel there. Nearly two centuries after, this little chapel passed into the hands of the monks of St. Benedict, who owned some lots, or *portions* of land, in the vicinity, whence came the name of *Portiuncula*, given first to those little plots of ground, and afterwards to the chapel itself. St. Bonaventure says that, later still, it was called "Our Lady of Angels," because the heavenly spirits frequently appeared there.

St. Francis, at the outset of his penitential life, going one day through the fields about Assisi, heard a voice which said to him: "Go, repair my house!" He thought the Lord demanded of him to repair the sanctuaries in which He was worshipped, and, amongst others, the Church of St. Damian, a little way from Assisi, which was falling to decay.

He went to work, therefore, begging in the streets of Assisi, and crying out: "He who giveth me a stone shall have one blessing—he who giveth me two, shall have two."

Meanwhile, Francis often bent his steps towards the little chapel of the Portiuncula, built about half a league from Assisi, in a fertile valley, in the midst of a profound solitude. The place had great charms for him, and he resolved to take up his abode there, but as the little chapel was urgently in need of repair, he undertook to do it, following, as he thought, the orders he had received from Heaven. He made himself a cell in the hollow of a neighboring rock, and there spent several years in great austerities. Some disciples, having joined him, inhabited caverns which they found in the rocks around, and some built themselves cells. This was the origin of the Order of St. Francis. The *Portiuncula*, or Our Lady of Angels, afterwards given to the holy penitent by the Benedictine Abbot of Monte Soubasio, thus became the cradle of the three orders founded by the Seraphic Patriarch, and is unspeakably dear to every child of St. Francis. [1]

[Footnote 1: The little chapel of the Portiuncula is now inclosed beneath the dome of the great basilica of Our Lady of Angels, built to preserve it from the injuries of the weather. It stands there still with its rough, antique walls, in all the prestige of its marvellous past. "I know not what perfume of holy poverty," says a pious author, "exhales from that venerable chapel. The pavement within is literally worn by the knees of the pious faithful, and their repeated and burning kisses have left their imprint on its walls."]

Francis, in the midst of his prodigious austerities, living always in the greatest privation, united, nevertheless, the most tender compassion for men and a marvellous love for poverty. He prayed above all, and with tears and groans, for the conversion of sinners. But one night—it was in October, 1221—Francis being inspired with a greater love and a deeper pity for men who were offending their God and Saviour, shedding torrents of tears, macerating his body, already attenuated by excessive mortifications, hears, all at once, the voice of an Angel commanding him to repair to the chapel of the Portiuncula. Ravished with joy, he rises immediately, and entering with profound respect into the chapel, he falls prostrate on the ground, to adore the majesty of God. He then sees Our Lord Jesus Christ, who appears to him, accompanied by His Holy Mother and a great multitude of Angels, and says to him: "Francis, thou and thy brethren have a great zeal for the salvation of souls; indeed, you have been placed as a torch in the world and as the support of the Church. Ask, then, whatsoever thou wilt for the welfare and consolation of nations, and for My glory."

In the midst of the wonders which ravished him, Francis made this prayer: "Our most holy Father, I beseech Thee, although I am but a miserable sinner, to have the goodness to grant to men, that all those who shall visit this Church may receive a plenary indulgence of all their sins, after having confessed to a priest; and I beseech the Blessed Virgin, Thy Mother, the advocate of mankind, to intercede, that I may obtain this favor."

The merciful Virgin interceded, and Our Lord said to Francis: "What thou dost ask is great, nevertheless thou shalt receive still greater favors. I grant it to thee, but I will that it be ratified on earth by him to whom I have given the power of binding and loosening."

The companions of the Saint overheard this colloquy between Our Lord and St. Francis; they beheld numerous troops of Angels, and a great light that filled the Church, but a respectful fear prevented them from approaching.

Next day Francis set out, accompanied by one of his brethren, and repaired to Perugia, where Pope Honorius III. then was. The Saint, introduced to the Pontiff, repeated the order he had received from Our Lord Jesus Christ Himself, and conjured him not to refuse what the Son of God had been pleased to grant him.

"But," said the Sovereign Pontiff, "thou askest of me something very great, and the Roman Court is not wont to grant such an indulgence." "Most Holy Father," replied Francis, "I ask it not of myself; it is Jesus Christ who sendeth me. I come on His behalf." Wherefore the Pope said publicly three times: *"I will that thou have it."*

The Cardinals made several objections; but Honorius, at length convinced of the will of God, granted most liberally, most gratuitously, and in perpetuity, this indulgence solicited so earnestly, yet with so much humility, *but only during one natural day, from evening till evening, including the night, till sunset on the following day.*

At these words, Francis humbly bowed his head. As he was going away, the Pope demanded of him: "Whither goest thou, simple man? What assurance hast thou of that which thou hast obtained?" "Holy Father," he replied, "thy word is sufficient for me; if this Indulgence be the work of God, He Himself will make it manifest. Let Jesus Christ, His holy Mother and the Angels be in that regard, notary, paper and witness; I ask no other authentic act." Such was the effect of the great confidence he felt in the truth of the apparition.

The Indulgence of the Portiuncula had been two years granted, and still the day when the faithful might gain it was not fixed. Francis waited till Jesus Christ, the first Author of a grace so precious, should determine it.

Meanwhile, one night, when Francis was at prayer in his cell, the tempter suggested to him to diminish his penances: feeling the malice of the demon, he goes into the woods, and rolls himself amongst briers and thorns until he is covered with blood. A great light shines around him, he sees a quantity of white and red roses all about, although it is the month of January, in a very severe winter. God had changed the thorny shrubs into magnificent rose-bushes, which have ever since remained green and without thorns, and covered with red and white roses. [1] Angels, who appeared then in great numbers, said to him: "Francis, hasten to the church; Jesus is there with His holy Mother." At the same moment, he was clothed in a spotless white habit, and having reached the church, after a profound obeisance, he made this prayer: "Our Father, Most Holy Lord of heaven and earth, Saviour of mankind, vouchsafe, through Thy great mercy, to fix the day for the Indulgence Thou hast had the goodness to grant." Our Lord replied that He would have it to be from the evening of the day on which the Apostle St. Peter was bound with chains till the following day. He then ordered Francis to present himself to his vicar, and give him some white and red roses in proof of the truth of the fact, and to bring some of his companions who might bear testimony of what they had heard.

[Footnote 1: "We have received from Rome," says the editor of the "Almanac of the Souls in Purgatory," "some leaves from these miraculous rose-bushes. We will willingly give some to the devout clients of St. Francis."]

The Pope, convinced by proofs so incontestable, confirmed the Indulgence with all its privileges.

The Indulgence of the Portiuncula, was soon known throughout the whole world; and the prodigies which were seen wrought every year at St. Mary of Angels, excited the devotion of the faithful to gain it. Many times there were seen there fifty thousand, and even a hundred thousand persons assembled together from all parts.

Meanwhile, in order to facilitate the means of gaining an Indulgence so admirable, the Sovereign Pontiffs extended it to all the churches of the three Orders of St. Francis, and it may be gained by all the faithful indiscriminately. "Of all Indulgences," said Bourdaloue, "that of the Portiuncula is one of the surest and most authentic that there is in the Church, since it is an Indulgence granted immediately by Jesus Christ, a privilege peculiar to itself, and this Indulgence has spread amongst all Christian people with a marvellous progress of souls, and a sensible increase of piety."

The Indulgence of the Great Pardon has another very special privilege; it is, that it may be gained *totus quotus*—that is to say, as often as one visits a church to which it is attached, and prays for the Sovereign Pontiff; and this privilege may be enjoyed from the 1st of August about two o'clock in the afternoon, till sunset on the following day.

Pope Boniface VIII. said that it is "most pious to gain that Indulgence several times for oneself; for, although by the first gaining of a plenary Indulgence, the penalty be remitted, by seeking to gain it again, one receives an augmentation of grace and of glory that crowns all their good works." Besides, this Indulgence can be applied to the Souls in Purgatory, as it can be also gained for the living by way of satisfaction, provided they be in the state of grace.

It was one day revealed to St. Margaret of Cortona that the Souls in Purgatory eagerly look forward every year to the Feast of Our Lady of Angels, because it is a day of deliverance for a great number of them.

While speaking of the Indulgence of the Portiuncula, we are naturally disposed to say a few words in regard to the grievous outrage recently committed on that place, venerated for more than six hundred years by all Christian nations, and manifestly chosen as the object of divine predilection by all the prodigies there wrought.

The Italian government had unlawfully, and in a sacrilegious manner, possessed itself of the Convent of the Portiuncula; and notwithstanding the protest of all the members of the Order of St. Francis, and the indignation excited by so arbitrary an act in every Catholic heart, those iniquitous men put it up for sale, and actually sold it by public auction. The Minister General of the Franciscan Order, unwilling that this brightest gem of the Franciscan crown should fall into impious hands, resolved to have it purchased for him by a lay person. But how was this to be done, when he had no revenue, often not means enough for necessary expenses? a grave question, truly, for the children of St. Francis, who might have seen themselves bereft of the cradle of their Order, were it not that, at the critical moment, a man of a truly Christian heart came forward and advanced the thirty-four thousand francs, the price to which their precious relic had been raised. Thus, God would not permit that so many memories connected with His servant Francis should be effaced from the earth, although they would still have lived in the hearts of his children, and the Friars Minors are still the owners and possessors of that venerable sanctuary. [1]— *Almanac of the Souls in Purgatory*, 1881.

[Footnote 1: Nevertheless, means must be taken to pay back this sum so seasonably advanced. Hence it is, that at the request of the Minister General of the Franciscans, Father Marie, of Brest, has made a touching appeal to all friends of the Order and of justice, and has opened subscription lists wherever there are children of St. Francis, and there are children of St. Francis all over the world. These lists, with the names of the pious donors, shall be sent to Assisium, to be preserved there in the very sanctuary of the Portiuncula.—ED. AL.]

CATHERINE OF CARDONA.

Catherine of Cardona was born in the very highest rank. She was but eight years old when she lost her father, Raymond of Cardona, who was descended from the kings of Aragon. Catherine had already made herself remarkable by her love of prayer, solitude, and mortification, and by her admirable fidelity to grace she had drawn down upon herself, at an age still so tender, the signal favor of Heaven.

One day, whilst absorbed in prayer in her little oratory, her father appeared to her enveloped in the flames of Purgatory, and, conjuring her to deliver him, he said to her: "Daughter, I shall remain in this fire until thou hast done penance for me." With a heart full of compassion, Catherine promised her father to satisfy the divine justice for him, and the vision disappeared.

From that moment Catherine, rising above the weakness of her age and sex, applied herself to those amazing austerities which have made her a prodigy of penance. To open Heaven to her father, she freely sheds, in bloody scourgings, the first fruits of that virginal blood which is to flow for half a century in innumerable torments. Magnanimous child, she is already the martyr of filial piety, but her tears, her mortifications, her prayers have disarmed the divine justice and discharged the paternal debt. Raymond, resplendent with the glory of the blessed, appears again to his daughter, and addresses her in these words: "God has accepted thy penance, my daughter, and I go to enjoy His glory. By that penance, thou hast become so pleasing to Jesus Christ that He has chosen thee for His spouse. Continue all thy life to immolate thyself as a victim for the salvation of souls; such is His divine will."

With these words, which filled the heart of Catherine with joy unspeakable, he goes to Heaven to sing the mercies of his God, and to intercede with Him, in his turn, for the beloved daughter who was his liberator.

Oh! happy, thrice happy Catherine! Whilst accomplishing an act of filial piety, she gained the title of Spouse of Christ, and secured for herself a powerful intercessor in heaven.—*Almanac of the Souls in Purgatory, 1881.*

The life of the little Catherine was so admirable that we cannot resist the desire of giving some extracts from it here. It will be so much the more appropriate that her whole life was consecrated to the relief of the souls in Purgatory and the salvation of men.

Overwhelmed with the happiness of seeing herself chosen for the spouse of the God of Virgins, Catherine consecrates herself entirely to Him, and promises inviolable fidelity to Him. Rejoiced to belong to the same Spouse as the Agathas and Agnesses, she makes a vow of perpetual virginity, and exclaims in the fullness of her bliss: "Thou alone, mine Adorable Beloved, Thou alone shalt reign over my heart, Thou alone shalt have dominion over it for all eternity!" Then Jesus invisibly places on her finger the marriage ring, and endows with strength her who aspires only to die with Him on the cross.

Catherine, who, after the death of her father, was placed under the care of the Princess of Salerno, a near relative of her mother, leads in the palace of the

160

princess a life no less rigorous than that of the penitents of the desert; but she will have no other witness of it than He by whom she alone desires to be loved. Condemned by her rank to wear rich clothing, she values only the glorious vesture of the soul, which is grace. The hair-cloth that macerates her flesh is her chosen garment. At that age, when people allow themselves to be dazzled by the world, Catherine of Cardona has trampled it beneath her feet, and later on, becoming entirely free from the slavery of the world, she retires to the Capuchin Convent at Naples, and there prepares, by a seclusion of twenty-five years, to give to the great ones of the earth an example of the most sublime virtues. Called by the Princess of Salerno to share her disfavor with the king, she hesitates not to quit her dear solitude, and repairs to Spain, in 1557. Her presence at Valladolid was an eloquent sermon, and produced the happiest fruits in souls. The Princess died at the end of two years; and Philip II., knowing the wisdom of Catherine, kept her at the Court, appointing her as governess to Don Carlos, his son, and the young Don Juan of Austria, afterwards the hero of Lepanto.

In 1562, Our Lord, in a vision, says to Catherine: "Depart from this palace; retire to a solitary cave, where thou mayest more freely apply thyself to prayer and penance." At these words, the soul of Catherine is inundated with joy, and she feels that no worldly obstacle could restrain her. She would fain set out forthwith, but her spiritual guides opposed her doing so. Finally, after many trials, whilst she was in prayer, before the dawn, the crucifix she wore hanging from her neck, suddenly rose into the air, and said: "Follow me!" She followed it to a window on the ground-floor; and although it was fastened with great iron bars, Catherine, without knowing how, found herself in the street. Transported with joy at this new miracle, she flew to the place where the Hermit of Alcada and another priest were waiting to conduct her to the desert. Seeing the heroic virgin, they blessed Him who had thus broken her chains. In order that she might not be recognized they cut off her hair, gave her a hermit's robe, and set out without delay. Arriving at a small hill about four leagues from Roda, Catherine said to her guides: "Here it is that God will have me take up my abode; let us go no farther." After a careful search they discovered amongst thorny hedges difficult to get through, a species of grotto sufficiently deep; but the entrance thereto was so narrow, and the roof so low, that Catherine, who was of medium height and rather full figure, could hardly stand upright in it. The two guides of the holy recluse, taking leave of her, left her some instruments of penance, and three loaves, for all provision. There it was that the daughter of the Duke of Cardona commenced, in 1562, that admirable life which has been the wonder of all succeeding ages.

Teresa, the seraphic Teresa, who lived at that time not far from Catherine's solitude, cried out in a transport of admiration: "Oh! how great must be the love that transported her, since she thought neither of food, nor danger, nor the disgrace her flight might bring upon her; what must be the intoxication of that holy soul, flying thus to the desert, solely engrossed by the desire of enjoying there without obstacle the presence of her Spouse! And how firm must be her resolution to break with the world, since she thus fled from all its pleasures!"

161

St. Teresa adds that Catherine spent more than eight years in this desert cave, that after having exhausted the small provision of three loaves left her by the hermit who had served her as a guide, she had lived solely on roots and wild herbs, but that, after several years, she met with a shepherd, who thenceforward faithfully supplied her with bread, of which she, nevertheless, ate but once in three days. The discipline which she took with a large chain lasted often for an hour and a half, and sometimes two hours. Her hair-cloth was so rough that a woman, returning from a pilgrimage, having asked hospitality of her, told me (it is still St. Teresa who speaks), that feigning sleep, she saw the holy recluse take off her hair-cloth and wipe it clean, for it was full of blood. The warfare she had to sustain against the demons made her suffer still more than her austerities; she told our sisters that they appeared to her, now in the form of great dogs who sprang on her shoulders, and now in that of snakes; but do as they might, they could not make her afraid.

She heard Mass in a convent of the Sisters of Mercy, a quarter of a league distant; sometimes she made the journey on her knees. She wore a tunic of coarse serge, and over that a robe of drugget so fashioned that she was taken for a man.

Nevertheless, the fame of her sanctity soon spread everywhere, and the people conceived so great a veneration for her that they flocked from every side, so that, on certain days, the surrounding country was covered with vehicles full of people going to see her.

"About this time," says St. Teresa, "she was seized with a great desire to found near her cave a monastery of religious, but being undecided in her choice of the order, she postponed for a time the execution of her design. One day while at prayer before a crucifix which she always carried about her, Our Lord showed her a white mantle, and gave her to understand that she was to found a monastery of barefooted Carmelites. She knew not till then that such an order existed, as she had never heard it mentioned; indeed, we had then but two monasteries of reformed Carmelites, that of Moncera and that of Pastrana. Catherine was speedily informed of the existence of this last. As Pastrana belonged to the Princess of Eboli, her former friend, she set out for that town with the firm resolution of doing what Our Lord had enjoined her to do. It was at Pastrana, in the church of our religious, that the Blessed Catherine took the habit of Our Lady of Mount Carmel, having no intention, notwithstanding that act, to embrace the religious life. Our Lord conducted her by another way, and she never felt any attraction towards that state. What kept her away from it was the fear of being obliged through obedience to moderate her austerities and quit her solitude."

As she had worn man's apparel ever since she had been in the desert, she would not now change it. So, in laying aside her hermit's robe, and assuming that of Carmel, she took a habit like that of the barefooted Carmelite monks, and wore it till her last breath. In this Catherine was led by a very special way.

Catherine had been preceded at Pastrana by the account of the wonders which had marked the eight years she had spent in her cave; she was thus greeted as a saint as soon as she appeared; no one was surprised to see her in her Carmelite habit, a cowl on her head, a white mantle on her shoulders, a robe of coarse drugget, and a leathern girdle. God permitted the appearance of Catherine at the court of Philip II. as a virgin with the heart of a man, victorious over all the weakness, of her sex, and rivalling in her austerities the most famous penitents of the desert. At the Escurial, she observed the same abstinence as in her hermitage; there, as in her cave, she took but one hour's sleep, and gave to prayer the rest of the time at her disposal.

From the Escurial, Catherine returned to Madrid. From the carriage in which she rode, she gave her blessing to the multitudes who crowded the road as she passed. … The Nuncio, having sent for her, reproached her for wearing the apparel of a man, and for taking it upon her to give her blessing, like a bishop. The humble virgin heard all prostrate on the ground. When the Nuncio had finished speaking, she arose and justified herself with that holy simplicity peculiar to herself. The legate of the Holy See, perceiving then that God was leading the Blessed Catherine by an extraordinary way, left her at liberty to wear that costume, blessed her, and recommended himself to her prayers.

In Madrid Catherine again met Don Juan of Austria, who had been appointed Generalissimo of the Christian fleet directed against the Turks. He gave her the name of mother, and regarded her as a Saint. After having given some wise counsel to the young prince, she predicted to him that he should obtain a victory over the enemies of the Christian name. It was a happy day in the life of Don Juan on which he heard these prophetic words. Kneeling on the ground, with clasped hands and tearful eyes, the future liberator of Christendom asked Catherine's blessing, and arose with a heart strengthened by an invincible hope.

The Carmelites of Toledo, amongst whom she spent some time, endeavoring to persuade her to diminish her austerities a little, she replied in these memorable words, which reveal to us the secret of her life: "When one has seen, as I have, what Purgatory and Hell are, one cannot do too much to draw souls from one, and preserve them from the other; I may not spare myself, since I have offered myself in sacrifice for them."

On the 7th October, 1571, Catherine was warned by a light from above that the great combat against the Turks was to take place that day. She macerated herself with fearful rigor, and offered herself as a victim to the anger of God, justly indignant at the sins of His people. She addressed to the Saviour of men the most tender supplications, when, all at once, seized with a holy transport, she uttered in a distinct voice these words, which were heard by several persons of the Court: "O Lord, the hour is come, help Thy Church; give the victory to the Catholic chiefs; have pity on so many kingdoms which are Thine own, preserve them from ruin! The wind is against us: my God, if Thou order it not to change, we perish!"

Some time after, she cried out in a still stronger voice: "Blessed be Thou, O Lord, Thou hast changed the wind at the needful moment; finish what Thou hast begun!" After these words she prayed in silence for a long space of time. Then, starting up joyfully, she offered to God the most lively thanksgivings for the victory He had just granted to His Church.

163

Soon, in fact, the news of the victory of Lepanto confirmed the miraculous vision of Catherine. Don Juan wrote immediately to the venerable Catherine of Cardona, thanking her for her prayers, and sent her, as a memento, some spoils taken from the enemy.

Catherine having received, at the Court and elsewhere, sufficient means to found her monastery, regained her solitude in the month of March, 1572. She lived there five years longer. It has been considered as a supernatural thing that mortifications so extraordinary as hers had not ended her life sooner. She died on the 11th of May, 1577.

"One day," says St. Teresa, "after having received communion in the church of this monastery (that which Catherine had founded), I entered into a profound recollection, which was soon followed by an ecstasy. Whilst I was thus ravished out of myself, that holy woman appeared to my intellectual vision, resplendent with light like a glorified body, and surrounded by angels. She said to me: 'Weary not of founding monasteries, but rather pursue that work with ardor.' I understood, albeit that she did not say so, that she was assisting me with God. This apparition left me exceedingly comforted, and inflamed with the desire of working for Our Lord's glory. Hence, I hope from His divine goodness and the powerful prayers of that Saint, that I may be able to do something for His service."

THE EMPEROR NICHOLAS PRAYING FOR HIS MOTHER.

Heretics or Schismatics care very little about contradicting themselves. It is of the nature of the iniquity of lying. The *Anti de la Religion*, of March 1, 1851, judiciously observes:

"It is well known that the Russian Church pretends not to admit the doctrine of Purgatory, which one of its principal prelates set down as '*a crude modern invention.*' Nevertheless, the manifesto recently published by the Emperor Nicholas, on the death of his mother, the Grand Duchess Elizabeth, Duchess of Nassau, concludes with these words: 'We are convinced that all our faithful subjects will unite their prayers with ours, *for the repose of the soul* of the deceased.' How are we to reconcile this request for prayers with the denial of Purgatory, coming as it does from the mouth of the supreme pontiff of the Church of Russia?"—"*Christian Anecdotes.*"

FUNERAL ORATION ON PIUS VI.
REV. ARTHUR O'LEARY, O S F.

Thou hast lifted me up, and cast me down. My days are like a shadow; that declineth, and I am withered like grass; but thou, O Lord, shall, endure forever.—Ps. cii., verses 10, 11, 12.

Yes! O my God! You lift up and you cast down; you humble and you exalt the sons of men. You cut off the breath of princes, and are terrible to the kings of the earth. It is then we know your power, when, by the stroke of death, we feel what we are, that our life is but as a shadow that declineth, a vapor dispersed by the beams of the rising sun, or as the grass which loses at noon the verdure it had acquired from the morning dew. It is a truth of which we, are made sensible upon this mournful occasion, and in this sacred temple, where the trophies of death are displayed, and its image reflected on every side. The mournful accents of the solemn dirge, the sable drapery that lines these walls, the vestments of the ministers of the sacred altar, this artificial darkness which is a figure of the darkness of the grave;— the tapers that blaze around the sanctuary to put us in mind that when our mortal life is extinct, there is an immortal life beyond the grave, in a kingdom of light and bliss reserved for those who walk on earth by the light of the gospel;—that tomb, in which the tiara and the sceptre, the Pontifical dignity, and the power of the temporal prince, are covered over with a funeral shroud,—every object that strikes the eye, and every sound that vibrates on the ear, is an awful memento which reminds us of our approaching dissolution, points out the vanity and nothingness of all earthly grandeur, and convinces, us that in holiness of life, which unites us to God and secures an immortal crown in the enjoyment of the sovereign good, consists the greatness as well as the happiness of man. An awful truth exemplified in many great characters, hurled from the summit of power and grandeur into an abyss of woe, whose unshaken virtue supported them under the severest trials, and whose greatness of soul shone conspicuous in their fall as well as in their elevation. A truth particularly exemplified in His Holiness Pope Pius VI., whose obsequies we are assembled to solemnize on this day—Pius VI. great in prosperity; Pius VI. great in adversity.

When his life is written by an impartial hand, when his contemporaries are dead, when history lays open the hidden and mysterious springs of the events connected with his reign, and posterity erects a tribunal, at which it is to judge, without dread of giving offence, then his virtues and wisdom will appear in their true light, as the symmetry and proportion of those beautiful statues, which are placed in the porticoes or entrance of temples and public edifices, are better discovered, and seen to a greater advantage at a certain distance.

* * * * *

Though His life was spotless, yet as the judgments of God are unsearchable, as there is such a quantity of dross mixed with our purest gold, such chaff with our purest grain, our purest virtues tarnished with so many imperfections, that on appearing in the presence of God, into whose Kingdom the slightest stain is not admitted, who can say, "My soul is pure; I have nothing to answer for?" as in our belief, divine justice may inflict temporary as well as eternal punishments beyond the grave, according to the quality of unexpiated offences, let us perform the sacred rites of our holy religion for the repose of his soul. [1]

[Footnote 1: These extracts are taken from the funeral oration on Pius VI, delivered at St. Patrick's Chapel, Soho, in presence of Monsignore Erskine, Papal Auditor, on the 10th Nov., 1799.]

FROM THE FUNERAL ORATION ON THE REV. ARTHUR. O'LEARY, O.S.F.

REV. MORGAN D'ARCY.

My brethren, as it is God alone, that searcher of hearts, who can truly appreciate the merits of His elect, as it belongs only to the Holy Catholic Church,

165

"*that pillar and ground of truth*," to canonize them, as we know that nothing impure can enter into heaven, and that Moses himself, that great legislator, and peculiar favorite of heaven, was not entirely spotless in the discharge of his ministry, nor exempt from temporal punishment at his death, let us no longer interrupt the awful mysteries and impressive ceremonies of religion, but, uniting, and, as it were, embodying our prayers and fervent supplications, let us offer a holy violence to heaven; while we mingle our tears with the precious blood of the spotless Victim offered in sacrifice on our hallowed altar, let us implore the Father of Mercies, through the merits and passion of His adorable Son, our merciful Redeemer, to purify this His minister, and admit him to a participation of the never-ending joys of the heavenly Jerusalem. May he rest in peace. *Amen.*

DE MORTUIS. OUR DECEASED PRELATES.

[From a Sermon delivered by Most Rev. ARCHBISHOP CORRIGAN, of NEW YORK, at the THIRD PLENARY COUNCIL of BALTIMORE.]

Remember your prelates who have spoken the Word of God to you. Heb. c. xiii. v. 2.

Of the forty-six Fathers who sat in the Second Plenary Council, only sixteen still survive. More than this. During the few years that have since elapsed not only have thirty bishops and archbishops gone to the house of their eternity, but in several instances, their successors, too, have passed away, so that the Solemn Requiem offered this morning for the prelates who have died since the last Council is chanted for forty-two consecrated rulers. For these, "as it is a good and wholesome thought to pray for the dead," we send up our sighs and our prayers in the spirit of fraternal charity, and as a tribute of love and gratitude to our Fathers in the faith who had the burden of the day and the heat, and who now rest from their labors. "Blessed are the dead who die in the Lord. From henceforth now, saith the Spirit,... for their works follow them."

In the commemorative services and solemn supplications offered in this cathedral, the first place, dear brethren, is deservedly due to your own lamented archbishops.... Besides these, memory turns, with fond regret, to a long list of Right Reverend Prelates, who were all present at the late Plenary Council, and who have since, one by one, passed away.... As we repeat each well-known name, hosts of pleasant memories come crowding on the mind just as by-gone scenes are awakened to new life by some sweet strain of once familiar music. Venerable forms loom up again before us with the paternal kindness, the distinguished presence, the winning ways we knew so well of old; and while the vision lasts we seem to hear a still small voice saying: "To-day for me, to- morrow for thee," or the echo of the words spoken by the wise woman of Thecua to the king on his throne: "We all die, and fall down into the earth, like waters that return no more."

"Star differeth from star in glory." The bishops, whose virtues we commemorate, differed in gifts of mind, in habits of thought, in nationality, in early training, in personal experience, in almost everything else but their common faith. This golden bond united them to each other and to us. There was still another point of resemblance and another link that bound them all together—the

166

participation in the divine work of the Good Shepherd which was laid upon them all....

PART IV.
THOUGHTS OF VARIOUS AUTHORS ON PURGATORY.

The fuel justice layeth on,
And mercy blows the coals,
The metal in this furnace wrought
Is men's defiled souls.—SOUTHWELL.

THOUGHTS OF VARIOUS AUTHORS ON PURGATORY.
PURGATORY.
CARDINAL NEWMAN.

Thus we see how, as time went on, the doctrine of Purgatory was brought home to the minds of the faithful as a portion or form of penance due for post-baptismal sin. And thus the apprehension of this doctrine, and the practice of Infant Baptism, would grow into general reception together. Cardinal Fisher gives another reason for Purgatory being then developed out of earlier points of faith. He says: "Faith, whether in Purgatory or in Indulgences, was not so necessary in the Primitive Church as now; for then love so burned that every one was ready to meet death for Christ. Crimes were rare; and such as occurred were avenged by the great severity of the Canons.... The doctrine of post-baptismal sin, especially when realized in the doctrine of Purgatory, leads the inquirer to fresh developments beyond itself. Its effect is to convert a Scripture statement, which might seem only of temporary application, into a universal and perpetual truth. When St. Paul and St. Barnabas would 'confirm the souls of the disciples,' they taught them 'that we must, through much tribulation, enter into the kingdom of God.' It is obvious what very practical results would follow on such an announcement in the instance of those who accepted the apostolic decision; and, in like manner, a conviction that sin must have its punishment, here or hereafter, and that we all must suffer, how overpowering will be its effect, what a new light does it cast on the history of the soul, what a change does it make in our judgment of the external world, what a reversal of our natural wishes and aims for the future! Is a doctrine conceivable which would so elevate the mind above this present state, and teach it so successfully to dare difficult things, and to be reckless of danger and pain? He who believes that suffer he must, and that delayed punishment may be the greater, will be above the world, will admire nothing, fear nothing, desire nothing. He has within his breast a source of greatness, self-denial, heroism. This is the secret spring of strenuous efforts and persevering toil; of the sacrifice of fortune, friends, ease, reputation, happiness. There is, it is true, a higher class of motives which will be felt by the Saints; who will do from love what all Christians who act acceptably do from faith. And, moreover, the ordinary measures of charity which Christians possess suffice for securing such respectable attention to religious duties as the routine necessities of the Church require. But, if we would raise an army of devoted men to resist the world, to oppose sin and error, to relieve misery, or to propagate truth, we must

167

be provided with motives which keenly affect the many. Christian love is too rare a gift, philanthropy is too weak a material, for that occasion. Nor is there an influence to be found to suit our purpose besides this solemn conviction, which arises out of the very rudiments of Christian theology, and is taught by its most ancient masters,—this sense of the awfulness of post-baptismal sin. It is in vain to look out for missionaries for China or Africa, or evangelists for our great towns, or Christian attendants on the sick, or teachers of the ignorant, on such a scale of numbers as the need requires, without the doctrine of Purgatory. For thus the sins of youth are turned to account by the profitable penance of manhood; and terrors, which the philosopher scorns in the individual, become the benefactors, and earn the gratitude of nations."—*Essay on the Development of Christian Doctrine*, [1] p. 386.

[Footnote 1: Nevertheless, means must be taken to pay back this sum so seasonably advanced. Hence it is, that at the request of the Minister General of the Franciscans, Father Marie, of Brest, has made a touching appeal to all.]

OUR DEBT TO THE DEAD.
CARDINAL MANNING

The Saints, by their intercession and their patronage, unite us with God. They watch over us; they pray for us; they obtain graces for us. Our guardian angels are round about us: they watch over and protect us. The man who has not piety enough to ask their prayers must have a heart but little like to the love and veneration of the Sacred Heart of Jesus. But there are other friends of God to whom we owe a debt of piety. They are those who are suffering beyond the grave, in the silent kingdom of pain and expiation—in the dark and yet blessed realm of purification; that is to say, the multitudes who pass out of this world, washed in the Precious Blood, perfectly absolved of all guilt of sin, children and friends of God, blessed souls, heirs of the kingdom of Heaven, all but Saints; nevertheless, they are not yet altogether purified for His kingdom. They are there detained— kept back from His presence—until their expiation is accomplished. You and I, and every one of us, will pass through that place of expiation. Neither you nor I are Saints, nor, upon earth, ever will be; therefore, before we can see God, we must be purified by pain in that silent realm. But those blessed souls are friends of God next after His Saints; and in the same order they ought to be the objects of our piety; that is, of our love and compassion, of our sympathy and our prayers. They can do nothing now for themselves: they have no longer any Sacraments; they do not even pray for themselves. They are so conformed to the will of God that they suffer there in submission and in silence. They desire nothing except that His will should be accomplished. Therefore, it is our duty to help them—to help them by our prayers, our penances, our mortifications, our alms, by the Holy Sacrifice of the Altar. There may be father and mother, brother and sister, friend and child, whom you have loved as your own life: they may now be there. Have you forgotten them? Have you no pity for them now, no natural piety, no spirit of love for them? Do you forget them all the day long? Look back upon those who made your home in your early childhood, the light of whose faces you can still see shining in your memories, and the sweetness of whose voice is still in your ears—do you forget them because they are no longer seen? Is it, indeed, "out of sight, out of mind"? What an impiety of heart is this!

The Catholic Church, the true mother of souls, cherishes, with loving memory, all her departed. Never does a day pass but she prays for them at the altar; never does a year go by that there is not a special commemoration of all her children departed on one solemn day, which is neither feast nor fast, but a day of the profoundest piety and of the deepest compassion. Surely, then, if we have the spirit of piety in our hearts, the holy souls will be a special object of our remembrance and our prayers. How many now are there whom we have known in life? There are those who have been grievously afflicted, and those who have been very sinful, but, through the Precious Blood and a death-bed repentance, have been saved at last. Have you forgotten them? Are you doing nothing for them? There may also be souls there for whom there is no one to pray on earth; there may be souls who are utterly forgotten by their own kindred, outcast from all remembrance; and yet the Precious Blood was shed for their sakes. If no one remember, them now, you, at least, if you have in your hearts the gift of piety, will pray for them.—*Internal Mission of the Holy Ghost, p.* 247.

PURGATORY
CARDINAL WISEMAN.

I need hardly observe, that there is not a single liturgy existing, whether we consider the most ancient period of the Church, or the most distant part of the world, in which this doctrine is not laid down. In all Oriental liturgies, we find parts appointed, in which the Priest or Bishop is ordered to pray for the souls of the faithful departed; and tables were anciently kept in the churches, called the *Dyptichs,* on which the names of the deceased were enrolled, that they might be remembered in the Sacrifice of the Mass and the prayers of the faithful. The name of Purgatory scarcely requires a passing comment. It has, indeed, been made a topic of abuse, on the ground that it is not to be found in Scripture. But where is the word Trinity to be met with? Where is the word *Incarnation* to be read in Scripture? Where are many other terms, held most sacred and important in the Christian religion? The doctrines are, indeed, found there; but these names were not given, until circumstances had rendered them necessary. We see that the Fathers of the Church have called it a purging fire—a place of expiation or purgation. The idea is precisely, the name almost, the same.

It has been said by divines of the English Church, that the two doctrines which I have joined together, of prayers for the dead and Purgatory, have no necessary connection, and that, in fact, they were not united in the ancient Church. The answer to this assertion I leave to your memories, after the passages which I have read you from the Fathers. They surely speak of purgation by fire after death, whereby the imperfections of this life are washed out, and satisfaction made to God for sins not sufficiently expiated; they speak, at the same time, of our prayers being beneficial to those who have departed this life in a state of sin; and these propositions contain our entire doctrine on Purgatory. It has also been urged that the established religion, or Protestantism, does not deny or discourage prayers for the dead, so long as they are independent of a belief in Purgatory; and, in this respect, it is stated to agree with the primitive Christian Church. But, my brethren, this distinction is exceedingly fallacious. Religion is a lively, practical profession; it is to be ascertained and judged by its sanctioned practices and outward demonstration, rather than by the mere opinions of the few. I would at once fairly appeal to the judgment of any Protestant, whether he has been taught, and has understood that such is the doctrine of his Church. If, from the services which he attended, or the Catechism which he has learned, or the discourses heard, he has been led to suppose that praying for the dead, in terms however general, was noways a peculiarity of Catholicism, but as much a permitted practice of Protestantism. It is a practical doctrine in the Catholic Church, it has an influence highly consoling to humanity, and eminently worthy of a religion that came down from heaven to second all the purest feelings of the heart. Nature herself seems to revolt at the idea that the chain of attachment which binds us together in life, can be rudely snapped asunder by the hand of death, conquered and deprived of its sting since the victory of the cross. But it is not to the spoil of mortality, cold and disfigured, that she clings with affection. It is but an earthly and almost unchristian grief, which sobs when the grave closes over the bier of a departed loved one: but the soul flies upward to a more spiritual affection, and refuses to surrender the hold which it had upon the love and interest of the spirit that has fled. Cold and dark as the sepulchral vault is the belief that sympathy is at an end when the body is shrouded in decay, and that no further interchange of friendly offices may take place between those who have lain down to sleep in peace and us, who for awhile strew fading flowers upon their tomb. But sweet is the consolation to the dying man, who, conscious of imperfection, believes that even after his own time of merit is expired, there are others to make intercession on his behalf; soothing to the afflicted survivors the thought, that instead of unavailing tears they possess more powerful means of actively relieving their friend, and testifying their affectionate regret, by prayer and supplication. In the first moments of grief, this sentiment will often overpower religious prejudice, cast down the unbeliever on his knees beside the remains of his friend, and snatch from him an unconscious prayer for rest; it is an impulse of nature, which for the moment, aided by the analogies of revealed truth, seizes at once upon this consoling belief. But it is only like the flitting and melancholy light which sometimes plays as a meteor over the corpses of the dead; while the Catholic feeling, cheering, though with solemn dimness, resembles the unfailing lamp which the piety of the ancients is said to have hung before the sepulchres of their dead. It prolongs the tenderest affections beyond the gloom of the grave, and it infuses the inspiring hope that the assistance which we on earth can afford to our suffering brethren, will be amply repaid when they have reached their place of rest, and make of them friends, who, when *we* in our turns fail, shall receive us into everlasting mansions. [1]

[Footnote 1: "Lectures on the Catholic Church," often called the "Moorfield

Lectures," from being delivered in St. Mary's Moorfields, in the Lent of 1836. Vol. I., Lecture xi, pp 65,68. This lecture upon Purgatory is an admirable exposition of the Catholic doctrine, supported by numberless testimonies from the Fathers.]

REPLY TO SOME MISSTATEMENTS ABOUT PURGATORY. ARCHBISHOP SPALDING, OF BALTIMORE.

"The Synod of Florence," says this writer, [1] "was the first which taught the doctrine of Purgatory, as an article of faith. It had, indeed, been held by the Pope and by many writers, and it became the popular doctrine during the period under review; but it was not decreed by any authority of the universal, or even the whole Latin Church. In the Eastern Church it was always rejected."

[Footnote 1: Rev. Wm. A. Palmer of Worcester College, Oxford, in his "Compendium of Ecclesiastical History."]

Even admitting, for the sake of argument, that the Council of Florence was the first which defined this doctrine as an article of faith, would it thence follow that the doctrine itself was of recent origin? It could only be inferred that it was never before questioned, and that, therefore, there was no need of any definition on the subject. Would it follow from the fact, that the Council of Nice was the first general synod which defined the doctrine of the consubstantiality of the Son with the Father, that this, too, was a new doctrine, unknown to the three previous centuries? Mr. Palmer himself admits that this tenet of Purgatory "had become the popular doctrine during the period under review;" which, in connection with the solemn promises of Christ to guard His Church from error, clearly proves that it was an article of divine revelation,—on the principles even of our Oxford divine!

It is not true that "it was always rejected in the Eastern Church." The Greek Church admitted it in the Council of Florence and, at least, impliedly, in that of Lyons. It had never been a bar to union between the churches, however their theologians may have differed on the secondary question, whether the souls detained in this middle place of temporary expiation are purified by a material fire. "The ancient Fathers, both of the Greek and Latin Church, who had occasion to refer to the subject, had unanimously agreed in maintaining the doctrine, as could be easily shown by reference to their works. All the ancient liturgies of both Churches had embodied this same article of faith. And even at present, not only the Greek Church, but all the Oriental sectaries still hold it as doctrine, and practice accordingly."

COUNT DE MAISTRE ON PURGATORY.

You have heard, in countries separated from the Roman Church, the *doctors of the law* deny at once Hell and Purgatory. You might well have taken the denial of a word for that of a thing. An enormous power is that of words! The minister who would be angry at that of Purgatory will readily grant us a *place of expiation*, or an *intermediate state*, or perhaps even *stations*, who knows? without thinking it in the least ridiculous. One of the great motives of the sixteenth century revolt was precisely *Purgatory*. The insurgents would have nothing less than Hell, pure and simple. Nevertheless, when they became philosophers, they set about denying the

171

eternity of punishment, allowing, nevertheless, a *hell for a time*, only through good policy and for fear of putting into heaven at one stroke Nero and Messalina side by side with St. Louis and St. Teresa. But a temporary hell is nothing else than Purgatory; so that having broken with us because they did not want Purgatory, they broke with us anew because they wanted Purgatory only.

WHAT THE SAINTS THOUGHT OF PURGATORY.

In the Special Announcement of the "Messenger of St. Joseph's Union" for 1885-6, we find the following interesting remarks in relation to the devotion to the Souls in Purgatory: "St. Gregory the Great, speaking of Purgatory, calls it 'a penitential fire harder to endure than all the tribulations of this world.' St. Augustine says that the torment of fire alone endured by the holy souls in Purgatory, exceeds all the tortures inflicted on the martyrs; and St. Thomas says that there is no difference between the fire of Hell and that of Purgatory. Prayer for the souls in Purgatory is a source of great blessings to ourselves. It is related of a holy religious who had for a long time struggled in vain to free himself from an impure temptation, and who appealed earnestly to the Blessed Virgin to deliver him, that she appeared to him and commanded him to pray earnestly for the souls in Purgatory. He did so, and from that time the temptation left him. The duration of the period of confinement in Purgatory is probably much longer than we are inclined to think. We find by the Revelations of Sister Francesca of Pampeluna that the majority of souls in Purgatory with whose sufferings she was made acquainted, were detained there for a period extending from thirty to sixty years; and, as many of those of whom she speaks were holy Carmelites, some of whom had even wrought miracles when on earth, what must be the fate of poor worldlings who seldom think of gaining an indulgence either for themselves or their departed friends and relatives? Father Faber commenting on this subject— the length of time that the holy souls are detained in Purgatory—says very justly: 'We are apt to leave off too soon praying for our parents, friends, or relatives, imagining with a foolish and unenlightened esteem for the holiness of their lives, that they are freed from Purgatory much sooner than they really are.' Can the holy souls in Purgatory assist us by their prayers? Most assuredly. St. Liguori says: 'Though the souls in Purgatory are unable to pray or merit for themselves, they can obtain by prayer many favors for those who pray for them on earth.' St. Catherine of Bologna has assured us that she obtained many favors by the prayers of the holy souls in Purgatory which she had asked in vain through the intercession of the saints. The Holy Ghost says: 'He who stoppeth his ear against the cry of the poor, shall also cry himself and shall not be heard,' and St. Vincent Ferrer says, in expounding that passage, that the holy souls in Purgatory cry to God for justice against those who on earth refuse to help them by their prayers, and that God will most assuredly hear their cry. Let us, therefore, do all in our power to relieve the holy souls in Purgatory, and avert from ourselves the punishment that God is sure to inflict on those whose faith is too dead, or whose hearts are too cold to heed the cry that rises, day and night, from that sea of fire: 'Have pity on me, have pity on me, at least you my friends!'" Job xix. 21.

PURGATORY.
CHATEAUBRIAND.

That the doctrine of Purgatory opens to the Christian poet a source of the marvellous which was unknown to antiquity will be readily admitted. [1] Nothing, perhaps, is more favorable to the inspiration of the muse than this middle state of expiation between the region of bliss and that of pain, suggesting the idea of a confused mixture of happiness and of suffering. The graduation of the punishments inflicted on those souls that are more or less happy, more or less brilliant, according to their degree of proximity to an eternity of joy or of woe, affords an impressive subject for poetic description. In this respect, it surpasses the subjects of heaven and hell, because it possesses a future which they do not.

[Footnote 1: Some trace of this dogma is to be found in Plato and in the doctrine of Zeno. (See Diog. Laer.) The poets also appear to have had some idea of it (Æneid, v. vi), but these notions are all vague and inconsequent.]

The river Lethe was a graceful appendage of the ancient Elysium; but it cannot be said that the shades which came to life again on its banks exhibited the same poetical progress in the way to happiness that we behold in the souls of Purgatory. When they left the abodes of bliss to reappear among men, they passed from a perfect to an imperfect state. They re-entered the ring for the fight. They were born again to undergo a second death. In short, they came forth to see what they had already seen before. Whatever can be measured by the human mind is necessarily circumscribed. We may admit, indeed, that there was something striking and true in the circle by which the ancients symbolized eternity; but it seems to us that it fetters the imagination by confining it always within a dreaded enclosure. The straight line extended *ad infinitum* would, perhaps, be more expressive, because it would carry our thoughts into a world of undefined realities, and would bring together three things which appear to exclude each other—hope, mobility, eternity.

The apportionment of the punishment to the sin is another source of invention which is found in the purgatorial state, and is highly favorable to the sentimental.... If violent winds, raging fires, and icy cold, lend their influence to the torments of hell, why may not milder sufferings be derived from the song of the nightingale, from the fragrance of flowers, from the murmur of the brook, or from the moral affections themselves? Homer and Ossian tell us of the joy of grief *aruerou tetarpo mesthagolo.*

Poetry finds its advantage also in that doctrine of Purgatory which teaches us that the prayers and other good works of the faithful may obtain the deliverance of souls from their temporal pains. How admirable is this intercourse between the living son and the deceased father—between the mother and daughter—between husband and wife— between life and death. What affecting considerations are suggested by this tenet of religion! My virtue, insignificant being as I am, becomes the common property of Christians; and, as I participate in the guilt of Adam, so also the good that I possess passes to the good of others. Christian poets! the prayers of your Nisus will be felt, in their happy effects, by some Euryalus beyond the grave. The rich, whose charity you describe, may well share their abundance with the poor, for the pleasure which they take in performing this simple and grateful act will receive its regard from the Almighty in the release of their parents from the expiatory flame. What a beautiful feature in our religion to impel the heart of man to virtue by the power of love, and to make him feel that the very coin which gives bread for the moment to an indigent fellow-being, entitles, perhaps, some rescued soul to an eternal position at the table of the Lord. [1]

[Footnote 1: "Genius of Christianity." Book II., Chap. xv. pp. 338- 340.]

MARY AND THE FAITHFUL DEPARTED.

BY BROTHER AZARIAS.

Mary, from her nearness to Jesus, has imbibed many traits of the Sacred Heart of Jesus. She shares, in a preeminent degree, His Divine compassion for sorrow and suffering. Where He loves and pities, she also loves and pities. Nay, may we not well say that all enduring anguish of soul and writhing under the pangs of a lacerated heart, are especially dear to both Jesus and Mary? Was not Jesus the Man of Sorrows? and did He not constitute Mary the Mother of suffering and sorrowing humanity? And even as His Divine breast knew keenest sorrow, did not a sword of sorrow pierce her soul? She participated in the agony of Jesus only as such a Mother can share the agony of such a Son; in the tenderest manner, therefore, does she commiserate sorrow and suffering wherever found. Though now far beyond all touch of pain and misery, still as the devoted Mother of a pain-stricken race, she continues to watch, to shield, to aid and to strengthen her children in their wrestlings with these mysterious visitants.

II.

Nor does Mary's interest cease upon this side of the grave. It accompanies souls beyond. And when she beholds those souls undergoing their final purgation, before entering upon the enjoyment of the beatific vision, she pities them with a pity all the more heartfelt because their suffering is so much greater than any they could have endured in this life. See the state of those souls. They are in grace and favor with God; they are burning with love for Him; they are yearning, with a yearning boundless in its intensity, to drink refreshment of life, and love, and sanctification, and to be replenished with goodness and truth, and to perfect their natures at the Fountain-head of all truth, all goodness, all love, and all perfection. They are yearning; but so clearly and piercingly does the white light of God's truth and God's holiness shine through them and penetrate every fold and recess of their moral natures, and reveal to them every slightest imperfection, that they dare not approach Him and gratify their intense desire to be united with Him. Their weaknesses and imperfections; the traces in them of, and the attachments in them to, former sins, incident upon the frailties of feeble human nature, still cling to them, and must needs be consumed in the fiery ordeal of suffering before their enjoyment of the beatific vision can be completed and their union with the Godhead consummated.

III.

That there should be for souls after death such a state of purgation is all within the grasp of human reason. It is a doctrine that was taught in the remotest ages of the world. Here is a condensed version of the tradition as handed down in clearest terms, beautifully expressed by one of the world's greatest thinkers and writers: "All things are distinctly manifest in the soul after it has been divested of the body; and this is true both of the natural disposition of the soul and of the affections that the man has acquired from his various pursuits. When therefore the soul comes before the Judge ... the Judge finds all things distorted through pride and falsehood and whatsoever is unrighteous, for as much as the soul has been nurtured with untruth ... and he forthwith sends it to a prison state where it will undergo the punishment it deserves. But it behooveth that he that is punished, if he be justly punished, either become better and receive benefit from his punishment, or become a warning to others.... *But whoso are benefited ... are such as have been guilty of curable transgressions; their benefit here and hereafter [1] accrues to them through pains and torments; for it is impossible to get rid of injustice by other manner of means.*" This reads like a page torn from one of the early Fathers of the Church. [2] More than five centuries before the Christian era it was penned by Plato. [3] Clearly does he draw the line between eternal punishment for unrepented crimes and temporal punishment for curable *Idmpa* trangressions. Virgil in no uncertain tone echoes the same doctrine, making no exception to the rule that some corporeal stains and traces of ill follow all beyond the grave; *and therefore do they suffer punishment and pay the penalty of old wrongs.* [4] What antiquity has handed down, and reason has found to be just and proper, the Church has defined and decreed. She has gone further. She has supplemented and completed the pagan conception of expiation by that of intercession; and she has added thereto, for the comfort and consolation of the living and the dead, that the souls so suffering "may be helped by the suffrages of the faithful, but principally by the acceptable Sacrifice of the Altar." [5] And in her prayers for deceased friends, relatives and benefactors, she is mindful of Mary's sweet influence with her Son, and asks their deliverance through her intercession. [6]

[Footnote 1: Kai enthude kai en Aidou]

[Footnote 2: There is a passage in Clement of Alexandria, not unlike this in statement of the same doctrine ("Stromaton" 1. vi. m. 14, p. 794 Ed. Potter). The passage is quoted in "Faith of Catholics." Vol. Ill p. 142.]

[Footnote 3: Gorgias, cap. lxxx, lxxxi.]

[Footnote 4: Æneid, lib. vi. 735, 740.]

[Footnote 5: Council of Trent, Sess. xxv. Decret. de Purgatorio, p. 204.]

[Footnote 6: Beata Maria semper virgine intercedente.]

The tendency to commune with the dead, and to pray for them, is strong and universal. It survives whatever systems or whatever creeds men may invent for its suppression. Samuel Johnson is professedly a staunch Protestant, bristling with prejudices, but a delicate moral sense enters the rugged manhood of his nature. Instinctively he seeks to commune with his departed wife, after the manner dear to the Catholic heart, but forbidden to the Protestant. He keeps the anniversary of her death. He composes a prayer for the repose of her soul, beseeching God "to grant her whatever is best in her present state, and finally to receive her to eternal happiness." [1]

[Footnote 1: Boswell's Johnson, vol. 1, p. 100. Croker's Ed. There is pathos in this entry, remembering the man: "Mar. 28, 1753. I kept this day as the anniversary of my Tetty's death, with prayer and tears in the morning. In the evening I prayed for her conditionally, if it were lawful." *Ibid.* p. 97.]

IV

Of the nature and intensity of the sufferings of souls undergoing this purgation, we on earth can form but the faintest conception. Not so Mary. She sees things as they are. She sees the great love animating those I holy souls. She sees their eager desire to be united to God, the sole centre and object of their being. She sees and appreciates the struggle going on in them between that intense desire—that great yearning—that groping after perfect union—that unfilled and unsatiated vagueness arising from their privation of the only fulness that could replenish them, on the one hand, and on the other, the sense of their unfitness, keen, strong, deep, intense, overwhelming them and driving them back to the flames of pain and soul-hunger and soul-thirst until they shall have satisfied God's justice to the last farthing, and even the slightest stain has been cleansed, and they stand forth in the light of God's sanctity, whole and spotless. She sees the terrible struggle; and her motherly heart goes out in tender pity to these her children, washed and ransomed by the Blood of her Divine Son, and she is well disposed to extend to them the aid of her powerful intercession. She is fitly called the Mother of Mercy. Her merciful heart goes out to these, the favored ones of her Son, all the more lovingly and tenderly because they are unable to help themselves.

V.

But whilst Mary looks upon those souls with an eye of tender mercy and sweet compassion, and whilst Jesus is prepared to admit them to the beatific vision as soon as they become thoroughly purified, still the assuaging of their pains and the abridging of their time of purgation depend in a great measure upon the graces and the merits that are applied to them by us, their brethren upon earth. According to the earnestness of the prayers we say for them, and the measure of the good works we do for them, will the intercession of Mary and all the saints be efficacious with Jesus in their behalf. It is unspeakably consoling to the living and the dead to know that the members of the Church militant upon earth have it within their power to aid and relieve the members of the Church suffering. It is therefore really and indeed a holy and a wholesome thought for us of the one to pray for those of the other. It is more: it is an imperative duty we owe the faithful departed. They are our brethren in Christ, bought at the same price, nurtured by the same graces, living by the same faith, and sanctified by the same spirit. Many of them may have been near and dear to us in this life; and of these, many again may now suffer because of us; whether it was that we led them directly into wrong-doing, or whether it was that, in their loving kindness for us, they connived at, permitted, aided or abetted us, in what their consciences had whispered them not to be right. In each and every case it is our bounden duty to do all in our power to assuage sufferings to which we may have been accessory. In heart-rending accents do they cry out to us: "*Have pity on me, have pity on me, at least ye my friends!*" [1] And as we would have others do by us under like circumstances, so should we not turn a deaf ear to their petition.

[Footnote 1: Job, xix. 21.]

VI.

Daily does the Angel of Death enter our houses, and summon from us those that are rooted in our affections, and for whom our heart-throbs beat in love and esteem. Daily must we bow our heads in reverent silence and submission to the decree that snatches from us some loved one. Perhaps it is a wife who mourns the loss of her husband. She finds comfort and companionship in praying for the repose of his soul; in the words of Tertullian, "she prays for his soul, and begs for him in the interim refreshments, and in the first resurrection companionship, and maketh offerings on the anniversary day of his falling asleep." [1] Perhaps it is a husband whose loving wife has gone to sleep in death. Then will he hold her memory sacred, and offer thereto the incense of unceasing prayer, so that it may be said of him as St. Jerome wrote to Pammachius: "Thou hast rendered what was due to each part; giving tears to the body and alms to the soul.... There were thy tears where thou knewest was death; there were thy works where thou knewest was life.... Already is she honored with thy merits; already is she fed with thy bread, and abounds with thy riches." [2] Perhaps it is a dear friend around whom our heart-strings were entwined, and whose love for us was more than we were worthy of: whose counsels were our guide; whose soul was an open book in which we daily read the lesson of high resolve and sincere purpose; whose virtuous life was a continuous inspiration urging us on to noble thought and noble deed; and yet our friendship may have bound his soul in ties too earthly, and retarded his progress in perfection; in consequence he may still dread the light of God's countenance, and may be lingering in this state of purgation. It behooves us in all earnestness, and in friendship's sacred claim, to pray unceasingly for that friend, beseeching God to let the dews of Divine mercy fall upon his parching soul, assuage his pain, and take him to Himself, to complete his happiness.

[Footnote 1: "De Monogam," n. x. p 531. "Faith of Catholics," Vol. III., p. 144.]

[Footnote 2: Ep. XXXVII]

So the sacred duty of prayer for the dead runs through all the relations of life. From all comes the cry begging for our prayers. We cannot in justice ignore it; we cannot be true to ourselves and unmindful of our suffering brethren. Every reminder that we receive is a voice coming from the grave. Now it is the mention of a name that once brought gladness to our hearts; or we come across a letter written by a hand whose grasp used to thrill our souls—that hand now stiffened and cold in death; or it is the sight of some relic that vividly recalls the dear one passed away; or it is a dream—and to whom has not such a dream occurred?—in

177

which we live over again the pleasant past with the bosom friend of our soul, and he is back once more, in the flesh, re-enacting the scenes of former days, breathing and talking as naturally as though there were no break in his life or ours and we had never parted. When we awaken from our dream, and the pang of reality, like a keen blade, penetrates our hearts, let us not rest content with a vain sigh of regret, or with useless tears of grief; let us pray God to give the dear departed soul eternal rest, and admit it to the perpetual light of His Presence. And in like manner should we regard all other reminders as so many appeals to the charity of our prayers. In this way will the keeping of the memory of those gone before us be to them a blessing and to us a consolation.

VII.

Furthermore, every prayer we say, every sacrifice we make, every alms we give for the repose of the dear departed ones, will all return upon ourselves in hundredfold blessings. They are God's choice friends, dear to His Sacred Heart, living in His grace and in constant communing with Him; and though they may not alleviate their own sufferings, their prayers in our behalf always avail. They can aid us most efficaciously. God will not turn a deaf ear to their intercession. Being holy souls, they are grateful souls. The friends that aid them, they in turn will also aid. We need not fear praying for them in all faith and confidence. They will obtain for us the special favors we desire. They will watch over us lovingly and tenderly; they will guard our steps; they will warn us against evil; they will shield us in moments of trial and danger; and when our day of purgatorial suffering comes, they will use their influence in our behalf to assuage our pains and shorten the period of our separation from the Godhead. And so may we, in constant prayer, begging in a special manner the intercession of Mary the Mother of Mercy, say to our Lord and Saviour: "_Deliver them from gloom and darkness, and snatch them from sorrow and grief; enter not into judgment with them, nor severely examine their past life; but whether in word or deed they have sinned, as men clothed with flesh, forgive and do away with their transgressions." [1]

[Footnote 1: From prayer for the Faithful Departed in the Syriac Liturgy. See "Faith of Catholics," Vol. III, p. 203]

DR. JOHNSON ON PRAYERS FOR THE DEAD.

BOSWELL. What do you, think, sir, of Purgatory, as believed by the Roman Catholics?

JOHNSON. Why, sir, it is a very harmless doctrine. They are of opinion that the generality of mankind are neither so obstinately wicked as to deserve everlasting punishment, nor so good as to merit being admitted into the society of blessed spirits; and therefore that God is graciously pleased to allow of a middle state, where they may be purified by certain degrees of suffering. You see, sir, that there is nothing unreasonable in this.

BOSWELL. But then, sir, their Masses for the dead?

JOHNSON. Why, sir, if it be once established that there are souls in Purgatory, it is as proper to pray for them as for our brethren of mankind who are yet in this life.

178

BOSWELL. The idolatry of the Mass?

JOHNSON. Sir, there is no idolatry in the Mass. They believe God to be there, and they adore Him.

* * * * *

BOSWELL. We see in Scripture that Dives still retained an anxious concern about his brethren?

JOHNSON. Why, sir, we must either suppose that passage to be metaphorical, or hold with many divines, and all purgatorians, that departed souls do not all at once arrive at the utmost perfection of which they are capable.

* * * * *

BOSWELL. Do you think, sir, it is wrong in a man who holds the doctrine of Purgatory to pray for the souls of his deceased friends?

JOHNSON. Why, no, sir.

* * * * *

He states, that he spent March 22, 1753, in prayers and tears in the morning; and in the evening prayed for the soul of his deceased wife, "conditionally, if it be lawful." The following is his customary prayer for his dead wife: "And, O Lord, so far as it may be lawful in me, I commend to Thy fatherly goodness the soul of my departed wife; beseeching Thee to grant her whatever is best in her present state, and finally to receive her into eternal happiness."—*Boswell's "Life of Johnson,"* Pages 169, 188.

THE DOCTRINE OF PURGATORY.
BURNETT [1]

[Footnote 1: From his work, "The Path which Led a Protestant Lawyer to the Catholic Church," p. 637.]

The Council of Trent declared, as the faith of the Catholic Church, "*that there is a Purgatory, and that the souls there detained are helped by the suffrages of the faithful, but principally by the acceptable sacrifice of the altar.*"

This is all that is required to be believed. As to the kind and measure of the purifying punishment, the Church defines nothing. This doctrine has been very much misrepresented, and has most generally been attacked by sarcasm and denunciation. But is this a satisfactory method to treat a grave matter of faith, coming down to us from the olden times? The doctrine of Purgatory is most intimately connected with the doctrine of sacramental absolution and satisfaction, and legitimately springs from it. That there is a distinction in the guilt of different sins, must be conceded. All our criminal laws, and those of all nations, are founded upon this idea. To say that the smallest transgression, the result of inadvertence, is equal in enormity to the greatest and most deliberate crime, is utterly opposed to the plain nature of all law, and to the word of God, which assures us that men shall be punished or rewarded according to their works (Rom. ii. 6), as not to require any refutation. Our Lord assures us that men must give an account in the day of judgment for every idle word they speak (Matt, xii. 36), and St. John tells us that nothing denied shall enter heaven (Rev. xxi. 27). Then St. John says there is a sin unto death, and there is a sin which is not unto death (I

179

John, v. 16), and he also tells us that "all unrighteousness is sin; and there is a sin not unto death." So we are told by the same apostle, that if we confess our sins, God is faithful and just to forgive us (I John, i. 9). Now we must put all these texts together, and give them their full, harmonious, and consistent force. We must carry out the principles laid down to their fair and logical results. Suppose, then, a man speak an idle word, and die suddenly, before he has time to repent and confess his sin, will he be lost everlastingly? Must there not, in the very nature of Christ's system, be a middle state, wherein souls can be purged from their lesser sins?

MALLOCK ON PURGATORY. [1]

[Footnote 1: William Hurrell Mallock, the author of "Is Life Worth Living," from which this extract is given, and of several other recent works, was, at the time when the above was written, as he says himself in his dedication, "an outsider in philosophy, literature, and theology," and not, as might be supposed, a Catholic. It has been positively asserted, and as positively denied, that he has since entered the Church. But it is certain that he has not done so. Mallock is not a Catholic.—COMPILER'S NOTE.]

To those who believe in Purgatory, to pray for the dead is as natural and rational as to pray for the living. Next, as to this doctrine of Purgatory itself—which has so long been a stumbling-block to the whole Protestant world—time goes on, and the view men take of it is changing. It is becoming fast recognized on all sides that it is the only doctrine that can bring a belief in future rewards and punishments into anything like accordance with our notions of what is just or reasonable. So far from its being a superfluous superstition, it is seen to be just what is demanded at once by reason and morality, and a belief in it to be not an intellectual assent, but a partial harmonizing of the whole moral ideal.—*W. H. Mattock, "Is Life Worth Living,"* Page 297.

BOILEAU-DESPRÉAUX AND PRAYER FOR THE DEAD.

We love to see the truth of our dogmas proclaimed from amid the great assemblies of choice intelligences. Boileau did not hesitate to do homage to the Catholic doctrine of Purgatory on the following solemn occasion:—

On the death of Furetière, the French Academy deliberated whether they would have a funeral service for him, according to the ancient custom of the establishment. Despréaux, who had taken no part in the expulsion of his former associate, gave expression, when he was no more, to the language of courageous piety. He feared not to express himself in these words: "Gentlemen, there are three things to be considered here—God, the public, and the Academy. As regards God, He will, undoubtedly, be well pleased if you sacrifice your resentment for His sake and offer prayers to Him for the repose of a fellow-member, who has more need of them than others, were it only on account of the animosity he showed towards you. Before the public, it will be a glorious thing for you not to pursue your enemy beyond the grave. And as for the Academy, its moderation will be meritorious, when it answers insults by prayers, and does not deny a Christian the resources offered by the Church for appeasing the anger of

God, all the more that, besides the indispensable obligation of praying to God for your enemies, you have made for yourselves a special law to pray for your associates."

ALL SAINTS AND ALL SOULS. [1]

[Footnote 1: New York *Tablet*, Nov. 12, 1870]

MRS. J. SADLIER.

OF all the sublime truths which it is the pride and happiness of Christians to believe, none is more beautiful, more consoling than that of the Communion of Saints. Do we fully realize the meaning of that particular article of our faith? From their earliest infancy Christian children repeat, at their mother's knee, "I believe in the Communion of Saints;" but it is only when the mind has attained a certain stage of development that they begin to feel the inestimable privilege of being in the Communion of Saints.

But how sad to think that even in later life many of those whose childhood lisped "I believe in the Communion of Saints," neither know, nor care to know, what it means. Outside the Church who believes in the Communion of Saints?— who rejoices in the glory of the glorified, or invokes their intercession with God? Who believes in that state of probation whereby the earth-stains are washed from the souls of men? Who has compassion on "the spirits who are in prison?" To Catholics only is the Communion of Saints a reality, a soul-rejoicing truth. How inestimable is the privilege of being truly and indeed "of the household of faith,"—within and of "the Church of the Saints," the Church that alone connects the life which is and that which is to come, the living and the dead!

Year by year we are reminded of this truth, so solemn and so beautiful, the Communion of Saints, by the double festival of All Saints and All Souls—when the Church invites her children of the Militant Church to rejoice with her on the glory of her Saints, and to pray with her for the holy dead who are still in the purgatorial fire that is to prepare them for that blessed abode into which "nothing defiled can enter."

Grand and joyous is the feast of the Saints, when we lovingly honor all our brethren who have gained their thrones in Heaven, and with faith and hope invoke their powerful aid, that we, too, may come where they are, and be partakers in their eternal blessedness; solemn and sad, but most sweetly soothing to the heart of faith, is the day of All Souls, when the altars are draped in black, and the chant is mournful, and sacrifice is offered, the whole world over, for the dead who have slept in Christ, with the blessing of the Church upon them. For them, if they still have need of succor, are all the good works of the faithful offered up, and the prayers of all the Saints and all the Angels invoked, not only on the second day of November, but on every day of that mournful month.

Thus do we, who are still on earth, honor the glorified Saints of God, and invoke them for ourselves and for the blessed souls who may yet be debarred from the joys of Heaven. And this is truly the Communion of Saints—the Church on earth, the Church in Heaven, the Church in Purgatory, distinct, yet united, the children of one common Father, who is God; of one common

Mother, who is Mary, the Virgin ever Blessed.

LEIBNITZ [1]

[Footnote 1: Gottfried Wilhelm von Leibnitz, the eminent Protestant philosopher. The above is from his "Systema Theologicum."]

ON THE MASS AS A PROPITIATORY SACRIFICE.

No new efficacy is superadded to the efficacy of the Passion from this propitiatory Sacrifice, repeated for the remission of sins; but its entire efficacy consists in the representation and application of the first bloody Sacrifice, the fruit of which is the Divine Grace bestowed on all those who, being present at this tremendous sacrifice, worthily celebrate the oblation in unison with the priest. And since, in addition to the remission of eternal punishment, and the gift of the merits of Christ for the hope of eternal life, we further ask of God, for ourselves and others, both living and dead, many other salutary gifts (and amongst those, the chief is the mitigation of that paternal chastisement which is due to every sin, even though the penitent be restored to favor); it is therefore clearly manifest that there is nothing in our entire worship more precious than the sacrifice of this Divine Sacrament, in which the Body of Our Lord itself is present.

EXTRACTS FROM "A TROUBLED HEART."

How often have I been touched at the respect paid the dead in Catholic countries; at the reverence with which the business man, hastening to fulfil the duties of the hour, pauses and lifts his hat as the funeral of the unknown passes him in the street! What pity streams from the eyes of the poor woman who kneels in her humble doorway, and, crossing herself, prays for the repose of the soul that was never known to her in this life; but the body is borne towards the cemetery, and she joins her prayer to the many that are freely offered along the solemn way (pp. 151-2).

* * * * *

So passes the faithful soul to judgment; after which, if not ushered at once into the ineffable glory of the Father, it pauses for a season in the perpetual twilight of that border-land where the spirit is purged of the very memory of sin. Even as Our Lord Himself descended into Limbo; as He died for us, but rose again from the dead and ascended into heaven, so we hope to rise and follow Him,— sustained by the unceasing prayers of the Church, the intercession of the Saints, and all the choirs of the just, who are called on night and day, and also by the prayers and pleadings of those who have loved us, and who are still in the land of the living.

The prayers that ease the pangs of Purgatory, the *Requiem*, the *Miserere*, the *De Profundis*—these are the golden stairs upon which the soul of the redeemed ascends into everlasting joy. Even the Protestant laureate of England has confessed the poetical justice and truth of this, and into the mouth of the dying Arthur—that worthy knight—he puts these words:

"Pray for my soul! More things are wrought by prayer
Than this world dreams of; wherefore let thy voice
Rise like a fountain for me night and day;

For, what are men better than sheep or goats
That nourish a blind life within the brain,
If, knowing God, they lift not hands of prayer
Both for themselves and those who call them friend?
For so the whole round earth is every way
Bound by gold chains about the feet of God." [1]

[Footnote 1: These exquisite lines will be found elsewhere in this volume in the full description of King Arthur's death from Tennyson. But they bear repetition.]

O ye gentle spirits that have gone before me, and who are now, I trust, dwelling in the gardens of Paradise, beside the river of life that flows through the midst thereof,—ye whose names I name at the Memorial for the Dead in the Holy Sacrifice of the Mass,—as ye look upon the lovely and shining countenances of the elect, and, perchance, upon the beauty of our Heavenly Queen, and upon her Son in glory,—O remember me who am still this side of the Valley of the Shadow, and in the midst of trials and tribulations. And you who have read these pages, written from the heart, after much sorrow and long suffering, though I be still with you in the flesh, or this poor body be gathered to its long home, —you whose eyes are now fixed upon this line, I beseech you,

Pray for me!—*Anon.*

EUGÉNIE DE GUÉRIN AND HER BROTHER MAURICE.

[In Eugénie de Guérin's journal we find the following beautiful words written while her loving heart was still bleeding for the early death of her best-loved brother, Maurice—her twin soul, as she was wont to call him.]

"O PROFUNDITY! O mysteries of that other life that separates us! I who was always so anxious about him, who wanted so much to know everything, wherever he may be now there is an end to that. I follow him into the three abodes; I stop at that of bliss; I pass on to the place of suffering, the gulf of fire. My God, my God, not so! Let not my brother be there, let him not! He is not there. What! his soul, the soul of Maurice, among the reprobate! ... Horrible dread, no! But in Purgatory, perhaps, where one suffers, where one expiates the weaknesses of the heart, the doubts of the soul, the half-inclinations to evil. Perhaps my brother is there, suffering and calling to us in his pangs as he used to do in bodily pain, 'Relieve me, you who love me!' Yes, my friend, by prayer. I am going to pray. I have prayed so much, and always shall. Prayer? Oh, yes, prayers for the dead, they are the dew of Purgatory."

All Souls'—How different this day is from all others, in church, in the soul, without, within. It is impossible to tell all one feels, thinks, sees again, regrets. There is no adequate expression for all this except in prayer.... I have not written here, but to some one to whom I have promised so long as I live, a letter on All Souls'....

O my friend, my brother, Maurice! Maurice! art thou far from me? dost thou hear me? What are they, those abodes that hold thee now? ... Mysteries of another life, how profound, how terrible ye are— sometimes, how sweet!

PASSAGES FROM THE VIA MEDIA.

[Written while Cardinal Newman was still an Anglican]

Now, as to the punishments and satisfactions for sins, the texts to which the minds of the early Christians seem to have been principally drawn, and from which they ventured to argue in behalf of these vague notions, were these two: 'The fire shall try every man's work,' etc., and 'He shall baptize you with the Holy Ghost and with fire.' These passages, with which many more were found to accord, directed their thoughts one way, as making mention of fire, whatever was meant by the word, as the instrument of trial and purification; and that, at some time between the present time and the Judgment, or at the Judgment. As the doctrine, thus suggested by certain striking texts, grew in popularity and definiteness, and verged towards its present Roman form, it seemed a key to many others. Great portions of the books of Psalms, Job, and the Lamentations, which express the feelings of religious men under suffering, would powerfully recommend it by the forcible and most affecting and awful meaning which they received from it. When this was once suggested, all other meanings would seem tame and inadequate.

To these may be added various passages from the prophets, as that in the beginning of the third chapter of Malachi, which speaks of fire as the instrument of purification, when Christ comes to visit His Church.

Moreover, there were other texts of obscure and indeterminate meaning, which seem on this hypothesis to receive a profitable meaning; such as Our Lord's words in the Sermon on the Mount, "Verily, I say unto thee, thou shalt by no means come out thence till thou hast paid the uttermost farthing;" and St. John's expression in the Apocalypse, that, "no man in heaven, nor in earth, neither under the earth, was able to open the book."—*Via Media, pp.* 174-177.

Most men, to our apprehensions, are too little formed in religious habits either for heaven or for hell; yet there is no middle state when Christ comes in judgment. In consequence, it is obvious to have recourse to the interval before His coming, as a time during which this incompleteness may be remedied, as a season, not of changing the spiritual bent and character of the soul departed, whatever that be, for probation ends with mortal life, but of developing it in a more determinate form, whether of good or evil. Again, when the mind once allows itself to speculate, it will discern in such a provision a means whereby those who, not without true faith at bottom, yet have committed great crimes, or those who have been carried off in youth while still undecided, or who die after a barren, though not immoral or scandalous life, may receive such chastisement as may prepare them for heaven, and render it consistent with God's justice to admit them thither. Again, the inequality of the sufferings of Christians in this life compared one with another, leads the mind to the same speculations; the intense suffering, for instance, which some men undergo on their death-bed, seeming as if but an anticipation in their case of what comes after death upon others, who, without greater claims on God's forbearance, live without chastisement and die easily. The mind will inevitably dwell upon such thoughts, unless it has been taught to subdue them by education or by the fear of the experience of their dangerousness.— *Via Media, pp. 174-177.*

ALL SOULS.
FROM THE FRENCH.

November is come; and the pleasant verdure that the groves and woods offered to our view in the joyous spring is fast losing its cheerful hue, while its withered remains lie trembling and scattered beneath our feet. The grave and plaintive voice of the consecrated bell sends forth its funereal tones, and, recalling the dead to our pensive souls, implores, for them the pity of the living. Oh! let us hearken to its thrilling call; and may the sanctuary gather us together within its darkened walls, there to invoke our Eternal Father, and breathe forth cherished names in earnest prayer!

When the solemn hour of the last farewell was come for those we loved, and their weakened sight was extinguished forever, it seemed as if our hearts' memory would be eternal, and as if those dear ones would never be forgotten. But time has fled, their memory has grown dim, and other thoughts reign paramount in our forgetful hearts, which barely give them from time to time a pious recollection.

Nevertheless, they loved us, perhaps too well, lavish of a love that Heaven demanded. How devoted was their affection; and shall we now requite it by a cruel forgetfulness? Oh! if they suffer still on our account; if, because of their weakness, they still feel the wrath of God's justice, shall we not pray, when their voices implore our help, when their tears ascend towards us?

Alas! in this life what direful contamination clings to the steps of irresolute mortals! Who has not wavered in the darksome paths into which the straight road so often deviates?

The infinite justice of the God of purity perhaps retains them in the dungeons of death. Alas! for long and long the Haven of eternal life may be closed against them! Oh, let us pray; our voices will open the abode of celestial peace unto the imprisoned soul. The God of consolation gave us prayer, that love might thus become eternal.— *The Lamp*, Nov. 5, 1864.

AN ANGLICAN BISHOP PRAYING FOR THE DEAD.

Foremost among later Anglican divines in piety, in learning, and in the finer qualities of head and heart, stands the name of Reginald Heber, Bishop of the Establishment, whose gentle memory,—embalmed in several graceful and musical poems, chiefly on religious subjects,—is still revered and cherished by his co-religionists, respected and admired even by those who see in him only the man and the poet—not the religious teacher. I am happy to lay before my readers the following extract from a letter of Bishop Heber, in which that amiable and accomplished prelate expresses his belief in the efficacy of prayers for the departed:

"Few persons, I believe, have lost a beloved object, more particularly by sudden death, without feeling an earnest desire to recommend them in their prayers to God's mercy, and a sort of instinctive impression that such devotions might still be serviceable to them.

* * * * *

"Having been led attentively to consider the question, my own opinion is, on the whole, favorable to the practice, which is, indeed, so natural and so comfortable, that this alone is a presumption that it is neither unpleasing to the Almighty nor unavailing with Him.

"The Jews, so far back as their opinions and practices can be traced since the time of Our Saviour, have uniformly recommended their deceased friends to mercy; and from a passage in the Second Book of Maccabees, it appears that, from whatever source they derived it, they had the same custom before His time. But if this were the case, the practice can hardly be unlawful, or either Christ or His Apostles would, one should think, have, in some of their writings or discourses, condemned it. On the same side it may be observed that the Greek Church, and all the Eastern Churches, pray for the dead; and that we know the practice to have been universal, or nearly so, among the Christians a little more than one hundred and fifty years after Our Saviour. It is spoken of as the usual custom by Tertullian and Epiphanius. Augustine, in his *Confessions*, has given a beautiful prayer which he himself used for his deceased mother, Monica; and among Protestants, Luther and Dr. Johnson are eminent instances of the same conduct. I have, accordingly, been myself in the habit, for some years, of recommending on some occasions, as, after receiving the sacrament, etc., my lost friends by name to God's goodness and compassion, through His Son, as what can do them no harm, and may, and I hope will, be of service to them."

THE "PURGATORY" OF DANTE.
MARIOTTI.

In the course of his remarks upon the *Divina Comedia* of Dante, a bitter opponent of the Holy See and of everything Catholic, Mariotti, [1] an apostle of United Italy, expresses his views upon the ancient doctrine of Purgatory. These views are but an instance of how its beauty and truthfulness to nature strike the minds of those who have strayed from the centre of Christian unity.

[Footnote 1: Mariotti, author of "Italy Past and Present," an unscrupulous opponent of the Papacy and of the Church.]

"To say nothing of its greatness and goodness, the poem of Dante," says Mariotti, "is the most curious of books. The register of the past, noting down every incident within the compass of man's nature.... Dante is the annalist, the interpreter, the representative of the Middle Ages.... The ideas of mankind were in those '*dark*' ages perpetually revolving upon that 'life beyond life,' which the omnipresent religion of that *fanatical* age loved to people with appalling phantoms and harrowing terrors. Dante determined to anticipate his final doom, and still, in the flesh, to break through the threshold of eternity, and explore the kingdom of death.... No poet ever struck upon a subject to which every fibre in the heart of his contemporaries more readily responded than Dante. It is not for me to test the soundness of the Roman Catholic doctrine of Purgatory, or to inquire which of the Holy Fathers first dreamt of its existence. It was, however, a sublime contrivance, unscriptural though it may be—a conception full of love and charity, in so far as it seemed to arrest the dead on the threshold of eternity; and making his final welfare partly dependent on the pious exertions of those who were left behind, established a lasting interchange of tender feelings, embalmed the memory of the departed, and by a posthumous tie wedded him to the mourning survivor.... Woe to the man, in Dante's age, who sunk into his grave without bequeathing a heritage of love; on whose sod no refreshing dew of sorrowing affection descended. Lonely as his relics in the sepulchre, his spirit wandered in the dreaded region of probation; alone he was left defenceless, prayerless, friendless to settle his awful score with unmitigated justice. It is this feeling, unrivalled for poetic beauty, that gives color and tone to the second division of Dante's poem. The five or six cantos, at the opening, have all the milk of human nature that entered into the composition of that miscalled saturnine mind. With little more than two words, the poet makes us aware that we have come into happier latitudes. Every strange visitor breathes love and forgiveness. The shade we meet is only charged with tidings of joy to the living, and messages of good will. The heart lightens and brightens at every new stratum of the atmosphere in that rising region; the ascent is easy and light, like the gliding of a boat down the stream. The angels we become familiar with are angels of light, such as human imagination never before nor afterwards conceived. They come from afar across the waves, piloting the barge that conveys the chosen spirits to heaven, balancing themselves on their wide-spread wings, using them as sails, disdaining the aid of all mortal contrivance, and relying on their inexhaustible strength; red and rayless at first, from the distance, as the planet Mars when he appears struggling through the mist of the horizon, but growing brighter and brighter with amazing swiftness. They stand at the gate of Purgatory, they guard the entrance to each of the seven steps of its mountain—some with green vesture, vivid as new-budding leaves, gracefully waving and floating in simple drapery, fanned by their wings; bearing in their hands flaming swords broken at the point; others, ash-colored garments; others again, in flashing armor, but all beaming with so intense, so overwhelming a light, that dizziness overcomes all mortal ken, whenever directed to their countenance. The friends of the poet's youth one by one arrest his march, and engage him in tender converse. The very laws of immutable fate seem for a few moments suspended to allow full scope for the interchange of affectionate sentiments. The overawing consciousness of the place he is in, for a moment forsakes the mortal visitor so miraculously admitted into the world of spirits. He throws his arms round the neck of the beloved shade, and it is only by the smile irradiating its countenance that he is reminded of the intangibility of its ethereal substance. The episodes of "the Purgatory" are mostly of this sad and tender description. The historical personages introduced seem to have lost their own identity, and to have merged into a blessed calmness, characterizing medium of the region they are all travelling through." It is plain that, bitterly hostile as is this faithless Italian to the Church of his fathers, and the truth which it teaches, his poetic instinct, at least, rises above mere prejudice, and enables him to penetrate into that dim but holy atmosphere created by the poet's genius, and yet more fully by the poet's faith. This homage to the union of religious grandeur, natural tenderness, and supernatural fervent charity, which make this doctrine unconsciously dear to every human heart, is of value coming from the pen of so prejudiced a witness. It is but one of countless testimonies that in all times, and in all ages, have sprung from the heart of man, as it were in his own despite.

THE MOUTH OF NOVEMBER. [1]

[Footnote 1: New York *Tablet*, Nov. 26, 1859.]

MARY E. BLAKE (MARIE).

It is but a few days since the Church has celebrated the triumph of her saints, rejoicing in the eternal felicity of that innumerable throng whom she has given to the celestial Sion. She invites us to share her joy. She bids us look up from the rugged pathway of our thorn-strewn pilgrimage to that blissful abode which is to be the term and the reward of all our trials. Yet, like a true mother, she cannot forget that portion of her family who are sighing for their deliverance, in that region of pain to which they are consigned by eternal justice. On one day she sings with radiant brow and tones of jubilee her *Sursum Corda*; on the next, she kneels a suppliant, chanting with uplifted hands and tearful eyes her *Requiem Æternam*; and we, the companions of her exile, shall we not sympathize with every emotion of the heart of our tender Mother?

Among the pious customs which owe their existence to the fertile spirit of Catholic devotion is that which dedicates the month of November to the Suffering Souls in Purgatory. It would seem as though the annual circle of commemorative devotion were incomplete without this crowning fulfilment of charity.

Some years since, I met with a graphic description of a spectacle in the Catholic Cemetery of New Orleans. It was the 2d of November, when the friends and relatives of the dead came to scatter emblematic wreaths and sweet-scented flowers on their graves. This custom was observed by the French Catholics and their descendants; and the writer, although a Protestant, was deeply impressed with its beauty and significance. He asked why, among Americans, there was so little of this eloquent affection for the dead. He might have found an answer in the fact that the principle of faith was wanting—of that vivid and active faith which seeks and finds by such means its outward manifestation.

We, also, are the children of the Saints. We have inherited from them the same faith in all its integrity, and how does our *practice* correspond with it? What are we doing for that army of holy captives who cannot leave their prison till the uttermost farthing be paid? Let us not imitate those tepid Christians who are satisfied with erecting costly monuments, and observing, with scrupulous exactness, the usual period of "mourning," while the poor souls are left to pine forgotten, if they have gone with some-lingering stains—some earthly tarnish on their nuptial garment. Ah! there is so much that might be done if we would only reflect, and let our hearts be softened by the intense eloquence of their mute appeal....

188

These are a few of the thoughts suggested by the late solemnity, and perhaps they cannot be concluded more appropriately than by introducing the following poem, found in an old magazine. If the theme be sufficient to inspire thus one who had but faint glimmerings of divine truth, what should be expected of us, who rejoice in the fullness of that light? I twine, then, this flower of the desert with the leaves I have gathered, and offer my humble wreath as a tribute of faith and affection on the altar dedicated to the dear departed.

November, 1859.

LITANY OP THE DEPARTED.

It is, therefore, a holy and wholesome thought to pray for the dead.—
II. Mach. xii. 26.

For the spirits who have fled
From the earth which once they trod;
For the loved and faithful dead,
We beseech the living God!
Oh! receive and love them!
By the grave where Thou wert lying,
By the anguish of Thy dying,
Spread Thy wings above them;
Grant Thy pardon unto them,
Dona eis requiem!

Long they suffered here below,
Outward fightings, inward fears;
Ate the cheerless bread of woe,—
Drank the bitter wine of tears:—
Now receive and love them!
By Thy holy Saints' departures,
By the witness of Thy martyrs,
Spread Thy wings above them.
On the souls in gloom who sit,
Lux eterna luceat!

Lord, remember that they wept,
When Thy children would divide;
Lord, remember that they slept
On the bosom of Thy Bride;
And receive and love them!
By the tears Thou couldst not smother;
By the love of Thy dear Mother,
Spread Thy wings above them.
To their souls, in bliss with Thee,
Dona pacem, Domini!

Grant our prayers, and bid them pray,
O thou Flower of Jesse's stem;
Lend a gracious ear when they,

Plead for us, as we for them.
Deus Angelorum,
Dona eis requiem,
Et beatitudinem.
Cordibus eorum
Jesu, qui salutam das
Micat lumen animas!
　　—*Acolytus.*

ALL SOULS' DAY [1]

[Footnote 1: New York *Tablet*, Nov. 12, 1864.]

MRS. J. SADLIER.

Nothing in the whole grand scheme of Religion is more beautiful than the tender care of the Church over her departed children. Not content with providing for their spiritual wants during their lives, and sending them into eternity armed with and strengthened by the last solemn Sacraments, blessing their departure from, as she blessed their entrance into, this world, her maternal solicitude follows them beyond the grave, and penetrates to the dreary prison in the Middle State where, happily, they may be, as the Apostle says, "cleansed so as by fire." With the tender compassion of a fond mother, the Church, *our* mother, yearns over the sufferings of her children, all the dearer to her because they suffer in the Lord, and by His holy will.

By every means within her power she aids these blessed souls who are at once so near Heaven, and so far from it; by solemn prayers, by sacrifice, by continual remembrance of them in all her good works, she gives them help and comfort herself, while encouraging the faithful to imitate her example in that respect by numerous and great Indulgences, and by the crown of eternal blessedness she holds out to those who perform faithfully and in her own proper spirit this Seventh Spiritual Work of Mercy—"to pray for the living *and the dead.*" In every Mass that is said the long year round on each of her myriad altars, a solemn commemoration is made for the Dead immediately after the Elevation of the Sacred Host, the great Atoning Sacrifice of the New Law; in all the other public offices of the Church, "the faithful departed" are tenderly remembered, and, to crown the efforts of her maternal charity, the second day of November of every year is set apart for the solemn remembrance of these her most beloved and most afflicted children, for whose benefit and relief all the Masses of that day throughout the whole Catholic world are specially offered up. Nay, more than that, the entire month of November is devoted to the Souls in Purgatory, and the good works and pious prayers of all the holy communities who spend their lives in commune with God are offered up with that benign intention during the month.

In Catholic countries, the faithful are touchingly reminded of this sad though pleasing duty to their departed brethren, by the tolling of the several convent and church bells at eight o'clock in the evening, at which time the different communities unite in reciting the solemn *De Profundis*, and other prayers for the dead. Solemn and sonorous we have heard that passing-bell, year after year, booming through the darkness and storm of the November night in a northern land [1] where the pious customs of the best ages of France, transplanted over two centuries ago, flourish still in their pristine beauty and touching fervor.

[Footnote 1: Eastern, or French Canada, now known as the Province of Quebec]

But, though all Catholics may not hear the *De Profundis* bell of November nights, nor all households kneel at evening hour to join in spirit with the pious communities who are praying then for the faithful departed, yet all Catholics know when, on the first of November, they celebrate the great and joyous festival of All Saints, that the next day will bring the mournful solemnity of All Souls, when the altars of the Church will be draped with black, and her ministers robed in the same sombre garb, whilst offering the "Clean Oblation" of the New Law for the souls who are yet in a state of purgation in the other life.

To the deep heart of Catholic piety nothing can be more sensibly touching than "the black Mass" of All Souls' Day. If the feast be not celebrated by the laity as it so faithfully is by the Church, it certainly ought to be, if the spirit of the faith be still amongst them. The funereal solemnity of the occasion touches the deepest, holiest sympathies in every true Catholic heart, reminding each of their loved and lost, and filling their souls with the soothing hope that the Great Sacrifice then offered up for all the departed children of the Church may release one or more of their nearest and dearest from the cleansing fires of Purgatory. Then, while the funeral dirge fills the sacred edifice, and the mournful *Dies Iræ* thrills the hearts of all, each one thinks of his own departed ones, and recalls with indescribable sadness other just such celebrations in the years long past, when those for whom they now invoke the mercy of Heaven were still amongst the living. Then comes, too, the solemn thought that some, perhaps many, of those then present in life and health may be numbered with the dead before All Souls' Day comes round again, and a voice from the depths of the Christian heart asks, "May not I, too, be then with the dead?"

When noting with surprise and regret how many Catholics neglect the celebration of All Souls' Day, we have often endeavored to account for such strange apathy. Surely, if the charity of the Church do not inspire them—if they do not feel, with the valiant Macchabeus of old, that "it is a holy and a wholesome thought to pray for the Dead that they may be loosed from their sins"—if natural affection, even, do not move them to think of the probable sufferings of their own near and dear—sufferings which they may have it in their power to alleviate —at least, a motive of self-interest ought to make them reflect that when they themselves are with the dead, retributive justice may leave them forgotten by their own flesh and blood, as they forget others now. But to those who do faithfully unite with the Church in her solemn commemoration of the faithful departed on All Souls' Day, nothing can be more soothing to the deep heart of human sadness, as nothing is more imposing, or more strikingly illustrative of that Catholic charity, that all-embracing charity which has its life and fountain within

191

the Church.

CEMETERIES.

THE respect due to cemeteries is too closely connected with the doctrine of Purgatory for us to omit observing here that those asylums of the dead, being the objects of pious reverence, even amongst infidels, ought to be still more so amongst us. It was in this connection that Mgr. Pelletan, Arch-priest of the Cathedral of Algiers, wrote thus on the 13th of March, 1843:

"Here in Algiers, do we not see, every Friday, the Mussulman Arab, wandering pensively through his cemetery, placing on some venerated and beloved grave bouquets of flowers, branches of boxwood; wrapped in his bornouse, he sits for hours beside it, motionless and thoughtful; lost in gentle melancholy, it would seem as though he were holding intimate and mysterious converse with the dear departed one whose loss he deplores....

"But for us, Christians, nourished, enlightened by the truth of God, what special homage, what profound reverence we should manifest towards the remains of our fathers, our brethren who died in the same faith! Oh, let us remember the first faithful—the martyrs—the catacombs! The cemetery is for us the land where grows invisibly the harvest of the elect; it is the sleeping world of intelligence; sheltered are its peaceful slumbers in the bosom of nature ever young, ever fruitful; the crowd of the dead pressed together beneath those crosses, under those scattered flowers, is the crowd that will one day rise to take possession of the infinite future, from which it is only separated by some sods of turf.

"Hence how lively, how motherly has ever been the solicitude of the Church in this respect! She wishes that the ground wherein repose the remains of her children be blessed and consecrated ground; she purifies it with hyssop and holy water; she calls down upon it by her humble supplications, the benediction of Him who disposes according to His will of things visible and invisible, of souls and of bodies; she wishes that the cross should rise in its midst, that her children may rest in peace in its shade while awaiting the grand awaking; even as a temple and a sanctuary, she banishes from it games, noise of all kinds, and even all that savors of levity or irreverence."—*Dictionnaire d'Anecdotes Chrétiens, p. 993.*

OPINIONS OF VARIOUS PROTESTANTS.

Some say, like Lessing in his "Treatise on Theology," "What hinders us from admitting a Purgatory? as if the great majority of Christians had not really adopted it. No, this intermediate state being taught and recognized by the ancient Church, notwithstanding the scandalous abuses to which it gave rise, should not be absolutely rejected."

Others, with Dr. Forbes (*controv. pontif. princip., anno* 1658): "Prayer for the dead, MADE USE OF FROM THE TIMES OF THE APOSTLES, cannot be rejected as useless by Protestants. They should respect the judgment of the primitive Church, and adopt a practice sanctioned by the continuous belief of so many ages. We repeat that prayer for the dead is a salutary practice."

Several others, rising to our point of view, drawing their inspiration from the sources of Catholic charity, tell you, with the theologian Collier (Part II. p. 100):

"Prayer for the dead revives the belief in the immortality of the soul, withdraws the dark veil which covers the tomb, and establishes relations between this world and the other. Had it been preserved, we should probably not have had amongst us so much incredulity. I cannot conceive why our Church, which is so remote from the primitive times of Christianity, should have abandoned or disdained a custom that had never been interrupted; which, on the contrary, as we have reason to believe from Scripture, existed in ancient times; which was practiced in the Apostolic age, in the time of miracles and revelations; introduced amongst the articles of faith, and never rejected, except by Arius."

"It was evidently in use in the Church in the time of St. Augustine, and down to the sixteenth century. If we do nothing for our dead, if we omit to occupy ourselves with them and pray for them, as was formerly done in the Holy Supper, we break off all intercourse with the Saints; and then, how could we dare to say that we remain in communion with the blessed? And if we break off in this way from the most noble part of the universal Church, may it not be said that we mutilate our belief and reject one of the articles of the Christian faith?"

"Yes," says the German Sheldon, in his turn, "prayer for the dead is one of the most ancient and most efficacious practices of the Christian religion."

You have just heard the sound of some bells; listen again and you shall hear something different.

You think, then, that there are Protestants who admit Purgatory and others who deny it? You are mistaken! There are some who at once admit and do not admit it. This is difficult to comprehend, but it is so, nevertheless, and this is how they take it:

On the one side, they will have nothing but hell, pure and simple; this is the Catholic side; but on the other is the philosophic side, the eternity of horrible pains is something too hard; and then, why not a hell that will end a little sooner, or a little later? For, in fine, there are small criminals and great criminals. So that their temporary hell—that is to say, having an end—being, after all, nothing more than one Purgatory, it follows that, having broken with us because they did not want Purgatory, they broke off again because they wanted Purgatory only.— *Dictionnaire d'Anecdotes*, 998-9.

Mr. Thorndike, a Protestant theologian, says: "The practice of the Church of interceding for the dead at the celebration of the Eucharist, is so general and so ancient, that it cannot be thought to have come in upon imposture, but that the same aspersion will seem to take hold of the common Christianity."

The Protestant translators of Du Pin observe, that St. Chrysostom, in his thirty-eighth homily on the Philippians, says, that to pray for the faithful departed in the tremendous mysteries, was decreed by the Apostles.

The learned Protestant divine, Dr. Jeremy Taylor, writes thus: "We find by the history of the Machabees, that the Jews did pray and make offerings for the dead, which appears by other testimonies, and by their form of prayer still extant, which they used in the captivity. Now, it is very considerable, that since our Blessed Saviour did reprove all the evil doctrines and traditions of the Scribes and

193

Pharisees, and did argue concerning the dead and the resurrection, yet He spake no word against this public practice, but left it as He found it; which He who came to declare to us all the will of His Father would not have done, if it had not been innocent, pious, and full of charity. The practice of it was at first, and was universal: it being plain both in Tertullian and St. Cyprian, and others."

"Clement," says Bishop Kaye, "distinguishes between sins committed before and after baptism: the former are remitted at baptism, the latter are purged by discipline.... The necessity of this purifying discipline is such, that if it does not take place in this life, it must after death, and is then to be effected by fire, not by a destructive, but a discriminating fire, pervading the soul which passes through it."—*Clem.*, ch. xii.

SOME THOUGHTS FOR NOVEMBER.

I stood upon an unknown shore,
A deep, dark ocean, rolled beside;
Dear, loving ones were wafted o'er
That silent and mysterious tide.

To most persons, the idea of Purgatory is simply one of pain; they try to avoid thinking about it, because the subject is unpleasant, and people's thoughts do not naturally revert to painful subjects; they feel that it is a place to which they must go at least, if they escape worse; they must suffer, they cannot help it, and so the less they think about it beforehand, the better. Purgatory and suffering are to them synonymous terms; perhaps fear keeps them from some sins which, without this salutary apprehension, they would readily fall into; but, on the whole, they take their chance, and hope for the best. This, perhaps, is the view of a large class of people, and of those who will scarcely own to themselves what they think on the subject; but their lives are the tell-tales, and we cannot but fear that to escape hell is the utmost effort of many who apparently are good Catholics. Still, we would not say that they do not love God, that they are not in many ways pleasing to Him; but, oh! how many there are who only want a little more generosity to become Saints! Then, there is another class, further on in their heavenward journey—souls who do love God, who do seek only to please Him, who are generous, often even noble-hearted, in their Master's service; souls who can say, "Our Father," and look up with child-like love to Heaven; but even with such, and perhaps with almost all, the feeling about Purgatory is much the same; it is a sort of necessary evil; a something that must be endured. They feel strongly all that justice demands; their very sanctity and goodness lead them to desire that that which is evil in them should be taken out, even by fire; but still there are few that do really see the deep, deep love of Purgatory. We are very far from wishing to hinder people from thinking less of its sufferings—nay, rather their very intenseness and severity only pleads our case more strongly. All that has been revealed to the Saints, all that has been made known to us by the Church or tradition, proclaims the same fact. Suffering, intense, unearthly anguish, is the portion of those most blessed souls; and it has been said that the pains of Purgatory only differ in duration from those of hell. Still, there is this difference

194

—oh! blessed be God, there is this difference, and it is all we could ask: in hell, the damned blaspheme their Master with the demons that torment them; in Purgatory, the holy souls love their God with the angelic choirs who await their entrance to the land of bliss. If the souls of the damned could love, hell would cease to be hell; if the souls of the blessed ones in prison could cease to love, Purgatory would be worse to them than a thousand such hells.

* * * * *

Yes; Purgatory is love, and if it be true that the love of God extends even to hell, because its torments might be worse, did not His infinite mercy temper His infinite justice, how much more truly may this be said of Purgatory! We have no wish to enter into any detailed account of what the pains of Purgatory are supposed to be; this is a subject for the pen of the theologian, or the raptures of the Saint. Awful and terrible we know they are. But there is one suffering which we wish to speak of, because we cannot but hope, if people reflected upon it seriously, that they would learn to think of Purgatory less as a necessary evil, and more as a most tender mercy, and be more inclined to enter into a hearty co-operation with those who are anxious to help the poor souls in this awful prison.

Surely, the one object of our whole lives is, not so much to get to Heaven because we shall be happy there, as to see Jesus forever and forever, to be near Him, to gaze on Him, and to love Him without fear; for then love will be fearless, because suffering and sin will have ceased.

And what will happen when we die? Oh! if we were sent to Purgatory without seeing Jesus, we might bear it better. There have been souls on earth privileged to suffer for months the pains of the holy souls, and they have lived and borne the pain, and longed, if it were possible, even for more; but they had not seen Jesus as we shall see Him at the moment of our death. The very thought makes us shudder and our life- blood run cold. What if we should indeed be saved, we who have so trembled and feared, and known not whether we were worthy of love or hatred? What if we should behold the face of Divinest Majesty gaze upon us even for one moment in tenderness? And yet, unless we see it in unutterable wrath, this will be. But what then? Shall we see it forever? Shall our eyes gaze on and on, and feast themselves on that sight for all eternity? ... Ah! not yet; we must lose sight of that vision of delight; it must be withdrawn from us—not, thank God, in anger, but in sorrow. Oh! what are the pains of Purgatory, what the burning of its fire, in comparison with the suffering which the soul endures when separated, even for a moment, from her God? Who can tell, who can understand, who can even faintly guess, what will be the anguish of longing which shall consume our very being? But why must this be? Why does love, infinite, tender love, inflict such intense pain? Why does the parent turn away from his child, and forbid him his presence for a time? Is it that he loves him less than when he lavished on him the tenderest caresses? ... Why, but because suffering is needed as an atonement to justice, because love cannot be perfected without fear. "It is here tried and purified, but hath in Heaven its perfect rest." Oh! the love of Purgatory! we shall never know it, or understand it, until we are there. Yes, we cannot but think that

195

the greatest, the keenest suffering of the soul will be the remembrance of that which it has seen for a passing moment, and the pining to behold again and forever the face of God. It has been revealed to Saints that so intense is this desire, that the soul would gladly place itself even in the most fearful tortures, could it thus become more quickly purged from that which withholds it from the presence of God. Did we but well consider, and enter into this feeling, we should be much more careful about our imperfections and our venial sins.

* * * * *

The Saints have ever desired suffering, and consider it as the greatest favor which could be bestowed upon them; not that it is in itself desirable, but because it perfects love. Let us, then, we who are not Saints, think of Purgatory with more affection; let us rejoice that, if we are not privileged to have keen, unearthly anguish in this life, we shall yet suffer, and suffer intensely, in the next. Our love will be purified; our dross be purged away; the weary pain which we feel continually when we think how vile we are in the sight of God, how the eye of Jesus, with all its tenderness, must often turn from us in sorrow—the weary pain, the deep degradation of misery and sin, will one day cease; we shall not tremble under our Father's eye, or long to hide ourselves from our Father's countenance. Now we must often feel, when trying with our whole hearts to please God, how impure, how sullied we are before Him. Our pride, our vanity, our impatience, our self-love, are all there. God sees them; how can He, then, look on us as we desire He should? And often we almost long to be in those purging flames, even should it be for years and years, that this vileness might be burned away.

PART V.
LEGENDARY AND POETICAL.

Well beseems
That we should help them wash away the stains
They carried hence; that so, made pure and light,
They may spring upward to the starry spheres.
Ah! so may mercy tempered justice rid
Your burdens speedily; that ye have power
To stretch your wing, which e'en to your desire
Shall lift you.

—DANTE.
LEGENDARY AND POETICAL.
DIES IRÆ.

The day of wrath, that dreadful day
Shall the whole world in ashes lay,
As David and Sybils say.

What horror will invade the mind,
When the strict Judge, who would be kind,
Shall have few venial faults to find!

The last loud trumpet's wondrous sound
Must thro' the rending tombs rebound,

196

And wake the nations underground.
   Nature and death shall with surprise
Behold the pale offender rise,
And view the Judge with conscious eyes.

   Then shall with universal dread,
The sacred mystic book be read,
To try the living and the dead.

   The Judge ascends His awful throne,
He makes each secret sin be known,
And all with shame confess their own.

   O then! what int'rest shall I make,
To save my last important stake,
When the most just have cause to quake!

   Thou mighty formidable King!
Thou mercy's unexhausted spring!
Some comfortable pity bring.

Forget not what my ransom cost,
Nor let my dear-bought soul be lost,
In storms of guilty terror tost.

   Thou, who for me didst feel such pain,
Whose precious blood the cross did stain,
Let not those agonies be vain.

   Thou whom avenging powers obey,
Cancel my debt (too great to pay)
Before the said accounting day.

   Surrounded with amazing fears,
Whose load my soul with anguish hears,
I sigh, I weep, accept my tears.

   Thou, who wast mov'd with Mary's grief,
And by absolving of the thief,
Hast given me hope, now give relief.

   Reject not my unworthy prayer,
Preserve me from the dangerous snare,
  Which death and gaping hell prepare.

  Give my exalted soul a place
Among the chosen right hand race,
The sons of God, and heirs of grace.

   From that insatiate abyss,
Where flames devour and serpents hiss,
Promote me to Thy seat of bliss.

   Prostrate, my contrite heart I rend,
My God, my Father, and my Friend:
Do not forsake me in my end.

   Well may they curse their second birth,

Who rise to a surviving death.
Thou great Creator of mankind,
Let guilty man compassion find.—*Amen.*

AUTHORSHIP OF THE DIES IRÆ.
O'BRIEN. [1]

[Footnote 1: Rev. John O'Brien, A.M., Prof. of Sacred Liturgy in Mount St. Mary's College, Emmettsburg, Md.]

The authorship of the "Dies Iræ" seems the most difficult to settle. This much, however, is certain: that he who has the strongest claims to it is Latino Orsini, generally styled *Frangipani*, whom his maternal uncle, Pope Nicholas III. (Gætano Orsini), raised to the cardinalate in 1278. He was more generally known by the name of Cardinal Malabranca, and was, at first, a member of the Order of St. Dominic. (See *Dublin Review*, Vol. XX., 1846; Gavantus, Thesaur. Sacr. Rit., p. 490.)

As this sacred hymn is conceded to be one of the grandest that has ever been written, it is but natural to expect that the number of authors claiming it would be very large. Some even have attributed it to Pope Gregory the Great, who lived as far back as the year 604. St. Bernard, too, is mentioned in connection with it, and so are several others; but as it is hardly necessary to mention all, we shall only say that, after Cardinal Orsini, the claims to it on the part of Thomas de Celano, of the Order of Franciscans Minor, are the greatest. There is very little reason for attributing it to Father Humbert, the fifth general of the Dominicans in 1273; and hardly any at all for accrediting it to Augustinus de Biella, of the Order of Augustinian Eremites. A very widely circulated opinion is that the "Dies Iræ," as it now stands, is but an improved form of a Sequence which was long in use before the age of any of those authors whom we have cited. Gavantus gives us, at page 490 of his "Thesaurus of Sacred Rites," a few stanzas of this ancient sequence. [1]

[Footnote 1: We subjoin this Latin stanza: Cum recordor moriturus,
Quid post mortem sum futurus
Terror terret me venturus,
Queru expecto non securus.]

* * * * *

To repeat what learned critics of every denomination under heaven have said in praise of this marvellous hymn, would indeed be a difficult task. One of its greatest encomiums is, that there is hardly a language in Europe into which it has not been translated; it has even found its way into Greek and Hebrew—into the former, through an English missionary of Syria, named Hildner; and into the latter, by Splieth, a celebrated Orientalist. Mozart avowed his extreme admiration of it, and so did Dr. Johnson, Sir Walter Scott, and Jeremy Taylor, besides hosts of others. The encomium passed upon it by Schaff is thus given in his own words: "This marvellous hymn is the acknowledged master-piece of Latin poetry and the most sublime of all uninspired hymns. The secret of its irresistible power lies in the awful grandeur of the theme, the intense earnestness and pathos of the poet, the simple majesty and solemn music of its language, the stately metre, the triple rhyme, and the vocal assonances, chosen in striking adaptation—all combining to produce an overwhelming effect, as if we heard the final crash of the universe, the commotion of the opening graves, the trumpet of the archangel summoning the quick and the dead, and saw the King 'of tremendous majesty' seated on the throne of justice and mercy, and ready to dispense everlasting life, or everlasting woe." (See "Latin Hymns," Vol. I. p. 392, by Prof. March, of Lafayette College, Pa.)

The music of this hymn formed a chief part in the fame of Mozart; and it is said, and not without reason, that it contributed in no small degree to hasten his death, for so excited did he become over its awe- enkindling sentiments while writing his celebrated "Mass of Requiem," that a sort of minor paralysis seized his whole frame, so

Terret dies me terroris,

Dies irae, ac furoris,

Dies luctus, ac moeroris,

Dies ultrix peccatoris,

Dies irae, dies illa, etc, etc.

that he was heard to say: "I am certain that I am writing this Requiem for myself. It will be my funeral service." He never lived to finish it; the credit of having done so belongs to Sussmayer, a man of great musical attainments, and a most intimate friend of the Mozart family.— *Dublin Review*, Vol. I., May, 1836.

The allusion to the sibyl in the third line of the first stanza, "Teste David cum Sybilla," [1] has given rise to a good deal of anxious inquiry; and so very strange did it sound to French ears at its introduction into the sacred hymnology of the Church, that the Parisian rituals substituted in its place the line, *Crucis expandens vexilla*. The difficulty is, however, easily overcome if we bear in mind that many of the early Fathers held that Almighty God made use of these sibyls to promulgate His truths in just the same way as He did of Balaam of old, and many others like him. The great St. Augustine has written much on this subject in his "City of God;" and the reader may form some idea of the estimation in which these sibyls were held, when he is told that the world-renowned Michael Angelo made them the subject of one of his greatest paintings…. In the opinions of the ablest critics it was the Erythrean sibyl who uttered the celebrated prediction about the advent of our Divine Lord and His final coming at the last day to judge the living and the dead…. The part of the sibyl's response which referred particularly to the Day of Judgment was written (as an acrostic) on the letters of Soter, or Saviour. It is given as follows in the translation of the "City of God" of St. Augustine:

[Footnote 1: As David and Sibyls say.]

"Sounding, the archangel's trumpet shall peal down from heaven, Over the wicked who groan in their guilt and their manifold sorrows, Trembling, the earth shall be opened, revealing chaos and hell. Every king before God shall stand on that day to be judged; Rivers of fire and of brimstone shall fall from the heavens."

199

DANTE'S "PURGATORIO."

The bright sun was risen
More than two hours aloft; and to the sea
My looks were turned. "Fear not," my master cried.
"Assured we are at happy point. Thy strength
Shrink not, but rise dilated. Thou art come
To Purgatory now. Lo! there the cliff
That circling bounds it. Lo! the entrance there,
Where it doth seem disparted."…

Reader! thou markest how my theme doth rise;
Nor wonder, therefore, if more artfully
I prop the structure. Nearer now we drew,
Arrived whence, in that part where first a breach
As of a wall appeared. I could descry
A portal, and three steps beneath, that led
For inlet there, of different color each;
And one who watched, but spake not yet a word,
As more and more mine eye did stretch its view,
I marked him seated on the highest step,
In visage such as past my power to bear.
Grasped in his hand, a naked sword glanced back
The rays so towards me, that I oft in vain
My sight directed. "Speak from whence ye stand,"
He cried; "What would ye? Where is your escort?
Take heed your coming upward harm ye not."

"A heavenly dame, not skilless of these things,"
Replied the instructor, "told us, even now,
'Pass that way, here the gate is.'" "And may she,
Befriending, prosper your ascent," resumed
The courteous keeper of the gate. "Come, then,
Before our steps." We straightway thither came.

The lowest stair was marble white, so smooth
And polished, that therein my mirrored form
Distinct I saw. The next of hue more dark
Than sablest grain, a rough and singed block
Cracked lengthwise and across. The third, that lay
Massy above, seemed porphyry, that flamed
Red as the life-blood spouting from a vein.
On this God's Angel either foot sustained,
Upon the threshold seated, which appeared
A rock of diamond. Up the trinal steps
My leader cheerily drew me. "Ask," said he,
"With humble heart, that he unbar the bolt."
Piously at his holy feet devolved

I cast me, praying him, for pity's sake,
That he would open to me; but first fell
Thrice on my bosom prostrate. Seven times
The letter that denotes the inward stain,
He, on my forehead, with the blunted point
Of his drawn sword, inscribed. And "Look," he cried,
"When entered, that thou wash these scars away."
Ashes, or earth ta'en dry out of the ground,
Were of one color with the robe he wore.
From underneath that vestment forth he drew
Two keys, of metal twain; the one was gold,
Its fellow, silver. With the pallid first,
And next the burnished, he so plyed the gate,
As to content me well. "Whenever one
Faileth of these that in the key-hole straight
It turn not, to this alley then expect
Access in vain." Such were the words he spake.
"One is more precious, but the other needs
Skill and sagacity, large share of each,
Ere its good task to disengage the knot
Be worthily performed. From Peter these
I hold, of him instructed that I err
Rather in opening, than in keeping fast;
So but the suppliant at my feet implore."
   Then of that hallowed gate he thrust the door.
Exclaiming, "Enter, but this warning hear:
He forth again departs who looks behind."
   As in the hinges of that sacred ward
The swivels turned, sonorous metal strong.
Harsh was the grating; nor so surlily
Rocked the Tarpeian when by force bereft
Of good Metellus, thenceforth from his loss
To leanness doomed. Attentively I turned,
Listening the thunder that first issued forth;
And "We praise Thee, O God," methought I heard,
In accents blended with sweet melody.
The strains came o'er mine ear, e'en as the sound
Of choral voices, that in solemn chant
With organ mingle, and, now high and clear
Come swelling, now float indistinct away.—*Canto IX*.
   * * * * *

   Hell's dunnest gloom, or night unlustrous, dark,
Of every planet reft, and palled in clouds,
Did never spread before the sight a veil

In thickness like that fog, nor to the sense
So palpable and gross. Entering its shade,
Mine eye endured not with unclosed lids;
Which marking, near me drew the faithful guide,
Offering me his shoulder for a stay.

　　As the blind man behind his leader walks,
Lest he should err, or stumble unawares
On what might harm him, or perhaps destroy;
I journeyed through that bitter air and foul,
Still listening to my escort's warning voice,

　　"Look that from me thou part not." Straight I heard
Voices, and each one seemed to pray for peace,
And for compassion to the Lamb of God
That taketh sins away. The prelude still
Was "Agnus Dei;" and, through all the choir,
One voice, one measure ran, that perfect seemed
The concord of their song. "Are these I hear
Spirits, O Master?" I exclaimed; and he,
"Thou aim'st aright: these loose the bonds of wrath."—*Canto*
XVI.

　　　* * * * *

　　Forthwith from every side a shout arose
So vehement, that suddenly my guide
Drew near, and cried: "Doubt not, while I conduct thee."
"Glory!" all shouted (such the sounds mine ear
Gathered from those who near me swelled the sounds),
"Glory in the highest be to God!" We stood
Immovably suspended, like to those,
The shepherds, who first heard in Bethlehem's field
That song: till ceased the trembling, and the song
Was ended: then our hallowed path resumed,
Eyeing the prostrate shadows, who renewed
Their customed mourning. Never in my breast
Did ignorance so struggle with desire
Of knowledge, if my memory do not err,
As in that moment; nor, through haste, dared I
To question, nor myself could aught discern.
So on I fared, in thoughtfulness and dread.—*Canto XX.*

　　　* * * * *

　　Now the last flexure of our way we reached;
And, to the right hand turning, other care
Awaits us. Here the rocky precipice
Hurls forth redundant flames; and from the rim
A blast up-blown, with forcible rebuff

202

Driveth them back, sequestered from its bound.
  Behooved us, one by one, along the side,
That bordered on the void, to pass; and I
Feared on one hand the fire, on the other feared
Headlong to fall: when thus the instructor warned:
"Strict rein must in this place direct the eyes.
A little swerving and the way is lost."
  Then from the bosom of the burning mass,
"O God of mercy!" heard I sung, and felt
No less desire to turn. And when I saw
Spirits along the flame proceeding, I
Between their footsteps and mine own was fain
To share by turns my view. At the hymn's close
They shouted loud, "I do not know a man;" [1]
Then in low voice again took up the strain.-*Canto XXV.*
  [Footnote 1: *I do not know a man.* St. Luke, i. 34.]
  * * * * *

  Now was the sun [1] so stationed, as when first
His early radiance quivers on the heights
Where streamed his Maker's blood; while Libra hangs
Above Hesperian Ebro; and new fires,
Meridian, flash on Ganges' yellow tide.
So day was sinking, when the Angel of God
Appeared before us. Joy was in his mien.
Forth of the flame he stood—upon the brink;
And with a voice, whose lively clearness far
Surpassed our human, "Blessed are the pure
In heart," he sang; then, near him as we came,
"Go ye not further, holy spirits," he cried,
"Ere the fire pierce you; enter in, and list
Attentive to the song ye hear from thence."
I, when I heard his saying, was as one
Laid in the grave. My hands together clasped,
And upward stretching, on the fire I looked,
And busy fancy conjured up the forms,
Erewhile beheld alive, consumed in flames.—*Canto XXVII.*
  [Footnote 1: At Jerusalem it was dawn, in Spain midnight, and in India noonday,
while it was sunset in Purgatory]

HAMLET AND THE GHOST.
SHAKESPEARE.

  HAMLET. Where wilt thou lead me? Speak, I'll go no further.
GHOST. Mark me.
HAM. I will.
GHOST. My hour is almost come,

When I to sulphurous and tormenting flames
Must render up myself.
HAM. Alas! poor ghost!
GHOST. Pity me not, but lend thy serious hearing
To what I shall unfold.
HAM. Speak, I am bound to hear.
GHOST. So art thou to revenge, when thou shalt hear.
HAM. What?
GHOST. I am thy father's spirit;
Doomed for a certain time to walk the night;
And, for the day, confined to fast in fires,
Till the foul crimes, done in my days of nature,
Are burnt and purged away. But that I am forbid
To tell the secrets of my prison-house,
I could a tale unfold, whose lightest word
Would harrow up thy soul; freeze thy young blood;
Make thy two eyes, like stars, start from their spheres;
Thy knotted and combined locks to part,
And each particular hair to stand on end,
Like quills upon the fretful porcupine;
But this eternal blason must not be
To ears of flesh and blood.

CALDERON'S "PURGATORY OF ST. PATRICK."

In a work of this nature, it is essential to its purpose that the compiler should take cognizance of the many legends, wild and extravagant as some of them are, which have been current at various times and amongst various peoples, on the subject of Purgatory. For they have, indeed, a deep significance, proving how strong a hold this belief in a middle state of souls has taken on the popular mind. They are, in a certain sense, a part of Catholic tradition, and have to do with what is called Catholic instinct. They prove that this dogma of the Church has found a home in the hearts of the people, and become familiar to them, as the tales of childhood whispered around the winter hearth. If it appear now and then, in some such uncouth disguise, as that which we, are about to present to our readers, we see, nevertheless, through it all the truth, or rather the fragments of truth, such as is often found floating about through Europe on the breath of tradition. The curious legend has been turned by Calderon from dross into precious gold. He presents it to us in his "Purgatory of St. Patrick" with a beauty that divests it of much of its native wildness. He presumably drew his materials for the drama from a work, "The Life and Purgatory of St. Patrick," published in Spain in 1627 by Montalvan, a Spanish dramatist. It was translated into French by a Franciscan priest and doctor of theology, François Bouillon; as also into Portuguese by Father Manuel Caldeira. When this work was issued Calderon was wish the army in Flanders. He must have seen it, his brilliant imagination at once taking hold of it as the groundwork for a splendid effort of his genius.

204

We cite here an extract from an introduction by Denis Florence MacCarthy to his translation of Calderon's "Purgatory of St. Patrick." It will be of interest as following the thread of this weird legend:

The curious history of Ludovico Enio, on which the principal interest of this play depends, has been alluded to, and given more or less fully by many ancient authors. The name, though slightly altered by the different persons who have mentioned him, can easily be recognized as the same in all, whether as Owen, Oien, Owain, Eogan, Euenius, or Ennius. Perhaps the earliest allusion to him in any printed English work is that contained in 'Ranulph Hidgen's Polychronicon,' published at Westminster by Wynkin de Worde, in 1495: 'In this Steven's tyme, a knyght that hyght Owen wente into the Purgatory of the second Patrick, abbot, and not byshoppe. He came agayne and dwelled in the abbaye of Ludene of Whyte Monks in Irlonde, and tolde of joycs and of paynes that he had seen.'

The history of Enio had, however, existed in manuscript for nearly three centuries and a half before the Polychronicon was printed; it had been written by Henry, the Monk of Salterey, in Huntingdonshire, from the account which he had received from Gilbert, a Cistercian monk of the Abbey of the Blessed Virgin Mary of Luden, or Louth, above mentioned. [1] Colgan, after collating this manuscript with two others on the same subject, which he had seen, printed it nearly in full in his "Trias." ... Matthew Paris had, however, before this, in his "History of England," under date 1153, given a full account of the adventures of OEnus in the Purgatory. ... Sir Walter Scott mentions, in his "Border Minstrelsy," that there is a curious Metrical Romance in the Advocates' Library of Edinburgh, called "The Legend of Sir Owain," relating his adventures in St. Patrick's Purgatory; he gives some stanzas from it, descriptive of the knight's passage of "The Brig o' Dread;" which, in the legend, is placed between Purgatory and Paradise. This poem is supposed to have been written early in the fourteenth century.

[Footnote 1: Colgan's "Trias Thanmaturgæ," p. 281, Ware's "Annals of Ireland," A.D. 1497.]

A second extract on the subject, taken from the Essay by Mr. Wright on the "Purgatory of St. Patrick," published in London in 1844, gives still further information with regard to it.

"The mode," he says, "in which this legend was made public is thus told in the Latin narrative. Gervase (the founder and first Abbot of Louth, in Lincolnshire) sent his monk, Gilbert, to the king, then in Ireland, to obtain a grant to build a monastery there. Gilbert, on his arrival, complained to the king, Henry II., that he did not understand the language of the country. The king said to him,' I will give you an excellent interpreter,' and sent him the knight Owain, who remained with him during the time he was occupied in building the monastery, and repeated to him frequently the story of his adventures in Purgatory. Gilbert and his companions subsequently returned to England, and there he repeated the story, and some one said he thought it was all a dream, to which Gilbert answered: 'That there were some who believed that those who entered the Purgatory fell into a trance, and saw the vision in the spirit, but that the knight had denied this, and declared that the whole was seen and felt really in the body.' Both Gilbert, from whom Henry of Salterey received the story, and the bishop of the diocese, assured him that many perished in this Purgatory, and were never heard of afterwards." It is clear from the allusion to it in Cæsarius of Heisterbach, that already, at the beginning of the thirteenth century, St. Patrick's Purgatory had become famous throughout Europe. 'If any one doubt of Purgatory,' says this writer, 'let him go to Scotland (i. e., Ireland, to which this name was anciently given), and enter the Purgatory of St. Patrick, and his doubts will be expelled.' This recommendation was frequently acted upon in that, and particularly in the following century, when pilgrims from all parts of Europe, some of them men of rank and wealth, repaired thither. On the patent rolls in the Tower of London, under the year 1358, we have an instance of testimonials given by the king, Edward III., on the same day, to two distinguished foreigners, one a noble Hungarian, the other a Lombard, Nicholas de Becariis, of their having faithfully performed this pilgrimage. And still later, in 1397, we find King Richard II. granting a safe conduct to visit the same place to Raymond, Viscount of Perilhos, Knight of Rhodes, and Chamberlain of the King of France, with twenty men and thirty horses. Raymond de Perilhos, on his return to his native country, wrote a narrative of what he had seen, in the dialect of the Limousin (*Lemosinalingna*), of which a Latin version was printed by O'Sullivan in his '_Historia Catholica Ibernica.' ... This is a mere compilation from the story of 'Henry of Salterey,' and begins, like that, with an account of the origin of the Purgatory. He represents himself as having been first a minister to Charles V. of France, and subsequently the intimate friend of John I. of Aragon, after whose death (in 1395) he was seized with the desire of knowing how he was treated in the other world, and determined, like a new Æneas, to go into St. Patrick's Purgatory in search of him. He saw precisely the same sights as the knight, Owain, but (as in Calderon) only twelve men came to him in the hall instead of fifteen, and in the fourth hall of punishments he saw King John of Aragon, and many others of his friends and relations.

We will now select from the drama of "Calderon" a few characteristic passages, to show how this subject was treated by the glowing pen and fervid fancy of the greatest of all the poets of Catholic Spain, whose poetry, indeed, is deserving of more widespread appreciation than it has yet received at the hands of the Catholic reading public. We will begin with those lines in which Ludovico Enio, the hero of the tale, makes known his identity to King Egerio.

LUDOVICO. Listen, most beautiful divinity,
For thus begins the story of my life.
Great Egerio, King of Ireland, I
Am Ludovico Enio—a Christian also—
In this do Patrick and myself agree,
And differ, being Christians both,
And yet as opposite as good from evil.

But for the faith which I sincerely hold
(So greatly do I estimate its worth),
I would lay down a hundred thousand lives—
Bear witness, thou all-seeing Lord and God.
      . . . . . . All crimes,
Theft, murder, treason, sacrilege, betrayal
Of dearest friends, all these I must relate.
For these are all my glory and my pride.
In one of Ireland's many islands I
Was born, and much do I suspect that all
The planets seven, in wild confusion strange,
Assisted at my most unhappy birth.

    He proceeds with a catalogue of his crimes, most dark, indeed, and relates how St. Patrick, who was present, had saved him from shipwreck. The King, however, who is a pagan, takes the Knight into his service, while he bids the Saint begone. Before they part Patrick asks of him a favor:

PATRICK. This one boon I ask—
LUDOVICO. What is it?
PATRICK. That, alive or dead, we meet
In this world once again.
LUDOVICO. Dost thou demand
So strange and dread a promise from me?
PATRICK. Yes.
LUDOVICO. I give it to thee then.
PATRICK. And I accept it.

    What follows is from a conversation between Patrick and the King, wherein are explained many of the truths of faith, including the existence of heaven and of hell. Thus the Saint:

PATRICK. There are more places
In the other world than those of
Everlasting pain and glory:
Learn, O King, that there's another,
Which is Purgatory; whither
Flies the soul that has departed
In a state of grace; but bearing
Still some stains of sin upon it:
For with these no soul can enter
God's pure kingdom—there it dwelleth
Till it purifies and burneth
All the dross from out its nature;
Then it flieth, pure and limpid,
Into God's divinest presence.

    KING. So you say, but I have nothing,
Save your own words, to convince me;

Give me of the soul's existence
Some strong proof—some indication—
Something tangible and certain—
Which my hands may feel and grasp at.
And since you appear so powerful
With your God, you can implore him,
That to finish my conversion,
He may show some real being,
Not a mere ideal essence,
Which all men can touch; remember,
But one single hour remaineth
For this task: this day you give us
Certain proofs of pain or glory,
Or you die: where we are standing
Let your God display his wonders—
And since we, perhaps, may merit
Neither punishment nor glory,
Let the other place be shown us,
Which you say is Purgatory.
   PATRICK then prays, concluding with the words:
   "I ask, O Lord, may from Thy hand be given,
That Purgatory, Hell, and Heaven
May be revealed unto those mortals' sight."
   An Angel then descends and speaks as follows:
   ANGEL. Patrick, God has heard thy prayer,
He has listened to thy vows;
And as thou hast ask'd, allows
Earth's great secrets to lie bare.
Seek along this island ground
For a vast and darksome cave,
Which restrains the lake's dark wave,
And supports the mountains round;
He who dares to go therein,
Having first contritely told
All his faults, shall there behold
  Where the soul is purged from sin.
He shall see with mortal eyes
Hell itself—where those who die
In their sins forever lie,
In the fire that never dies.
He shall see, in blest fruition,
Where the happy spirits dwell.
But of this be sure as well—
He who without true contrition

Enters there to idly try
What the cave may be, doth go
To his death—he'll suffer woe
While the Lord doth reign on high.
Who this day shall set you free
From this poor world's weariness;
  He shall grant to you, in pity,
Bliss undreamed by mortal men—
Making thee a denizen
Of his own celestial city.
He shall to the world proclaim
His omnipotence and glory,
By the wondrous Purgatory,
Which shall bear thy sainted name.

    Polonia, the King's daughter, whom Ludovico had married and deserted, having first tried to kill her, appears upon the scene just as the King, Patrick, and some others, who have set out upon their quest for the Purgatory, have reached a gloomy mountain and a deep cave. Polonia relates the wonders and the terrors of the cavern through which she has passed. Patrick then speaks as follows:

    PATRICK. This cave, Egerio, which you see, concealeth
Many mysteries of life and death,
Not for him whose hardened bosom feeleth
Nought of true repentance or true faith.
But he who freely enters, who revealeth
All his sins with penitential breath,
Shall endure his Purgatory then,
And return forgiven back again.

  Later in the drama we find Ludovico desiring
  "To enter
Into Patrick's Purgatory;
Humbly and devoutly keeping
Thus the promise that I gave him."

  Again, he says:
  "I have faith and firm reliance
That you yet shall see me happy,
If in God's name blessed Patrick,
  "Aid me in the Purgatory."

    Having confessed his sins and made due preparation, he enters the cave. On his return hence, the Priest, or Canon as he is called, bids him relate the wonders he has seen. He finds himself first "in thick and pitchy darkness," he hears horrid clangor, and falls down at length into a hall of jasper, where he meets with twelve grave men, who encourage him, and bid him keep up his courage amid the fearful sights he is to behold later on. At length he reaches the Purgatory:

  "I approached another quarter;

There it seemed that many spirits
I had known elsewhere, were gathered
Into one vast congregation,
Where, although 'twas plain they suffered,
Still they looked with joyous faces,
Wore a peaceable appearance,
Uttered no impatient accents,
But, with moistened eyes uplifted
Towards the heavens, appeared imploring
Pity, and their sins lamenting.
This, in truth, was Purgatory,
Where the sins that are more venial
Are purged out."

He then alludes to that Bridge or "Brig o' Dread," to which allusion will be
made in another portion of our volume. As this passage is celebrated, it is well to
give it in full:

LUDOVICO. To a river did they lead me,
Flowers of fire were on its margin,
Liquid sulphur was its current,
Many-headed hydras—serpents—
Monsters of the deep were in it;
It was very broad, and o'er it
Lay a bridge, so slight and narrow
That it seem'd a thin line only.
It appear'd so weak and fragile,
That the slightest weight would sink it.
"Here thy pathway lies," they told me,
"O'er this bridge so weak and narrow;
And, for thy still greater horror,
Look at those who've pass'd before thee."
Then I look'd, and saw the wretches
Who the passage were attempting
Fall amid the sulphurous current,
Where the snakes with teeth and talons
Tore them to a thousand pieces.
Notwithstanding all these horrors,
I, the name of God invoking,
Undertook the dreadful passage,
And, undaunted by the billows,
Or the winds that blew around me,
Reached the other side in safety.
Here within a wood I found me,
So delightful and so fertile,
That the past was all forgotten.

On my path rose stately cedars,
Laurels—all the trees of Eden.

After having described some of the glories of this abode of bliss, he relates his meeting with "the resplendent, the most glorious, the great Patrick, the Apostle"—and was thus enabled to keep his early promise. The poem ends with the following somewhat confused list of authorities:

"For with this is now concluded
The historic legend told us
By Dionysius, the great Carthusian,
With Henricus Salteriensis,
Cæsarius Heisterbachensis,
Matthew Paris, and Ranulphus,
Monbrisius, Marolicus Siculus,
David Rothe, and the judicious
Primate over all Hibernia,
Bellarmino, Beda, Serpi,
Friar Dymas, Jacob Sotin,
Messingham, and in conclusion
The belief and pious feeling
Which have everywhere maintained it."

From Alban Butler's notes to "Lives of the Saints," Vol. I. p. 103, we subjoin the following:

"St. Patrick's Purgatory is a cave on an island in the Lake Dearg (Lough Derg), in the County of Donegal, near the borders of Fermanagh. Bollandus shows the falsehood of many things related concerning it. Upon complaint of certain superstitious and false notions of the vulgar, in 1497, it was stopped up by an order of the Pope. See Bollandus, 'Tillemont,' p. 287, Alemand in his 'Monastic Hist. of Ireland,' and Thiers, 'Hist. des. Superst.' I. 4 ed. Nov. It was soon after opened again by the inhabitants; but only according to the original institution, as Bollandus takes notice, as a penitential retirement for those who voluntarily chose it, probably in imitation of St. Patrick, or other saints, who had there dedicated themselves to a penitential state. They usually spent several days here, living on bread and water, lying on rushes, praying and making stations barefoot."

THE BRIG O' DREAD.
SIR WALTER SCOTT.

In connection with the extracts which we have given from the celebrated Drama of Calderon, the "Purgatory of St. Patrick," and in particular of that one which relates to the passage of Ludovico over the bridge which leads from Purgatory to Paradise, it will be interesting to quote the following from Sir Walter Scott's "Minstrelsy of the Scottish Border:"

"There is a sort of charm, sung by the lower ranks of Roman Catholics, in some parts of the north of England, while watching a dead body previous to interment. The tone is doleful and monotonous, and, joined to the mysterious import of the words, has a solemn effect. The word sleet, in the chorus, seems to be corrupted from selt or salt; a quantity of which, in compliance with a popular superstition, is frequently placed on the breast of a corpse. The mythologic ideas of the dirge are common to various creeds. The Mahometan believes that, in advancing to the final judgment seat, he must traverse a bar of red-hot iron, stretched across a bottomless gulf. The good works of each true believer, assuming a substantial form, will then interpose between his feet and this 'Bridge of Dread;' but the wicked, having no such protection, fall headlong into the abyss." Passages similar to this dirge are also to be found in "Lady Culross' Dream," as quoted in the second Dissertation, prefixed by Mr. Pinkerton to his select Scottish Ballads, 2 vols. The dreamer journeys towards heaven, accompanied and assisted by a celestial guide:

"Through dreadful dens, which made my heart aghast,
He bore me up when I began to tire.
Sometimes we clamb o'er craggy mountains high,
And sometimes stay'd on ugly braes of sand.
   "They were so stay that wonder was to see;
But when I fear'd, he held me by the hand.
Through great deserts we wandered on our way—
Forward we passed a narrow bridge of trie,
O'er waters great, which hideously did roar."

Again, she supposes herself suspended over an infernal gulf:

"Ere I was ware, one gripped me at the last,
And held me high above a flaming fire.
The fire was great, the heat did pierce me sore;
My faith grew-weak; my grip was very small.
I trembled fast; my faith grew more and more."

A horrible picture of the same kind, dictated probably by the author's unhappy state of mind, is to be found in Brooke's "Fool of Quality." The Russian funeral service, without any allegorical imagery, expresses the sentiment of the dirge in language alike simple and noble: "Hast thou pitied the afflicted, O man? In death shalt thou be pitied. Hast thou consoled the orphan? The orphan will deliver thee. Hast thou clothed the naked? The naked will procure thee protection."— *Richardson's "Anecdotes of Russia."*

But the most minute description of the Brig o' Dread occurs in the legend of Sir Owain, No. XL. in the MS. collection of romances, W. 4. I, Advocates' Library, Edinburgh. Sir Owain, a Northumbrian knight, after many frightful adventures in St. Patrick's Purgatory, at last arrives at the bridge, which, in the legend, is placed betwixt Purgatory and Paradise:

"The fendes han the Knight ynome,
To a stink and water thai ben ycome,
He no seigh never er non swiche;
It stank fouler than ani hounde,
And mani mile it was to the grounde,
And was as swart as piche.

"And Owain seigh ther ouer ligge
A swithe, strong, naru brigge:
The fendes seyd tho;
Lo, Sir Knight, sestow this,
This is the brigge of Paradis,
Here ouer thou must go.
    "And we the schul with stones prowe
And the winde the schul ouer blow,
And wirche the ful wo;
Thou no schalt for all this unduerd,
Bot gif thou falle a midwerd, To our fewes [1] mo.
    [Footnote 1: Sir Walter Scott says probably a contraction of "fellows."]
    "And when thou art adoun yfalle,
Than schal com our felawes alle,
And with her hokes the hede;
We schul the teche a newe playe:
Thou hast served ous mani a day,
And into helle the lede.
    "Owain biheld the brigge smert,
The water ther under blek and swert,
And sore him gan to drede;
For of othing he tok yeme,
Never mot, in sonne beme,
Thicker than the fendes yede.
    "The brigge was as heigh as a tower,
And as scharpe as a rasour,
And naru it was also;
    "And the water that ther run under,
Brend o' lighting and of thonder,
That thocht him michel wo.
    "Ther nis no clerk may write with ynke,
No no man no may bithink, No no maister deuine;
That is ymade forsoth ywis,
Under the brigge of paradis Halven del the pine.
    "So the dominical ous telle,
Ther is the pure entrae of helle,
Seine Poule [1] verth witnesse;
Whoso falleth of the brigge adown,
Of him nis no redempcion, Neither more nor lesse.
    [Footnote 1: St. Paul.]
    "The fendes seyd to the Knight tho,
'Ouer this brigge might thou nowght go,
For noneskines nede;
Fie peril sorwe and wo,

213

And to that stede ther thou com fro,
Wel fair we schul the lede.'
  "Owain anon began bithenche,
Fram hou mani of the fendes wrenche,
God him saved hadde;
He sett his fot opon the brigge,
No feld he no scharpe egge,
No nothing him no drad.
  "When the fendes yseigh tho,
That he was more than half ygo,
Loude thai gun to crie:
Allas! Allas! that he was born!
This ich night we habe forlorn
Out of our baylie."—*Minstrelsy of Scottish Border.*

SHELLEY AND THE PURGATORY OF ST. PATRICK.

It will be of interest to quote the following passage from one of Shelley's best known works, "The Cenci," of which he himself says: "An idea in this speech was suggested by a most sublime passage in 'El Purgatorio de San Patricio,' of Calderon."

"But I remember, Two miles on this side of the fort, the road Crosses a deep ravine; 'tis rough and narrow, And winds with short turns down the precipice; And in its depths there is a mighty rock Which has, from unimaginable years, Sustained itself with terror and with toil Over the gulf, and with the agony With which it clings seems slowly coming down; Even as a wretched soul, hour after hour, Clings to the mass of life; yet clinging, leans; And leaning, makes more dark the dread abyss In which it fears to fall; beneath this crag Huge as despair, as if in weariness, The melancholy mountain yawns."

ON A GREAT FUNERAL. [1]

[Footnote: The above lines apply with peculiar impressiveness to the funeral of General Grant, so lately occupying public attention.]

AUBREY DE VERE.

No more than this? The chief of nations bears Her chief of sons to his last resting-place; Through the still city, sad and slow of pace, The sable pageant streams; and as it nears That dome, to-day a vault funereal, tears Run down the gray-hair'd veteran's wintry face; Deep organs sob and flags their front abase; And the snapt wand the rite complete declares. Soul, that before thy Judge dost stand this day, Disrobed of strength and puissance, pomp and power; O soul! defrauded at thine extreme hour Of man's sole help from man, and latest stay, Swells there for thee no prayer from all that host, And is this burial but a nation's boast?

"MORTE D'ARTHUR."

TENNYSON.

Then loudly cried the bold Sir Bedivere,
"Ah! my Lord Arthur, whither shall I go?
Where shall I hide my forehead and my eyes?

214

For now I see the true old times are dead,
When every morning brought a noble chance,
And every chance brought out a noble knight.
Such times have been not since the light that led
The holy Elders with the gift of myrrh.
But now the whole Round Table is dissolved
Which was an image of the mighty world;
And I, the last, go forth companionless,
And the days darken round me, and the years,
Among new men, strange faces, other minds."
  And slowly answered Arthur from the barge:
"The old order changeth, yielding place to new,
And God fulfils Himself in many ways.
Lest one good custom should corrupt the world.
Comfort thyself: what comfort is in me?
I have lived my life, and that which I have done
May He within Himself make pure! but thou,
If thou shouldst never see my face again,
Pray for my soul.
More things are wrought by prayer
Than this world dreams of.
Wherefore, let thy voice
Rise like fountain for me night and day.
For what are men better than sheep or goats
That nourish a blind life within the brain,
If, knowing God, they lift not hands of prayer
Both for themselves and those who call them friend?
For so the whole round earth is every way
Bound by gold chains about the feet of God.
But now farewell!
I am going a long way
With these thou seest—if indeed I go
(For all my mind is clouded with a doubt)
To the island-valley of Avilion;
Where falls not hail, or rain, or any snow;
Nor ever wind blows loudly; but it lies
Deep-meadowed, happy, fair with orchard lawns
And bowery hollows crowned with summer sea,
Where I will heal me of my grievous wound."
  So said he, and the barge with oar and sail
Moved from the brink, like some full-breasted swan.
That, fluting a wild carol, ere her death,
Ruffles her pure cold plume, and takes the flood
With swarthy webs.

Long stood Sir Bedivere
Revolving many memories, till the hull
Looked one black dot against the verge of dawn,
And on the meer the wailing died away.

GUIDO AND HIS BROTHER.
COLLIN DE PLANCY.

The brother who forgets his brother is no longer a man, he is a monster.—Sr. John Chrysostom.

Peter the Venerable relates the story of a lord of his time, named Guy or Guido, who had lost his life in battle; this was very common in the Middle Ages, when the nobles were beyond all else great warriors. As this Guido had not been able to make his last confession, he appeared fully armed, to a priest, some time after his death.

"Stephanus," said he (that was the name of the priest), "I pray thee go to my brother Anselm; thou shalt tell him that I conjure him to restore an ox which I took from a peasant," naming him; "and also to repair the damage I did to a village which did not—belong to me, by wrongfully imposing taxes thereupon. I was unable to confess, or to expiate these two sins, for which I am grievously tormented. As an assurance of what I tell thee," continued the apparition, "I warn thee that, when thou returnest to thy dwelling, thou shalt find that the money thou hast saved to make the pilgrimage of St. James has been stolen."

The priest, on his return, actually found that his strongbox had been broken open and his money carried off; but he could not discharge his commission, because Anselm was absent.

A few days after, the same Guido appeared a second time, to reproach Stephanus for his neglect. The good priest excused himself on the impossibility of finding Anselm; but learning that he had returned to his manor, he repaired thither, and faithfully fulfilled his commission.

He was received very coolly. Anselm told him that he was not obliged to do penance for the sins of his brother; and with these words he dismissed him.

The dead man, who experienced no relief, appeared a third time, and bemoaning his brother's harshness, he besought the worthy servant of God to have compassion himself on his distress, and assist him in his extremity. Stephanus, much affected, promised that he would, He restored the price of the stolen ox, gave alms to the wronged village, said prayers, recommended the deceased to all the good people he knew, and then Guido appeared no more.

BERTHOLD IN PURGATORY.
COLLIN DE PLANCY.

Miseremini mei, miseremini mei, saltem vos, amici moi.—JOB xix.

A short time after the death of Charles the Bald, there is found in Hincmar a narrative which it may be well to introduce here; it is the journey of Berthold, or Bernold, to Purgatory in the spirit.

Berthold was a citizen of Rheims, of good life, fulfilling his Christian duties and enjoying public esteem. He was subject to ecstasies, or syncope, which sometimes lasted a good while. Then, whether he had visions, or that his soul transported itself or was transported out of his body—an effect which, is evidently produced in our days by magnetism—he made, in his ecstasies, several journeys into Purgatory.

Having fallen seriously ill when already well advanced in age, he received all the sacraments which console the conscience; after which he remained four entire days in a sort of ecstasy, during which he took no nourishment of any kind. At the end of the fourth day he had become so weak that there was hardly any breath in him. About midnight, however, he begged his wife to send quickly for his confessor. He afterwards remained motionless. But, at the end of a quarter of an hour, he said to his wife:

"Place a seat here, for the priest is coming."

He entered the moment after, and recited the beautiful prayers for the departing soul, to which Berthold responded clearly and exactly. After this he had again a moment of ecstasy; and, coming out of it, he related his several visits to Purgatory, and the commissions wherewith he had been charged by many suffering souls.

He was conducted by a spirit, an Angel doubtless. Amongst those who were being purified, in ice or in fire, he found Ebbon, Archbishop of Rheims; Pardule, Bishop of Laon; Enée, Bishop of Paris, and some other prelates, clothed in filthy garments, torn and rusty. Their faces were wrinkled, haggard, and sallow. Ebbon besought him to ask the clergy and people of Rheims to pray for him and his companions, who made him the same request. He charged himself with all these commissions.

He found, farther on, or in another visit, the soul of Charles the Bald, extended in the mud and much exhausted. The ex-king asked Berthold to recommend him to Archbishop Hincmar and the princes of his family, acknowledging that he was principally punished for having given ecclesiastical benefices to courtiers and worldly laics, as had been done by his ancestor, Charles Martel. Berthold promised to do what he could.

Farther on, and perhaps also on another occasion, he saw Jesse, Bishop of Orleans, in the hands of four dark spirits, who were plunging him alternately into a well of boiling pitch and one of ice-cold water. Not far from him, Count Othaire was in other torments. The two sufferers recommended themselves, like the others, to the pious offices of Berthold, who faithfully executed the commissions of the souls in pain. He applied, on behalf of the bishops, to their clergy and people; for King Charles the Bald, to Archbishop Hincmar. He wrote besides—for he was a lettered man—to the relatives of the deceased monarch, making known to them the state wherein he had seen him. He went to urge the wife of Othaire, his vassals and friends, to offer up prayers and give alms for him; and in a last visit which he was permitted to make, he learned that Count Othaire and Bishop Jessé were delivered; King Charles the Bald had reached the term of his punishment; and he saw the Bishops Ebbon, Enée, and Pardule, who thanked him as they went forth from Purgatory, fresh and robed in white.

217

After this account, whereto Berthold subjoined that his guide had promised him some more years of life, he asked for Holy Communion, received it, felt himself cured, left his bed on the following day, and his life was prolonged for fourteen years.

A LEGEND OF ST. NICHOLAS.

Let us quote here, says Collin de Plancy, a good English religious whose journey has been related by Peter the Venerable, Abbot of Cluny, and by Denis the Carthusian. This traveller speaks in the first person:

"I had St. Nicholas for a guide," he says; "he led me by a level road to a vast horrible space, peopled with the dead, who were tormented in a thousand frightful ways. I was told that these people were not damned, that their torment would in time come to an end, and that it was Purgatory I saw. I did not expect to find it so severe. All these unfortunates wept hot tears and groaned aloud. Since I have seen all these things I know well that if I had any relative in Purgatory, I would suffer a thousand deaths to take him out of it.

"A little farther on, I perceived a valley, through which flowed a fearful river of fire, which rose in waves to an enormous height. On the banks of that river it was so icy cold that no one can have any idea of it. St. Nicholas conducted me thither, and made me observe the sufferers who were there, telling me that this again was Purgatory."

"DREAM OF GERONTIUS."
CARDINAL NEWMAN.

ANGEL. Thy judgment now is near, for we are come Into the veiled presence of our God.

SOUL. I hear the voices that I left on earth.

ANGEL. It is the voice of friends around thy bed,
Who say the "Subvenite" with the priest.
Hither the echoes come; before the
Throne Stands the great Angel of the Agony,
The same who strengthened Him, what time He knelt
Lone in that garden shade, bedewed with blood.
That Angel best can plead with Him for all
Tormented souls, the dying and the dead.

ANGEL OF THE AGONY. Jesu! by that shuddering dread which fell on Thee;
Jesu! by that cold dismay which sicken'd Thee;
Jesu! by that pang of heart which thrill'd in Thee;
Jesu! by that mount of sins which crippled Thee;
Jesu! by that sense of guilt which stifled Thee;
Jesu! by that innocence which girdled Thee;
Jesu! by that sanctity which reign'd in Thee;
Jesu! by that Godhead which was one with Thee;
Jesu! spare these souls which are so dear to Thee;
Who in prison, calm and patient, wait for Thee;
Hasten, Lord, their hour, and bid them come to Thee,

To that glorious Home, where they shall ever gaze on Thee.

SOUL. I go before my Judge. Ah! …

ANGEL. … Praise to His Name! The eager spirit has darted from my hold,
And, with the intemperate energy of love,
Flies to the dear feet of Emmanuel;
But, ere it reach them, the keen sanctity,
Which, with its effluence, like a glory, clothes
And circles round the Crucified, has seized,
And scorch'd, and shrivell'd it; and now it lies
Passive and still before the awful Throne.
O happy, suffering soul! for it is safe,
Consumed, yet quicken'd, by the glance of God.

SOUL. Take me away, and in the lowest deep
There let me be, And there in hope the lone night-watches keep,
Told out for me.
There, motionless and happy in my pain,
Lone, not forlorn,—There will I sing my sad, perpetual strain,
Until the morn.
There will I sing, and soothe my stricken breast,
Which ne'er can cease
To throb, and pine, and languish, till possess'd
Of its Sole Peace.
There will I sing my absent Lord and Love:—Take me away,
That sooner I may rise, and go above,
And see Him in the truth—of everlasting day.

ANGEL. Now let the golden prison ope its gates,
Making sweet music, as each fold revolves
Upon its ready hinge.
And ye, great powers,
Angels of Purgatory, receive from me
My charge, a precious soul, until the day,
When from all bond and forfeiture released,
I shall reclaim it for the courts of light.

SOULS IN PURGATORY

1. Lord, Thou hast been our refuge: in every generation;

2. Before the hills were born, and the world was: from age to age, Thou art God.

3. Bring us not, Lord, very low: for Thou hast said, Come back again, ye sons of Adam!

4. A thousand years before Thine eyes are but as yesterday: and as a watch of the night which is come and gone.

5. The grass springs up in the morning: at evening-tide it shrivels up and dies.

6. So we fall in Thine anger: and in Thy wrath are we troubled.

219

7. Thou hast set our sins in Thy sight: and our round of days in the light of Thy countenance.

8. Come back, O Lord! how long: and be entreated for Thy servants.

9. In Thy morning we shall be filled with Thy mercy: we shall rejoice and be in pleasure all our days.

10. We shall be glad according to the days of our humiliation: and the years in which we have seen evil.

11. Look, O Lord, upon Thy servants and upon Thy work: and direct their children.

12. And let the beauty of the 'Lord our God be upon us: and the work of our hands, establish Thou it.

Glory be to the Father, and to the Son: and to the Holy Ghost.

As it was in the beginning, is now, and ever shall be: world without end. Amen.

ANGEL. Softly and gently, dearly-ransom'd soul, In my most loving arms I now enfold thee, And, o'er the penal waters, as they roll, I poise thee, and I lower thee, and hold thee.

And carefully I dip thee in the lake, And thou, without a sob, or a resistance, Dost through the flood thy rapid passage take, Sinking deep, deeper, into the dim distance.

Angels, to whom the willing task is given, Shall tend, and nurse, and lull thee, as thou liest; And Masses on the earth, and prayers in heaven, Shall aid thee at the throne of the Most High.

Farewell, but not for ever! brother dear, Be brave and patient on thy bed of sorrow; Swiftly shall pass thy night of trial here, And I will come and wake thee on the morrow.

ST. GREGORY RELEASES THE SOUL OF THE EMPEROR TRAJAN
MRS. JAMESON.

In a little picture in the Bologna Academy he is seen praying before a tomb, on which is inscribed "TRAJANO IMPERADOR;" beneath are two angels, raising the soul of Trafan out of flames. Such is the usual treatment of this curious and poetical legend, which is thus related in the "Legenda Aurea": "It happened on a time, as Trajan was hastening to battle at the head of his legions, that a poor widow flung herself in his path, and cried aloud for justice, and the emperor stayed to listen to her; and she demanded vengeance for the innocent blood of her son, killed by the son of the emperor. Trajan promised to do her justice when he returned from his expedition. 'But, sire', answered the widow, 'should you be killed in battle, who will then do me justice?' 'My successor,' replied Trajan. And she said, 'What will it signify to you, great emperor, that any other than yourself should do me justice? Is it not better that you should do this good action yourself than leave another to do it?' And Trajan alighted, and having examined into the affair, he gave up his own son to her in place of him she had lost, and bestowed on her likewise a rich dowry. Now, it came to pass that as Gregory was one day meditating in his daily walk, this action of the Emperor Trajan came into his mind, and he wept bitterly to think that a man so just should be condemned to eternal punishment. And entering a church, he prayed most fervently that the soul of the good emperor might be released from torment. And a voice said to him, 'I have granted thy prayer, and I have spared the soul of Trajan for thy sake; but because thou hast supplicated for one whom the justice of God had already condemned, thou shalt choose one of two things: either thou shalt endure for two days the fires of Purgatory, or thou shalt be sick and infirm for the remainder of thy life.' Gregory chose the latter, which sufficiently accounts for the grievous pains and infirmities to which this great and good man was subjected, even to the day of his death."

This story of Trajan was extremely popular in the Middle Ages; it is illustrative of the character of Gregory.... Dante twice alludes to it. He describes it as being one of the subjects sculptured on the walls of Purgatory, and takes occasion to relate the whole story.

"There was storied on the rock Th'exalted glory of the Roman Prince, Whose mighty worth moved Gregory to earn This mighty conquest—Trajan the Emperor. A widow at his bridle stood attired In tears and mourning. Round about them troop'd Full throng of knights: and overhead in gold The eagles floated, struggling with the wind The wretch appear'd amid all these to say: 'Grant vengeance, sire! for woe, beshrew this heart, My son is murder'd!' He, replying, seem'd: 'Wait now till I return.' And she, as one Made hasty by her grief: 'O, sire, if thou Dost not return?'—'Where I am, who then is, May right thee.'—'What to thee is others' good, If thou neglect thine own?'—'Now comfort thee,' At length he answers: 'It beseemeth well My duty be perform'd, ere I move hence. So justice wills and pity bids me stay.'"—*Purg. Canto X.*

It was through the efficacy of St. Gregory's intercession that Dante afterwards finds Trajan in Paradise, seated between King David and King Hezekiah.—*Purg. Canto XX.*

ST. GREGORY AND THE MONK

There was a monk who, in defiance of his vow of poverty, secreted in his cell three pieces of gold. Gregory, on learning this, excommunicated him, and shortly afterwards the monk died. When Gregory heard that the monk had perished in his sin, without receiving absolution, he was filled with grief and horror, and he wrote upon a parchment a prayer and a form of absolution, and gave it to one of his deacons, desiring him to go to the grave of the deceased and read it there: on the following night the monk appeared in a vision, and revealed to him his release from torment.

This story is represented in the beautiful bas-relief in white marble in front of the altar of his chapel; it is the last compartment on the right.

In chapels dedicated to the Service of the Dead, St. Gregory is often represented in the attitude of supplication, while on one side, or in the background, angels are raising the tormented souls out of the flames.—*Sacred and Legendary Art, Vol. I.*

THE LEGEND OF GEOFFROID D'IDEN.

It is related by Peter the Venerable, Abbot of Cluny, that, in the first half of the

221

twelfth century, the Lord Humbert, son of Guichard, Count de Beaujeu, in the Mâçonnais, having made war on some other neighboring lords, Geoffroid d'Iden, one of his vassals, received in the fight a wound which instantly killed him. Two months after his death, Geoffroid appeared to Milon d'Ansa, who knew him well; he begged him to tell Humbert de Beaujeu, in whose service he had lost his life, that he was in Purgatory, for having aided him in an unjust war and not having expiated his sins by penance, before his unlooked-for death; that he besought him, therefore, most urgently, to have compassion on him, and also on his own father, Guichard, who, although he had led a religious life at Cluny in his latter days, had not entirely satisfied the justice of God for his past sins, and especially for a portion of his wealth, which, as his children knew, was ill gained; that, in consequence thereof, he prayed him to have the Holy Sacrifice of the Mass offered for him and for his father, to distribute alms to the poor, and to recommend both sufferers to the prayers of good people, in order to shorten their time of penance. "Tell him," added the apparition, "that if he hear thee not, I must go myself to announce to him that which I have now told to thee."

The lof Ansa (now Anse) faithfully discharged the task imposed upon him. Humbert was frightened; but he neither had prayers nor Masses offered up, made no reparation, and distributed no alms.

Nevertheless, fearing lest Guichard his father or Geoffroid d'Iden might come to disturb him, he no longer dared to remain alone, especially by night; and he always had some of his people around him, making them sleep in his chamber.

One morning, as he was still in bed, but awake, he saw appear before him Geoffroid d'Iden, armed as on the day of the battle. Showing him the mortal wound which he had received, and which appeared still fresh, he warmly reproached him for the little pity he had for himself and for his father, who was groaning in torment; and he added: "Take care lest God may treat thee in His rigor, and refuse thee the mercy thou dost not grant to us; and for thee, give up thy purpose of going to the war with Amadeus. If thou goest thither, thou shalt lose thy life and thy possessions."

At that moment, Richard de Marsay, the Count's squire, entered, coming from Mass; the, spirit disappeared, and thenceforward Humbert de Beaujeu went seriously to work to relieve his father and his vassal, after which he made the journey to Jerusalem to expiate his own sins.

THE QUEEN OF PURGATORY.
BY FREDERICK WILLIAM FABER, D. D.

Oh! turn to Jesus, Mother! turn,
And call Him by His tenderest names;
Pray for the Holy Souls that burn
This hour amid the cleansing flames.

Ah! they have fought a gallant fight;
In death's cold arms they persevered;
And, after life's uncheery night,
The harbor of their rest is neared.

In pains beyond all earthly pains
Fav'rites of Jesus, there they lie,
Letting the fire wear out their stains,
And worshipping God's purity.

Spouses of Christ they are, for He
Was wedded to them by His blood;
And angels o'er their destiny
In wondering adoration brood.

They are the children of thy tears;
Then hasten, Mother! to their aid;
In pity think each hour appears
An age while glory is delayed!

See, how they bound amid their fires,
While pain and love their spirits fill;
Then, with self-crucified desires,
Utter sweet murmurs, and lie still.

Ah me! the love of Jesus yearns
O'er that abyss of sacred pain;
And, as He looks, His bosom burns
With Calvary's dear thirst again.

O Mary! let thy Son no more
His lingering spouses thus expect;
God's children to their God restore,
And to the Spirit His elect.

Pray then, as thou hast ever prayed;
Angels and Souls all look to thee;
God waits thy prayers, for He hath made
Those prayers His law of charity.

THE DEAD PRIEST BEFORE THE ALTAR.
REV. A. J. RYAN.

Who will watch o'er the dead young priest,
People and priests and all?
No, no, no, 'tis his spirit's feast,
When the evening shadows fall.
Let him rest alone—unwatched, alone,
Just beneath the altar's light,
The holy Hosts on their humble throne
Will watch him through the night.

The doors were closed—he was still and fair,
What sound moved up the aisles?
The dead priests come with soundless prayer,
Their faces wearing smiles.
And this was the soundless hymn they sung:
"We watch o'er you to-night;

Your life was beautiful, fair and young,
Not a cloud upon its light.
To-morrow—to-morrow you will rest
With the virgin priests whom Christ has blest."
    Kyrie Eleison! the stricken crowd
Bowed down their heads in tears
O'er the sweet young priest in his vestment shroud.
Ah! the happy, happy years!
They are dead and gone, and the Requiem Mass
Went slowly, mournfully on,
The Pontiff's singing was all a wail,
The altars cried and the people wept,
The fairest flower in the Church's vale
Ah me! how soon we pass!
In the vase of his coffin slept. —*From In Memoriam.*

MEMORIALS OF THE BEAD.

R. R. MADDEN. [1]

[Footnote 1: Author of "Lives and Times of United Irishmen."]
    'Tis not alone in "hallowed ground,"
At every step we tread
Midst tombs and sepulchres, are found
Memorials of the dead.
    'Tis not in sacred shrines alone,
Or trophies proudly spread
On old cathedral walls are shown
Memorials of the dead.
    Emblems of Fame surmounting death,
Of war and carnage dread,
They were not, in the "Times of Faith,"
Memorials of the dead.
    From marble bust and pictured traits
The living looks recede,
They fade away: so frail are these
Memorials of the dead.
    On mural slabs, names loved of yore
Can now be scarcely read;
A few brief years have left no more
Memorials of the dead.
    Save those which pass from sire to son,
Traditions that are bred
In the heart's core, and make their own
Memorials of the dead.

A CHILD'S REQUIESCAT IN PACE.
ELIZA ALLEN STARR.

With the gray dawn's faintest break,
Mother, faithfully I wake,
Whispering softly for thy sake
Requiescat in pace!

When the sun's broad disk at height
Floods the busy world with light,
Breathes my soul with sighs contrite,
Requiescat in pace!

When the twilight shadows lone
Wrap the home once, once thine own,
Sobs my heart with broken moan,
Requiescat in pace!

Night, so solemn, grand, and still,
Trances forest, meadow, rill;
Hush, fond heart, adore His will,
Requiescat in pace!

THE SOLITARY SOUL.

I died; but my soul did not wing its flight straight to the heaven- nest, and there repose in the bosom of Him who made it, as the minister who was with me said it would. Good old man! He had toiled among us, preaching baptizing, marrying, and burrying, until his hair had turned from nut-brown to frost-white; and he told me, as I lay dying, that the victory of the Cross was the only passport I needed to the joys of eternity; that a life like mine would meet its immediate reward. And it did; but, O my God! not as he had thought, and I had believed.

As he prayed, earth's sights and sounds faded from me, and the strange, new life began. The wrench of agony with which soul and body parted left me breathless; and my spirit, like a lost child, turned frightened eyes towards home.

I stood in a dim, wind-swept space. No gates of pearl or walls of jacinth met my gaze; no streaming glory smote my eyes; no voice bade me enter and put on the wedding garment. Hosts of pale shapes circled by, but no one saw me. All had their faces uplifted, and their hands—such patient, pathetic hands—were clasped on their hearts; and the air was heavy with the whisper, "Christ! Christ!" that came unceasingly from their lips.

Above us, the clouds drifted and turned; about us, the horizon was blotted out; mist and grayness were everywhere. A voiceless wind swept by; and as I gazed, sore dismayed and saddened, a rent opened in the driving mass, and I saw a man standing with arms upraised. He was strangely vestured; silver and gold gleamed in his raiment, and a large cross was outlined upon his back. He held in his hands a chalice of gold, in which sparkled something too liquid for fire, too softly brilliant for water or wine.

As this sight broke on our vision, two figures near me uttered a cry, whose rapturous sweetness filled space with melody; and, like the up- springing lark,

225

borne aloft by the beauty of their song, they vanished; and those about me bowed their heads, and ceased their moan for a moment.

"What is it?" I cried. "Who is the man? What was it he held in his hand?"

But there was none to answer me, and I drove along before the wind with the rest, helpless, bewildered.

How long this lasted I do not know; for there was neither night nor day in the sad place; and a fire of longing burnt in my breast, so keen, so strong, that all other sensation was swallowed up.

And then, too, my grief! There were many deeds of my life to which I had given but casual regret. When the minister would counsel us to confess our sins to God, I had knelt in the church and gone through the form; but here, where the height and depth and breadth of God's perfection dawned upon me, and grew hourly clearer, they seemed to rend my heart, and to far outweigh any little good I might have done. Oh! why did no one ever preach the justice of God to me, and the necessity of personal atonement! Why had they only taught me, "Believe, and you shall be saved?"

Time by time, the shapes about me rose and vanished with the same cry as the two I saw liberated in my first hour; and sometimes—like an echo—the sound of human voices would go through space—some choked with tears, some low with sadness, some glad with hope.

"Eternal rest grant to them, O Lord!"

"And let perpetual light shine upon them!"

"May they rest in peace!"

And the "Amen" tolled like a silver bell, and I would feel a respite.

But no one called me by name, no one prayed for my freedom. My mother's voice, my sister's dream, my father's belief—all were that I was happy before the face of God. And friends forgot me, except in their pleasures.

At seasons, through the mist would loom an altar, at which a man, in black robes embroidered with silver, bowed and bent. The chalice, with its always wonderful contents, would be raised, and a disc, in whose circle of whiteness I saw Christ crucified. From the thorn-wounds, the Hands, the Feet, the Side, shot rays of dazzling brightness; and my frozen soul, my tear-chilled eyes, were warmed and gladdened; for the man who held this wondrous image would himself sigh: "For *all* the dead, sweet Lord!" And to me, even me, would come hope and peace.

But, oh! the agony, oh! the desolateness, to be cut off from the sweet guerdon of immediate release! Oh! the pain of expiating every fault, measure for measure! Oh, the grief of knowing that my own deeds were the chains of my captivity, and my unfulfilled duties the barriers that withheld me from beholding the Beatific Vision!

Sometimes a gracious face would gleam through the mist—a face so tender, so human, so full of love, that I yearned to hear it speak to *me*, to have those radiant eyes turned on *me*. My companions called her "Mary!" and I knew it was the Virgin of Nazareth. Often she would call them by name, and say: "My child, my

Son bids thee come home."

Why had I never known this gentle Mother! Why could I not catch her mantle, and clinging to it, pass from waiting to fulfilment!

Once when I had grown grief-bowed with waiting, worn with longing, I saw again the vision of the Church. At a long railing knelt many young girls, and they received at the hands of the priest what I had learned to discern as the Body of the Lord. One—God bless her tender heart!— whispered as she knelt: "O dearest Lord, I offer to Thee this Holy Communion for the soul *that has no one to pray for her.*"

And through the grayness rang at last *my* name, and straight to heaven I went, ransomed by that mighty price, freed by prayer from prison.

O you who live, who have voices and hearts, for the sake of Christ and His Holy Mother; by the love you bear your living, and the grief you give your dead, pray for those whose friends do not know how to help them; for the suddenly killed; for the executed criminal; and for those who, having suffered long in Purgatory, need one more prayer to set them free.—*Ave Maria*, November 10, 1883.

THE STORY OF THE FAITHFUL SOUL.

Founded on an old French Legend.

ADELAIDE ANNE PROCTER.

The fettered spirits linger In purgatorial pain,
With penal fires effacing
Their last faint earthly stain,
Which Life's imperfect sorrow
Had tried to cleanse in vain.

Yet, on each feast of Mary
Their sorrow finds release,
For the great Archangel Michael
Comes down and bids it cease;
And the name of these brief respites
Is called "Our Lady's Peace."

Yet once—so runs the legend—
When the Archangel came,
And all these holy spirits
Rejoiced at Mary's name,
One voice alone was wailing,
Still wailing on the same.

And though a great Te Deum
The happy echoes woke, I
This one discordant wailing
Through the sweet voices broke:
So when St. Michael questioned,
Thus the poor spirit spoke:—

I am not cold or thankless,

Although I still complain;
I prize Our Lady's blessing,
Although it comes in vain
To still my bitter anguish,
Or quench my ceaseless pain.

   "On earth a heart that loved me
Still lives and mourns me there,
And the shadow of his anguish
Is more than I can bear;
All the torment that I suffer
Is the thought of his despair.

   "The evening of my bridal
Death took my Life away;
Not all Love's passionate pleading
Could gain an hour's delay.
And he I left has suffered
A whole year since that day.

   "If I could only see him—
If I could only go
And speak one word of comfort
And solace—then, I know
He would endure with patience,
And strive against his woe."

   Thus the Archangel answered:
"Your time of pain is brief,
And soon the peace of Heaven
Will give you full relief;
Yet if his earthly comfort
So much outweighs your grief,

   "Then, through a special mercy,
I offer you this grace—
You may seek him who mourns you
And look upon his face,
And speak to him of Comfort,
For one short minute's space.

   "But when that time is ended,
Return here and remain
A thousand years in torment,
A thousand years in pain;
Thus dearly must you purchase
The comfort he will gain."

   The lime-trees shade at evening
Is spreading broad and wide;
Beneath their fragrant arches

Pace slowly, side by side,
In low and tender converse,
A Bridegroom and his Bride.
   The night is calm and stilly,
No other sound is there
Except their happy voices:—
What is that cold bleak air
That passes through the lime-trees,
And stirs the Bridegroom's hair?
   While one low cry of anguish,
Like the last dying wail
Of some dumb, hunted creature,
Is borne upon the gale—
Why dogs the Bridegroom shudder
   And turn so deathly pale?
   Near Purgatory's entrance
The radiant Angels wait;
It was the great St. Michael
Who closed that gloomy gate,
When the poor wandering spirit
Came back to meet her fate.
   "Pass on," thus spoke the Angel:
"Heaven's joy is deep and vast;
Pass on, pass on, poor spirit,
For Heaven is yours at last;
In that one minute's anguish,
Your thousand years have passed."

GENÉRADE, THE FRIEND OF ST. AUGUSTINE.
J. COLLIN DE PLANCY.

ST. AUGUSTINE reckoned among his friends the physician Genérade, highly honored in Carthage, where his learning and skill were much esteemed. But by one of those misfortunes of which there are, unhappily, but too many examples, while studying the admirable mechanism of the human body, he had come to believe matter capable of the works of intelligence which raise man so far above other created beings. He was, therefore, a materialist; and St. Augustine praying for him, earnestly besought God to enlighten that deluded mind.

One night while he slept, this doctor, who believed, as some do still, that "when one is dead, all is dead"—we quote their own language—saw in his dreams a young man, who said to him: "Follow me." He did so, and was conducted to a city, wherein he heard, on the right, unknown melodies, which filled him with admiration. What he heard on the left he never remembered. But on awaking he concluded, from this vision, that there was, somewhere, something else besides this world.

Another night he likewise beheld in sleep the same young man, who said to him:

229

"Knowest thou me?"

"Very well," answered Genérade.

"And wherefore knowest thou me?"

"Because of the journey we made together when you showed me the city of harmony."

"Was it in a dream, or awake, that you saw and heard what struck you then?"

"It was in a dream."

"Where is your body now?"

"In my bed."

"Knowest thou well that thou now seest nothing with the eyes of the body?"

"I know it."

"With what eyes, then, dost thou see me?"

As the physician hesitated, and could not answer, the young man said to him:

"Even as thou seest and hearest me, now that thine eyes are closed and thy senses benumbed, so, after thy death, thou shalt live, thou shalt see, thou shalt hear—but with the organs of the soul. Doubt, then, no more!"

ST. THOMAS AQUINAS AND FRIAR ROMANUS.

WE are about to treat of facts concerning which our fathers never had any hesitation, because they had faith. Nowadays, the truths which are above the material sight have been so roughly handled that they are much diminished for us. And if the goodness of God had not allowed some rays of the mysteries which He reserves for Himself to escape, if some gleams of magnetism and the world of spirits occupying the air around us had not a little embarrassed those of our literati who make a merit of not believing, we would hardly dare, in spite of the grave authorities on which they rest, to represent here some apparitions of souls departed from this world. We shall venture to do so, nevertheless.

One day, when St. Thomas Aquinas was praying in the Church of the Friars, Preachers, at Naples, the pious friar Romanus, whom he had left in Paris, where he replaced him in the chair of Theology, suddenly appeared beside him. Thomas, seeing him, said:

"I am glad of thine arrival. But how long hast thou been here?"

Romanus answered: "I am now out of this world. Nevertheless, I am permitted to come to thee, because of thy merit."

The Saint, alarmed at this reply, after a moment's recollection, said to the apparition: "I adjure thee, by Our Lord Jesus Christ, tell me simply if my works are pleasing to God!"

Romanus replied: "Persevere in the way in which thou art, and believe that what thou doest is agreeable unto God."

Thomas then asked him in what state he found himself.

"I enjoy eternal life," answered Romanus. "Nevertheless, for having carelessly executed one clause of a will which the Bishop of Paris gave me in charge, I underwent for fifteen days the pains of Purgatory."

St. Thomas again said: "You remind me that we often discussed the question whether the knowledge acquired in this life remain in the soul after death. I pray you give me the solution thereof."

Romanus made answer: "Ask me not that. As for me, I am content with seeing my God."

"Seest thou him face to face?" went on Thomas.

"Just as we have been taught," replied Romanus, "and as I see thee."

With these words he left St. Thomas greatly consoled.

THE KEY THAT NEVER TURNS.
ELEANOR C. DONNELLY.

"In Purgatory, dear," I said to-day, Unto my pet, "the fire burns and burns, Until each ugly stain is burned away—And then an Angel turns A great, bright key, and forth the glad soul springs Into the presence of the King of kings."

"But in that other prison?" "Sweetest love! The same fierce fire burns and burns, but thence None e'er escapes." The blue eyes, raised above, Were fair with innocence. "Poor burning souls!" she whispered low, "ah me! No Angel ever comes to turn *their* key!"

THE BURIAL.
THOMAS DAVIS.

"ULULU! ululu! wail for the dead,
Green grow the grass of
Fingal on his head;
And spring-flowers blossom, ere elsewhere appearing,
And shamrocks grow thick on the martyr for Erin.
Ululu! ululu! soft fall the dew
On the feet and the head of the martyred and true."

For a while they tread
In silence dread—
Then muttering and moaning go the crowd,
Surging and swaying like mountain cloud,
And again the wail comes wild and loud.

"Ululu! ululu! kind was his heart!
Walk slower, walk slower, too soon we shall part.
The faithful and pious, the
Priest of the Lord,
His pilgrimage over, he has his reward.

"By the bed of the sick, lowly kneeling,
To God with the raised cross appealing—
He seems still to kneel, and he seems still to pray,
And the sins of the dying seem passing away.

"In the prisoner's cell, and the cabin so dreary,
Our constant consoler, he never grew weary;
But he's gone to his rest,
And he's now with the blest,
Where tyrant and traitor no longer molest—
Ululu! ululu! wail for the dead!

231

Ululu! ululu! here is his bed."
   Short was the ritual, simple the prayer,
Deep was the silence, and every head bare;
The Priest alone standing, they knelt all around,
Myriads on myriads, like rocks on the ground.
Kneeling and motionless.—
"Dust unto dust."
   "He died as becometh the faithful and just—
Placing in God his reliance and trust;"
   Kneeling and motionless—
"Ashes to ashes"—
Hollow the clay on the coffin-lid dashes;
Kneeling and motionless, wildly they pray,
But they pray in their souls, for no gesture have they—
Stern and standing—oh! look on them now!
Like trees to one tempest the multitude bow.

HYMN FOR THE DEAD.
NEWMAN.

   Help, Lord, the souls which Thou hast made,
The souls to Thee so dear,
In prison, for the debt unpaid
Of sins committed here.
   Those holy souls, they suffer on,
   Resign'd in heart and will,
Until Thy high behest is done,
And justice has its fill.
For daily falls, for pardon'd crime,
They joy to undergo
The shadow of Thy cross sublime,
The remnant of Thy woe.
   Help, Lord, the souls which Thou hast made,
The souls to Thee so dear,
In prison, for the debt unpaid Of sins committed here.
   Oh! by their patience of delay,
Their hope amid their pain,
Their sacred zeal to burn away
Disfigurement and stain;
Oh! by their fire of love, not less
In keenness than the flame,
Oh! by their very helplessness,
Oh! by Thy own great Name,
   Good Jesu, help! sweet Jesu, aid
The souls to Thee most dear,
In prison, for the debt unpaid

Of sins committed here.

THE TWO STUDENTS.

The Abbé de Saint Pierre, says Collin de Plancy, has given a long account, in his works, of a singular occurrence which took place in 1697, and which we are inclined to relate here:

In 1695, a student named Bezuel, then about fifteen years old, contracted a friendship with two other youths, students like himself, and sons of an attorney of Caen, named D'Abaquène. The elder was, like Bezuel, fifteen; his brother, eighteen months younger. The latter was named Desfontaines. The paternal name was then given only to the eldest; the names of those who came after were formed by means of some vague properties....

As the young Desfontaines' character was more in unison with Bezuel's than that of his elder brother, these two students became strongly attached to each other.

One day during the following year, 1696, they were reading together a certain history of two friends like themselves, who had promised each other, with some solemnity, that he of the two who died first would come back to give the survivor some account of his state. The historian added that the dead one really did come back, and that he told his friend many wonderful things. Young Desfontaines, struck by this narrative, which he did not doubt, proposed to Bezuel that they should make such a promise one to the other. Bezuel was at first afraid of such an engagement. But several months after, in the first days of June, 1697, as his friend was going to set out for Caen, he agreed to his proposal.

Desfontaines then drew from his pocket two papers in which he had written the double agreement. Each of these papers expressed the formal promise on the part of him who should die first to come and make his fate known to the surviving friend. He had signed with his blood the one that Bezuel was to keep. Bezuel, hesitating no longer, pricked his hand, and likewise signed with his blood the other document, which he gave to Desfontaines.

The latter, delighted to have the promise, set out with his brother. Bezuel received some days after a letter, in which his friend informed him that he had reached his home in safety, and was very well. The correspondence between them was to continue. But it stopped very soon, and Bezuel was uneasy.

It happened that on the 31st of July, 1697, being about 2 o'clock in the afternoon, in a meadow where his companions were amusing themselves with various games, he felt himself suddenly stunned and taken with a sort of faintness, which lasted for some minutes. Next day, at the same hour, he felt the same symptoms, and again on the day after. But then— it was Friday, the 2d of August—he saw advancing towards him his friend Desfontaines, who made a sign for him to come to him. Being in a sitting posture and under the influence of his swoon, he made another sign to the apparition, moving on his seat to make place for him.

The comrades of Bezuel moving around saw this motion, and were surprised.

As Desfontaines did not advance, Bezuel arose to go to him. The apparition then took him by the left arm, drew him aside some thirty paces, and said:

"I promised you that, if I died before you, I would come to tell you. I was drowned yesterday in the river at Caen, about this hour. I was out walking; it was so warm that we took a notion to bathe. A weakness came over me in the river, and I sank to the bottom. The Abbé de Menil-Jean, my companion, plunged in to draw me out; I seized his foot; but whether he thought it was a salmon that had caught hold of him, or that he felt it actually necessary to go up to the surface of the water to breathe, he shook me off so roughly that his foot gave me a great blow in the chest, and threw me to the bottom of the river, which is there very deep."

Desfontaines then told his friend many other things, which he would not divulge, whether the dead boy had prayed him not to do so, or for other reasons.

Bezuel wanted to embrace the apparition, but he found only a shadow. Nevertheless, the shadow had squeezed his arm so tightly, that it pained him after.

He saw the spirit several times, yet always a little taller than when they parted, and always in the half-clothing of a bather. He wore in his fair hair a scroll on which Bezuel could only read the word *In*. His voice had the same sound as when he was living, he appeared neither gay nor sad, but perfectly tranquil. He charged his friend with several commissions for his parents, and begged him to say for him the Seven Penitential Psalms, which had been given him as a penance by his confessor, three days before his death, and which he had not yet recited.

The apparition always ended by a farewell expressed in words which signified: "Till we meet again! (*Au revoir!*)" At last, it ceased at the end of some weeks; and the surviving friend, who had constantly prayed for the dead, concluded from this that his Purgatory was over.

This Monsieur Bezuel finished his studies, embraced the ecclesiastical state, became *curé* of Valogne, and lived long, esteemed by his parishioners and the whole city, for his good sense, his virtuous life, and his love of truth.

THE PENANCE OF DON DIEGO RIEZ.

A Legend of Lough Derg. [1]

[Footnote 1: Lough Derg, in Donegal, was a place famous for pilgrimage from a very early period, and was much resorted to out of France, Italy, and the Peninsula, during the Middle Ages, and even in the sixteenth and seventeenth centuries. In Mathew Paris, and Froissart, as well as in our native annals, and in O'Sullivan Beare, there are many facts of its extraordinary history.]

T. D. MCGEE.

There was a knight of Spain—Diego Riaz,
Noble by four descents, vain, rich and young,
Much woe he wrought, or the tradition lie is,
Which lived of old the Castilians among;
His horses bore the palm the kingdom over,
His plume was tall, costliest his sword,
The proudest maidens wished him as a lover,
The *caballeros* all revered his word

234

But ere his day's meridian came, his spirit
Fell sick, grew palsied in his breast, and pined—
He fear'd Christ's kingdom he could ne'er inherit,
The causes wherefore too well he divined.
Where'er he turns, his sins are always near him,
Conscience still holds her mirror to his eyes,
Till those who long had envied came to fear him,
To mock his clouded brow and wintry sighs.
   Alas! the sins of youth are as a chain
Of iron, swiftly let down to the deep,
How far we feel not—till when, we'd raise't again
We pause amid the weary work and weep.
Ah, it is sad a-down Life's stream to see.
So many agèd toilers so distress'd,
And near the source—a thousand forms of glee
Fitting the shackle to Youth's glowing breast.
   He sought peace in the city where she dwells not,
He wooed her amid woodlands all in vain,
He searches through the valleys, but he tells not
The secret of his quest to priest or swain,
Until, despairing evermore of pleasure,
He leaves his land, and sails to far Peru;
There, stands uncharm'd in caverns of treasure,
And weeps on mountains heavenly high and blue.
   Incessant in his ears rang this plain warning—
"Diego, as thy soul, thy sorrow lives";
He hears the untired voice, night, noon, and morning,
Yet understanding not, unresting grieves.
One eve, a purer vision seized him, then he
Vow'd to Lough Derg, an humble pilgrimage—
The virtues of that shrine were known to many,
And saving held even in that skeptic age.
   With one sole follower, an Esquire trustful,
He pass'd the southern cape which sailors fear,
And eastward held: meanwhile his vain and lustful
Past works more loathsome to his soul appear.
Through the night-watches, at all hours o' day,
He still was wakeful as the pilot, and
For grace, his vow to keep, doth always pray,
And for his death to lie in the saints' land.
   But ere his eyes beheld the Irish shore, Diego died.
Much gold he did ordain
To God and Santiago—furthermore,
His Esquire plighted, ere he went to Spain,

To journey to the Refuge of the Lake;
Before St. Patrick's solitary shrine,
A nine days' vigil for his rest to make,
Living on bitter bread and penitential wine. [1]
[Footnote 1: The brackish water of the lake, boiled, is called wine by the pilgrims.]
   The vassal vow'd; but, ah! how seldom pledges
Given to the dying, to the dead, are held!
The Esquire reach'd the shore, where sand and sedge is
O'er melancholy hills, by paths of eld;
Treeless and houseless was the prospect round,
Rock-strewn and boisterous the lake before;
A Charon-shape in a skiff a-ground—
The pilgrim turned, and left the sacred shore.
   That night he lay a-bed hard by the Erne—
The island-spangled lake—but could not sleep—
When lo! beside him, pale, and sad, and stern,
Stood his dead master, risen from the deep.
"Arise," he said, "and come." From the hostelrie
And over the bleak hills he led the sleeper,
And when they reach'd Derg's shore, "Get in with me,"
He cried; "nor sink my soul in torments deeper."
   The dead man row'd the boat, the living steer'd,
Each in his pallor sinister, until
The Isle of Pilgrimage they duly near'd—
"Now hie thee forth, and work thy master's will!"
So spoke the dead, and vanish'd o'er the lake,
The Squire pursued his course, and gain'd the shrine,
There, nine days' vigil duly he did make,
Living on bitter bread and penitential wine.
   The tenth eve shone in solemn, starry beauty,
As he, rejoicing, o'er the old paths came,
Light was his heart from its accomplished duty,
All was forgotten, even the latest shame—
When these brief words some disembodied voice
Spoke near him: "Oh, keep sacred, evermore,
Word, pledge, and vow, so may you still rejoice,
And live among the Just when Time is o'er!"

THE DAY OF ALL SOULS.
ELIZA ALLEN STARR.
   FROM the far past there comes a thought of sweetness,
From the far past a thought of love and pain;
A voice, how dear! a look of melting kindness,
A voice, a look, we ne'er shall know again.

A fresh, young face, perchance of boyish gladness,
An aged face, perchance of patient love;
My heart-strings fail, I sob in utter anguish,
As past my eyes these lovely spectres move.

The chill morn breaks, the matin star still flaming;
The hushed cathedral's massive door stands wide;
Through the dim aisles I pass, in silent weeping,
From mortal eyes my sorrowing tears to hide.

Already morn has touched the painted windows;
The yellow dawn creeps down the storied panes;
Already, in the early solemn twilight,
The sanctuary's taper softly wanes.

My faltering step before the altar pauses;
My treasur'd dead I see remembered here;
All climes, all nations, lost on land or ocean,
They on whose grave none ever drop a tear.

The Church, their single mourner, drapes in sorrow
The festal shrines she loves with flowers to dress;
And "Kyrie! Kyrie!" sighs, while lowly bending
To Thee, O God! to shorten their distress.

"*Dies iræ, dies illa,*" sobs the choir;
"*In pace, pace,*" from the altar rises higher;
"*Lux æterna,*" daylight floods the altar,
Priest and choir take up the holy psalter.
"*Requiescant in pace!*"
Amen, amen, in pace!

THE MESSAGE OF THE NOVEMBER WIND.
BY ELEANOR C. DONNELLY.

I.

Wrapped in lonely shadows late,
(Bleak November's midnight gloom),
As I kneel beside the grate
In the silent sitting-room:
Down the chimney moans the wind,
Like the voice of souls resigned,
Pleading from their prison thus,
"Pray for us! pray for us!
Gentle Christian, watcher kind,
Pray for us, oh! pray for us!"

II.

Melt mine eyes with sudden tears—
Old familiar tones are there;
Dear ones lost in other years,
Breathing Purgatory's prayer.

Through my fingers pass the beads,
Tender heart, responsive bleeds,
As the wind, all tremulous,
"Pray for us! pray for us!"
Seems to murmur "Love our needs—
Pray for us! oh, pray for us!"

A LEGEND OF THE TIME OF CHARLEMAGNE.

We read in the *Gesta Caroli Magni* that Charlemagne had a man-at-arms who served him faithfully till his death. Before breathing his last he called a nephew of his, to make known to him his last will:

"Sixty years," said he, "have I been in the service of my prince; I have never amassed the goods of this world, and my arms and my horse are all I have. My arms I leave to thee, and I will that my horse be sold immediately after my death; I charge thee with the care of this matter, if thou wilt promise me to distribute the full price amongst the poor."

The nephew promised to execute the will of his uncle, who died in peace, for he was a good and loyal Christian. But when he was laid in the earth the young man, considering that the horse was a very fine one, and well-trained, was tempted to keep him for himself. He did not sell him, and gave no money to the poor. Six months after, the soul of the dead man appeared to him and said: "Thou hast not accomplished that which I had ordered thee to do for the welfare of my soul, and for six months I have suffered great pains in Purgatory. But behold God, the strict Judge of all things, has decreed, and His angels will execute the decree, that my soul be placed in eternal rest, and that thine shall undergo all the pains and torments which I had still to undergo for the expiation of my sins."

Thereupon the nephew, being instantly seized with a violent disease, had barely time to confess to a priest, who had just been announced. He died shortly after, and went to pay the debt he had undertaken to discharge.

THE DEAD MASS.

It has been, and still is believed, that the mercy of God sometimes permits souls that have sins to expiate, to come and expiate them on earth. Of this the following is an example:

Polet, the principal suburb of Dieppe, is still inhabited almost exclusively by fishermen, who, in past times, more especially, have ever been solid and faithful Christians. The Catholic worship was formerly celebrated with much solemnity in their church, consecrated under the invocation of "Our Lady of the Beach" (Notre Dame des Grèves); and the mothers of the worthy fishermen who give to Polet an aspect so picturesque, have forgotten only the precise date of the adventure we are about to relate.

The sacristan of Notre Dame des Grèves dwelt in a little cottage quite close to the church. He was an exact and pious man; he had the keys of the sacred edifice and the care of the bells. Several worthy priests were attached to the lovely church; the earliest Masses were never rung except by the honest sacristan. Now, one morning, during the Christmas holydays, he heard, before day, the tinkle of

238

one of his bells announcing a Mass. He rose immediately and ran to the window. The snow- covered roofs enabled him to see objects so distinctly that he thought the day was beginning to dawn. He hastened to put on his clothes and go to the church. The total solitude and silence reigning all around him made him understand that he was mistaken and that day was not yet breaking. He tried to go into the church, however, but the door was closed.

How, then, could he have heard the bell? If robbers had got in, they would certainly have taken good care not to touch the bell. He listens; not the slightest noise in the holy place. Should he return home? Not so, for having heard the bell, he must go in.

He opens a little door leading into the sacristy; he passes through that, and advances towards the choir.

By the light of the small lamp burning before the tabernacle and that of a taper already lighted, he perceives, at the foot of the altar, a priest robed in a chasuble, and in the attitude of a celebrant about to commence Mass. All is prepared for the Holy Sacrifice. He stops in dismay. The priest, a stranger to him, is extremely pale; his hands are as white as his alb; his eyes shine like the glow-worm, the light going forth, as it were, from the very centre of the orbits.

"Serve my Mass," he said gently to the sacristan.

The latter obeyed, spell-bound with terror. But if the pallor of the priest and the singular fire of his eyes frightened him, his voice, on the contrary, was mild and melancholy.

The Mass goes on. At the elevation of the Sacred Host the limbs of the priest tremble and give forth a sound like that of dry reeds shaken by the wind. At the *Domine, non sum dignus*, his breast, which he strikes three times, sounds like the coffin when the first shovel-full of earth is cast upon it by the grave-digger. The Precious Blood produces in his whole body the effect of water which, in the silence of the night, falls drop by drop from the roof.

When he turns to say *Ita Missa est*, the priest is only a skeleton, and that skeleton speaks these words to the server:

"Brother, I thank thee! In my life-time, I was a priest; I owed this Mass at my death. Thou hast helped me to discharge my debt; my soul is freed from a heavy burden."

The spectre then disappeared. The sacristan saw the vestments fall gently at the foot of the altar, and the burning taper suddenly went out. At that moment, a cock crowed somewhere in the neighborhood. The sacristan took up the vestments, and passed the rest of the night in prayer.

THE EVE OF ST. JOHN.
SIR WALTER SCOTT.

"O fear not the priest who sleepeth to the east!
For to Dryburgh the way he has ta'en;
And there to say Mass, till three days do pass,
For the soul of a Knight that is slayne."

He turned him round, and grimly he frowned;

Then he laughed right scornfully—
"He who says the Mass-rite for the soul of that Knight,
May as well say Mass for me."
   Then changed, I trow, was that bold baron's brow,
From dark to the blood-red high;
"Now tell me the mien of the Knight thou hast seen,
For by Mary he shall die."
   "O hear but my word, my noble lord,
For I heard her name his name,
And that lady bright, she called the Knight
Sir Richard of Coldinghame."
   The bold baron's brow then chang'd, I trow,
From high blood-red to pale—
"The grave is deep and dark—and the corpse is stiff and stark—
So I may not trust thy tale.
   "The varying light deceived thy sight,
And the wild winds drown'd the name,
For the Dryburgh bells ring, and the white monks do sing,
For Sir Richard of Coldinghame."
   It was near the ringing of matin-bell,
The night was well-nigh done,
When the lady looked through the chamber fair,
On the eve of good St. John.
   The lady looked through the chamber fair,
By the light of a dying flame;
And she was aware of a knight stood there—
Sir Richard of Coldinghame.
   "By Eildon-tree for long nights three,
In bloody grave have I lain,
The Mass and the death-prayer are said for me,
But, lady, they are said in vain.
   "By the baron's hand, near Tweed's fair stand,
Most foully slain I fell;
And my restless sprite on the beacon's height,
For a space is doom'd to dwell."
   He laid his left palm on an oaken beam,
His right upon her hand;
The lady shrunk, and fainting sunk,
For it scorched like a fiery brand.

THE BEQUEST OF A SOUL, IN PURGATORY.

[From "A Collection of Spiritual Hymns and Songs on Various Religious
Subjects," published by Chalmers & Co., of Aberdeen, Scotland, in 1802.
Its quaint and touching simplicity, redolent of old-time faith, will
commend it to the reader]

240

From lake where water does not go,
A prisoner of hope below,
To mortal ones I push my groans,
In hopes they'll pity me.
   O mortals that still live above,
Your faith, hope, prayers, and alms, and love,
Still merit place With God's sweet grace;
O faithful, pity me.
   My fervent groans don't merit here,
Strict justice only doth appear,
My smallest faults,
And needless talks Heap chains and flames on me.
   Though mortal guilt doth not remain,
I still am due the temp'ral pain, I did delay
To satisfy,
Past coldness scorcheth me.
   Tepidity and good works done
With imperfections mixt, here come;
All these neglects
And least defects,—
Great anguish bring on me.
   Though my defects here be not spared,
Yet endless glory for me's prepared,
I love in flames,
And hope in chains;
O friends, then, pity me!
   My God, my Father, is most dear,
For me your sighs and prayers He'll hear;
Though just laws scourge,
His mercies urge,
That you would pity me.
   Through pains and flames
I'll come to Him,
They purge me both from stain and sin;
When I'm set free,
Their friends I'll be
Who now do pity me.
   The smallest thing that could defile
Keeps me from bliss in this exile.
God loves to see
That you me free;
For His love pity me!
   For me who alms give, fast, or pray,
Great store of grace will come their way;

241

Try this good thought—
Great help is brought,
And souls from sin set free.
 If you for me now do not pray,
The utmost farthing I must pay;
The time is hid
That I'll be rid,
Unless you pity me.
 In mortal sin who yields his breath,
Pray not for him behind his death.
All mortal crime
I quit in time;
O faithful, pity me!
 For me good works may be practised,
Thus some were for the dead baptized.
Suet pains endure
For me, and sure
You'll help and pity me!
 For his good friend, as Scriptures say,
Onesiphorus, Paul did pray, [1]
His words, you see,
Urge, then, for me;
And thus you'll pity me.
 [Footnote 1: II. Tim., i. 16, 18.]
 This third place clear in writ you spy,
Where all your works the fire will try,
From death game rose,
Sure then all those
From third place were set free.
 In hell there's no redemption found;
God ne'er degrades whom
He once crowned—These judgments both
Confirmed by oath
And absolute decree.
 For all the Saints prayer should be made,
Who stand in need, alive or dead.
I stand in need
That you with speed
Should help and pity me.
 In presence of our sweetest Lord,
For dead they, prayed, as all accord.
Christ did not blame
What I now claim;
Oh! haste and pity me!

To a third place Christ's soul did go.
And preached to spirits there below;
This in the Creed
And Writ you read,
That you may pity me.

When Christ on earth would stay no more,
These captives freed He brought to glore;
There I will be,
And soon set free,
If you would pity me.

Mind, then, Communion of the Saints;
All should supply each other's wants:
In pains and chains,
And scorching flames,
I languish; pity me!

Eternal rest, eternal glore,
Eternal light, eternal store,
To them accord,
O sweetest Lord!
There's mercy still with Thee!

Let mercy stay Thy just revenge,
Their scorching flames to glory change;
The precious flood
Of Thine own blood
For them we offer Thee!

ALL SOULS.
BY MARION MUIR.

FOR all the cold and silent clay
That once, alive with youth and hope,
Rushed proudly to the western slope-
O brothers, pray!

For all who saw the orient day
Rise on the plain, the camp, the flood,
The sudden discord drowned in blood-
O brothers, pray!

For all the lives that ebbed away
In darkness down the gulf of tears;
For all the gray departed years-
O brothers, pray!

For all the souls that went astray
In deserts hung with double gloom;
For all the dead without a tomb-
O brothers, pray!

For we have household peace; but they

Who led the way, and held the land,
Are homeless as the heaving sand-
Oh! let us pray!

THE DEAD.

(From the French of Octave Cremacie.)

ANNA T. SADLIER.

O dead, ye sleep within your tranquil graves;
No more ye bear the burden that enslaves
Us in this world of ours.
For you outshine no stars, no storms rave loud,
No buds has spring, the horizon no cloud,
The sun marks not the hours.

The while, with anxious thought oppress'd, we go,
Each weary day but bringing deeper woe,
Silently and alone
Ye list the sanctuary chant arise,
That downwards first to you, remounts the skies,
Sweet pity's monotone.

The vain delights whereto our souls incline,
Are naught beside the prayer to love divine,
Alms-giving of the heart,
Which reaching to you warms your chilly dust
And brings your name enshrined a sacred trust,
Swift to the throne of God!

Alas! love's warmest memory will fade
Within the heart, ere yet the mourning shade
Has ceased to mark the garb.
Forgetfulness, our meed to you, outweighs
The leaded coffin as it dully lays
Upon your lifeless bones.

Our selfish hearts but to the present look,
And see in you the pages of a book
Now laid aside long read.
For loving in our fev'rish joy or pain
But those who serve our hate, pride, love of gain,
No more can serve the dead.

To cold ambition or to joy's sweet store,
Ye dusty corpses minister no more,
We give to you neglect.
Nor reck we of that suff'ring world's pale bourne
Where you beyond the bridgeless barrier mourn
O'erpast the wall of death.

'Tis said that when our coldness grieves you sore,
Ye quit betimes that solitude's cold shore

Where ye forsaken dwell,
And flit about in darkness' sad constraint,
The while from spectral lips your mournful plaint
Upon the winds outswell.

When nightingales their woodland nests have left,
The autumn sky of gray, white-capped, cloud-reft,
Prepares the shroud which Winter soon shall spread
On frozen fields; there comes a day thrice blest,
When earth forgetting, all our musings rest
On those who are no more the dreamless dead.

The dead their graves forsake upon this day,
As we have seen doves mount with joyous grace,
Escape an instant from their prison drear,
Their coming brings us no repellent fear.
Their mien is dreamy, passing sweet their face,
Their fixed and hollow eyes cannot betray.

When spectral coming thus unseen they gaze
On crowds who, kneeling in the temple, pray
Forgiveness for them, one faint, joyful ray,
As light upon the opal, glittering plays,
On faces pale and calm an instant rests,
And brings a moment's warmth to clay-cold breasts.

They, the elect of God, with souls of saints,
Who bear each destined load without complaints,
Who walk all day beneath God's watching eye,
And sleep the night 'neath angels' ministry,
Nor made the sport of visions that arise
To show th' abyss of fire to dreaming eyes.

All they who while on earth, the pure of heart,
The heav'nly echoes hear, and who in part
Make smooth for man rude ways he has to tread,
And knowing earthly vanity, outspread
Their virtue like a carpet rich and rare,
And walk o'er evil, touching it nowhere.

When come sad guests from off that suff'ring shore,
Which Dante saw in dream sublime of yore,
Appearing midst us here that day most blessed,
'Tis but to those; for they alone have guessed
The secrets of the grave; alone they understand
The pallid mendicants, who ask for heav'n.

Of Israel's King the psalms, inspired cries,
With Job's sublime distress, commingled rise;
The sanctuary sobs them through the naves
While wak'ning subtle fear, the bell's deep toll

With fun'ral sounds, demanding pity's dole
For wand'ring ghosts, as countless as the waves.
   Give on this day, when over all the earth
The Church to God makes moan for parted worth;
Your own remorse, regret at least to calm
Awak'ning memory's dying flame, give balm,
Flow'rs for their graves, and prayer for each loved soul,
Those gifts divine can yet the dead console.
   Pray for your friends, and for your mother pray,
Who made less drear for you life's desert way,
For all the portions of your heart that lie
Shut in the tomb, alas, each youthful tie
Is lost within the coffin's close constraint,
Where, prey of worms, the dead send up their plaint
   For exiles far from home and native land,
Who dying hear no voice, nor touch no hand
In life alone, more lonely still in death.
With none for their repose, to breathe one prayer,
Cast alms of tears upon an alien grave,
Or heed the stranger lonely even there;
   For those whose wounded souls when here below,
But anxious thought and bitter fancies know,
With days all joyless, nights of dull unrest;
For those who in night's calm find all so blest
And meet, in place of hope with morning beams,
A horrid wak'ning to their golden dreams;
   For all the pariahs of human kind
Who, heavy burdens bearing, find
How high the steeps of human woe they scale.
Oh, let your heart some off'ring make to these,
One pious thought, one holy word of peace,
Which shall twixt them and God swift rend the veil.
   The tribute bring of prayers and holy tears,
That when your hour draws nigh of nameless fears,
When reached their term shall be your numbered days,
Your name made known above with grateful praise,
By those whose suff'rings it was yours to end,
Arriving there find welcome as a friend!
   Your loving tribute, white-winged angels take,
Ere bearing it unto eternal spheres,
An instant lay it on the grass-grown graves,
While dying flow'rs in church-yards raise each head
To life, refreshed by breath of prayer, awake
And shed their fragrance on the sleeping dead.

A REQUIEM.
SIR WALTER SCOTT.

No sound was made, no word was spoke,
Till noble Angus silence broke;
And he a solemn sacred plight
Did to St. Bryde of Douglas make,
That he a pilgrimage would take
To Melrose Abbey, for the sake
Of Michael's restless sprite.
Then each, to ease his troubled breast,
To some blessed saint his prayers addressed-
Some to St. Modan made their vows,
Some to St. Mary of the Lowes,
Some to the Holy Rood of Lisle,
Some to our Lady of the Isle;
Each did his patron witness make,
That he such pilgrimage would take,
And monks should sing, and bells should toll,
All for the weal of Michael's soul,
While vows were ta'en, and prayers were prayed.
Most meet it were to mark the day
Of penitence and prayer divine,
When pilgrim-chiefs, in sad array,
Sought Melrose, holy shrine.
With naked foot, and sackcloth vest,
And arms enfolded on his breast,
Did every pilgrim go;
The standers-by might hear aneath,
Footstep, or voice, or high-drawn breath.
Through all the lengthened row;
No lordly look, no martial stride,
Gone was their glory, sunk their pride,
Forgotten their renown;
Silent and slow, like ghosts, they glide,
To the high altar's hallowed side,
And there they kneeled them down;
Above the suppliant chieftains wave
The banners of departed brave;
Beneath the lettered stones were laid
The ashes of their fathers dead;
From many a garnished niche around,
Stern saint and tortured martyr frowned,
And slow up the dim aisle afar,
With sable cowl and scapular,

247

And snow-white stoles, in order due,
The holy Fathers, two and two,
In long procession came;
Taper, and host, and book they bare,
And holy banner, flourished fair
With the Redeemer's name;
Above the prostrate pilgrim band
The mitred Abbot stretched his hand,
And blessed them as they kneeled;
With holy cross he signed them all,
And prayed they might be sage in hall,
And fortunate in field.

The Mass was sung, and prayers were said,
And solemn requiem for the dead;
And bells tolled out their mighty peal,
For the departed spirit's weal;
And ever in the office close
The hymn of intercession rose;
And far the echoing aisles prolong
The awful burthen of the song—
Dies Irae, Dies Illa,
Salvet SÆlum in Favilla;
While the pealing organ rung,
Thus the holy father sung:

HYMN FOR THE DEAD.

The day of wrath, that dreadful day,
When heaven and earth shall pass away,
What power shall be the sinner's stay?
How shall he meet that dreadful day?
When, shrivelling like a parched scroll,
The flaming heavens together roll;
While louder yet, and yet more dread,
Swells the high trump that wakes the dead;
O! on that day, that wrathful day,
When man to judgment wakes from clay,
Be Thou the trembling sinner's stay,
Though heaven and earth shall pass away.

THE PENANCE OF ROBERT THE DEVIL.
COLLIN DE PLANCY.

In Normandy, the most sinister associations still remain connected with the name of Robert the Devil. By the people, who change historical details, but yet preserve the moral thereof, it is believed that Robert is undergoing his penance here below, on the theatre of his crimes, and that, after a thousand years, it is not yet ended. Messrs. Taylor and Charles Nodier have mentioned this tradition in

248

their "Voyage Pittoresque de l'Ancienne France" ("Picturesque Journey through Old France").

"On the left shore of the Seine," say they, "not far from Moulineaux, are seen the colossal ruins, which are said to be the remains of the castle, or fortress, of Robert the Devil. Vague recollections, a ballad, some shepherd's tales—these are all the chronicles of those imposing ruins. Nevertheless, the fame of Robert the Devil's doings still survives in the country which he inhabited. His very name still excites that sentiment of fear which ordinarily results only from recent impressions.

"In the vicinity of the castle of Robert the Devil every one knows his misdeeds, his violent conquests, and the rigor of his penance. The cries of his victims still reecho through the vaults, and come to terrify himself in his nocturnal wanderings, for Robert is condemned to visit the ruins and the dungeons of his castle.

"Sometimes, if the old traditions of the country are to be believed, Robert has been seen, still clad in the loose tunic of a hermit, as on the day of his burial, wandering in the neighborhood of his castle, and visiting, barefoot and bareheaded, the little corner of the plain where the cemetery must have been. Sometimes, a shepherd straying through the adjoining copse in search of his flock, scattered by an evening storm, has been frightened by the fearful aspect of the phantom, seen by the glare of the lightning, flitting about amongst the graves. He has heard him, in the pauses of the tempest, imploring the pity of their mute inhabitants; and on the morrow he shunned the place in horror, because the earth, freshly turned up, had opened on every side to terrify the murderer."

But there is another tradition which we cannot omit.

A band of those Northmen who, during the troubled reign of Charles III. of France—without any sufficient reason called Charles the Simple—had invaded that part of Neustria where Robert the Devil was born; a group of these fierce warriors were one evening warming themselves around a fire of brambles, and, joyous in a country more genial than their own, they sang, to a wild melody, the great deeds of their princes, when they saw, leaning against the trunk of a tree, an old man poorly clad, and of a sad, yet resigned aspect. They called to him as he passed along before the fortress of Robert the Devil, then only half ruined.

"Good man," said they, "sing us some song of this country."

The old man, advancing slowly, chanted in an humble yet manly voice, the beautiful prose of St. Stephen. It told how the first of the martyrs paid homage till the end to Jesus Christ, Our Lord; and how, expiring under their blows, he besought Heaven to forgive his murderers.

But this hymn displeased the rude band, who began brutally to insult the old man. The latter fell on one knee and uttered no complaint.

At this moment appeared a young man, before whom all the soldiers rose to their feet. His lofty mien and his tone of authority indicated the son of a mighty lord.

"You who insult a defenceless old man," said he, "your conduct is base and

249

cowardly. Away with you! those who insult women or old men are unworthy to march with the brave. For you, good old man, come and share my meal. It is for the chief to repair the wrong-doings of those he commands."

"Young man," said the stranger, "what you have just done is pleasing to God, who loveth justice; but it concerneth not me, who can bear no ill- will to any one."

He then told his name; related the hideous story of his crimes, then his conversion through the prayers of his mother, and his penance, which was to last yet a long time. He showed how the grace of faith and of repentance had entered into his heart.

"Exhausted with emotion," said he, "I sat down on a stone amid some ruins; I slept. Oh! blessed be my good angel for having sent me that sleep! Scarcely had I closed mine eyes when I had a vision. It seemed to me that the mountain on which rises the Castle of Moulinets darted up to heaven and formed a staircase. Up the steps went slowly a crowd of phantoms, in which I, alas! recognized my crimes. There were women and young maidens, whose death was my doing, hardworking vassals dishonored, old men driven from their dwellings, and forced to ask the bread of charity. I saw thus ascending not only men, but things, houses burned, crops destroyed, flocks, the hope and the care of a whole life of toil, sacrificed at a moment in some wild revel.

"And I saw an angel rising rapidly. Then did my limbs quiver like the leaves of the aspen. I said to that ascending angel:

"'Whither goest thou?' He answered: 'I bring thy crimes before the Lord, that they may bear testimony against thee.'

"Then all my members became as it were burning grass. 'O good angel!' I cried, 'could I not at least efface some of these images?' He replied: 'All, if thou wilt.' 'And how?' 'Confess them; the breath of thy avowal will disperse them. Weep them in penance, and thy tears will efface even the traces thereof.'"

The old man then told how he had made his confession, and what penance he did, wandering about in rags, without other food than that which he shared with the dogs.

"I had known," he added, "all the pleasures of the earth, and had known some of its joys. But I found them still more in the miseries, the life-long fatigue, the hard humiliations of penance, because they were expiating my faults. Thus, then, O strangers, whatever fate Heaven may decree for you, if you desire happiness, find Our Lord Jesus Christ, and practice His justice."

The old man was silent; the barbarians remained motionless. He, however, taking the young chief by the hand, led him to the esplanade of the castle, and showing him all that vast country which is watered by the Seine: "Young man," said he, "for as much as thou hast protected a poor old man, God will reward the noble heart within thee. Thou seest these lands so rich—they were once mine; and even now, after God, they have no other lawful owner. I give them to thee; make faith and equity reign there. I will rejoice in thy reign."

Now this chief, to whom the penitent Robert thus bequeathed his faith and his inheritance, was Rollo, first Duke of the Normans.

250

ALL SOULS' EVE.

Where the tombstones gray and browned,
And the broken roods around,
And the vespers' solemn sound,
Told an old church near;
I sat me in the eve,
And I let my fancy weave
Such a vision as I leave
With a frail pen here.

Methought I heard a trail
Like to slowly-falling hail
And the sadly-plaintive wail
Of a misty file of souls,
As they glided o'er the grass,
Sighing low: "Alas! alas!
How the laggard moments pass
In purgatorial doles!"

Through their garments' glancing sheen,
As if nothing were between,
Pierced the moon's benignant beam
To a grove of stunted pines;
In whose distant lightsome shade,
With their gilded coats arrayed,
Danced a fairy cavalcade,
To a fairy poet's rhymes.

Then a cloud obscured the moon,
And the fairy dance and rune
Faded down behind the gloom
Which along the upland fell,
And my ears could only hear,
In the church-yard lone and drear,
The tinkle soft and clear
Of the morning Mass's bell.
It eddied through the air,
And it seemed to call to prayer
All the waiting spirits there
Which the moon's beams showed,
But each tinkle sank to die
In a heart-distressing sigh,
And no worshippers drew nigh
With the penitential word.

Mute as statue, on each knoll
Stood a thin, transparent soul,
While the fresh breeze stole

From its long night's rest,
Till it bore upon its tongue,
Like a snatch of sacred song,
All the peopled graves among,
Ite Missa est!
   Then a cry, as Angels raise
In an ecstasy of praise,
When the Godhead's glowing rays
To their eager sight is given,
Shook the consecrated ground,
And the souls it lost were found
From their venial sins unbound,
In the happy fields of heaven!
   Where the tombstones gray and browned,
And the broken roods around,
And the vespers' solemn sound,
Told an old church near;
I sat me in the eve,
And I let my fancy weave
Such a vision as I leave
With a frail pen here.

ELEVENTH MONTH, NOVEMBER: THE HOLY SOULS.
COMMEMORATION OF ALL SOULS.
HARRIET M. SKIDMORE.

   O faithful church! O tender mother-heart,
That, 'neath the shelter of thy deathless love,
Shieldest the blood-bought charge thy Master gave;
Laving the calm, unfurrowed infant brow
With the pure wealth of Heaven's cleansing stream;
Breathing above the sinner's grief-bowed head
The mystic words that loose the demon-spell,
And bid the leprous soul be clean again;
Decking the upper chamber of the heart
For the blest banquet of the Lord of love;
Binding upon the youthful warrior's breast
The buckler bright, the sacred shield of strength,
The fair, celestial gift of Pentecost,
Borne on the pinions of the holy Dove!
And when, at last, life's sunset hour is near,
And the worn pilgrim-feet stand trembling on
The shadowy borders of the death-dark vale,
At thy command the priestly hand bestows
The potent unction in the saving Name,
And gives unto the parched and pallid lip

The blest Viaticum, the Bread of Life,
As staff and stay for that drear pilgrimage!
Thy prayers ascend, with magic incense-breath,
From the lone couch, where, fainting by the way,
The frail companion of the deathless soul
Parteth in pain from its immortal guest.
And when, at last, the golden chain is loosed,
And through the shadows of that mystic vale
The ransomed captive floateth swiftly forth,
In solemn tones thy *De Profundis* rings
O'er all the realms of vast eternity;
Thy tender litanies call gently down
The angel-guides, the white-robed band of Saints,
To lead the wanderer to "the great White Throne,"
To plead, with Heaven's own pitying tenderness,
For life and mercy at the judgment-seat.
The account is given, the saving sentence breathed,
Yet He who said that nought by sin defiled
Can take at once its blessed place amid
The spotless legion of His shining Saints,
Will find, upon the white baptismal robe,
Full many a blemish; stains too lightly held,
Half-cleansed by an imperfect sorrow's flood.
"The Christian shall be saved, yet as by fire;"
So, to the pain-fraught, purifying flame
The robe is given, till every blighting spot
Hath faded from its primal purity;
Still, faithful Church, thy blest Communion binds
Each suffering child unto thy mother's heart.
Full well thou know'st the wondrous power of prayer—
That 'tis a holy and a wholesome thought
To plead for those who in the drear abode
Of penance linger, "that they may be loosed
From all their sins;" that on each spotless brow
Love's shining hand may place the starry crown.
And so the holy Sacrifice ascends,
A sweet oblation for that wailing band
Thy regal form in mourning hues is draped,
Thy pleading *Miserere* ceaseth not
Till, at its blest entreaty, Love descends,
As erst, from His rent tomb, to Limbo's realm,
And leads again the freed, exultant throng,
Within the gleaming gates of gold and pearl,
To bask in fadeless splendor, where the flow

253

Of the "still waters" by the "pastures green"
Faints not, nor slackens, through the endless years.
O Christians, brethren by that holy tie
That links the living with the ransomed dead!
Children of one fond mother are ye all,
White-robed in heaven, militant on earth,
And sufferers 'mid the purifying flame.
O ye who tread the highway of our world,
Join now your voices with that mother's sigh!
And while the mournful autumn wind laments,
And sad November's ceaseless tear-drops fall
Upon "the Silent City's" marble roofs,
O'er lonely graves amid the pathless wild,
Or where the wayworn pilgrim sank to rest
In some lone cavern by the crested sea—
List to the pleading wail that e'er ascends
From the dark land of suffering and woe:
"Our footsteps trod your fair, sun-lighted paths,
Our voices mingled in your joyous songs,
Our tears were blended in one common grief;
Perchance our erring hearts' excessive love
For you, the worshipped idols of our lives,
Hath been the blemish on our bridal robes.
Plead for us, then, and let your potent prayer
Unlock the golden gates, that we who beat
Our eager wings against these prison bars,
May wing our flight to endless liberty!"

THE MEMORY OF THE DEAD.
FATHER FABER

[This poem scarcely comes within the scope of the present work, yet it is, by its nature, so closely connected therewith, and is, moreover, so exquisitely tender and pathetic, so beautiful in its mournful simplicity, that I decided on giving it a place amongst these funereal fragments.]

Oh! it is sweet to think
Of those that are departed,
While murmured Aves sink
To silence tender-hearted—
While tears that have no pain
Are tranquilly distilling,
And the dead live again
In hearts that love is filling.

Yet not as in the days
Of earthly ties we love them;
For they are touched with rays

From light that is above them;
Another sweetness shines
Around their well-known features;
God with His glory signs
His dearly-ransomed creatures.
　　Yes, they are more our own,
Since now they are God's only;
And each one that has gone
Has left one heart less lonely.
He mourns not seasons fled,
Who now in Him possesses
Treasures of many dead
In their dear Lord's caresses.
　　Dear dead! they have become
Like guardian angels to us;
And distant Heaven like home,
Through them begins to woo us;
Love that was earthly, wings
Its flight to holier places;
The dead are sacred things
That multiply our graces.
　　They whom we loved on earth
Attract us now to Heaven;
Who shared our grief and mirth
Back to us now are given.
They move with noiseless foot
Gravely and sweetly round us,
And their soft touch hath cut
Full many a chain that bound us.
　　O dearest dead! to Heaven
With grudging sighs we gave you;
To Him—be doubts forgiven!
Who took you there to save you:—
Now get us grace to love
Your memories yet more kindly,
Pine for our homes above
And trust to God more blindly.

THE HOLY SOULS.
WRITTEN FOR MUSIC BY THE AUTHOR OF "CHRISTIAN SCHOOLS AND SCHOLARS."

　　O Mary, help of sorrowing hearts,
Look down with pitying eye
Where souls the spouses of thy Son,
In fiery torments lie;

255

Far from the presence of their Lord
The purging debt they pay,
In prisons through whose gloomy shades
There shines no cheering ray.
   The fire of love is in their hearts,
Its flame burns fierce and keen;
They languish for His Blessed Face,
For one brief moment seen;
Prisoners of hope, their joy is there
To wait His Holy Will,
And, patient in the cleansing flames,
Their penance to fulfil.
   But dark the gloom where smile of thine,
Sweet Mother, may not fall,
Oh, hear us, when for these dear souls
Thy loving aid we call!
Thou art the star whose gentle beam
Sheds joy upon the night,
Oh, let its shining pierce their gloom
And give them peace and light.
   The sprinkling of the Precious Blood
From thy dear hand must come,
Quench with its drops their cruel flames,
And call them to their home;
Freed from their pains, and safe with thee,
In Jesu's presence blest,
Oh, may the dead in Christ receive
Eternal light and rest!

THE PALMER'S ROSARY.
ELIZA ALLEN STARR.

   No coral beads on costly chain of gold
The Palmer's pious lips at Vespers told;
No guards of art could Pilgrim's favor win,
Who only craved release from earth and sin.
He from the Holy Land his rosary brought;
From sacred olive wood each bead was wrought,
Whose grain was nurtured, ages long ago,
By blood the Saviour sweated in His woe;
Then on the Holy Sepulchre was laid
This crown of roses from His passion made;
The Sepulchre from which the Lord of all
Arose from death's dark bed and icy thrall.
   Yet not complete that wreath of joy and pain,
Which for the dead must sweet indulgence gain;

The pendant cross, on which with guileless art,
Some hand had graved what touches every heart,
The image of the Lamb for sinners slain,
From Bethlehem's crib, now shrine, his prayers obtain;
And tears and kisses tell the holy tale
Of pilgrim love and penitential wail.

  The love, the tears, which fed his pious flame,
May well be thine, my heart, in very same;
Since bead and cross, by Palmer prized so well,
At vesper-hour, these fingers softly tell,
And press, through them, each dear and sacred spot
Where God once walked, "yet men received Him not."
And still, with pious Palmer gray, of yore,
Thy lips can kiss the ground He wet with gore,
Still at the Sepulchre with her delay,
Who found Him risen ere the break of day;
And hover round the crib with meek delight
Where shepherds hasted from their flocks by night,
To there adore Him whom a Virgin blessed,
Bore in her arms and nourished at her breast.
My Rosary dear! my Bethlehem Cross so fair!

  No rose, no lily can with thee compare;
No gems, no gold, no art, or quaint device
Could be my precious Rosary's priceless price;
For Heaven's eternal joys at holier speed,
I trust to win through every sacred bead;
And still for suffering souls obtain release
From cleansing fires to everlasting peace.

A LYKE WAKE DIRGE.

[From Sir Walter Scott's "Minstrelsy of the Border," we take this fragment. The dirge to which the eminent author alludes in a before- quoted extract from his work, and which he erroneously styles "a charm," is here given in full. The reader will observe that it partakes not the least of the nature of a charm. It would seem to have some analogy with the "Keen," or Wail of the Irish peasantry.]

  This ae nighte, this ae nighte,
Every nighte and alle;
Fire and sleet, and candle lighte,
And Christe receive thye saule.

  When thou from hence away are paste,
Every nighte and alle;
To Whinny-muir thou comest at laste;
And Christe receive thye saule.

  If ever thou gavest hosen and shoon;
Every nighte and alle;

Sit thee down and put them on;
And Christe receive thye saule.
If hosen and shoon thou ne'er gavest nane,
Every nighte and alle,
The whinnes shall pricke thee to the bare bane;
And Christe receive thye saule.

    From Whinny-muir, when thou mayest passe,
Every nighte and alle;
To Brig o' Dread thou comest at laste;
And Christe receive thye saule.

    From Brig o' Dread when thou mayest passe,
Every nighte and alle;
To Purgatory fire thou comest at laste;
And Christe receive thye saule.

    If ever thou gavest meat or drink,
Every nighte and alle,
The fire shall never make thee shrinke;
And Christe receive thye saule.

    If meat or drink thou never gavest nane,
Every nighte and alle;
The fire will burn thee to the bare bane;
And Christe receive thye saule.

    This ae nighte, this ae nighte,
Every nighte and alle;
Fire and sleet, and candle lighte,
And Christe receive thye saule.

ALL SOULS' DAY.
SECOND VESPERS OF ALL SAINTS.

From "Lyra Liturgica."

    What means this veil of gloom
Drawn o'er the festive scene;
The solemn records of the tomb
Where holy mirth hath been:
As if some messenger of death should fling
His tale of woe athwart some nuptial gathering?

    Our homage hath been given
With gladsome voice to them
Who fought, and won, and wear in heaven
Christ's robe and diadem;
Now to the suffering Church we must descend,
Our "prisoners of hope" with succor to befriend.

    They will not strive nor cry,
Nor make their pleading known;
Meekly and patiently they lie,

Speaking with God alone;
And this the burden of their voiceless song,
Wafted from age to age, "How long, O Lord, how long?"
   O blessed cleansing pain!
Who would not bear thy load,
Where every throb expels a stain,
And draws us nearer GOD?
Faith's firm assurance makes all anguish light,
With earth behind, and heaven fast opening on the sight.
   Yet souls that nearest come
To their predestin'd gain,
Pant more and more to reach their home:
Delay is keenest pain
To those that all but touch the wish'd for shore,
Where sin, and grief that comes of sin, shall fret no more.
   And O—O charity,
For sweet remembrance sake,
These souls, to God so very nigh,
Into your keeping take!
Speed them by sacrifice and suffrage, where
They burn to pour for you a more prevailing prayer.
   They were our friends erewhile,
Co-heirs of saving grace;
Co-partners of our daily toil,
Companions in our race;
We took sweet counsel in the house of God,
And sought a common rest along a common road.
   And had their brethren car'd
To keep them just and pure,
Perchance their pitying God had spar'd,
The pains they now endure.
What if to fault of ours those pains be due,
To ill example shown, or lack of counsel true?
   Alas, there are who weep
In fierce, unending flame,
Through sin of those on earth that sleep,
Regardless of their shame;
Or who, though they repent, too sadly know
No help of theirs can cure or soothe their victim's woe.
   Thanks to our God who gives,
In fruitful Mass or prayer,
To many a friend that dies, yet lives,
A salutary share;
Nor stints our love, though cords of sense be riven,

259

Nor bans from hope the soul that is not ripe for heaven.
 Feast of the Holy Dead!
Great Jubilee of grace!
When angel guards exulting lead
To their predestin'd place
Souls, that the Church shall loose from bonds to-day
In every clime that basks beneath her genial sway.

THE SUFFERING SOULS.
BY E. M. V. BULGER.

 It is a holy and wholesome thought to pray for the dead.—II Mac. xii. 46.

 In some quiet hour at the close of day,
When your work is finished and laid away,
Think of the suffering souls, and pray.

 Think of that prison of anguish and pain,
Where even the souls of the Saints remain,
Till cleansed by fire from the slightest stain.

 Think of the souls who were dear to you
When this life held them; still be true,
And pray for them now; it is all you can do.

 Think of the souls who are lonely there,
With no one, perchance, to offer a prayer
That God may have pity on them and spare.

 Think of the souls that have longest lain
In that place of exile and of pain,
Suffering still for some uncleansed stain.

 Think of the souls who, perchance, may be
On the very threshold of liberty—
One "*Ave Maria*" may set them free!

 Oh, then, at the close of each passing day,
When your work is finished and folded away,
Think of the suffering souls, and pray!

 Think of their prison, so dark and dim,
Think of their longing to be with Him
Whose praises are sung by the cherubim!

 As you tell the beads of your Rosary,
Ask God's sweet Mother their mother to be;
Her immaculate hands hold Heaven's key.

 Oh, how many souls are suffering when
You whisper "Hail Mary" again and again,
May see God's face as you say "*Amen!*"
 —*Ave Maria*, November 24, 1883.

THE VOICES OF THE DEAD.

 'Twas the hour after sunset,
And the golden light had paled;

260

The heavy foliage of the woods
Were all in shadow veiled.
 Yet a witchery breathed through the soft twilight,
A thought of the sun that was set,
And a soft and mystic radiance
Through the heavens hung lingering yet.
 The purple hills stood clear and dark
Against the western sky,
And the wind came sweeping o'er the grass
With a wild and mournful cry:
 It swept among the grass that grows
Above the quiet grave,
And stirred the boughs of the linden-trees
That o'er the church-yard wave.
 And the low murmur of the leaves
All softly seemed to say,
 "It is a good and wholesome thought
For the dead in Christ to pray."
 Earth's voices all are low and dim;
But a human heart is there,
With psalms and words of holy Church,
To join in Nature's prayer.
 A Monk is pacing up and down;
His prayers like incense rise;
Ever a sweet, sad charm for him
Within that church-yard lies.
 Each morning when from Mary's tower
The sweet-toned *Ave* rings,
This herdsman of the holy dead
A Mass of Requiem sings.
 And when upon the earth there falls
The hush of eventide,
A dirge he murmurs o'er the graves
Where they slumber side by side.
 "Eternal light shine o'er them, Lord!
And may they rest in peace!"
His matins all are finished now,
And his whispered accents cease.
 But, hark! what sound is that which breaks
The stillness of the hour?
Is it the ivy as it creeps
Against the gray church tower?
 Is it the sound of the wandering breeze,
Or the rustling of the grass,

Or the stooping wing of the evening birds
As home to their nests they pass?
No; 'tis a voice like one in dreams,
Half solemn and half sad,
Freed from the weariness of earth,
Not yet with glory clad;
　Full of the yearning tenderness
Which nought but suffering gives;
Too sad for angel-tones—too full
Of rest for aught that lives.
　They are the Voices of the Dead
From the graves that lie around,
And the Monk's heart swells within his breast,
As he listens to the sound.
　"Amen! Amen!" the answer comes
Unto his muttered prayer;
"Amen!" as though the brethren all
In choir were standing there.
　The living and departed ones
On earth are joined again,
And the bar that shuts them from his ken
For a moment parts in twain.
　Over the gulf that yawns beneath,
Their echoed thanks he hears
For the Masses he has offered up,
For his orisons and tears.
　And as the strange responsory
Mounts from the church-yard sod,
Their mingled prayers and answers rise
Unto the throne of God. [1]

[Footnote 1: There is a story recorded of St. Birstan, Bishop of Winchester, who died about the year of Christ 944, how he was wont every day to say Mass and Matins for the dead; and one evening, as he walked in the church-yard, reciting his said Matins, when he came to the *Requiescat in Pace*, the voices in the graves round about him made answer aloud, and said, "Amen, Amen!"—*From the "English Martyrology" for October 22*]
　—*M. R., in "The Lamp," Oct. 31, 1863.*

THE CONVENT CEMETERY.
REV. ABRAM J. RYAN.

[This is an extract from Father Ryan's poem, "Their Story Runneth Thus."]

　And years and years, and weary years passed on
Into the past; one autumn afternoon,
When flowers were in their agony of death,

And winds sang "*De Profundis*" o'er them,
And skies were sad with shadows, he did walk
Where, in a resting-place as calm as sweet,
The dead were lying down; the autumn sun
Was half-way down the west—the hour was three,
The holiest hour of all the twenty-four,
For Jesus leaned His head on it, and died.
He walked alone amid the Virgins' graves,
Where calm they slept—a convent stood near by,
And from the solitary cells of nuns
Unto the cells of death the way was short.
   Low, simple stones and white watched o'er each grave,
While in the hollows 'twixt them sweet flowers grew,
Entwining grave with grave. He read the names
Engraven on the stones, and "Rest in peace"
Was written 'neath them all, and o'er each name
A cross was graven on the lowly stone.
He passed each grave with reverential awe,
As if he passed an altar, where the Host
Had left a memory of its sacrifice.
And o'er the buried virgin's virgin dust
He walked as prayerfully as though he trod
The holy floor of fair Loretto's shrine.
He passed from grave to grave, and read the names
Of those whose own pure lips had changed the names
By which this world had known them into names
Of sacrifice known only to their God;
Veiling their faces they had veiled their names.
The very ones who played with them as girls,
Had they passed there, would know no more than he,
Or any stranger, where their playmates slept.
And then he wondered all about their lives, their hearts,
Their thoughts, their feelings, and their dreams,
Their joys and sorrows, and their smiles and tears.
He wondered at the stories that were hid
Forever down within those simple graves.

ONE HOUR AFTER DEATH.
ELIZA ALLEN STARR.

   Oh! I could envy thee thy solemn sleep,
Thy sealed lid, thy rosary-folding palm,
Thy brow, scarce cold, whose wasted outlines keep
The "*Bona Mors*" sublime, unfathomed calm.
   I sigh to wear myself that burial robe
Anointed hands have blessed with pious care:

263

What nuptial garb on all this mortal globe
Could with thy habit's peaceful brown compare?
  Beneath its hallowed folds thy feeble dust
Shall rest serenely through the night of time;
Unharmed by worm, or damp, or century's rust,
But, fresh as youth, shall greet th' eternal prime
  Of that clear morn, before whose faintest ray
Earth's bliss will pale, a taper's flickering gleam;
I see it break! the pure, celestial day,
And stars of mortal hope already dim.
  "*In pace*" Lord, oh! let her sweetly rest
In Paradise, this very day with Thee:
Her faithful lips her dying Lord confessed,
Then let her soul Thy risen glory see!

A PRAYER FOR THE DEAD.
T. D. MCGEE.

  Let us pray for the dead!
For sister and mother,
Father and brother,
For clansman and fosterer,
And all who have loved us here;
For pastors, for neighbors,
At rest from their labors;
Let us pray for our own beloved dead!
That their souls may be swiftly sped
Through the valley of purgatorial fire,
To a heavenly home by the gate called Desire!
  I see them cleave the awful air,
Their dun wings fringed with flame;
They hear, they hear our helping prayer,
They call on Jesu's name.
  Let us pray for the dead!
For our foes who have died,
May they be justified!
For the stranger whose eyes
Closed on cold alien skies;
For the sailors who perished
By the frail arts they cherished;
Let us pray for the unknown dead.
  Father in heaven, to Thee we turn,
Transfer their debt to us;
Oh! bid their souls no longer burn
In mediate anguish thus.
Let us pray for the soldiers,

On whatever side slain;
Whose white bones on the plain
Lay unclaimed and unfathered,
By the vortex-wind gathered,
Let us pray for the valiant dead.
    Oh! pity the soldier,
Kind Father in heaven,
Whose body doth moulder
Where his soul fled self-shriven.
    We have prayed for the dead;
All the faithful departed,
Who to Christ were true-hearted;
And our prayers shall be heard,
For so promised the Lord;
And their spirits shall go
Forth from limbo-like woe—
And joyfully swift the justified dead
Shall feel their unbound pinions sped,
Through the valley of purgatorial fire,
To their heavenly home by the gate called Desire,
    By the gate called Desire,
In clouds they've ascended—
O Saints, pray for us,
Now your sorrows are ended!

THE DE PROFUNDIS BELL. [1]

[Footnote 1: Among the many beautiful and pious customs of Catholic countries, none appeals with more tender earnestness to the pitying heart than that of the *De Profundis* bell. While the shades of night are gathering over the earth, a solemn, dirge like tolling resounds from the lofty church towers. Instantly every knee is bent, and countless voices, in city and hamlet, from castle and cottage, repeat, with heartfelt earnestness, the beautiful psalm, "*De Profundis*," or, "Out of the depths," etc., for the souls of the faithful departed. Thus is illustrated, in a most touching manner, the blessed doctrine of the Communion of Saints. Thus does the Church Militant clasp, each day anew, the holy tie which binds her to the suffering Church of Purgation.

The compassionate heart of the Christian is stirred to its inmost depths by the plaintive call of that warning bell; and as, in the holy hush of nightfall, he obeys its tender appeal, how fully does he realize that "it is a holy and wholesome thought to pray for the dead."]

HARRIET M. SKIDMORE.

The day was dead; from purple summits faded
Its last resplendent ray,
And softly slept the wearied earth, o'ershaded
By twilight's dreamy gray;

Then flowed deep sound-waves o'er silence holy
Of nature's calm repose,
  As from its lofty dome, outpealing slowly
Through the still gloaming, rose
The deep and dirge-like swell
Of *De Profundis* bell.
  To heedful hearts each solemn cadence falling
Through twilight's misty veil,
An echo seemed of spirit-voices calling
With sad, beseeching wail;
And thus outspake the mournful intonation:
"Plead for us, brethren, plead!"
From the drear depths of woe and desolation
Our cry of bitter need
Floats upward in the swell
Of *De Profundis* bell.
Then bowed each knee, the plaintive summons heeding,
And rose the blended sigh.
As incense-breath of fond, united pleading
E'en to the throne on high:
"Hear, Lord, the cry of fervent supplication
Earth's children lift to Thee;
And from the depths of long and dread purgation
Thy faithful captives free,
Ere dies on earth the swell
Of *De Profundis* bell.
  "If, in Thy sight, scarce e'en the perfect whiteness
Of seraph-robe is pure,
Shall mortals brave Thine eye's eternal brightness?
Shall man its search endure?
Ah! trusting hope may meet the dazzling splendor
Of those celestial rays,
For with Thee, Lord, is pardon sweet and tender,
When contrite sorrow prays.
Ay, Thou wilt lead, from desert-waste of sadness,
Thine Israel's chosen band;
And Miriam's song of pure, triumphant gladness
Shall, in Thy promised land,
Succeed the dirge-like swell
Of *De Profundis* bell."

NOVEMBER.

ANNA. T. SADLIER.

  Robed in mourning, nave and chancel,
In the livery of the dead,

Hymns funereal are chanted.
Services sublime are read.
  Sounds the solemn *Dies Iræ*,
Fraught with echoes from the day
When the majesty of Heaven
Shall appear in dread array.
  Next the Gospel's weird recital,
Full of mystery and dread;
Holding message for the living,
Bringing tidings of the dead.
  With its resurrection promised—
Resurrection unto life,
With its full and true fruition,
And immunity from strife.
  Blest immunity from sorrow,
Primal man's unhappy dower;
While the evil shall find judgment
In the resurrection hour.
  To the Lord, the King of Glory,
Goes the voiceless, tuneless prayer,
From the deep pit to deliver,
From eternal pains to spare.
  All who wait the holy coming,
Wait the dawning of a day
That shall ope the gates of darkness,
Shall illume the watcher's way.
May the holy Michael lead them
To the fullness of the light
That of old, in prophet visions,
Burst on Adam's dazzled sight.
  May they pass from death to living—
Message that the Master's voice
Gave to Abraham the faithful,
Bade his exiled soul rejoice.
  May perpetual light descending
Touch their foreheads, dark with fear—
Dark with deadly torments suffered;
Sign them with the glory near!
  May they rest, O Lord, forever
In a peace that, unexpressed,
Shall bestow upon the pilgrims
Dual crowns of light and rest!
  Death's weird canticle is ringing
In its supplication strong—

In its far cry to the heavens,
Couched in wild, unearthly song.

Ay, this *Libera* o'ercomes us,
Requiem, at once, and dirge—
Makes this life with life immortal
In our consciousness to merge.

FOR THE SOULS IN PURGATORY.
ANONYMOUS.

Ye souls of the faithful who sleep in the Lord,
But as yet are shut out from your final reward,
Oh! would I could lend you assistance to fly
From your prison below to your palace on high!

O Father of Mercies! Thine anger withhold,
These works of Thy hand in Thy mercy behold;
Too oft from Thy path they have wandered aside,
But Thee, their Creator, they never denied.

O tender Redeemer, their misery see,
Deliver the souls that were ransomed by Thee;
Behold how they love Thee, despite all their pain;
Restore them, restore them to favor again!

O Spirit of Grace! O Consoler divine!
See how for Thy presence they longingly pine;
Ah! then, to enliven their sadness descend,
And fill them with peace and with joy in the end!

O Mother of Mercy! dear soother in grief!
Send thou to their torments a balmy relief;
Oh! temper the rigor of justice severe,
And soften their flames with a pitying tear.

Ye Patrons, who watched o'er their safety below,
Oh! think how they need your fidelity now;
And stir all the Angels and Saints in the sky
To plead for the souls that upon you rely!

Ye friends, who once sharing their pleasure and pain,
Now hap'ly already in Paradise reign,
Oh! comfort their hearts with a whisper of love,
And call them to share in your pleasures above!
O Fountain of Goodness! accept of our sighs:
Let Thy mercy bestow what Thy justice denies;
So may Thy poor captives, released from their woes,
Thy praises proclaim, while eternity flows!

All ye who would honor the Saints and their Head,
Remember, remember to pray for the dead—
And they, in return, from their misery freed,
To you will be friends in the hour of your need!

268

—Garland of Flowers.

ALL SOULS' EVE.

'Twas All Souls' Eve; the lights in Notre Dame
Blazed round the altar; gloomy, in the midst,
The pall, with all its sable hangings, stood;
With torch and taper, priests were ranged around,
Chanting the solemn requiem of the dead;
And then along the aisles the distant lights
Moved slowly, two by two; the chapels shone
Lit as they pass'd in momentary glare;
Behind the fretted choir the yellow ray,
On either hand the altar, blazing fell.
She thought upon the multitude of souls
Dwelling so near and yet so separate.
With dawn she sought Saint Jacques; the altars there
Had each its priest; the black and solemn Mass,
The nodding feathers of the catafalque,
The flaring torches, and the funeral chant,
And intercessions for the countless souls
In Purgatory still. With pity new
The Pilgrim pray'd for the departed. Long
She knelt before the Blessed Sacrament,
Beside Our Lady's altar. Pictured there,
She saw, imprisoned in the forked flames,
The suffering souls who ask the alms of prayer;
Her taper small an aged peasant lit,
To burn before Our Lady, that her voice,
Mother of mercy as she is, might plead
For one who left her still on earth to pray.
. . . . . Sable veils
Soon hid the altars; all things spoke of death,
And realms where those who leave the upper air
Wait till the stains of sin are cleansed, and pant
Amid the thirsty flames for Paradise. [1]

[Footnote 1: These verses are taken from an anonymous metrical work called
"The Pilgrim," published in England in 1867.]

OUR NEIGHBOR.
ELIZA ALLEN STARR.

Set it down gently at the altar rail,
The faithful, aged dust, with honors meet;
Long have we seen that pious face, so pale,
Bowed meekly at her Saviour's blessed feet.

These many years her heart was hidden where
Nor moth, nor rust, nor craft of man could harm;

269

The blue eyes, seldom lifted, save in prayer,
Beamed with her wished-for heaven's celestial calm.
　　As innocent as childhood's was the face,
Though sorrow oft had touched that tender heart;
Each trouble came as winged by special grace,
And resignation saved the wound from smart.
　　On bead and crucifix her finger kept,
Until the last, their fond, accustomed hold;
"My Jesus," breathed the lips; the raised eyes slept,
The placid brow, the gentle hand grew cold.
　　The choicely ripening cluster, ling'ring late
Into October on its shrivelled vine,
Wins mellow juices, which in patience wait
Upon those long, long days of deep sunshine.
　　Then set it gently at the altar rail,
The faithful, aged dust, with honors meet;
How can we hope, if such as she can fail
Before th' Eternal God's high judgment-seat?

PURGATORY.

OLD BELLS.

　　Ring out merrily,
Loudly, cheerily,
Blithe old bells from the steeple tower.
Hopefully, fearfully,
Joyfully, tearfully,
Moveth the bride from her maiden bower.
Cloud there is none in the bright summer sky,
Sunshine flings benison down from on high;
Children sing loud as the train moves along,
"Happy the bride that the sun shineth on."
　　Knell out drearily,
Measured out wearily,
Sad old bells from the steeple gray.
Priests chanting slowly,
Solemnly, slowly,
Passeth the corpse from the portal to-day.
Drops from the leaden clouds heavily fall,
Drippingly over the plume and the pall;
Murmur old folk, as the train moves along,
"Happy the dead that the rain raineth on."
　　Toll at the hour of prime,
Matin and vesper chime,
Loved old bells from the steeple high;
Rolling, like holy waves,

Over the lowly graves,
Floating up, prayer-fraught, into the sky.
Solemn the lesson your lightest notes teach,
Stern is the preaching your iron tongues preach;
Ringing in life from the bud to the bloom;
Ringing the dead to their rest in the tomb.
  Peal out evermore—
Peal as ye pealed of yore, Brave old bells, on each holy day.
In sunshine and gladness,
Through clouds and through sadness,
Bridal and burial have both passed away.
Tell us life's pleasures with death are still rife;
Tell us that death ever leadeth to life;
Life is our labor and death is our rest,
If happy the living, the dead are the blest.
  —*Popular Poetry.*

O HOLY CHURCH!
HARRIET M. SKIDMORE.

O holy Church! thy mother-heart
Still clasps the child of grace;
And nought its links of love can part,
Or rend its fond embrace.

  Thy potent prayer and sacred rite
Embalm the precious clay,
That waits the resurrection-light—
The fadeless Easter day.

  And loving hearts, by faith entwined,
True to that faith shall be,
And keep the sister-soul enshrined
In tender memory;

  Shall bid the ceaseless prayer ascend,
To win her guerdon blest;
The radiant day that hath no end,
The calm, eternal rest.

AN INCIDENT OF THE BATTLE OF BANNOCKBURN.
SIR WALTER SCOTT.

  Again he faced the battle-field—
Wildly they fly, are slain, or yield.
"Now then," he said, and couch'd his spear,
"My course is run, the goal is near;
One effort more, one brave career,
Must close this race of mine."
Then, in his stirrups rising high,
He shouted loud his battle-cry,

"St. James for Argentine!"
* * * * *

Now toil'd the Bruce, the battle done,
To use his conquest boldly won:
And gave command for horse and spear
To press the Southern's scatter'd rear,
Nor let his broken force combine,
When the war-cry of Argentine
Fell faintly on his ear!
"Save, save his life," he cried. "O save
The kind, the noble, and the brave!"
The squadrons round free passage gave,
The wounded knight drew near.
He raised his red-cross shield no more,
Helm, cuish, and breast-plate stream'd with gore.
Yet, as he saw the King advance,
He strove even then to couch his lance—
The effort was in vain!
The spur-stroke fail'd to rouse the horse;
Wounded and weary, in 'mid course
He tumbled on the plain.
Then foremost was the generous Bruce
To raise his head, his helm to loose:—
"Lord Earl, the day is thine!
My sovereign's charge, and adverse fate,
Have made our meeting all too late;
Yet this may Argentine,
As boon from ancient comrade, crave—
A Christian's Mass, a soldier's grave."
Bruce pressed his dying hand—its grasp
Kindly replied; but, in his clasp
It stiffen'd and grew cold—
And, "O farewell!" the victor cried,
Of chivalry the flower and pride,
The arm in battle bold,
The courteous mien, the noble race,
The stainless faith, the manly face!
Bid Ninian's convent light their shrine,
For late-wake of De Argentine.
O'er better knight on death-bier laid,
Torch never gleamd, nor Mass was said! [1]

[Footnote 1: It is said that the body of Sir Giles de Argentine was brought to Edinburgh, and interred with the greatest pomp in St. Giles' Church. Thus did the royal Bruce respond to the dying knight's request.]

272

—From "The Lord of the Isles"

PRAY FOE THE MARTYRED DEAD.

Pray for the Dead! When, conscienceless, the nations
Rebellious rose to smite the thorn-crowned Head
Of Christendom, their proudest aspirations
Ambitioned but a place amongst the dead.

Pray for the Dead! The seeming fabled story
of early chivalry, in them renewed,
Shines out to-day with an ascendent glory
Above that field of parricidal feud.

The children of a persecuted mother,
When nations heard the drum of battle beat,
Through coward Europe, brother leagued with brother,
Rallied and perished at her sacred feet.

O Ireland, ever waiting the To-morrow,
Lift up thy widowed, venerable head,
Exultingly, through thy maternal sorrow,
Not comfortless, like Rachel, for thy dead.

For, where the crimson shock of battle thundered,
From hosts precipitated on a few,
Above thy sons, outnumbered, crushed and sundered,
Thy green flag through the smoke and glitter flew.

Lift up thy head! The hurricane that dashes
Its giant billows on the Rock of Time,
Divests thee, mother, of thy weeds and ashes,
Rendering, at least, thy grief sublime.

For nations, banded into conclaves solemn,
Thy name and spirit in the grave had cast,
And carved thy name upon the crumbling column
Which stands amid the unremembered Past.

Pray for the Dead! Cold, cold amid the splendor
Of the Italian South our brothers sleep;
The blue air broods above them warm and tender,
The mists glide o'er them from the barren deep.

Pray for the Dead! High-souled and lion-hearted,
Heroic martyrs to a glorious trust,
By them our scorned name is re-asserted,
By them our banner rescued from the dust.
    —*Kilkenny Journal.*

IN WINTER
ELIZA ALLEN STARR.

How lonely on the hillside look the graves!
The summer green no longer o'er them waves;
No more, among the frosted boughs, are heard

273

The mournful whip-poor-will or singing bird.

The rose-bush, planted with such tearful care,
Stands in the winter sunshine stiff and bare;
Save here and there its lingering berries red
Make the cold sunbeams warm above the dead.

Through all the pines, and through the tall, dry grass,
The fitful breezes with a shiver pass,
While o'er the autumn's lately flowering weeds
The snow-birds flit and peck the shelling seeds.

Because those graves look lonely, bleak and bare,
Because they are not, as in summer, fair,
O turn from comforts, cheery friends, and home,
And 'mid their solemn desolation roam!

On each brown turf some fresh memorial lay;
O'er each dear hillock's dust a moment stay,
To breathe a "Rest in Peace" for those who lie
On lonely hillsides 'neath a wintry sky.

OSEMUS.

MARY E MANNIX

Welcome, ye sad dirges of November,
When Indian summer drops her brilliant crown
All withered, as in clinging mantle brown
She floats, away to die beneath the leaves;
Pressed are the grapes, gathered the latest sheaves;
O wailing winds! how can we but remember
The loved and lost? O ceaseless monotones!
Hearing your plaints, counting your weary moans
Like voices of the dead, like broken sighs
From stricken souls who long for Paradise,
We will not slight the message that ye bear,
Nor check a pitying thought, nor guide a prayer.
They have departed, we must still remember;
Welcome, ye sad, sad dirges of November!

FUNERAL HYMN.

From the French of Theodore Nisard

A. T. SADLIER

The bell is tolling for the dead,
Christians, hasten we to prayer,
Our brothers suffer there,
Consumed in struggles vain.

Have pity, have pity on them,
In torturing flames immersed,
The stains their souls aspersed
Retain them far from heav'n.

274

Since God has giv'n us power,
Oh, let us their woes relieve;
Their hope do not deceive,
Our protectors they will be.
    For these suff'ring ones we pray,
Lord Jesus, Victim blest,
Take them from pain to rest,
Thy children, too, are they.
    * * * * *

[As the translation is a very rude one, we add the French original, which, particularly when set to music, is full of a deep solemnity and pathos.]

CHANT FUNÈBRE.
NISARD
    La cloche tinte pour les morts
Chrétiens, mettons nous en prières!
Ceux qi gemissent sont des frères,
Se consumant en vains efforts.
Pitié pour eux! Pitié pour eux!
Ils tourbillonnent dans la flamme;
Les taches qui souillent leur âmes,
Les tiennent captifs loin des cieux.
Mettons un terme à leur douleurs,
Dieu nous en donne la puissance;
Ne trompons point leur espérance,
Puis ils seront nos protecteurs.
Disons pour nos fières souffrants:
Sauveur Jésus, Sainte Victime,
Tirez nos frères de l'abime,
Car, eux aussi, sont vos enfants.

REQUIESCAT IN PACE.
HARRIET M. SKIDMORE
    O Father, give them rest—
Thy faithful ones, whose day of toil is o'er,
    Whose weary feet shall wander never more
O'er earth's unquiet breast!
    The battle-strife was long;
Yet, girt with grace, and guided by Thy light,
They faltered not till triumph closed the fight,
Till pealed the victor's song.
    Though drear the desert path,
With cruel thorns and flinty fragments strewn,
Where fiercely swept, amid the glare of noon.
The plague-wind's biting wrath.
    Still onward pressed their feet;

275

For patience soothed with sweet celestial balm,
And, from the rocks, hope called her founts to calm
The Simoom's venom-heat.
     Their march hath reached its close,
Its toils are o'er, its Red Sea safely passed;
And pilgrim feet have cast aside at last
Earth's sandal-shoon of woes.
     Thou blissful promised land!
One rapturous glimpse of matchless glory caught,
One priceless vision, with thy beauty fraught,
Hath blessed that way-worn band.
     And to thy smiling shore
Their ceaseless messengers of longing went,
And blooms of bliss and fruitage of content,
Returning, gladly bore.
     Yet sadly still they wait;
For, past idolatries to gods of clay,
And past rebellions 'gainst the Master's sway,
Have barred the golden gate.
     The magic voice of prayer,
The saving rite, the sacrifice of love,
The human tear, the sigh of Saints above,
Blent in one off'ring fair—
     These, these alone, can win
The boon they crave: glad entrance into rest,
The fadeless crown, the garment of the blest,
Washed pure from stain of sin.
     Hear, then, our eager cry.
O God of mercy! bid their anguish cease;
To prisoned souls, ah! bring the glad release,
And hush the mourner's sigh.
     Mother of pitying love!
On sorrow's flood thy tender glances bend,
And o'er its dark and dreadful torrent send
The olive-bearing dove.
     Thy potent prayer shall be
An arch of peace, a radiant promise-bow,
To span the gulf, and shed its cheering glow
O'er the dread penance-sea.
     And on its pathway blest
The ransomed throng, in garments washed and white,
May safely pass to love's fair realm of light,
To heaven's perfect rest.

THE FEAST OF ALL SOULS IS THE COUNTRY.

From the French of Fontanes. [1]

[Footnote 1: Louis, Marquis de Fontanes, Peer of France, and Member of the French Academy.]

ANNA T. SADLIER

E'en now doth Sagittarius from on high,
Outstretch his bow, and ravage all the earth,
The hills, and meadows where of flowers the dearth
Already felt, like some vast ruins lie.

The bleak November counts its primal day,
While I, a witness of the year's decline,
Glad of my rest, within the fields recline.
No poet heart this beauty can gainsay,
No feeling mind these autumn pictures scorn,
But knows how their monotonous charms adorn.
Oh, with what joy does dreamy sorrow stray
At eve, slow pacing, the dun-colored vale;
He seeks the yellow woods, and hears the tale
Of winds that strip them of their lonely leaves;
For this low murmur all my sense deceives.
In rustling forests do I seem to hear
Those voices long since still, to me most dear.
In leaves grown sere they speak unto my heart.

This season round the coffin-lid we press,
Religion wears herself a mourning dress,
More grand she seems, while her diviner part
At sight of this, a world in ruins, grows.
To-day a pious usage she has taught,
Her voice opens vaults wherein our fathers dwell.
Alas, my memory doth keep that thought.
The dawn appeareth, and the swaying bell
Mingles its mournful sound with whistling winds,
The Feast of Death proclaiming to the air.
Men, women, children, to the Church repair,
Where one, with speech and with example binds
These happy tribes, maintaining all in peace.
He follows them, the first apostles, near,
Like them the pastor's holy name makes dear.

"With hymns of joy," said he, "but yesterday
We celebrated the triumphant dead
Who conquer'd heav'n by burning zeal, faith-fed.
For plaintive shades, whom sorrow makes his prey
We weep to-day, our mourning is their bliss,
All potent prayer is privileged in this,

Souls purified from sin by transient pain
It frees; we'll visit their most calm domain.
Man seeks it, and descends there every hour.
But dry our tears, for now celestial rays
The grave's dim region swift shall penetrate;
Yea, all its dwellers in their primal state
Shall wake, behold the light in mute amaze.
Ah, might I to that world my flight then wing
In triumph to my God, my flock recovered bring."
   So saying, offered he the holy rite,
With arms extended praying God to spare,
The while adoring knelt he humbly there.
That people prostrate! oh, most solemn sight
That church, its porticoes with moss o'ergrown,
The ancient walls, dim light and Gothic panes,
In its antiquity the brazen lamp
A symbol of eternity doth stamp.
A lasting sun. God's majesty down sent,
Vows, tears and incense from the altars rise,
Young beauties praying 'neath their mothers' eyes,
Do soften by their voices innocent,
The touching pomp religion there reveals;
The organ hush'd, the sacred silence round,
All, all uplifts, ennobles and inspires;
Man feels himself transported where the choirs
Of seraphim with harps of gold entone
Low at Jehovah's feet their endless song.
Then God doth make His awful presence known,
Hides from the wise, to loving hearts is shown:
He seeks less to be proved than to be felt. [1]
From out the Church the multitudes depart,
In separate groups unto th' abode they go
Of tranquil death, their tears still silent flow.
The standard of the Cross is borne apart,
Sublime our songs for death their sacred theme,
Now mixed with noise that heralds storms they seem;
Now lower above our heads the dark'ning clouds,
Our faces mournful, our funeral hymn
Both air and landscape in our grief enshrouds.
   Towards death's tranquil haven, on we fare,
The cypress, ivy, and the yew trees haunt
The spot where thorns seem growing everywhere.
Sparse lindens rise up grimly here and there,
The winds rush whistling through their branches gaunt.

278

Hard by a stream, my mind found there exprest
In waves and tombs a twofold lesson drest,
Eternal movement and eternal rest.
   Ah, with what holy joy these peasants fain
Would honor parent dust; they seek with pride
The stone or turf, concealing those allied
To them by love, they find them here again.
Alas, with us we may not seek the boon
Of gazing on the ashes of our dead.
Our dead are banish'd, on their rights we tread,
Their bones unhonored at hap-hazard strewn.
E'en now 'gainst us cry out their *Manes* pale,
Those nations and those times dire woes entail,
'Mongst whom in hearts grown weak by slow degree,
The *cultus* of the dead has ceased.
Here, here, at least have they from wrong been free,
Their heritage of peace preserving best.
No sumptuous marbles burden names here writ,
A shepherd, farmer, peasant, as is fit,
Beneath these stones in tranquil slumber see;
Perchance a Turenne, a Corneille they hide,
Who lived obscure, e'en to himself unknown.
But if from men he'd risen separate,
Sublime in camps, the theatre, the state,
His name by idol-loving worlds outcried,
Would that have made his slumber here more sweet?
   [Footnote 1: La Harpe said that these last twenty lines were the most beautiful
verses in the French tongue. They necessarily lose considerably in the translation.]

REQUIEM ÆTERNAM.

T. D. MCGEE.

[This beautiful requiem, written March 6th, 1868 (St. Victor's Day), on the death
of an intimate friend, acquires a new pathos and a new solemnity, from the fact
that its gifted author met his death at the hands of an assassin but one month
later, on the 7th of April of the same year. Like Mozart, he wrote his own
requiem]

   Saint Victor's Day, a day of woe,
The bier that bore our dead went slow
And silent gliding o'er the snow—
Miserere Domine!
   With Villa Maria's faithful dead,
Among the just we make his bed,
The cross, he loved, to shield his head—
Miserere Domine!
   The skies may lower, wild storms may rave

Above our comrade's mountain grave,
That cross is mighty still to save—
Miserere Domine!

Deaf to the calls of love and care,
He bears no more his mortal share,
Nought can avail him now but prayer—
Miserere Domine!

To such a heart who could refuse
Just payment of all burial dues,
Of Holy Church the rite and use?
Miserere Domine!

Right solemnly the Mass was said,
While burn'd the tapers round the dead,
And manly tears like rain were shed—
Miserere Domine!

No more St. Patrick's aisles prolong
The burden of his funeral song,
His noiseless night must now be long—
Miserere Domine!

Up from the depths we heard arise
A prayer of pity to the skies,
To Him who dooms or justifies—
Miserere Domine!

Down from the skies we heard descend
The promises the Psalmist penned,
The benedictions without end—
Miserere Domine!

Mighty our Holy Church's will
To shield her parting souls from ill,
Jealous of Death, she guards them still—
Miserere Domine!
The dearest friend will turn away,
And leave the clay to keep the clay,
Ever and ever she will stay—
Miserere Domine!

When for us sinners at our need,
That mother's voice is raised to plead,
The frontier hosts of heaven 'take heed—
Miserere Domine!

Mother of Love! Mother of fear,
And holy Hope, and Wisdom dear,
Behold we bring thy suppliant here—
Miserere Domine!

His glowing heart is still for aye,

That held fast by thy clemency,
Oh! look on him with loving eye—
Miserere Domine!

His Faith was as the tested gold,
His Hope assured, not over-bold,
His Charities past count, untold—
Miserere Domine!

Well may they grieve who laid him there,
Where shall they find his equal—where?
Nought can avail him now but prayer—
Miserere Domine!

Friend of my soul, farewell to thee!
Thy truth, thy trust, thy chivalry;
As thine? so may my last end be!
Miserere Domine!

APPENDIX

ASSOCIATION OF MASSES AND STATIONS OF THE CROSS FOR THE BELIEF OF THE HOLY SOULS.

It would be a great defect in a book such as this to omit all mention of an Association which exists in Montreal, Canada, for the special relief of the Souls in Purgatory. It is certain that there are Purgatorian societies, established in many other cities, both of Europe and America. But this Canadian one seems unique, in so far, that it has a triple aim: first, that of relieving the holy souls; second, that of the conversion of infidels; third, that of contributing to the support of the Mendicant Order of St. Francis. The money received is sent direct to these missionaries, by whom the Masses are said. Touching stories are told of the joy of these devoted apostles on receipt of such alms, which aid them so much in the various good works in which they are engaged.

The society has, as it were, two branches. In the first the associates merely bind themselves to make the Way of the Cross once a week, on a day fixed, with the primary object of relieving the holy souls, and particularly those most pleasing to God; and the secondary one of converting the infidels. At the end of this exercise, they make use of the following invocation: "Holy Souls in Purgatory, rest in peace, and pray for us."

The other branch has for its object the procuring of Masses for the deliverance of the suffering souls. Each associate must pay to the treasurer twenty-five cents a month, or three dollars a year; for which Masses will be said according to the intention of the subscriber, having always in view those souls which are most pleasing to God.

One may become a life member, on payment of twenty-five dollars. Foundations of Masses can also be made in connection with the Association. They are similar to those which came into existence at the time of the Crusades and at many other epochs in Christian history. Such foundations are sometimes made in wills. They are, of course, not within the reach of every one. It is

281

necessary to pay five hundred dollars into the hands of the Society. Every necessary security for its proper use is given, and the donor is entitled in perpetuity to a certain yearly rental to be expended in Masses for his soul. The sum may be paid in instalments, or several persons may club together in making the foundation. It is a sublime thought that the Holy Sacrifice will thus continue to be said for us, long after our memory has passed away from earth. But as the three dollars a year which constitutes one a member of the Association is much more within the reach of most of us, it may be well to lay more stress upon the advantages which we shall thereby gain for ourselves and our deceased friends. It entitles us after death to a special Mass and a Way of the Cross every year from each associate. The number of associates is very great; besides a share in all the Masses and Stations, we have also a share in the good works of the missionaries of St. Francis, and can gain Indulgences which have been granted to the members. These Indulgences, plenary and partial, are attached to all the principal, and to some of the minor feasts of the year.

In connection with the work, an almanac both in French and English is published every year at Montreal, and sold for the moderate sum of five cents. In this pamphlet a full account is given of the Association, and there is besides a great deal of useful and interesting reading, such as anecdotes relating to the dead, the opinions of various spiritual authors on Purgatory, and letters from foreign countries, or from various individuals concerning, the society and its progress. [1]

[Footnote 1: To become an associate one must address himself to the chaplain, Rev. F. Reid, 401 St. Denis Street, or to the treasurer, Louis Ricard, Esq., 166 St. Denis St, Montreal, Canada.]

EXTRACTS FROM "THE CATHOLIC REVIEW." [1]

[Footnote 1: November, 1885.]

"The Month of the Holy Souls" is at hand. In Catholic lands November is specially devoted by the faithful to increased suffrages for the repose of the holy and patient dead. Many reports reach us from experienced priests showing that the practice of requesting Requiem Masses for the dead is not increasing. Priests have what is, in some respects, a natural objection to urge upon their people perseverance in this old Catholic practice of piety and gratitude. It is one which can be easily understood. Yet, largely owing to this nice delicacy, they are, after their own deaths, forgotten by many bound to them through spiritual gratitude. One of the most experienced priests in New York tells us that for five priests that have died in his house he has not known ten Masses to be said at the request of the laity. How does friendship serve others less public and less popular? It gives a big funeral, a long procession of useless carriages, but no alms to the poor, and no Masses for the dead.

What a pity it is that in drawing so much that is Catholic and beautiful from Ireland, we did not adopt its truly Christian devotion for the forgotten and neglected dead, which makes every priest recite the *De Profundis* and prayers for the faithful departed, before he leaves the altar. We noticed some time ago that the Holy See sanctioned a Spanish practice of permitting to each priest three

Masses on All Souls' Day as on Christmas Day. No doubt, were it properly petitioned, it would likewise extend to all the churches drawing their faith from St. Patrick's preaching, that privilege, as well as the beautiful custom that now has the force of law in Ireland, and that recalls so much of her devotion to the dead and of her suffering for the Catholic faith. That _De Profundis is one of the chapters of "fossil history," which in all future periods will recall the generous endowments that Ireland once provided for her dead, and the ruthless confiscations by which they were robbed.

Not a Catholic American paper that we have received this November has failed to argue ably, generously, and most Christianly, for suffrages for those who have gone before and are anticipating the advent of final peace.

The letters which come to a Catholic newspaper office are a very sure barometer of the waves of thought in the Catholic atmosphere of the country. From those that we have received we can affirm that no devotion would be much more popular with the people than that which was pronounced in the days of the Maccabees "a holy and wholesome thought."

Every day now there is an agreeable record in the daily papers of New York of Requiem services held in the various churches for the repose of the soul of the late Cardinal. Church after church seems to surpass its predecessors in the grateful devotion of the people, who show that they remember their prelate. In St. Gabriel's the Cardinal's private secretary, Mgr. Farley, had the satisfaction of witnessing an exceptionally large gathering to honor his illustrious chief. The Paulist Fathers had a Requiem service that was worthy of their Church and their affection for the dead, to whom they were bound by so many ties.

Rome, if the city of the soul, is also pre-eminently the city of the dead. So many great and illustrious deaths are reported to it daily from the ends of the earth that to it death and greatness are familiar and almost unnoticeable facts. It is, therefore, not undeserving of remark to find the newspapers of the Eternal City marking their notices of the passing of our Cardinal with unusual signs of mourning. Their comments on the great loss of the American Church are toned by the *gravis mror* with which the Holy Father received by Atlantic Cable the sad news.

In the American College, Rev. Dr. O'Connell, the President, took immediate steps to pay to its illustrious patron the last homage that Catholic affection and loyalty can render to the great dead. From a letter to *The Catholic Review* we learn that the celebrant of the Solemn Mass of Requiem was the rector, Rev. Dr. O'Connell; Rev. John Curley, deacon; Rev. Bernard Duffy, sub-deacon; Rev. Thomas McManus and William Guinon, acolytes; Mr. William Murphy, thurifer; and Rev. Messrs. Cunnion and Raymond, masters of ceremonies. All these gentlemen are students from the diocese of New York.

A REQUIEM FOR THE CARDINAL IN PARIS.

PARIS, *October 30.*—A solemn funeral service of exceptional splendor was celebrated this morning at the Madeleine for the repose of the late Cardinal McCloskey, Archbishop of New York. The church was hung with black and was

283

resplendent with lights. Outside the portico, on the steps, were two large funeral torches, with green flames. Similar torches were visible in many parts of the edifice, including the lofty upper galleries. The catafalque was of large dimensions, and was flanked on either side by numerous lights and torches as well as by marble images. Over all was a sable canopy, suspended from the ceiling. A Cardinal's hat, with its tassels, lay on the pall. The late Cardinal's motto, "In the hope of life eternal," was repeated frequently in the decorations.

A DUTY OF NOVEMBER.
"HAVE PITY ON ME, AT LEAST YOU, MY FRIENDS."

(From the Texas Monitor.)

We have often repeated in our morning and night prayers the words of the Creed: "I believe in the communion of saints," without thinking, perhaps, that we were expressing our belief in one of the most beautiful and consoling doctrines of the Holy Catholic Church. I believe in the communion of saints—that is, I believe in the holy communion of prayer and intercession which exists between all the members of the Mystical Body of Christ—the Church, be they fighting the battles of the Lord against the Devil, the Flesh, and the World, in the ranks of the Church Militant on earth, or enjoying in the happy mansions of Heaven their eternal reward, as members of the Church Triumphant, or finally waiting in the dark prison of Purgatory until they shall have paid their debt to the Eternal Justice "*to the last farthing*," and be saved "yet, so as by fire." I believe in the communion of saints—that is, I believe that there exists no barrier between the members of Christ. Death itself cannot separate us from our brethren, who have gone before us. We believe that we daily escape innumerable dangers, both spiritual and temporal, through the prayers of our friends of the Triumphant Church; and we believe also that it is within our power to help by our prayers and sacrifices our friends who are for a time in the middle place of expiation, because "nothing defiled can enter the Kingdom of Heaven."

It has always been the practice of the Catholic Church to offer prayers and other pious works in suffrage for the dead, as is abundantly proved by the writings of the Latin Fathers, Tertullian, St. Cyprian, St. Augustine, St. Gregory, and of the Greek Fathers, St. Ephrem, St. Basil, and St. John Chrysostom. St. Chrysostom says:

"It was not without good reason ordained by the Apostles that mention should be made of the dead in the tremendous mysteries, because they knew well that these would receive great benefit from it." By the expression "tremendous mysteries" is meant the Holy Sacrifice of the Mass.

St. Augustine says, upon the same subject:

"It is not to be doubted that the dead are aided by prayers of the Holy Church and by the salutary sacrifice, and by the alms which are offered for their spirits that the Lord may deal with them more mercifully than their sins have deserved. For this, which has been handed down by the Fathers, the Universal Church observes."

St. Augustine also tells us that Arius was the first who dared to teach that it was of no use to offer up prayers and sacrifices for the dead, and this doctrine of Arius lie reckoned among heresies. (Heresy 53.)

The Church has always made a memento of the dead in the holy sacrifice of the Mass, and exhorted the faithful to pray for them. She urges us to pray for the souls in Purgatory, because not being able to merit, they cannot help themselves in the least. To their appeals for mercy the Almighty answers that His Justice must be satisfied, and that the night in which no one can any longer work has arrived for them (St. John ix., v. 4), and thus these poor souls have recourse to our prayers. According to the pious Gerson we may hear their supplications: "Pray for us because we cannot do anything for ourselves. This help we have a right to expect from you, you have known and loved us in the world. Do not forget us in the time of our need. It is said that it is in the time of affliction that we know our true friends; but what affliction could be compared to ours? Be moved with compassion." Have pity on us, at least you, our friends!

The Church being aware of the ingratitude and forgetfulness of men, and the facility with which they neglect their most sacred duties, has set apart a day to be consecrated to the remembrance of the dead. On the 2d day of November, All Souls' Day, she applies all her prayers to propitiate the Divine Mercy through the merits of the Precious Blood of Jesus Christ, her Divine Spouse, to obtain for the souls in Purgatory the remission of the temporal punishment due to their sins, and their speedy admission into the eternal abode of rest, light, and bliss. How holy and precious is the institution of All Souls' Day! How full of charity! It truly demonstrates the love and solicitude of the Church for all her children. In the first centuries of the Church, while the faithful were most exact in praying for their deceased friends and relatives and in having the holy sacrifice of the Mass offered for them, the Church had not yet appointed a special day for all the souls in Purgatory. But in 998 St. Odilon, Abbot of Cluny, having established in all the monasteries of his order the feast of the commemoration of the faithful departed, and ordered that the office be recited for them all, this devotion which was approved by the Popes, soon became general in all the Western Churches.

In doing away with the Christian practice of praying for the dead, the Protestant sects have despised the voice of nature, the spirit of Christianity, and the most ancient and respectable tradition.

The most efficacious means to help the suffering souls in Purgatory are prayer, fasting, almsgiving, and above all the holy sacrifice of the Mass. By fasting we mean all sorts of mortifications to abstain from certain things in our meals, to deprive ourselves of lawful amusements, to suffer with resignation trials and contradictions, humiliations and reverses of fortune. The alms we give for the dead prompt the Lord to be merciful to them. The sacrifice of the Mass, which was instituted for the living and the dead, is the most efficacious means of delivering them from their pains. "If the sacrifices which Job," says St. John Chrysostom, "offered to God for his children purified them, who could doubt that, when we offer to God the Adorable Sacrifice for the departed, they receive consolation therefrom, and that the Blood of Christ which flows upon our altars for them, the voice of which ascends to heaven, brings about their deliverance."

Not only charity and gratitude demand that we should pray for the souls in Purgatory, but it is also for us a positive duty, which we are in justice bound to fulfill. Perhaps some of these poor souls are suffering on our account. Perhaps they are relatives or friends who have loved us too much, or who have been induced to commit sin by our words or example. We are also prompted to pray for them by our own interest. What consolation will it not be for us to know that we have abbreviated their sufferings! How great will their gratitude be after their deliverance! They will manifest it by praying for us, and obtaining for us the help which is so necessary in this valley of tears. In prosperity men forget those who have helped them in adversity; but it will not be so with the souls in Purgatory. After being admitted to the kingdom of heaven through the help of our prayers, "they will solicit," says St. Bernard, "the most precious gifts of grace in our behalf, and because the merciful shall obtain mercy, we will receive after our death the reward of whatever may have been done for the souls of Purgatory during our life. Others will pray for us, and we shall share more abundantly in the suffrages which the Church offers without ceasing, for those who sleep in the Lord."

PURGATORIAL ASSOCIATION.
A CARD FROM REV. S. S. MATTINGLY.
(from the Catholic Columbian)

We wish to call the attention of the members of this Association to the near approach of the commemoration of all the faithful departed, which takes place on Monday, the second day of next November. Our Association is in its fourth year of existence. Its numbers have increased beyond our expectations.

Just now, on account of the season, applications begin to come in more rapidly, hence we wish to give again the conditions for membership, and the benefits derived from it. The members say one decade of the beads, or one "Our Father" and ten "Hail Marys" every day. They may take what mystery of the Holy Rosary devotion may prompt, and retain or change it at their own will, without reference to us. This is all that is required, and, of course, the obligation cannot bind under pain of even venial sin. Those families which say the Rosary every day need not add another decade unless they choose, but may say the Rosary in union with the Purgatorial Association, and thus gain the benefits for themselves and the faithful departed.

The benefits are one Mass every week, which is said for the poor souls, for the spiritual and temporal welfare of the members, according to their intention, and for the same intention a memento is made every day during Holy Mass for them.

There are many kind priests who are associated with us in this good work, and they, we are sure, remember us all in the Holy Sacrifice. We thank and beg them to continue to be mindful of us associated and bound together in this most charitable work of shortening, by our prayers and good works, the time of purgation for the souls in Purgatory. Those who desire to become members may send their names, with a postal card directed to themselves, so that their application may be answered. The applications for membership are directed to

Rev. S. S. Mattingly, McConnellsville, Morgan County, Ohio.

Some two or three times complaints have come to us, but in all cases the letters never came to hand. We have from time to time received letters not intended for us, and from this we judge our letters went elsewhere. We try to be prompt, though an odd time our absence on the mission may delay an answer.

Now, dear friends, there is another fact to which we must advert. Many of our dear associates, who were attracted by the charity of our work, are no longer among the living. Their friends have kindly reminded us of their death by letter, and we, grateful for this charity, always pray for them. Their day is passed. Our time is coming. Who can remember the kind faces which have gone out of our families and not shed tears at their absence? Their places are vacant. Love leaves the very chairs on which they sat unoccupied. We look around the room and at the places their forms filled within it. All these bring tears to our eyes, and make the heart too full for utterance. Thus fond imagination, sprung from love, wipes out the vacancy. We look through the mist of our tears and there again are the forms of our love, but alas! they do not speak to us. And days and months are run into years, yet our tears flow on; indeed we cannot and we do not want to forget them. We think of our sins and faults and how they caused theirs, and our cry of pardon for ourselves must come after or with that of mercy for them.

THE HOLY FACE AND THE SUFFERING SOULS.

The holy souls in Purgatory are ever saying in beseeching accents: "Lord, show us Thy Face," desiring with a great desire to see it; waiting, they longingly wait for the Divine Face of their Saviour. We should often pray for the holy souls who during life thirsted to see, in the splendor of its glory, the Human Face of Jesus Christ. We should often say the Litany of the Holy Face of Jesus, that our Lord may quickly bring these holy souls to the contemplation of His Adorable Countenance. We should pray to Mary, Mother All-Merciful, who, before all others, saw the Face of Jesus in His two-fold nativity in Bethlehem, and from the tomb, to plead for those holy souls; to St. Joseph, who saw the Face of Jesus in Bethlehem and Nazareth; to the glorious St. Michael, Our Lady's regent in Purgatory, one of the seven who stands before the throne and Face of God, who has been appointed to receive souls after death, and is the special consoler and advocate of the holy souls detained amidst the flames of Purgatory. We should also pray to St. Peter for the holy souls, he to whom Christ gave the keys of the kingdom of Heaven. The holy souls are suffering the temporal penalty due to sin. This Apostle had by his sin effaced the image of God in his soul, but Jesus turned His Holy Face toward the unfaithful disciple, and His divine look wounded the heart of Peter with repentant sorrow and love; also St. James and St. John, who with him saw the glory of the Face of Jesus on Mount Thabor, and its sorrow in Gethsemane, when, 'neath the olive trees, it was covered with confusion, and bathed in a bloody sweat for our sins. These great saints, dear to the Heart of Jesus, will surely hear our prayers in behalf of the holy souls. St. Mary Magdalen, who saw the Holy Face in agony on the cross, when its incomparable beauty was obscured under the fearful cloud of the sins of the world, and who assisted the

287

Virgin Mother to wash, anoint, and veil the bruised, pale, features of her Divine Son; the saint, whose many sins were forgiven her because she had loved much, will lend heed to our prayers for the holy souls. We should also invoke, for the holy souls, the Virgin Martyrs, because of their purity, love, and the sufferings they endured to see in Heaven the Face of their King.

Yet nothing can help these souls so much as the Holy Sacrifice of the Mass. By the "Blood of the Testament" these prisoners can be brought out of the pit. Even to hear Mass with devotion for the holy souls, brings them great refreshment. St. Jerome says: "The souls in Purgatory, for whom the priest is wont to pray at Mass, suffer no pain whilst Mass is being offered, that after every Mass is said for the souls in Purgatory some souls are released therefrom." Our Blessed Lady, the consoler of the afflicted, will always do much to aid the holy souls; in her maternal solicitude, she has *promised* to assist and console the devout wearers of the Brown Scapular of Mount Carmel detained in Purgatory, and also to speedily release them from its flames, the Saturday after their death, if *some* few conditions have been complied with during their life-time on earth. Bishop Vaughan says, "there can be no difficulty in believing thus, if we consider the meaning of a Plenary Indulgence granted by the Church, and applicable to the holy souls. The Sabbatine Indulgence is, in fact, a Plenary Indulgence granted by God, through the prayers of the Blessed Virgin Mary to the deceased who are in Purgatory, provided they have fulfilled upon earth certain specified conditions. The Sacred Congregation of the Holy Office by a Decree of February 13, 1613, forever settled any controversy that should arise on the subject of this Bull. St. Teresa, in the thirty-eighth chapter of her life, shows the special favor Our Lady exerts in favor of her Carmelite children and all who wear the Brown Scapular. She saw a holy friar ascending to Heaven without passing through Purgatory, and was given to understand, that because he had kept his rule well he had obtained the grace granted to the Carmelite Order by special bulls, as to the pains of Purgatory. So from their prison these waiting souls are ever crying out to us, patient and resigned, yet with a most burning desire, they are longing to be brought to the presence of God, and to gaze upon the glorified countenance of the Incarnate Word. They are far more perfectly members of the Mystical Body of Christ than we are, because they are confirmed in grace, and the doctrine of the Communion of Saints should hence prompt us to give the holy souls the charitable assistance of our alms, prayers, and good works. 'Bear ye one another's burdens, and so ye shall fulfill the law of Christ,' and thus one day with them enjoy the endless Vision of the Holy Face of Jesus Christ in its unclouded splendor in Heaven."

WHEN WILL THEY LEARN ITS SECRET?
HOW THE CARDINAL'S OBSEQUIES IMPRESSED A BAPTIST SPECTATOR.

(*From the Baptist Examiner.*)

For the third time in a quarter of a century the streets have been thronged, and an unending procession has filed by the dead. Long lines reached many blocks, both up and down Fifth avenue, and they grew no shorter through the best part of three days. This recognition of the eminence and power of the Cardinal, John McCloskey, has been very general.

All classes have paid homage. And why? He was a gentleman. He was learned, politic, able, far-sighted, clean. His energy was without measure. The rise and reach of his influence and work have no chance for comparison with the accomplishment of any other American clergyman. There is none to name beside him. He was a burning zealot all his life. Elevation and honors came to him. He became a prince in his Church. He swept every avenue of power and influence within his grasp into that Church. He lived singly for it. In his death, his Church exalts herself. She gives, after her faith, prayers, Masses, glory. In his, life he spoke only for Rome. In his death his voice is intensified. His life was one long gain to his people. In his, death they suffer no loss. His time and character and personality are so exalted, that, "being dead he yet speaketh."

The Church of Rome stands alone. It is forever strange. It is a law to itself. Thus it comes that this funeral does not belong to America, or to the century. Rome and the Middle Ages conducted the obsequies. The canons are prescribed. They have never changed. Behold then in New York, what might have been seen in ruined Melrose Abbey in its ancient day of splendor.

The Cardinal lies in state in his cathedral, that consummate flower of all his ministry. Saw you ever a Roman Pontiff lying in state? The high catafalque is covered with yellow cloth. The body, decked in official robes, uncoffined, reclines aslant thereon. The head is greatly elevated. A mighty candle shines on the bier at either corner. The Cardinal's red hat hangs at his feet. His cape is purple, his sleeves are pink drawn over with lace, his shirt is crimson and white lace covered. Purple gloves are on his hands. On his head is his tall white mitre. His pectoral cross lies on his pulseless breast. His seal ring glitters on his finger. To me it was an awful and uncanny figure. The man was old and disease wasted. The lips were sunken over shrunken gums. The chin was sharp and far-protruding. The colors of the cloths were garish and loud. It was a gay lay figure, red and yellow and white and black and purple and pink. It made me shudder. Yet lying there under the very roof his hands had builded, that reclining figure was immensely impressive.

The work—the work, in light and strength and glory stands; but the skilled and cunning workman is brought low, and lies cold and silent. The crowded and glorious, almost living cathedral—the richly bedecked body dismantled, deserted, dead. Was ever contrast so wide or suggestive? The white, shining arches and pinnacles, up-pointing in architectural splendor. The architect lies under them prone, unconscious, decaying. The beautiful windows, all storied in colors almost supernatural, and telling their histories and honoring their place. But the temple of the Cardinal's soul is in ruins, the windows are broken, and its day is darkness and mold.

So, silent he lies in his house, surrounded by his faithful, whose cries and lamentations he hears not, his cold hands clasped, his dead face uncovered, as though looking above its high vaulted roof.

289

I seemed to see again the bedizened skeleton of old St. Carlo Borromeo in the crypt of the Cathedral of Milan, as lying in his coffin of glass, his bones all bleached and dressed. But the careless throngs go thoughtlessly, noisily on. Some weep, some laugh, and Thursday, the day of sepulture, comes. What masses of people! What platoons of police! The magnificent temple is packed by pious thousands. The four candles about the bier become four shining rows. The glitter of royal violet velvet and cloth of gold add to the gorgeous trappings of the dead. The waiting multitudes look breathlessly at the black draped columns, the emblems of mourning put on here and there. Without announcement a single voice cries out from the dusky chancel the first lines of the office for the dead. A great Gregorian choir of boys takes up the wail, and their shrill treble is by-and-by joined by the hoarser notes of four hundred priests, in the solemn music of the Pontifical Requiem Mass. It has never been given to mortal ears to listen to such marvels of musical sound in this country. Anon the great organs and the united choirs render the master's most mournful music for the dead. Then processions, then eulogy. And what eulogy! Schools, colleges, convents, asylums, protectories, palaces, cathedrals, churches. What a vast and impressive testimony!

What a company rises up to call him blessed! This imposing pageantry is not an empty show. It is Rome's display of her resources and power. Who else can have such processions and vestments and music? Who can so minister to the inherent, perhaps barbaric remnant, love for display? In the wide world where can the ear of man catch such harmonies? The music, as a whole, was a deluge of lofty and inspiring expressions. Anguish, despair, devotion, submission, elevation! Ah, how the lofty Gothic arches thundered! How they sighed and cried and melted. The great assembly was swayed, awe-struck, like branches of forest trees in gales or in zephyrs. The influence of those melodies will not die. Oh! Rome is old, Rome is new; Rome is wise. Rome is the Solomon of the Churches.

Mark this well. The Cardinal is dead. What happens? Does the machinery stagger? Has a great and irreparable calamity fallen on the churches? Are any plans abandoned? Is the policy affected? Will aggression cease? Nothing happens but a great and imposing funeral. The plans are not affected. The lines do not waver. No work begun will be suspended. Everything goes on. If only a deacon should die out of some Baptist church, alas! my brethren, the plate returns empty to the altar. The minister puts on his hat. Consternation jumps on the ridge-pole and languishing, settles down. When shall we learn? When shall we plan harmoniously, unite our counsels, work within the lines, cease wasting resources, carry forward a common work, and when some man falls, put a new man in his place, move up the line, and keep step? To-day, when a gap is made here, we try to mend it, after a time, by seeking how great a gap we can create somewhere else. What wonder that good men get tired and go where no such folly flies, and where the current flows on and on forever!

And the old Cardinal rests in the crypt, under the high white altar. He sleeps in the mausoleum of the great. He has the reward of his labors. He carried into his tomb the insignia of his high office. Sealed up in his coffin is a parchment which future ages may read, long after we are all forgot, giving a condensed record of his long and active career. The bishops and priests have gone home to their parishes; and their tireless labors go on. They are thinking of the mighty but gentle and kindly Cardinal; of the telegrams from the Papal Court, the College of Cardinals, the Pope, and of the imposing funeral; of his own words which they wrung from him amidst the rigors of death:

"I bless you, my children, and all the churches." It was the parting of a prophet. And the priests will live for the Church and mankind. They are whispering, "The faithful are rewarded! Effort is acknowledged! O, Rome has shaken the earth! Rome is putting her armor together again." Sometimes I hear the creaking of her coat of mail as she mightily moves herself in exercise.

Manufactured by Amazon.ca
Acheson, AB

13285513R00160